Teaching Them t

Classic Edition

Delores Durkin

**With new foreword
by Dick Allington
University of Florida**

PEARSON

Boston   New York   San Francisco
Mexico City   Montreal   Toronto   London   Madrid   Munich   Paris
Hong Kong   Singapore   Tokyo   Cape Town   Sydney

Series Editor: Aurora Martinez
Editorial Assistant: Katrina Freddoso
Marketing Manager: Elizabeth Fogarty
Production Editor: Paul Mihailidis
Manufacturing Buyer: Andrew Turso
Cover Administrator: Joel Gendron
Electronic Composition: Omegatype Typography, Inc.

For related support materials, visit our online catalog at *www.ablongman.com.*

To obtain permission(s) to use material from this work, please submit a written request to
Allyn and Bacon, Permissions Department, 75 Arlington Street, Boston, MA 02116 or fax your
request to 617-848-7320.

A previous edition was published under Teaching Them to Read, Sixth Edition, copyright ©
1993, 1989, 1983, 1978, 1974, 1970, by Allyn & Bacon.

ISBN 0-205-40439-1

Printed in the United States of America

10   9   8   7   6   5   4   3   2   1   07   06   04   03

Contents

Part IV   Developing Comprehension Abilities   256

Part V   Materials   330

13 Basal Reader Series   332

14 Children's Literature   352

15 Content Area Textbooks   380

Part VI   Making Professional Decisions   402

16 Assessment and Classroom Organization   404

Foreword

Richard L. Allington
University of Florida

The director of the new U.S. Institute of Education Sciences, Grover Whitehurst (2002), has defined evidence-based instruction as: "The integration of professional wisdom with the best empirical evidence in making decisions about how to deliver instruction." This came some 30 years after Dolores Durkin wrote the first edition of *Teaching Them to Read,* an evidence-based professional text for teachers-to-be. So, 30 years after this mid-western researcher-teacher educator wrote this evidence-based book, Washington bureaucrats think that they have "discovered" a new, new idea—evidenced-based instructional decision-making. I will suggest that evidence-based instructional advice has been offered since Huey (1908), at least. And as the evidence expanded, so too did the advice on how best to teach reading. I will not claim that Durkin discovered evidence-based instructional advice, just that her work, and *Teaching Them to Read,* in particular, represents some of the finest examples of it.

Dolores Durkin pursued two broad themes as a researcher. First was her interest in early literacy development and children who learned to read early (1966; 1970; 1974–75; 1987a; 1987b). The second was classroom reading instruction, particularly comprehension instruction (1978–79; 1981a; 1981b; 1984; 1987c). *Teaching Them to Read* reflects both themes while extending well beyond just these interest areas. Well before they became hot commodities in educational circles, Durkin offered clear guidance about topics such as phonemic awareness, phonics, meta-language, comprehension strategies, and teaching reading and writing in kindergarten.

Durkin's research on early literacy extended professional understanding of emergent literacy and early literacy acquisition. Her then radical views about creating kindergarten (or even pre-kindergarten) classrooms that supported literacy development (many educators then viewed any attention to "academics" before first grade to be developmentally inappropriate) gave the field a vision of what a language- and literacy-rich early schooling environment might look like and might accomplish.

For me though, it is her research on comprehension instruction that makes Durkin such an important figure in modern thinking about reading instruction. That work provided the impetus for a whole-scale rethinking of what it means to teach children to better comprehend the texts they are reading.

Durkin conducted what is, perhaps, the classic article on reading comprehension instruction—or the lack of it. That study, "What classroom observations reveal about reading comprehension instruction", pointedly noted that comprehension skills and strategies were rarely taught. Instead, she coined and used the term "mentioning" to describe what passed for comprehension instruction. Mentioning meant that comprehension strategies, summarizing, for instance, were mentioned but never actually developed, explained, or modeled for students. In fact, much of what passed as comprehension instruction was, as Durkin pointed out, nothing more than assessment.

Her study found teachers asking lots of questions both during and after reading. She found that teachers reported that this use of questions was the "instruction" they offered. The questions teachers asked, by and large, provided some sense of who understood the story—or at least who recalled various bits of the story. But finding out your answer was wrong did not provide much help in figuring out what you needed to do differently in the future to improve your understanding (or recall). In other words, kids who responded incorrectly might learn the "right" answer in a lesson but almost never got much guidance in what sort of strategy might be added to the reading repertoire to improve understanding of the next story read.

Even teachers found the questions to be rather unhelpful in planning instruction because it was rarely obvious from the incorrect response just what had gone awry during reading. In other words, the questions, as assessments, rarely informed instruction. In a continuing investigation of this problem Durkin analyzed basal read series, studying the design of the lessons, the advice offered in the teachers' manuals, and the workbooks and other tasks students were assigned. She then studied teachers use of the basal manuals and materials. She placed the weight of the problems with comprehension instruction at the feet of the basal series publishers. Those widely used commercial reading programs provided darn little useful guidance for developing children's reading comprehension while providing lots of questions to be asked and worksheets to be completed.

I'm not sure that Durkin was justified in pointing so directly at the weaknesses in the basal reader series. Not to defend those series, but, honestly, her critiques appeared just as the research community was initiating the first studies of comprehension instruction from a constructivist framework. Durkin's criticism stimulated enormous interest, on the part of both publishers and researchers, in how to best help children develop useful comprehension skills and strategies. Durkin, herself, worked at the Center for the Study of Reading at the University of Illinois. That federally funded research center was focused on improving children's reading comprehension in an era of phonics-emphasis reading programs. Out of that research came such now well-known tools as Reciprocal Teaching, K-W-L, graphic organizers such a story maps, semantic feature charts, and character webs, routines for developing or activating background knowledge, and writing after reading.

Durkin was stellar researcher although little of her research was experimental in design. Instead, she conducted largely descriptive analyses. Analyses that were careful and theoretically-driven. These descriptions didn't just inform the profession but jolted it into action. As a classroom instruction-focused researcher, Durkin was a relative rarity even in her time. Today, of course, such research has been relegated to second-class status, almost unfundable given current federal research goals. But it was her time in classrooms that provided Durkin with the insights, the wisdom, she had about effective teaching. It was the thousands of hours of observing teachers teaching children to read that allowed her research to focus so clearly on important instructional issues. It is the lack of the same that leads researchers to mindlessly study what ultimately are found to be rather trivial components of the reading process (e.g., phonemic awareness; nonsense word reading), components that either produce few challenges for teaching or learning, or are ultimately found to be not very useful in the longer run of reading development, or both.

While it is obvious that Durkin's textbook writing was heavily influenced by what the research said about effective planning and practice, what might be overlooked is her reliance, while writing, on professional wisdom derived from extensive work in with teachers and in those teachers classrooms. She notes in her Preface that, "I relied on two sources of help that I always use to prepare for a textbook. I taught methods courses to undergraduates and to teachers and I observed many classrooms in a wide geographic area." (p. ix) Perhaps it is this process, integrating professional wisdom and research findings, that is central to the success of *Teaching Them to Read*.

Teaching undergraduates and teachers helped her write a "considerate" text—one that seems to be a "just right" book for most novices, neither too hard nor too theoretical, nor too simple or too practical. A text, in other words, that offered largely painless learning support. Her work in many classrooms provided her with a sense of what was critical for teachers to know and what they found hard to accomplish. These visits also provided vignettes that appear throughout the text, each providing a lesson summary, a snippet of conversation, or a glance at the instructional tasks that children are completing. It is in these vignettes that we see Durkin's professional wisdom holding forth. This professional wisdom is well integrated with empirical evidence throughout the book.

Every elementary teacher (and principal) and every reading researcher and reading teacher educator should be required to reread historically important books across their career. Rereading, for instance, Edmund Huey's (1908) hundred-year-old scientific treatise on teaching reading is a humbling experience. Reading Durkin's newer, but still classic, textbook reminds us of how much we know, and have known for awhile, about effective reading instruction.

Given how much we know, the question that bothers me is: Why are so few schools organized in ways that allow teachers to teach effectively? Why do most school districts (and some states) routinely plan (or mandate) an anti-scientific one-size-fits-all instructional plan? Why do our most effective teachers have to ignore central office plans for reading instruction in order to create classrooms such as those Durkin describes? If Durkin were still researching reading instruction in schools, perhaps those are the questions that she would be studying.

KEY REFERENCES:

Durkin, D. (1966). *Children who read early.* New York: Teachers College Press.

Durkin, D. (1970). A language arts program for pre-first grade children: A two year achievement report. *Reading Research Quarterly, 5,* 534–565.

Durkin, D. (1974–75). A six-year study of children who learned to read in school at the age of four. *Reading Research Quarterly, 10,* 9–61.

Durkin, D. (1978–79). What classroom observations reveal about reading comprehension instruction. *Reading Research Quarterly, 14,* 481–533.

Durkin, D. (1981a). Reading comprehension instruction in five basal reader series. *Reading Research Quarterly, 16*(4), 515–544.

Durkin, D. (1981b). Reading comprehension instruction in five basal reading series. *Reading Research Quarterly, 16,* 515–544.

Durkin, D. (1984). Is there a match between what elementary teachers do and what basal reader manuals recommend? *Reading Teacher* (9), 734–745.

Durkin, D. (1987a). A classroom observation study of reading instruction in kindergarten. *Early Childhood Research Quarterly, 2,* 275–300.

Durkin, D. (1987b). Influences on basal reader programs. *Elementary School Journal, 87,* 331–341.

Durkin, D. (1987c). Testing in the kindergarten. *Reading Teacher, 40,* 766–770.

Whitehurst, G. (2002). What is evidenced-based education? Downloaded on December 5, 2002 from: www.ed.gov/offices/OESE/SASA/eb/slide003.html

Preface

Between the publication of the Fifth Edition of *Teaching Them to Read* and the start of writing this Sixth Edition, I relied on two sources of help that I always use to prepare for a textbook. I taught methods courses to undergraduates and to teachers, and I observed many classrooms in a wide geographical area. The observations account for references to classrooms throughout *Teaching Them to Read*. Their inclusion is intended to add authenticity and interest to its contents.

The Introduction to the contents reviews strategies for acquiring and retaining information from text—specifically, from this book. It can be said, then, that from the beginning to its conclusion, this edition of *Teaching Them to Read* is concerned with comprehension. Chapter 1, for example, encourages readers not only to comprehend a brief piece of text but also to stand back, as it were, to examine what they did in order to achieve its comprehension. This procedure allows for calling attention to literal comprehension so that it can be contrasted with text-based and knowledge-based inferential comprehension.

Having scrutinized the reading process in Chapter 1, *Teaching Them to Read* turns next to the reading teacher. Chapter 2 distinguishes between different kinds of instruction—intentional and unintentional, for instance. The value of "teachable moments" is highlighted, too, for they are the times when the help a teacher provides is especially meaningful for students.

To conclude Part I, called "Background Information," Chapter 3 considers this question: Should the reading that is done in school be oral or silent? When each kind of reading is appropriate, or necessary, is discussed with illustrations.

Part II focuses on "Literacy at the Beginning." Because what occurs at the beginning has a lasting consequence for student achievement, the two chapters that make up Part II are very important. The first, Chapter 4, is entitled "Easing Young Children into Reading." The title reflects use of the concept *emergent literacy* to develop the content and to make recommendations. Implementing the recommendations is the concern of Chapter 5, "A Beginning Literacy Program." The hope is that Chapter 5 will serve as an antidote for what is still seen in too many kindergartens and even nursery schools: whole-class instruction in phonics, which is equated with beginning reading instruction. In its treatment of beginning literacy, Chapter 5 discusses invented spelling and the initial efforts of young children to write.

The five chapters that constitute Part III, "Developing Reading Vocabularies," are an acknowledgment that comprehending connected text—whether a sentence or a book—requires a reader to know most of the words of which the text is composed. These chapters further recognize that knowing words at the level of automaticity is especially helpful for comprehension. This explains why Chapter 6, "Whole

Word Methodology," takes the time to distinguish between word recognition and word identification and why it assigns importance to, and makes suggestions for, word practice.

Even though naming words directly for children is required at first, a prolonged use of nothing but whole word instruction does not permit students to acquire the ability to cope with new and forgotten words themselves. Because it is the use of relevant cues—contextual, graphophonic, and structural—that allows independence to flourish, the three kinds of cues provide subject matter for the remaining chapters in Part III. Chapter 7 deals with contextual cues by tracing how instruction about them progresses over time. How they continue to function for readers over time enters into the content of this and subsequent chapters. Chapter 8, "Graphophonic Cues: Content," is directed to teachers and prospective teachers who want to know enough about phonics so they can move away from commercially produced materials toward teaching what needs to be taught *when* students need to learn it. How to do the teaching is the subject of Chapter 9. Chapter 10, "Structural Cues," focuses on strategies for dealing with unfamiliar words that are more complex than a root—specifically, inflected and derived words. As the chapter goes about realizing this goal, it demonstrates how knowing prefixes and suffixes helps not only with pronunciations but also with meanings.

Word meanings are central to Chapter 11, the first of the two chapters in Part IV, "Developing Comprehension Abilities." Without neglecting the fact that the meanings of many words are dependent on the text in which they are embedded, Chapter 11 covers how teachers at all levels can add to students' oral vocabularies and thus to their potential to become accomplished readers. Chapter 12, "Comprehension: Connected Text," reviews ideas presented in Chapter 1 and then adds to them in ways that make distinctions between facilitating, teaching, and assessing comprehension. Other distinctions are made between narrative, expository, and procedural text. Subsequently, topics for instruction that are appropriate for different kinds of text are identified. Some of these topics figure in lessons in which interchanges take place between teachers and students.

By the time readers reach Part V of *Teaching Them to Read,* they are aware that *instructional material* is defined as anything that displays written words. It thus encompasses not only textbooks but also trade books, magazines, newspapers, brochures, timetables, maps, menus, road signs, recipes, and labels on boxes, cans, packages, and bottles. In spite of the vast array of materials that are instructive for reading, the three chapters in Part V limit their content to basal reader series, trade books, and content area textbooks. (The term *trade book* refers to books written for the library and bookstore market.)

Preparations for writing Chapter 13, "Basal Reader Series," began with an analysis of current basal programs, for they are different in some ways from their predecessors. Like their predecessors, however, they require selective use—if used at all. The position taken in Chapter 13 is that new teachers need something like a basal program but that they should use it selectively and in conjunction with literature and environmental text.

How to use children's literature to complement basal reader selections is one topic covered in Chapter 14. As in earlier chapters, the importance of daily read-alouds by teachers and of well-stocked classroom libraries is emphasized. The need to allot time in the daily schedule for students' self-selected reading is another topic in Chapter 14. How these more enjoyable kinds of reading can at least reduce the number of exercise sheets still being assigned is illustrated.

As its title suggests, Chapter 15, "Content Area Textbooks," focuses on expository text—in particular, on the text students are expected to read for subjects such as social studies, science, and health. Why these textbooks are difficult is explained, as are ways to make it possible for students to comprehend them.

Chapter 16, "Assessment and Classroom Organization," brings the book to a close. Underlying all the recommendations in this chapter for assessment, for selecting instructional objectives, and for organizing a class is a portrayal of the teacher that entered into previous chapters: a knowledgeable decision maker who strives daily to provide instruction and materials that advance not only the ability of students to read but also their desire to do so.

One final word about *Teaching Them to Read*. Because the majority of persons who make decisions in kindergarten and elementary school classrooms are women, feminine pronouns are used whenever references are made to teachers. The exceptions are cases in which a specific teacher is a man. To avoid ambiguity, masculine pronouns are used to refer to students, again with the exception of times when a specific girl is the referent.

Dolores Durkin

Introduction

TEACHERS WHO KNOW HOW to go about acquiring information from text are likely to be ready to help students learn how to read for the same purpose. This Introduction, therefore, is intended to review some procedures that promote learning from textbooks such as *Teaching Them to Read*.

The fact that students—even some in prestigious universities—need to acquire strategies for learning from text has been verified many times. For example, after questioning college students about their study habits, one researcher concluded that

> the typical approach of 90 percent of these students was to start at the beginning of the chapter and read straight ahead. No attempt was made to survey the chapter, note marginal headings, or first read the recapitulation paragraph in which the whole structure and summary of the chapter were given. Thus, none of the clues and signals provided as a basis for raising questions were used to identify specific purposes for reading. (2, p. 196)

In conversations I myself have had with college students, some laughingly conclude that steps like the following describe how *they* study:

1. Sit down.
2. Find the assignment.
3. Count the pages.
4. Look at their watch.
5. Start reading.

One central message of the textbook you are now reading is that there are more productive and efficient ways to learn. Because these procedures start by getting acquainted with the whole of the text to be read, this Introduction begins with a brief description of the overall structure of *Teaching Them to Read*.

OVERVIEW

As the Table of Contents shows, *Teaching Them to Read* is divided into Parts, each composed of chapters that cover related topics. The subject matter of the Parts is sketched at the time each part begins.

Chapters also start with Previews and, in addition, end with Summaries. Reading the Previews and Summaries before chapters are started should promote both comprehension and retention of their content (1, 3, 4, 5).

You will also find an outline facing each Preview. Examining the headings and subheadings in the outline—again, before you begin a chapter—will show the parts of that chapter as well as how the parts fit together. Knowing the organization of a chapter ahead of time also facilitates both understanding and recall of the information presented.

READERS OF THIS BOOK

Successful readers of textbooks start a chapter with the intention of acquiring certain kinds of information. Their reading, therefore, can be portrayed as *intentional thinking.* It is purposeful.

Purposes for reading a chapter in a textbook are often defined by an instructor when the chapter is assigned. In the case of *Teaching Them to Read,* you yourself can establish purposes by looking ahead to the Review section at the end of every chapter. Having purposes in mind should help you decide how to do your reading; you now are in a position to know what to attend to with care, what can be read more quickly, and what might even be skipped. This suggests that good reading is not one unchanging kind of behavior. Rather, it is behavior that changes as purposes change.

Comprehension monitoring also accounts for some of the flexible behavior that characterizes proficient reading. As the term suggests, comprehension monitoring is the self-checking that readers do by comparing what they are learning with what they need or want to learn. Purposes for reading and comprehension monitoring, therefore, are closely connected. Together, they keep readers from wandering aimlessly through a chapter, only to end up with little or no new information.

FEATURES OF CHAPTERS

To help you monitor your comprehension of the information in *Teaching Them to Read,* terms introduced in a chapter appear initially in italic print. Use the special type as a signal to make sure you understand the term, which is always directly or indirectly explained. (Based on your reading of this Introduction, the meaning of *intentional thinking* and *comprehension monitoring* should be clear. The inability to explain one or both suggests the need to remedy the problem by returning to the text that provided explanations.)

Other features of chapters reflect the reason *Teaching Them to Read* was written: to provide information about reading and reading instruction from kindergarten through the elementary grades that is sufficiently clear and specific that it will be helpful to anyone who is, or will be, teaching reading. Because of this objective, chapters include many references to actual classrooms that I and other people have observed. Sometimes the references are brief; at other times, they are detailed. In the latter case, what is described is often analyzed. All of these references are meant to be helpful to prospective teachers by allowing them to see life in classrooms. For experienced teachers, they provide opportunities to sit in a corner to learn what other teachers do or do not do in their classrooms.

Adding still more to the specificity of the content are descriptions of instruction presented in a variety of formats. How teachers can make sure that students see the value of what they are learning is described, too. Not neglected are the many different kinds of materials that contribute either to getting reading started or to keeping it progressing.

A REMINDER

Not all of you have taught reading; nonetheless, you all *have* learned to be readers in the settings of a number of classrooms. Therefore, this allows you to compare your own experiences with what a chapter says about a topic. Again, the comparisons should have a positive effect on comprehension, as new learnings are acquired most easily when they relate to what is already known or has been experienced.

All this is to say that successful comprehenders are anything but passive individuals. Instead, they make their way through a piece of text consciously guided by pre-established purposes that become goals to be attained with the reading.

SUMMARY

"Learning How to Learn from Text" is one possible title for this Introduction. Because it deals with *planful* reading, the Introduction could also be called "Learning How to Be a Strategic Reader." Strategies offered for maximizing knowledge acquisition from *Teaching Them to Read* suggest that you:

1. Read the Preview and Summary before a chapter is begun in order to get a sense of the overall content.

2. Examine the outline of a chapter, which shows the parts of the content and how they are interrelated.

3. Read the Review section in order to identify some of the most important content and to establish purposes for your reading.

4. Note key terms in a chapter, which are in italics. Your ability to define these terms, coupled with your ability to summarize the content of each part of a chapter, are signs of adequate comprehension. If the definitions or the summaries do not come readily to mind, remedial action in the form of rereading may be necessary.

5. Compare, as you read, what is said with what you yourself have experienced in classrooms. The involvement this creates will enhance comprehension, too.

PART I

Each of the three chapters in Part I of *Teaching Them to Read* provides background information for the study of subsequent chapters. Chapter 1 focuses on the reading process. It discusses reading in a nontechnical way that still takes into account research findings about this complex, highly useful ability.

Having focused on the reading process in Chapter 1, the book moves on to consider teachers and teaching in Chapter 2. Even though effec-

tive instruction is the concern of the whole of *Teaching Them to Read,* an early discussion of features of instruction that either facilitate or impede the attainment of its objectives should be helpful. Chapter 2 discusses these features. Other chapters complement its content with descriptions of specific lessons designed to realize the numerous objectives that an instructional program must achieve.

Chapter 3 continues to provide background

Background Information

information by looking at reading in relation to the two modes in which it can be done: silently and orally. This third chapter, "Reading: Silent or Oral?," should clarify the circumstances in which each mode is appropriate and also the times when a combination of silent reading and oral reading is desirable or, as the case may be, undesirable. Chapter 3 thus shows the need for teachers to be introspective about how they use their time as well as the time of students. As you will

soon learn, "*Why* am I doing what I'm doing?" is a question that teachers must constantly ask if they hope to improve what they do to help all students learn to read.

As you now prepare to start Chapter 1, keep in mind the guidelines for learning from expository text discussed in the Introduction.

CHAPTER 1

The Reading Process

Traditionally, the opening chapter in a textbook like this one begins by defining *reading*. Instead of adhering to tradition, this initial chapter attempts to involve you consciously with the reading process before providing definitions. First, though, the kinds of text commonly read are discussed.

Once such text is discussed and your active involvement with comprehending ends, the definitions of *reading* that are offered should be meaningful. Also, by then you should understand why children can know all the words in a piece of text yet not be able to comprehend it.

As you make your way through Chapter 1, try to keep the following questions in mind:

1. What am I learning about reading that I did not know before?
2. Am I finding any unexpected statements about reading?
3. Based on what I have experienced as a reader, do I disagree with anything in the chapter?

Keeping these concerns in mind should minimize the possibility of your reading Chapter 1 without a purpose. It should also permit you to *monitor* your comprehension, as you can now ask, How am I doing insofar as those questions are concerned? Later, when Chapter 15 deals with content subject textbooks, *comprehension monitoring* is cited as something teachers need to foster in students' reading, especially of text designed to provide information. If you now develop the habit of monitoring your own comprehension, helping children do the same will come naturally. In fact, if you develop the habit of following the recommendations made earlier in the Introduction, you will develop into a highly strategic (planful) reader who succeeds in achieving whatever goals you set for your reading.

MOST OF THE READING WE DO is of *connected text.* (Common exceptions are lists of groceries to buy or errands to run.) Connected text consists of words arranged, or sequenced, in ways that yield something meaningful. Such text can be as limited as two words (e.g., *bright sunshine*) or as many as needed to write a novel.

CONNECTED TEXT AND COHESIVE TIES

Whenever connected text exceeds a sentence, comprehending it requires readers to make both intrasentence (within a sentence) connections and intersentence (among sentences) connections. Certain words, appropriately called *cohesive ties,* help readers to do this.

Below, in what seems on the surface to be simple text, notice how cohesive ties—in this instance, mostly pronouns and adverbs—link parts of sentences together and, at other times, make connections across sentences. (Numbers make apparent the semantic connections that are implied.)

>   [1]   [2] [2] [1]   [2]
> The <u>children</u> can hardly wait to get <u>there.</u> <u>It</u> is <u>their</u> favorite <u>park.</u> Now
> [1]   [1]   [3]
> <u>they</u> are getting ready for the picnic. <u>Two</u> are making lemonade, because <u>it</u>
>   [3] [1]   [4] [4] [1]   [1]
> is a warm <u>day.</u> <u>Another</u> is looking for <u>games that they</u> can play when <u>they</u>
>   [2]
> get <u>there.</u>

How a word like *nevertheless* functions in connected text is illustrated next.

> It took only five minutes for the bus to come. Nevertheless, Sharon's nose was red and her hands felt numb.

In the text above, *nevertheless* ties two sentences together, thus serving as a cohesive tie. The use of *nevertheless* makes it unnecessary for the author to write something as tedious as:

> It took only five minutes for the bus to come. Even though it took only five minutes for the bus to come, Sharon's nose was red and her hands felt numb.

The examples of connected text that have now been considered should be enough to explain why cohesive ties provide subject matter for comprehension instruction—a topic left for later chapters.

KINDS OF CONNECTED TEXT

Connected text can be categorized in various ways. Three kinds that students need to know how to comprehend are (a) expository, (b) narrative, and (c) procedural.

Expository Text

The Introduction focuses on expository text. It does that because, like other expository material, textbooks are written to provide information. Articles in newspapers and magazines may serve the same function.

Expository text usually deals with one or more topics about which major ideas are presented. Often, the ideas are embellished with details that provide clarification or further information that is related. How an author puts all this together is referred to as the *macrostructure* of the text. As the Introduction states, knowing about the macrostructure of expository material helps readers understand and retain the information presented.

Narrative Text

Another kind of connected text, narration, is often equated with stories; however, not all narrative texts are stories. For instance, an account of a special relationship between a young boy and his grandfather is narrative in nature, but it does not tell a story.

Like expository text, stories have a structure. In the most simple stories, the structure is composed of a setting, main character, and plot. The plot is made up of attempts to solve a problem that the main character is experiencing. The resolution of the problem brings the story to an end. It is generally thought that children's knowledge of story structure, whether tacit or explicit, fosters both understanding and recall (3, 5, 9).

Procedural Text

A third kind of connected text is procedural in nature. It is portrayed this way because its purpose is to describe procedures for doing or making something, or for getting somewhere. As most of us know, procedural text can be a source of considerable stress—at least when it gives directions for assembling a toy, completing an income tax form, or using a computer.

In addition to being incomprehensible some of the time, procedural text is found everywhere—on the containers of household cleaning products, in cookbooks and telephone directories, on job applications, and at the top of countless numbers of workbook pages and other exercise sheets. In spite of its omnipresence and, at times, incomprehensibility, too little is done in classrooms to help students learn how to succeed with procedural text. Probably the best way, therefore, to end this brief discussion of expository, narrative, and procedural materials is to say that none of the three should receive so much attention in school that any one or two are neglected.

EXPERIENCING COMPREHENSION

Adults who are far removed in time from their own efforts to acquire reading ability are not in the best position to appreciate all that is necessary for comprehending even simple text. Because reading for such individuals is usually a taken-for-granted, unexamined behavior, most adults are not likely to think very much about what they have to do and know to be a reader. This suggests that anyone who is, or will be, responsible for teaching reading must make an effort to become consciously aware of the requirements of comprehension. Such conscious knowledge is important, because it helps identify what has to be done to help students begin to read or to add to the abilities they already possess. Conscious awareness of what is involved in comprehending also helps teachers establish correct priorities for instructional programs.

With these comments in the background, it seems fitting to start a textbook (whose purpose is to describe reading instruction) with an effort to get its readers actively and consciously involved with the comprehension process. To do that, I am going to ask you to list now what you would put into the picture suggested by the sentence below.

Marty opened her umbrella just in time and held it tightly.

On the assumption that you have completed your list, let me tell you about the contents of the mental image that the sentence evoked for me. As I do this, you can compare your picture with mine.

To begin, I have one woman in the picture. She is outdoors walking in the rain on a windy day. She is wearing a raincoat and carrying a purse with an over-the-shoulder strap. (At first, I assumed Marty was a man; however, the word *her,* which I inferred pertained to *Marty,* identified the person as female. She could be a child or an adult; for no particular reason, I envisioned an adult.) The woman in my picture has an opened umbrella above her head. Because I inferred that *it* meant the umbrella, I show the woman having her two hands wrapped firmly around the handle of the umbrella. (To free both hands is the reason I have her carrying a shoulder bag.) I inferred from the words *just in time* that rain began to fall recently and suddenly. That is why I omitted puddles from my picture.

CONTRIBUTORS TO COMPREHENSION

To draw the picture, I used (a) the eleven words that make up the sentence; (b) inferences that the words suggest (text-based inferences); and (c) inferences based on my own knowledge (knowledge-based inferences). Each of the three sources of help is discussed next.

An Author's Words

Even though how to pronounce written words receives considerable attention in classrooms, it is meaning that makes a difference for readers. The fact that I know "Marty" is a person's name and that I understand the meaning of *umbrella, opened umbrella, just in time,* and *held tightly* contributed substantially to my ability to envision a picture. Stated differently, understanding all the words that make up the sentence allowed for comprehending it at a literal level. (As is the case with listening comprehension, another contributor is my familiarity with English syntax.)

Inferences: Text-Based

As the explanation of how I went about "drawing" my mental picture indicated, inferential as well as literal comprehension figured in my decisions. Let me start with the inferences that derived from the author's words.

To begin, *her* implied that Marty is female. (Authors imply; readers infer.) The words *opened her umbrella just in time* further implied that Marty is outdoors and, in addition, that rain began to fall suddenly.

While reading the sentence, I inferred that the author used *it* to avoid repeating *umbrella*. With that in mind, *held it tightly* implied that one or even both of Marty's hands are wrapped tightly around the handle of the umbrella. (Even though the author does not use the word *handle*, I inferred that *held it* implied "held the handle.") Based on the words *held it tightly*, I also inferred that the day is windy as well as rainy.

Inferences: Knowledge-Based

What I know about rainy weather tells me that, at such times, people often carry umbrellas and may wear raincoats. That is why I dressed Marty in a raincoat. I could have added some kind of a hat and even boots. Based on what I know, I could also have Marty's body postured in a way that shows her walking ahead even while the wind nudges her backwards. None of this contradicts the author's text, nor does it contradict anything known about the behavior and dress of individuals caught in a rainstorm on a windy day.

CONTRIBUTORS TO COMPREHENSION: ADDITIONAL COMMENTS

The discussion of (a) literal comprehension, (b) text-based inferential comprehension, and (c) knowledge-based inferential comprehension is not meant to obscure the fact that it is sometimes difficult—even impossible—to make precise distinctions between the sources that successful readers use when they go about constructing the meaning of text. In fact, you may have found yourself disagreeing with the way I identified sources for the content of my picture. It is likely, for instance, that some of you may have thought that the reader's own relevant knowledge—not a text-based inference—suggests it is a handle that Marty held tightly.

Not to be overlooked, however, is that some texts *do* have clearly identifiable sources of help. Take the following sentence as an example:

> Of the three girls, only Bonnie can reach the shelf on which their mother keeps the cookies.

It seems reasonable to predict that most people will agree with the distinctions shown in Figure 1.1.

Two conclusions can be drawn from this discussion of factors that contribute to comprehension. First, the meaning that readers construct derives from an author's words, from what the words imply, and from what the readers themselves know that

Text: Of the three girls, only Bonnie can reach the shelf on which their mother keeps the cookies.

Literal Comprehension	Inferential Comprehension	
	Text-Based	*Knowledge-Based*
There are three girls. Bonnie can reach the shelf.	[their mother] The three girls, one of which is Bonnie, are sisters. [only Bonnie can reach the shelf] Bonnie is the tallest. None of her sisters are tall enough to reach the shelf. [the shelf on which] The cookies are kept on a shelf.	The three girls are in a kitchen. The cookies are in a container that has been put on a shelf.

FIGURE 1.1   Sources for Understanding Text

is relevant. Parts of the constructed message derive from one source and, at other times, from a combination of sources. Second, identifying sources for understanding text is much less important than is the recognition that reading is *not* merely naming written words correctly. That is, reading is not a translation but, rather, a transaction between author and reader in which both contribute to "making meaning" (7, 8). This is why it is correct to think of comprehension as an *interactive* process in which both the author and the reader contribute to the construction of something meaningful (1, 2, 7, 8).

CHARACTERIZATIONS OF THE READING PROCESS AND THEIR IMPLICATIONS FOR TEACHING

Thus far, reading has been characterized as intentional thinking during which meaning is constructed through interactions between text and reader. This characterization should allow you to see why the text is sometimes referred to as a *blueprint* to which readers add details by making inferences.

Still another characterization views the author's words as the *external text* and the constructed meaning as the *internal, mental* text. Examples of both follow.

External Text	**Internal Text,**
Of the three girls, only Bonnie can reach the shelf on which their mother keeps the cookies.	Bonnie and her two sisters are in the kitchen. Because their mother keeps cookies in a jar on a high shelf, only Bonnie, the tallest of the girls, can get to the cookies.

The sample of an internal text allows for making explicit two more points about comprehending that are significant for teachers. One is that comprehending is *not* a matter of constructing any message that a reader feels like constructing. Instead, the message is always constrained by the author's words. For instance, if the text about the girls and the cookies had been something like *As the girls walked home from school, they looked forward to a snack. Only Bonnie can reach the shelf on which their mother keeps the cookies,* an internal text that indicates the girls are in a kitchen shows deficiencies in literal comprehension (*As the girls walked home from school...*). The first point, therefore, is that the content of an internal text embellishes but also reflects the external text. This means that literal comprehension is hardly unimportant even though it may be insufficient.

The second point is that comprehending is not always as objective as it is sometimes thought to be. This is the case because, as has been illustrated, knowledge-based inferences often vary from one reader to another simply because the experiences and knowledge of people vary. The fact that comprehending may be partially subjective is something teachers need to keep in mind whenever they use questions to assess comprehension (4, 6). Even though many such questions have only one right answer, others allow for a variety of responses. Distinctions between the two kinds of questions should be in the minds of teachers and also clarified for students, as many children go through school believing that every question has but one right answer, which is "on the page."

The fact that answers or parts of answers may be in the reader's head should suggest to teachers the need to encourage students to use what they know that is relevant *to help themselves* comprehend. Unfortunately, such encouragement is not always given. This can be illustrated with an incident that occurred during a visit to one fourth grade during social studies. The following interchange took place before the students started a chapter in their textbook. The book had a sociological orientation, which seemed much too advanced for the observed students:

Teacher: Who can give us an example of a group?
Student 1: A fight.
Teacher: When we find out the four reasons that make a group, you'll see that a fight isn't a group.
Student 2: When you're on a bus in Chicago.
Teacher: Once we read about the rules of a group, that will fit.

Evidence of the failure to encourage students to use what has been experienced to help themselves comprehend was also found in a first grade. In this case, the teacher and children were engaged in a postreading discussion:

Teacher: Where were the children going?
Student: To Krannert. [This is the name of an auditorium in the community in which the students live.]
Teacher: The story doesn't say that. It says, "They are going to a play."
Student: But Krannert is where we go to see plays!
Teacher: Let's get back to the story. Who...?

In addition to minimizing the value for reading of what has been experienced, the two teachers just referred to were assigning—at least during the observations—too much importance to individual words and too little to the fact that reading and comprehending are synonymous. Specifically, does it not seem correct to conclude that the first grader who referred to a particular auditorium had successfully comprehended *They are going to a play*? And in the following interchange, is it not equally likely that another child in a different classroom understood the text *They looked everywhere*? In this instance, a teacher and a group of second graders were discussing a story that had just been read:

Teacher: Where did they look for her?
Student: All over.
Teacher: That's not what it said. The story says they looked "everywhere."

Before anyone concludes because of the comments just made that the philosophy underlying *Teaching Them to Read* is that an author's words are relatively unimportant, let me be quick to point out that a number of the chapters in this book are included *because* an author's words *are* critical. What is being attempted here is to make the point that the essence of reading is comprehending. Keeping that equation in mind, effective teachers take the time to reward successful efforts to comprehend without undermining the fundamental importance of the text. In the case of the child who used her experiences in going to plays to answer a question, the teacher might have responded with the following feedback: "You certainly did understand where the children were going. In our city, we do go to Krannert for plays, but Krannert—let me write it on the board—is not mentioned in the story, is it? Maybe the person who wrote this story hasn't even heard of Krannert. Maybe that's why the author wrote, "They are going to a play."

Teacher comments like those just suggested correctly reflect the interactive nature of the comprehension process. In no way, therefore, do they take anything away from the importance of the words on a page; nor do they overlook the contributions that experiences and knowledge make to successful comprehension.

SUMMARY

This first chapter began by describing three kinds of connected text we often read: expository, narrative, and procedural. Connected text was explained with the help of words that serve as cohesive ties.

Even though mental processes can hardly be put on display for purposes of examination and study, Chapter 1 next tried to make the reading process "visible." It did this by requesting a picture of the mental image evoked by a sentence. The content of the picture was then described and analyzed. The first intent of the analysis was to show the difference between literal and inferential comprehension. The second goal was to differentiate between text-based and knowledge-based inferences. The three kinds of comprehension (literal comprehension, text-based inferential comprehension, and knowledge-based inferential comprehension) were then brought together in a comparison of an external text and an internal text. Along the way, various definitions of comprehension were provided.

What should have emerged from the discussion is the active role students must play if they are to succeed in comprehending. How that role is performed was implied when reading was defined as an interactive process during which readers construct meaning. The significance of this definition for teachers was then discussed. Especially emphasized was the importance of encouraging students to use what they know to help themselves comprehend.

REVIEW

1. Let's start with a request for answers to questions posed in the Preview: What did you learn about the reading process in Chapter 1? Was any of what you learned unexpected? Did you disagree with anything in the chapter? If so, *why* did you disagree?

2. The word *text* occurred frequently in Chapter 1:

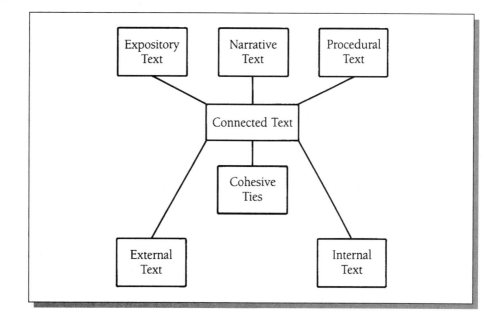

a. Explain each of the six uses of *text*.
b. What are cohesive ties?

3. It should not have been surprising to find many uses of the word *reading* in Chapter 1, which was defined in a variety of ways. Specifically, reading was said to be: (a) intentional thinking; (b) an interactive process; and (c) a "meaning making" process. Explain the three definitions.

4. What is meant by the following statement, which is in Chapter 1?
Literal comprehension is hardly unimportant even though it may be insufficient.

5. A common misunderstanding is that inferences are required only for difficult text. To show this is not the case, identify inferences that figure in constructing the meaning of the two pieces of text shown below. Next, state whether each inference is text-based or knowledge-based. Finally, explain why you categorized the source of each inference in the way that you did.
   a. Jack and Annabel are playing ball with their dad. Jack has a big glove on his left hand.
   b. "Look at that butterfly," said the caterpillar. "It reminds me of my future."

6. Tell what the statement below means:
An external text puts constraints on the content of the internal text.

7. The following sign was seen at a newspaper stand in an airport:

> This in not a library.
> The newspapers and magazines are for sale!

For this external text, compose an internal text.

REFERENCES

1. Anderson, Richard C. "The Notion of Schemata and the Educational Enterprise." In R. C. Anderson, R. J. Spiro, and W. E. Montague (Eds.), *Schooling and the Acquisition of Knowledge.* Hillsdale, N.J.: Lawrence Erlbaum, 1977.

2. Anderson, Richard C.; Reynolds, Ralph E.; Schallert, Diane L.; and Goetz, Ernest T. "Frameworks for Comprehending Discourse." *American Educational Research Journal* 14 (Fall, 1977), 367–381.

3. Mandler, J. M., and Johnson, N. S. "Remembrance of Things Passed: Story Structure and Recall." *Cognitive Psychology* 9 (March, 1977), 111–151.

4. Nessel, Denise. "The New Face of Comprehension Instruction: A Closer Look at Questions." *Reading Teacher* 40 (March, 1987), 604–606.

5. Omanson, Richard C.; Warren, William H.; and Trabasso, Tom. "Goals, Inferential Comprehension, and Recall of Stories by Children." *Discourse Processes,* 1 (October, 1978), 337–354.

6. Raphael, Taffy E. "Teaching Question-Answer Relationships, Revisited." *Reading Teacher* 39 (February, 1986), 516–522.

7. Rosenblatt, Louise M. *The Reader, the Text, the Poem: The Transactional Theory of Literary Work.* Carbondale: Southern Illinois University Press, 1978.

8. Rosenblatt, Louise M. *Writing and Reading: The Transactional Theory* (Technical Report No. 416). Urbana-Champaign: University of Illinois, Center for the Study of Reading, 1988.

9. Stein, Nancy L. *How Children Understand Stories: A Developmental Analysis* (Technical Report No. 69). Urbana-Champaign: University of Illinois, Center for the Study of Reading, 1978.

CHAPTER 2

The Reading Teacher

· · · · · · ·
PREVIEW

Now that Chapter 1 has helped you to think about the reading process, Chapter 2 encourages you to think about the reading teacher.

The fact that the selected focus of the chapter is teachers in classrooms is not a denial of the effectiveness of other teachers. It is recognized, for instance, that some children learn as much about how to read out of school as they do in school. Not to be overlooked *in* school is the success that children may have in teaching their peers. And, lest we forget, some children are remarkably successful in teaching themselves. This last point is important, because it reminds us that learning is the product of much more than what is usually thought of as instruction. To sum up, then, even though teachers, teaching, and learning do come in many different sizes and forms, the concern of Chapter 2 is the classroom teacher. More specific concerns are the instruction she provides and the materials she uses.

For purposes of discussion, instruction is divided into three kinds: planned and intentional; unplanned but intentional; and unplanned, unintentional. Each kind is illustrated with examples originating in classrooms that have been observed. As explained earlier in the Introduction, one reason for including references to actual classrooms is to add both specificity and authenticity to points being made. The points that *are* being made should not be overlooked when accounts of classrooms are read.

As we know from our own experiences, teaching reading in American classrooms has been associated for a long time with commercially prepared materials known as basal readers and basal workbooks. Although Chapter 2 refers to these materials briefly—they are discussed in more detail later—the emphasis in the chapter is on the need for teachers to make greater use of more authentic materials, including the text that is liberally displayed in the environment.

Because basal materials continue to enjoy a prominent place in classrooms, the consequences of a dependent use of them by teachers is also considered. It is in this section that you become acquainted with Teacher A and Teacher B, to whom many references are made in subsequent chapters. Predictably, then, one postreading question for Chapter 2 is, What is meant by "Teacher A" and "Teacher B"?

· · · · · · ·

WHETHER FOR READING OR MATHEMATICS or some other subject, most people think of school instruction in the context of lessons. Some of us have also experienced lessons out of school—for instance, piano and swimming lessons.

Regardless of the topic, lessons aim toward the achievement of one or more goals. At times, goals have to be changed because the individuals being instructed show evidence of having already attained them or, as the case may be, of not yet being ready to achieve them.

Typically, lessons include practice, initially done under the instructor's supervision. This allows for monitoring what has or has not been achieved. For the students, it provides opportunities to raise questions or, perhaps, to request one more explanation or demonstration. Subsequently, independent practice by students is expected.

Whether a lesson has to do with reading or swimming, its success is measured by the extent to which the reading or swimming is better than it was before the lesson began.

Given the fact that lessons like those just described are generally familiar, this chapter starts by considering the components of lessons for reading. They are grouped under the heading "preplanned, intentional instruction." Later sections discuss (a) unplanned, intentional instruction, and (b) unplanned, unintentional instruction. Brief descriptions of the three follow.

1. *Planned, intentional instruction:* A teacher offers instruction designed to achieve a preestablished objective.
2. *Unplanned, intentional instruction:* Something occurs by chance that has the potential to be instructive. The teacher consciously attempts to realize the potential.
3. *Unplanned, unintentional instruction:* An event occurs that teaches students something.

PLANNED, INTENTIONAL INSTRUCTION

The four components of planned, intentional instruction are listed below:

Components of a Lesson
1. Objective
2. Instruction
3. Practice
   a. Supervised
   b. Independent
4. Application

Each component is discussed in the sections that follow.

Objective

Like travelers with a destination, teachers offering planned, intentional instruction have a goal. Their goal or objective is what they intend students will know, understand, or be able to do as a consequence of instruction. Sample objectives follow:

- Students will know the referent for a pronoun when the pronoun precedes the referent in a sentence. [E.g., *Even though they are thin, the dogs eat well.*]
- Students will recognize evidence that shows parts of a biography are fiction. [E.g., A conversation between the subject of a biography and her brother when they were young children.]
- Students will understand the meaning of an unfamiliar word when an appositive explains it. [E.g., *The merino, a variety of sheep that originated in Spain, produces fine wool.*]

The most important point to make about objectives is that they are worth realizing only if they will be useful. To spend time, for example, on appositives when nothing that students are, or soon will be, reading contains appositives is senseless. Actually, the lack of connections between what is taught and what children can use in their reading has been the subject of much criticism over the years (10, 12). In recent times, the most vocal critics have been associated with the *whole language movement* (1, 16), which emphasizes making connections ("wholeness") not only within an area such as reading but also across the curriculum.

When an objective *is* worth pursuing, plans for achieving it should be made with care. Having said that, let me add right away that once plans begin to be implemented, student reactions—or their absence—may suggest the need for modifications. Plans for lessons, therefore, should be viewed not as a script to follow but as a carefully arranged journey that may take unexpected detours. Because the detours in executing plans directly reflect the students being instructed, they can be the most enlightening parts of a lesson.

Instruction

Traditionally, we think of instructing as providing explanations, information, demonstrations, examples, and—for the purpose of clarifying—nonexamples. Posing questions also serves a number of purposes: to maintain student involvement, to check what is being learned, and to see whether the pace of the lesson is suitable. Because questions from students often serve similar functions, they should be both encouraged and respected.

Just as interest in the processes involved in comprehending has increased, so, too, has interest in instruction referred to as *modeling*. In the case of reading, modeling is displaying mental processes that might be used to reach a goal or to solve a problem encountered while reading. "Making thinking public" is the way Scott Paris characterizes modeling (18). Were a teacher to model how to get acquainted with a new textbook, procedures could be clarified with a "think-aloud" by the teacher (6) that might begin as follows:

> Because this is a new textbook, I think I'll take a look at the Table of Contents to see the names of the chapters.... It looks as if we'll be studying different parts of the United States this year. Last year, our textbook had a glossary in the back. I think I'll see what's at the end of this book that might be helpful....

When teachers choose modeling to instruct, it is sometimes followed by a request for modeling from one or more students. This provides not only additional instruction but also the chance to learn whether the teacher's modeling has succeeded in communicating clear explanations. When students do the modeling, they often need help—especially when modeling is a new experience or when what is being made visible is complex. At such times, *scaffolding* should be provided. This term refers to the support—hence the name *scaffolding*—that teachers give when students are attempting something new or difficult (3). A combination of encouragement plus prompts, reminders, and questions from a teacher is often enough to move students from doing something with support to doing it independently.

Practice

The brief reference to scaffolding should be enough to show that instruction and supervised practice are not always distinctly different. In fact, the components of a lesson listed earlier should not be thought of as discrete steps, because one often blends with another. Nor should the components be thought of as occurring in an unbroken sequence. After all, the information that teachers pick up when supervised practice is occurring may signal that students are ready to move immediately to applying what they learned. On the other hand, it may reveal the need to start over because, for whatever reason, the instruction provided earlier was insufficiently helpful.

Application

In a sense, application is the most important part of a lesson because it allows students the opportunity to use in their reading what they have been asked to learn or do. Experiencing the value of instruction adds substantially to students' interest in learning still more.

PLANNED, INTENTIONAL INSTRUCTION: SOME PRECAUTIONS

In theory, it is difficult to dispute the efficacy of offering lessons made up of the components just discussed. Each component contributes to successful, efficient learning. Nonetheless, putting into practice what seems theoretically desirable may have undesirable consequences. Objectives that do not reflect the requirements of reading or of students' needs, practice and application that never get beyond workbook exercises to authentic reading—these are some problems that are possible but not inevitable. To bring the discussion of planned, intentional instruction to a close, therefore, guidelines are offered that should keep lessons from becoming monotonous, unexamined routines.

Guidelines for Teaching

Objectives
- Whether instruction is planned or spontaneous, a definite objective ought to guide its development. The objective should be one that, if realized, advances students' reading ability.
- Objectives should relate directly to students' reading because this makes them useful immediately. In fact, if students do not experience the practical value of

what is taught, then lessons become little more than something they reluctantly learn to endure.

- Keeping the objective in mind (*"Why* am I doing what I'm doing?") minimizes the likelihood of wandering away from what is necessary for realizing the objective.
- Whenever instruction is offered at the time students demonstrate they do not understand something, no need exists to explain the significance of the instruction. In such instances, the value for solving a real problem is apparent.

The Instruction Itself

- Teaching reading should not be equated with delivering one lecture after another. To view it that way runs the risk of replacing reading with lessons about reading.
- Instruction should not be allowed to become an end in itself. Keeping it in close contact with students' current reading (assigned or voluntary) helps avoid that pitfall.
- Just as variety is the spice of life so, too, does variety characterize instruction that keeps students attentive. Replacing tedious explanations with modeling and, for instance, involving students by posing problems and questions allow for variety as well as the likelihood that students will listen and watch and think.
- Whatever form instruction takes, it should be no longer or more detailed than achievement of the objective requires. Teachers, like preachers and authors, need to work at knowing when to quit.
- The pace of instruction should be matched to students' abilities. Some children require detailed help; others profit most from instruction that moves along at a brisk pace.

Practice and Application

- With practice, "rules were made to be broken." Even though it was recommended that instruction should be followed by supervised and independent practice, there are times when instruction is so obviously successful (or students are so obviously bright) that application can follow the instruction.
- Practice should be connected with, not detached from, meaningful reading. This calls into question the heavy reliance on workbook exercises still seen in some classrooms. Whenever practice is carried on in the context of authentic reading, it closely resembles application.
- One of the best ways to provide both practice and application is to allow students time for self-selected, uninterrupted reading.

What has now been said can be summed up by stating that superior teachers do not rely on recipes—not even on good recipes. Rather, they have cookbooks in their heads from which they make selections based on what needs to be taught to whom.

UNPLANNED, INTENTIONAL INSTRUCTION

The description "unplanned, intentional instruction" refers to occasions when (a) something not anticipated happens that has the potential to be instructive for students, and (b) a teacher takes advantage of the occasion to make it instructive. The examples used initially to explain such instruction focus on students' erroneous responses because, first, they are inevitable and, second, they offer opportunities for on-the-spot help. The second group of examples are commonly called teachable moments.

Using Incorrect Responses

Because asking questions is something teachers do with noticeable frequency, students' errors are often incorrect responses to questions. Unfortunately, such errors are not always used productively. In fact, classroom-observation research spanning three decades identifies repeated use of an IRE pattern: teacher *initiates,* student *responds,* teacher *evaluates* (5, 7, 12, 14, 17). An elaboration of the pattern follows:

1. Teacher poses a question about a piece of text students have read and calls on one student to answer.
2. If the answer is correct, the teacher asks another question.
3. If the answer is incorrect, additional students are called on (or volunteer) until one offers the desired response.
4. Another question is then asked.

Even though the above sequence is familiar to us all, it hardly constitutes the best use of anyone's time. Assuming a question has but one right answer, students should at least receive feedback that helps them understand *why* their response is unacceptable. Should students give a series of incorrect responses, one teacher might decide to stop responding to each incorrect answer and, instead, switch to an attempt to walk the students through the text so that she can make explicit the act of answering questions. More specifically, if the student who responded first said, "A hundred gold coins" when the correct answer is "A hundred silver coins," the teacher might begin as follows (15, p. 23):

> Let's go back through the story to answer the question again. The question is, "What was Anna to bring to court?" Read the first paragraph silently.... Does any sentence in that paragraph tell what Anna was to bring to court?... Jack, read the sentence that says what Anna is supposed to bring....

In the face of the same series of wrong answers, another teacher may also decide that corrective instruction is needed; however, her decision is to take the time to think through a lesson before offering it the following day. The next day's lesson falls under the heading "planned, intentional instruction."

Using Teachable Moments

Let me continue the discussion of *un*planned, intentional instruction with a reference to a teachable moment that occurred when a teacher was reading to her second-grade class from a book that provided information about a topic they were studying: pollution in the environment. The last sentence at the bottom of a page that was about to be turned ended with the word *smog;* as the teacher turned the page, she inquired, "Does anyone know what 'smog' is?" Nobody did. The teacher then answered her own question ("It's smoky fog.") and continued reading. Even though excessive interruptions should be avoided, I believe this was a time when stopping to do the following would have been a positive addition to the reading.

Adhering to the important guideline *Don't just talk about it—show it*! the teacher could have written three words on the chalkboard, which was behind her:

> smoke
>
> > > smog
>
> > fog

With the help of the words, the teacher could have shown how *smog* makes use of both *smoke* and *fog*—appropriately so, as it is a combination of the two.

An account of another teachable moment, described by the teacher who took advantage of it, is in Figure 2.1. The detailed description is useful in showing how productive activities can originate in an unexpected happening.

Earlier, when instruction was being discussed, examples and nonexamples were cited as possible contributors to instruction. Nonexamples were named because they help to clarify by providing contrasts. With that in mind, I want to describe a contrast to the teacher who took advantage of the interest shown in a boy's very colorful shirt. This contrasting teacher also teaches third grade.

When the observation started, the teacher had just begun to work with five boys who were much more interested in a pencil than in the reader they were being told to open. The pencil's attraction was both the die attached to one end and the advertisement for a new furniture store printed on its side. The latter said, "Don't gamble on quality. See us first." At the time the pencil was taken from its owner, he and the other boys were doing their best to read the two sentences. Because they did anything but try hard to read the story in the reader—they repeatedly stated that they had read it in second grade—a question had to be raised about why the textbook was not temporarily laid aside in order to allow for attention to the slogan on the pencil because it had so much potential for comprehension. To illustrate, the meaning of "Don't gamble on quality" could have been contrasted with the meaning of "Don't gamble on a horse," immediately establishing the opportunity to talk about literal and figurative language. Or, the words *die* and *dice* could have been written and discussed in the framework of unusual ways to form plural nouns. Words like *quantity* and *quality* might have been considered along with such questions as, When is quality more important than quantity? Is quantity ever more important than quality? Instead of doing anything like this, the teacher spent the time on some very poor oral reading, while the boys insisted they had read the story when they were in second grade.

Even though the reference to this classroom incident is *not* intended to convey the notion that instructional programs should proceed according to students' whims, it *is* meant to emphasize that teachable moments do occur and that they may have greater potential than the most carefully planned instruction.

I teach third grade. My class is made up primarily of students whose achievement in reading is hampered by a limited knowledge of word meanings. That is why I'm always looking for opportunities to give attention to vocabulary. Thanks to a boy who arrived Monday wearing an unusually colorful shirt, I'm giving time this week to the concept "pattern." Because the boy's shirt attracted much attention but little in the way of specific descriptions, I decided to work on patterns with the entire class.

Today (Tuesday) after lunch, everyone was surprised to find a large male paper doll on a bulletin board. Mr. Fashion was wearing a polka dot hat, a striped shirt, and checkered pants. Once the class quieted down, we discussed ways to describe his clothing. Eventually, "polka dot," "checkered," and "striped" were printed on the chalkboard next to the bulletin board. I explained that all referred to patterns, after which I wrote *pattern.* (With the help of my questions, "pattern" was defined as "something that is repeated.") After the group reread the words on the board, I held up three cards on which the words for the patterns had been printed. As each was reread, I attached the card to the bulletin board next to the appropriate piece of clothing that Mr. Fashion was wearing. We then talked about other places where the same three patterns are found. (References were made to such things as tablecloths, food packaging, and games.) Finally, I suggested that it might be fun for everybody to draw their own Mr. Fashion, using the same patterns. I also mentioned the possibility of writing about their Mr. Fashion, once the pictures were done.

Originally, I thought I'd follow the same procedures tomorrow afternoon, this time using a Ms. Fashion paper doll. (We talked earlier in the year about *Ms.* when we were discussing abbreviations.) However, because almost nobody wanted to do any writing, I changed plans. (Ms. Fashion will wear a hat made of a print fabric, a solid colored blouse, and a plaid skirt.) Everything will be done the same way except for the drawing and writing.

Tomorrow, I'll show the students store catalogues and sports magazines that will be left on one of the larger tables. I'll show them five large envelopes, each displaying words for one of the patterns. Now the suggestion will be to look through the catalogues and magazines whenever free time is available in order to cut out examples of the patterns. If, for instance, a baseball player is pictured in a striped uniform, that picture will be placed in the envelope labeled *striped.* I will remind everyone that if any of the pattern words cannot be recalled, the cards next to Mr. and Ms. Fashion on the bulletin board will help. I also plan to say that on Friday afternoon we'll take a look at each envelope to see what has been found and, in particular, to learn if the patterns were identified correctly. Only time will tell how the plan works.

FIGURE 2.1 Making the Most of Teachable Moments

UNPLANNED, UNINTENTIONAL INSTRUCTION

For good or bad, unplanned, unintentional instruction is probably more common *and* effective than anybody realizes. The fact, for instance, that children are known to carry in their heads misconceptions about the nature of reading may be attributed to the frequent, persistent practice of having students take turns reading aloud while others follow the text silently. This activity, commonly called round robin reading, may account for one researcher's hearing a fourth-grade student claim that the most important reason for reading her basal textbook was "to learn to say all the words right and with expression" (21, p. 351).

Unintentionally, one or more teachers who have round robin reading daily may account for a conversation overheard in a doctor's waiting room. The conversation is approximated below:

Woman: I see you like to read.
Girl: It's okay.
Woman: It looks as if lots of children have looked at that book (referring to a dog-eared book that the girl was scanning).
Girl: I guess so.
Woman: I bet you're a good reader.
Girl: No, I'm not.
Woman: You're not?
Girl: No. I don't read loud enough.

On the positive side, the most important thing a student might learn when his teacher takes time to find a book about castles is that reading ability is a highly useful possession. This may be the case even though the teacher's only conscious intention was to satisfy a student's curiosity about castles.

In any discussion of unplanned, unintentional instruction, parents should not be forgotten. It is not accidental, for instance, that when children who acquire initial reading ability at home are studied (9, 13), a typical finding is that one or both parents are avid readers. This is not surprising when it is remembered that just hearing people chuckle as they read adds a positive note to that ability. Nor is it surprising that parents who spend their free time watching television often have children who are fans of television, not of books.

The effectiveness of what is being categorized as unplanned, unintentional instruction accounts for well-known maxims like:

"Attitudes are as much caught as they are taught."
"I can't hear what you're saying for the noise of what you're doing."
"Don't do what I do. Do as I say."

THREE KINDS OF INSTRUCTION: A SUMMARY

One characteristic of effective instruction is the use of reviews that permit students to see and compare what is different but related—for example, similes and metaphors, facts and opinions. To review now, examples of the three kinds of instruction that have been discussed are in Figure 2.2.

INSTRUCTIONAL MATERIALS

Several references are made in the chapter to basal reader materials. Basal series, made up of readers and workbooks for students and manuals for teachers, have been used in classrooms for a long time. Their continued presence explains why it is almost inevitable to find references to basal materials when classroom events related to reading are reported.

For as long as basal series have been used, they have been criticized. The 1980s, however, may end up as the decade of basal bashing because, in retrospect, those years witnessed more frequent criticism of basal series than occurred previously. This is related to the fact that, during the same decade, a substantial increase occurred in the number of researchers reporting classroom-observation studies.

Teachers' Use of Materials

When researchers who observed in elementary classrooms began to report their findings, similar conclusions had to be drawn. Few, for example, saw instruction; however, many found what came to be called "mentioning," defined as "saying just enough about a topic to allow for an assignment related to it" (12, p. 505). More often than not, the assignments originated in workbooks and exercise sheets that schools purchase from basal reader publishers. Large amounts of time were also spent on round robin reading and on comprehension assessment questions asked in ways not likely to make them instructive for students.

A more general conclusion supported by the classroom studies is that, in many instances, the major thrust behind classroom procedures is not to teach students but to move them through commercially prepared materials (2, 8, 11, 12). Or, to state the same conclusion differently, the observation data suggest that the planning many teachers do focuses not on what they will help students learn but on what they will have students do.

Because what students continue to do in a large number of classrooms are assignments originating in a basal series, the essence of the conclusions reached by classroom observers can be summed up with a reference to what I call in this textbook Teacher A and Teacher B. Both are depicted in Figure 2.3 (p. 28).

The classroom studies portray Teacher B as being more concerned about covering commercially prepared materials than about teaching particular children. Because Teacher B abides by the recommendations in these materials, she is characterized in Figure 2.3 as an assistant to them. Among the by-products of such a role is too little incentive to become more knowledgeable about reading and reading instruction. For Teacher B herself, the most undesirable consequence may be the omission of reflection about the meaning and significance of her work as a teacher.

Whereas Teacher B is subordinate to materials in the sense that she allows them to dictate what will be taught, how it will be taught, and even when it will be taught,

1. Unplanned, Unintentional Instruction

    During postreading discussions, a teacher habitually asks so many comprehension assessment questions that some inevitably deal with insignificant details.

    Outcome: Students reach an incorrect conclusion about the nature of proficient reading, namely, that it requires paying attention to, and remembering, every detail in a piece of text.

2. Unplanned, Unintentional Instruction

    A teacher who is an avid reader of novels often comments to her fifth graders about the characters in the book she is currently reading. (E.g., "Last night, I have to admit, I cried a little when Alex died in a car accident. Interestingly, I didn't even finish the novel I started last week because I found I didn't care what happened to the characters. They were more like puppets than real people.")

    Outcome: Some students begin to pay more attention to how the authors of the novels they read portray characters.

3. Unplanned, Intentional Instruction

    A teachable moment occurs when a student refers to whales as "fish." The teacher responds by explaining why whales are mammals, not fish.

    Outcome: Students learn why a whale is not a fish.

4. Planned, Intentional Instruction

    To provide further corrective instruction, the teacher just referred to reads a colorfully illustrated expository book on the following day that tells about whales and dolphins. The book explains why whales and dolphins are both mammals, not fish.

    Outcome: Students have a more detailed understanding of the differences between fish and mammals.

5. Planned, Intentional Instruction

    Three derived words (*unhurt, playful, careless*) with familiar roots are in the basal reader selection that will be assigned next. Prior to making the assignment, a teacher explains the nature of derived words with the help of the three examples. She tells the students that these words are in the story they will soon be reading.

    Outcome: Students begin to learn that some words are roots and that certain letters can be added to them, both at the beginning and the end, to form different but related words.

6. Planned, Intentional Instruction

    The basal reader manual that one teacher uses describes procedures for teaching the contrasting meanings of *or* and *and*. Because the description suggests suitable illustrations, includes clear explanations, and refers to sentences in the next basal selection that include *or* and *and,* the teacher follows the manual's recommendations.

    Outcome: Students understand the meanings of *or* and *and* and demonstrate their understanding by correctly explaining how text like *pie* and *cake* and *pie* or *cake* differ in meaning. In the postreading discussion, they are also able to explain the meaning of *and* and *or* in sentences in the basal selection.

FIGURE 2.2 Examples of Three Kind of Instruction

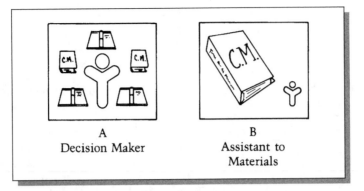

FIGURE 2.3   Contrasting Teachers

Teacher A makes key decisions herself. Once decisions *are* made about necessary instructional objectives, Teacher A uses whatever materials are likely to forward her efforts to attain them. Although not directed by materials, Teacher A is knowledgeable about what is available—more knowledgeable than Teacher B.

Correct Understanding of Instructional Materials

It must be said that teachers who equate instructional materials with basal reader materials have an exceedingly circumscribed perspective that cannot help but result in classroom routines marked by boredom. In contrast, an underlying assumption of this book is that anything that displays text has the potential to be instructive. Instructional materials, therefore, include bumper stickers, catalogs, grocery lists, newspapers, magazines, posters, greeting cards, pencils and ads with slogans, recipes, maps, and labeled boxes, packages, bottles, and cans.

To specify the instructional potential of the unorthodox textbook, a few examples are listed in Figure 2.4. Not noted there are two other benefits of using unorthodox textbooks: They are of interest to students and, further, they help bridge the gap between life in classrooms and what is seen and experienced outside its doors.

Instructional Materials: A Whole Language View

Whole language supporters have been especially effective in their criticisms of inauthentic text—that is, of materials developed expressly for the purpose of teaching reading. Not unexpectedly, a common target of the complaints is basal reader materials. One specific complaint is the inclusion in basal readers of abridged versions of good stories. To counteract this practice, a more generous use of literature has been endorsed. Two problems with obvious solutions have accompanied both partial and complete acceptance of the recommendation. The first problem is lopsided programs in the sense that they have overlooked the need for students to learn how to comprehend expository and procedural text. One survey reports, for

Source	Text	Helpful for Teaching
Sign in lot where bank is being constructed	"New Quarters for Your Quarters"	Multiple meanings of *quarters*. One function of underlining.
Sign on restaurant door	"No shirt. No shoes. No service."	Implicit cause-effect relationship.
Bumper sticker on truck	"Love they neighbor. Tune thy piano."	Dependence of comprehension on world knowledge. Implied relationship between sentences.

FIGURE 2.4   Instructional Value of Environmental Text

example, that "fully 75 percent of all books used [in literature-based programs] are fiction" (4, p. 2).

In some classrooms in which the use of literature replaces basal readers, instruction is also overlooked. This problem is illustrated in an account of a second grade (see Figure 2.5).

CONCLUDING COMMENTS

The account in Figure 2.5 allows for making several comments, which add up to an appropriate way to conclude a chapter concerned with teachers, teaching, and instructional materials.

To begin, providing instruction is a desirable use of a teacher's time only when (a) its objective has not yet been achieved by the students being instructed, and (b) the objective relates directly to what children need or want to read. What students do read should be some combination of narrative, expository, and procedural text. Even though many wonderful, beautifully illustrated stories are available, the mixture is a realistic reflection of literacy needs. A mixture of assigned reading—assigned for some good reason—and self-selected reading is also desirable.

The desirability of providing authentic materials, timely instruction, and meaningful application for *all* students should also be apparent. This point is made because I am seeing too many classrooms in which the best readers get the goodies while the poorest get the workbooks. If we are going to work hard to assemble better ways to produce literacy, it is vitally important that *all* students profit from such efforts.

In this second grade, tremendous variability in reading ability exists. The teacher said she had four reading groups because of the differences. All but the top group were doing workbook pages. Following is a description of the best readers, who were sitting at a table with the teacher.

The children took turns reading *Little Red Hen* stories they themselves had written and illustrated. The books were nicely done. The children read their books with pride and enjoyment. The teacher then passed out copies of *Frog and Toad Are Friends.* She reminded the group that this was a familiar story because they had heard it earlier in the Listening Center. She then said:

> Open to the very first page. This is the title page, and it tells you who wrote the book and who publishes it. (A brief discussion of "publish" followed. Nothing was written on the board.) Turn to the next page. Here it says "For Barbara Barack." That means the author wrote the book for someone he liked. This is called a "dedication." (Again: Nothing written. Teacher remains seated.) Turn to the next page. What does that say? Nobody knows? The <u>c</u> makes a /k/ sound—the word is "Contents." This page tells what's in the book. Look at the word "Spring." Why is number 4 next to it? Now a student responds, "It starts on page 4," after which the teacher suggests, "Let's check to see if that's true."

The children continued to look at the Table of Contents to check to see if chapters began on the pages listed. Then the teacher told them that the story was about "two guys who are the best of friends." She directed the children to read in their heads and, if there were words they didn't know, to ask for help. The teacher stayed with the children, sitting at the table. As it turned out, they asked for help with many words. All the teacher did was name them directly.

What could have been done differently and, perhaps, better? This teacher did introduce the book effectively; however, she missed opportunities to be a teacher. For example, when she said that *c* in the word *Contents* records /k/, she could have written the word and talked about the generalization for the hard and soft sounds of *c*. (This is certainly something these second graders should know.) Also, instead of telling the students to ask for help with an unfamiliar word, she could have pretaught words likely to cause problems. I suggest this because, as it turned out, the children did need help with many words and often with the same ones. Had she at least made a list of the words, they could have been considered later. But, she didn't do that, either.

These children might have been better prepared to read *Frog and Toad Are Friends* independently had the teacher asked them what they recalled about the story from hearing it in the Listening Center. Activating their knowledge of the story might have helped when they met an unknown word. That is, they could use both the context in the story and the content in their heads about the whole story in order to decide what it said.

In summary, I think this teacher provided the students with some useful information but not with instruction that could help them become better readers. Children do learn to read by reading—but they are likely to learn even more with a little relevant instruction offered at appropriate times.

FIGURE 2.5   Absence of Instruction in a Second-Grade Classroom

SUMMARY

What is commonly thought of as lessons was described first in Chapter 2 under the heading "Planned, Intentional Instruction." The description was detailed because such instruction is always necessary. A detailed consideration of lessons is also warranted because lessons lend themselves to becoming unexamined routines. That is why the fairly lengthy section "Some Precautions" was included. In a sense, the gist of the precautions is stated in the belief that the most important question teachers can ask themselves is, "*Why* am I doing what I'm doing?"

The next type of instruction discussed, unplanned but intentional, is especially characteristic of highly effective teachers. As Chapter 2 explained, on-the-spot instruction stands a good chance of being successful because students see it as an attempt to solve a problem. Such instruction thus comes across as being less contrived than does some of the intentional, planned instruction that is seen.

The third kind of instruction considered, unplanned and unintentional, is an acknowledgment that students learn many things from what a teacher says, asks, or does even though what was said or done was never thought, or intended, to be instructive. The maxim "We teach what we are" reflects both the existence *and* effectiveness of unplanned, unintentional instruction.

The need to link the objectives of instruction and the materials that students need or want to read explains why the treatment of instruction in the chapter was followed by a section on instructional materials. Traditionally, teaching reading has been tied to textbooks known as basal readers; consequently, references were made to unorthodox "textbooks" that come in such forms as bumper stickers and highway signs. How these kinds of text allow for instruction was illustrated.

The common reliance on textbooks and teaching manuals also accounts for the discussion of teachers in the context of Teacher A, the decision maker, and Teacher B, the assistant to commercial materials. Such a context made it natural to point out how the commercialization of instruction often results in greater concern for covering material than for teaching students.

REVIEW

1. Explain with examples the meaning of (a) planned, intentional instruction, (b) unplanned, intentional instruction, and (c) unplanned, unintentional instruction. Use examples different from those in Chapter 2.

2. The discussion of planned, intentional instruction concluded with reminders of ways to make it maximally effective as well as meaningful for students. Name some of the reminders. As you do, explain the connection between a reminder and the importance of teachers' acquiring the habit of asking themselves, "*Why* am I doing what I'm doing?"

3. Explain: Scaffolding, which may figure in instruction, shows that instruction and supervised practice are not always essentially different.

4. Describe Teacher A and Teacher B.

5. What is meant by the commercialization of instruction?

6. What is the difference between (a) planning that concentrates on learning, and (b) planning that is concerned with doing?

7. Round robin reading refers to what? Why was it discussed under the heading "Unplanned, unintentional instruction"? The chapter cited one negative consequence when round robin reading is used routinely. What is that consequence and why is it an undesirable one?

8. Chapter 1 discussed narrative, expository, and procedural text. Why does Chapter 2 refer again to these kinds of text?

REFERENCES

1. Altwerger, Bess; Edelsky, Carole; and Flores, Barbara M. "Whole Language: What's New?" *Reading Teacher* 41 (November, 1987), 144–154.

2. Alvermann, Donna E.; O'Brien, David G.; and Dillon, Deborah R. "What Teachers Do When They Say They're Having Discussions of Content Area Reading Assignments: A Qualitative Analysis." *Reading Research Quarterly* 25 (1990, No. 4), 296–322.

3. Applebee, Arthur N., and Langer, Judith A. "Instructional Scaffolding: Reading and Writing as Natural Language Activities." *Language Arts* 60 (February, 1983), 168–175.

4. Association of American Publishers. "Reading Initiative News," Vol. 1, No. 1 (Winter, 1990), 2.

5. Cazden, Courtney B. *Classroom Discourse: The Language of Teaching and Learning.* Portsmouth, N.H.: Heinemann, 1988.

6. Davey, Beth. "Think Aloud—Modeling the Cognitive Process of Reading Comprehension." *Journal of Reading* 27 (October, 1983), 44–47.

7. Duffy, Gerald G. "From Turn-Taking to Sense-Making: Toward a Broader Definition of Reading Teacher Effectiveness." *Journal of Educational Research* 76 (January–February, 1983), 134–139.

8. Duffy, Gerald G.; Roehler, Laura R.; and Putnam, Joyce. "Putting the Teacher in Control: Basal Reading Textbooks and Instructional Decision Making." *Elementary School Journal* 87 (January, 1987), 355–366.

9. Durkin, Dolores. *Children Who Read Early.* New York: Teachers College Press, Columbia University, 1966.

10. Durkin, Dolores. "Dolores Durkin Speaks on Instruction." *Reading Teacher* 43 (March, 1990), 472–476.

11. Durkin, Dolores. "Matching Instruction with Reading Abilities." *Remedial and Special Education* 11 (May/June, 1990), 23–28.

12. Durkin, Dolores. "What Classroom Observations Reveal about Comprehension Instruction." *Reading Research Quarterly* 14 (1978–79, No. 4), 481–533.

13. Greaney, Vincent. "Parental Influences on Reading." *Reading Teacher* 39 (April, 1986), 813–818.

14. Guszak, Frank J. "Teacher Questioning and Reading." *Reading Teacher* 21 (December, 1967), 227–234.

15. Meyer, Linda A. *Strategies for Correcting Students' Wrong Responses.* Technical Report No. 354. Urbana: University of Illinois, Center for the Study of Reading, December, 1985.

16. Newman, Judith M., and Church, Susan M. "Myths of Whole Language." *Reading Teacher* 44 (September, 1990), 20–26.

17. O'Flahavan, J. F.; Hartman, Douglas K.; and Pearson, P. David. *Teacher Questioning and Feedback Practices after the Cognitive Revolution.* Technical Report No. 461. Urbana: University of Illinois, Center for the Study of Reading, February, 1989.

18. Paris, Scott G. "Using Classroom Dialogues and Guided Practice to Teach Comprehension Strategies." In Theodore L. Harris and Eric J. Cooper (Eds.), *Reading, Thinking, and Concept Development.* New York: College Entrance Board, 1985, 133–144.

19. Shannon, Patrick. "Commercial Reading Materials, a Technological Ideology, and the Deskilling of Teachers." *Elementary School Journal* 87 (January, 1987), 307–329.

20. Thomas, Karen F. "Early Reading as a Social Interaction Process." *Language Arts* 62 (September, 1985), 469–475.

21. Wixson, Karen K.; Bosky, Anita B.; Yochum, M. Nina; and Alvermann, Donna E. "An Interview for Assessing Students' Perceptions of Classroom Reading Tasks." *Reading Teacher* 37 (January, 1984), 346–352.

CHAPTER 3

Reading: Silent or Oral?

Chapter 1 looks at the reading process; Chapter 2, at the reading teacher. The concern now is when should reading be silent and when should students read orally. This question is raised as early as Chapter 3 because some teachers and many parents equate teaching reading with listening to children read aloud.

Even though oral reading *is* common in classrooms, it is likely that you took for granted that the many references to reading in the previous chapters were to reading done silently. That is an expected conclusion, given the fact that relatively little oral reading is done outside of school.

To reinforce its scarcity, recall the last time you found oral reading was necessary. Perhaps somebody in your home asked you to read a telephone number aloud or to read the weather forecast from the newspaper. Although there *are* times when the reason to read makes it necessary to read aloud, a request to recall when silent reading was used would result in a long list of examples, including the reading of this Preview right now.

To underscore with recollections and comparisons the significance of silent reading out of school is not meant to suggest that oral reading ought to be eliminated *in* school. In fact, the central purpose of Chapter 3 is to help teachers and prospective teachers make knowledgeable decisions about when to allot time to silent reading and when to have students read orally.

Like life itself, the rest of this book attends mostly to silent reading; in contrast, Chapter 3 allots generous space to oral reading. Initially, its use with young children is covered. That reading and comprehending are synonymous explains why the next section concentrates on the role oral reading plays in comprehension instruction. The chapter then deals with oral reading from a broader perspective in order to identify more generally its contributions to instructional programs.

Once positive uses of oral reading are identified, the focus shifts to a critique of a questionable use: round robin reading, during which one child reads aloud while other members of the group follow the same text silently. Although round robin reading is usually associated with the primary grades, it is also used with older students. When it is, poor readers generally are the participants. On the other hand, when round robin reading is the means used to get through something like a social studies textbook, an entire class is likely to be involved. You may, in fact, remember all this from your own days in elementary school. Keep those experiences in mind as you make your way through Chapter 3.

TWO APPROPRIATE USES of oral reading are with children who are just starting to read. The two are referred to briefly because they are discussed in Chapter 4. After that, oral reading for comprehension instruction is considered.

ORAL READING FOR THE BEGINNER

One of the many things teachers need to help beginners understand is that written words are not as strange as they may at first appear to be—that, in fact, the squiggles on a page "say" what the children themselves might say. One of the best ways to promote this understanding is to write what a child says and to read back aloud whatever *was* said. Teachers commonly do this as early as nursery school; often, the dictated text is about a child's art.

Once children begin to do a little reading themselves, it is important to provide overt evidence of this newly acquired ability. Encouraging them to read something aloud is an effective way to confirm an "I can read!" conclusion. To allow even brief readings to be cognitive in nature, teachers can have children read to themselves something as limited as *two yellow chicks,* after which the teacher poses questions: "Do these words say something about children?... Do they tell about the weather?...Whom *do* these words tell about? Read them aloud so that I'll know what they say."

The recommendation to have young beginners read to themselves may have prompted the question, But *can* they read silently? Here, a distinction needs to be made between reading silently and reading to oneself. Young children *can* read to themselves but, usually, they cannot do this without being heard. As their competence accumulates, the ability to read silently increases, too.

Now let's switch the focus to the role that oral reading plays in comprehension instruction.

ORAL READING FOR COMPREHENSION INSTRUCTION

Teaching students how to go about constructing the meaning of connected text is the essence of comprehension instruction. In the discussion of connected text in Chapter 1, cohesive ties is cited as a topic that provides subject matter for such instruction. Topics requiring the use of oral reading are the concern now.

Typographic Signals

Authors use a variety of typographic signals to help readers construct the meaning of the text they have composed. The examples of typographic signals that follow will remind you of their prominence in connected text: periods, commas, colons, semicolons, question marks, exclamation marks, underlining, italics, boldface type, quotation marks, indented lines.

The large number of typographic signals that authors of fiction use for conversations is one reason that so-called easy stories can be difficult for beginning readers. This is why publishers present conversations in formats like those shown in Figure 3.1. In the first example, the person speaking is pictured; in the second, extra space signals a shift from one speaker to another. At some point, however, students need to be able to use typographic signals only in order to decide who is saying what to whom.

Sometimes, instruction for typographic signals consists of imparting information. In these cases, oral reading is unnecessary. On the other hand, when the need

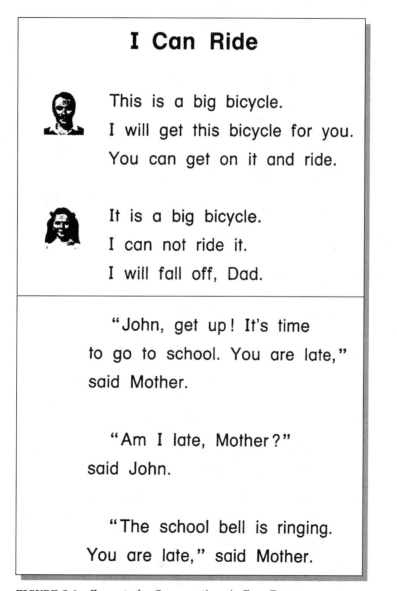

FIGURE 3.1 Formats for Conversations in Easy Text

Source: From *All Through the Town and Morning Bells of the World of Reading Program,* © 1989 Silver, Burdett & Ginn Inc. Used with permission.

Instruction: Typographic Signals	
Objective: Imparting Information *[Oral reading: not required]*	*Objective: Effect on Meaning* *[Oral reading: required]*

Comma: a. indicates person being addressed
  b. sets off appositive
  c. keeps units of meaning together
	Comma: need for brief pause

Period: a. signals abbreviation b. signals end of sentence	*Period:* need for longer pause
Question mark: signals question	*Question mark:* possible need for rising intonation at end of sentence
Exclamation mark: signals end of sentence expressing emotion or excitement	*Exclamation mark:* need for reading text with certain emotion (e.g., anger, surprise)
Underlined word(s): may signal title, heading, subheading, or special stress	*Underlined word(s):* possible need for special stress
Quotation marks: may signal title or exact words spoken	
Indented line: may signal new paragraph and, possibly, shift in focus	

FIGURE 3.2   Distinctions in Attention Given Typographic Signals

is to clarify how typographic signals affect the meaning of text, the material under consideration must be read aloud. The contrasts shown in Figure 3.2 are intended to clarify these distinctions.

Times when oral reading is or is not required are described more specifically in the following examples.

If commas are receiving attention in order to explain how they set off appositives that add information about the subject of a sentence (e.g., *Andy, the only one in his family to go to college, has the best job*), text should be examined but does not have to be read aloud. However, if the goal is to explain that commas signal brief pauses that are essential for achieving meaning, then sentences like the one just referred to, as well as others such as *Tracy is tall, slender, and very bright,* need to be read orally so that pauses can be demonstrated and their relevance for meaning discussed. The old traditional tale, *The Little Red Hen,* shows the significance of all this even for simple stories (p. 39):

> When she went out walking with her friends, the goose,
> the cat, and the pig,...

To cite another example, if the purpose of instruction is to inform students that interrogative sentences end with question marks, oral reading is unnecessary. In contrast, if the intent is to make explicit the rise in intonation when certain kinds of questions are posed, oral reading must be used so that the change in pitch is heard and its significance for meaning understood. In this case, reading aloud yes/no questions like *Will you do me a favor?* and tag questions like *You'll do me a favor, won't you?* demonstrates how rising intonation clarifies the author's message.

As is often the case with all kinds of instruction, contrasts help in work done with typographic signals. Identical strings of words like the following, for example, are useful in clarifying the significance for meaning of the placement of commas:

> Tom, my son is your age.
> Tom, my son, is your age.

Teacher-questions about the meaning of the two sentences, coupled with an appropriate oral reading of each, serve well in highlighting the function of commas and pauses in constructing meaning.

More contrasts that show how typographic signals alter meaning follow:

> For her birthday, they had ice cream, cake, and juice.
> For her birthday, they had ice cream cake and juice.

Other sentences illustrate how typographic signals help readers chunk text into meaningful units—an ability required for comprehending that is not common among poor readers (25, 30). The same examples reillustrate the value of oral reading for highlighting "same words but different message":

> His mother said who will be invited.
> His mother said, "Who will be invited?"

> Andria said her brother is not home.
> "Andria," said her brother, "is not home."

How authors signal the need to assign special stress to a word and, more important, how the stress affects meaning, can be explained with oral readings of contrasts like these:

> This is my <u>new</u> coat.   I <u>care.</u>
> This is <u>my</u> new coat.   <u>I</u> care.

Again, probing by a teacher is essential: "In the first sentence, we have to give special stress to *new*. Listen as I read the sentence.... What am I especially trying to let you know by the way I read the sentence?...Yes, I'm letting you know that the coat I'm referring to is a new one. I'll read the very same words again, but this time I'll stress *my*. Listen.... What did I do my best to tell you this time?...That's right. I wanted to be very certain you knew that *I* have a new coat. That's why I said, 'This is *my* new coat'."

Rather than continue with examples of helpful questions, let me instead conclude with an observation made for teachers by a linguist, Alfred Hayes:

> Remember that you are *not* teaching children stress and intonation; they already use them naturally when they talk. You *are* teaching them to respond to print in a way which helps them understand its meaning. (17, p. 5)

The connection between typographic signals and understanding text is further illustrated in Figure 3.3.

Inferences about Dialogues

As the previous section points out, understanding typographic features of text is an early requirement for readers because quoted speech is a part of stories. In addition to having to know who is saying what to whom, knowing *how* something is said may be important, too. In some instances, authors provide direct help (e.g., "Joel snapped back,…" or "Amy pleaded,…"). In other cases, it is up to a reader to infer intonation and emotions. To see how students learn to make these inferences, let's follow one fourth-grade teacher's efforts.

On this particular day, some students are reading a story in which the main character, a boy named Eddy, displays a variety of emotions as the plot progresses. In the end, he loses what he wants most because of his quick, uncontrolled temper. Once the plot of the story is reviewed during the postreading discussion, the teacher and students move through the story again, first to find sections in which the author specifies how dialogue is spoken and then to find other sections in which readers must draw their own conclusions based on text that precedes the dialogue. For each

---

"I mean, could I have known that Max, who is always trying to work up the nerve to talk to Dawn Sharington, would get upset when I broke the ice by writing her a love letter and signing his name to it?"

(16, p. 21)

Thurgood wondered what good it did to have it all written out in the Constitution that everyone was supposed to enjoy "equal rights." His father tried to explain that the Constitution stated things as they were *supposed* to be. Everyone knew there was a difference between what things were supposed to be and what they actually *were.*

(9, p. 21)

Hard? How her father, Pa, would have laughed. *Hard* was tracking through knee-deep snow for three days to catch a bear for food, he'd tell her.
Hard was a cloud of grasshoppers, the noise of their chewing filling the air as they ate every leaf, every stem of the precious food Pa had planted.

(16, p. 8)

FIGURE 3.3   Examples of Typographic Signals in Fifth-Grade Textbooks

of the latter passages, the teacher's questions are, "Who can read what is being said here just the way it might sound?…What emotion were you trying to express when you read that?…What made you think that was how it was said?"

The instruction just portrayed clarifies for students exactly how to go about making inferences based on text whose meaning they have constructed. It reflects, therefore, the *cognitive* view of reading discussed in Chapter 1. This contrasts with an *elocutionary* view that erroneously portrays reading as a performance. Teacher suggestions like the following, both heard in classrooms and both concerned with conversations, foster an elocutionary concept in which good reading is equated with appropriate expression:

> Connie is certainly disappointed, isn't she? Who wants to read what she says in a way that shows how disappointed she is?
>
> Josh is really scared—and no wonder. I would be, too. Kelli, read what Josh says there so that we can hear the fear in his voice.

When teachers routinely name the emotional state that oral reading should display—as did the teachers just referred to—they are turning suitable expression into an end in itself. More important, they are obscuring the fact that reading is a cognitive process that is concerned not with expressing a message but with building one.

What all these comments about dialogues and oral reading suggest is that oral reading is not something that should be eliminated from classrooms. Rather, it is an activity that ought to be used at appropriate times in appropriate ways.

ORAL READING FOR SHARING

One obviously appropriate function for oral reading is sharing. Before examples of oral reading done for this purpose are given, two other topics are discussed briefly: (a) prerequisites for this oral reading and (b) ways to foster effectiveness.

Prerequisites

When oral reading is a medium for sharing, teachers need to make sure that two requirements are met. The first is the availability of a genuine audience. By genuine I mean one or more individuals who have the desire, or at least a willingness, to listen. Whether a genuine audience is likely to exist depends on a combination of factors, one of which is the material being read. If it is dull, too familiar, or excessively long, nobody should be surprised if the expected listeners fail to pay attention. On the other hand, if the material is something like an announcement of a forthcoming surprise, attention is practically guaranteed.

A second factor that determines the likelihood of a genuine audience is the quality of the reading. This suggests the second requirement for oral reading done to share: preparation. If the material is short and simple, a quick skimming of the text is usually sufficient. If it is difficult or lengthy, adequate preparation might require a complete, careful (and silent) prereading.

Because meaningful preparation depends on understanding the essence of effective oral reading, ways to define and promote effectiveness are discussed next.

Fostering Effective Oral Reading

To begin, it is important to remember that some students will never be more than minimally successful oral readers. This is so because how well anyone reads aloud is partially dependent on factors like personality and quality of speech. Fortunately, schools have no obligation to produce students who read telephone directories with gusto. Instead, the aim is a moderate amount of ability. In some instances, individuals go beyond this; in other cases, they will not reach the goal. But that is not a major worry because it is comprehension that is important.

The fact that comprehension *is* what matters is not always reflected in classroom practices. Here I cannot help but recall a conversation with a third-grade teacher who works with low achievers. Surprisingly, her overwhelming concern was for an effective oral delivery, expressed with the complaint, "I can never get these children to read smoothly even when I have them practice reading the same material again and again."* Such a worry suggests that this teacher may have an elocutionary concept of reading in which success is equated with expressive oral reading. Yet with her students, who are still struggling to overcome basic deficiencies, such reading is like frosting on a cake—nice but not necessary.

To work on the frosting when this seems appropriate, teachers can allow time for activities that both demonstrate and promote effective oral reading. Some are considered now.

Reading to Students. One assumption of this book is that good oral reading is as much caught as it is taught. This assumption suggests one of the many reasons teachers ought to read effectively to students on a regular basis. Ideally, their reading demonstrates the importance of careful pronunciation and enunciation of words, appropriate volume, and an expression that succeeds in communicating feelings as well as facts.

An article by Sterl Artley (3) reminds us how students both enjoy and remember being read to. The article is based on responses from junior and senior education majors who were asked to recall elementary school experiences that "turned them on or off reading." After describing the bleak picture drawn by the responses, Artley shifts to the positive and notes:

> The greatest number said that teachers reading to the class on any level was the thing they remembered and enjoyed most. In some cases the teacher read the opening chapter of a book or an interesting episode from it as a starter, the pupils then finishing it themselves, in some instances having to wait in turn because of the book's sudden popularity. Other teachers read a book to completion, chapter by chapter.... Some students reported that their teachers frequently talked about books they thought some of them might enjoy, and in other cases a teacher told about a book that she was reading for her own information or enjoyment. In this way the pupils saw that reading was important to the teacher. (3, p. 27)

---

*In prior years, reading "smoothly" during oral reading was called fluency. Now, reflecting the cognitive view of reading, the term describes reading in which words are known so well that readers can give total attention to the meaning of connected text.

Choral Reading. Another way to foster effective oral reading is with choral reading (group oral reading). For students whose potential for oral reading is diminished by shyness, choral reading can be especially effective because it reduces fears. Not to be forgotten is that the repetition of words commonly found in material suitable for choral reading ensures word practice that is not tedious.

The most important point to remember about choral reading is that a perfect performance is not the goal. Instead, it is a way to allow for better oral reading *and* enjoyment. With the twin goals in the foreground, choral reading will be handled with an appropriate amount of seriousness. Publications are available to help teachers choose material, organize students, and plan the details of a reading (19, 22, 31).

A recent observation in a third grade demonstrated that choral reading may not always be preplanned. Instead of having students read a two-page selection in a basal reader (see Figure 3.4), the teacher had decided to read it to the class herself. And she did this very effectively. Aware of how much the children had enjoyed the text, she read it a second time. Now, the students tried spontaneously—but with little success—to join in whenever the teacher came to the four-line refrain. Taking advantage of the interest, the teacher promised to have copies of the lines available the next day. By spending a little time on the words, she explained, everyone would be able to respond when she read the selection again.

Commercial Recordings. Like the oral reading that teachers do, commercial recordings of stories can provide models. They have the added advantage of allowing students to analyze why the recordings are excellent, average, or perhaps ineffective. Some students also enjoy comparing a professional recording with their own taped reading of the same material. (Comparisons should be made privately unless a student is fairly skillful.) A comparison can be made systematic with a checklist like the one in Figure 3.5, once a teacher has clarified the criteria listed.

Examples of Oral Reading for Sharing

Having dealt with the two prerequisites for oral reading done to share—preparation and an audience—and, in addition, with some ways to foster effective oral reading, let me now add to the discussion descriptions of activities that students can do on their own. Each suggestion for oral reading is followed by comments.

> Prepare written descriptions of objects and scenes. Have students draw a picture that corresponds to a description. Later, each student displays his drawing and reads the description. Others listen in order to see whether all the details are in the picture.

Comment. This suggestion illustrates how one activity can achieve multiple goals. First, students practice reading aloud to communicate to an audience; next, they practice reading silently in order to visualize a picture suggested by text. Notice, too, that the oral reader has a chance to preread the material and that the audience has a definite purpose for listening.

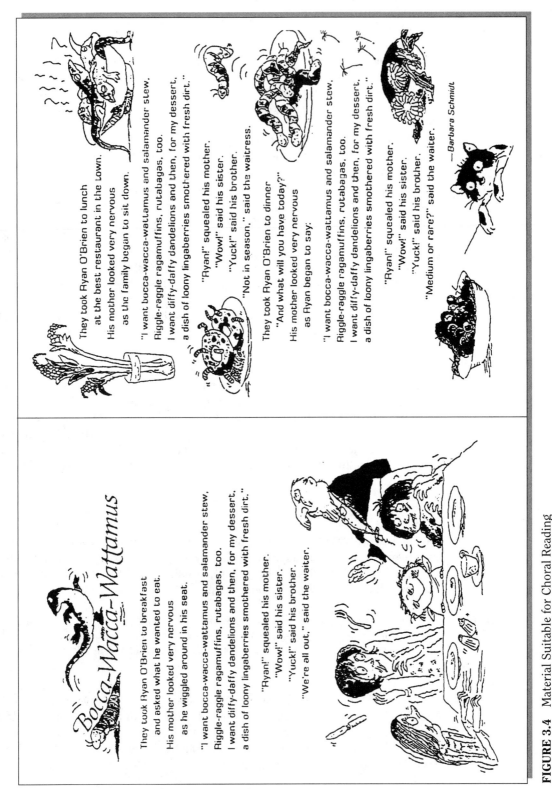

FIGURE 3.4 Material Suitable for Choral Reading

Source: From *A Soft Pillow for an Armadillo,* Heath Reading series, © 1989. Used with permission.

Oral Reading

When I read aloud, do I: Yes   No

1. Pronounce all the words correctly?   _____   _____

2. Enunciate each word so that it can
   be understood?   _____   _____

3. Read smoothly, not stopping when
   there is no reason to stop?   _____   _____

4. Read loudly enough to be easily
   heard?   _____   _____

5. Read with an expression that
   helps my audience understand
   and enjoy what am I reading?   _____   _____

Things I do well:

Things I need to work on:

FIGURE 3.5   Self-Evaluation Checklist for Oral Reading

Let students work in pairs. One member of each pair will be responsible, first, for finding material likely to be of interest to a partner (e.g., a short magazine article or a chapter in a book) and, second, for preparing to read it to the partner by a prespecified date. Following the reading, the text can be discussed. The next time the pairs get together, the second partner does the reading.

Comment.   Whenever students are unaccustomed to doing something, preparation is usually required. With the activity just described, a teacher can show what is expected before the paired reading starts. To do this, she selects a student to be her partner and then demonstrates the meaning of the request.

Periodically, have able readers write questions about material they have been reading that deals with one or more topics currently being studied in social studies or science. (After checking the questions, type them so that they can be distributed.) The second responsibility of a student is to prepare to read the material aloud to less able classmates whose responsibilities are threefold: (a) read the questions silently, (b) listen to the reader, and (c) answer the questions.

Comment.   This suggestion provides one solution (not to be overdone) for a problem that middle- and upper-grade teachers refer to regularly—the need to use textbooks even when a number of students are unable to read them. As time passes and the activity described above is used more than once, able readers can usually direct the postreading discussions without help, thus freeing a teacher to give time to other students.

> To foster interest in word meanings and word histories, give members of an instructional group copies of books that tell about words. (Examples of such books are listed in Chapter 11.) Have each student skim a book to find a word with an especially interesting history. Allow time for reading the selection silently before it is read to the group. Prior to each reading, write the word (or have a student do this) so that the others can see what it looks like. Following each reading, encourage discussion.

Comment.   This activity also aims toward more than a single objective. In addition to allowing for reading aloud to an audience, it can promote interest in words, provide practice in skimming, and encourage participation in a discussion. Because many words in English are tied to myths, the same activity might kindle an interest in mythology.

> To provide motivation for improving oral reading, let volunteers take turns reading aloud to younger children—kindergartners and first graders, for instance.

Comment.   If older students select stories or informational books that are appropriate in content and length (with the help of a teacher or librarian) and preparations are adequate, a most appreciative, attentive audience will be their reward. On the other hand, if the material is inappropriate or the reading poor, they will learn promptly that they made some mistakes along the way. (One study [21] has documented improvement in the reading ability of low-achieving fifth graders who participated in a program that had them read to kindergartners.)

> Using wordless picture books covering a wide variety of topics, have interested students compose anything from brief captions to a well-developed text to go with the pictures. Later, composers can read what they wrote while you or a student display the illustrations to the audience.

Comment.   Reading their own material is something children enjoy. As described, the material on some occasions can be written in connection with picture books. Another possible stimulus is a student's own artwork. Either way, an audience should be available for the oral reading. Because the purpose is to communicate, not to get feedback on the quality of the writing, the text should be better than a first draft.

The final example of oral reading done to share is reported by a classroom observer in Figure 3.6.

Teachers' Questions about Oral Reading for Sharing

Before the discussion of oral reading done to share ends, two questions that teachers often ask are addressed. The first is, "When students are reading aloud to others and are unable to identify a word, should I tell them what it says?" As with many other concerns, the solution for this one is found in a consideration of purpose and goals. (Remember? *Why* am I doing what I'm doing?) Because in this case the

In the second grade that I visited this morning, I saw oral reading used appropriately and effectively near the end of the reading period. The teacher explained that the children had written ghost stories for Hallowe'en and that she had discussed the need to read only a few at a time "so that they could really enjoy them." Three children were practicing in the library corner while the rest of the class and the teacher talked about the following.

Courtesy: The children related personal experiences at movies and concerts and described good listening.

Role of Announcer: After one child said that Johnny Carson is an announcer, the group discussed what an announcer should say (the person's name and the title of the story). An announcer was quickly chosen and went to the library area to get the necessary information from the three children.

Showing Appreciation: One child asked if they should clap at the end, which resulted in practicing "courteous" clapping. Why yelling was not the best way to show appreciation was the final topic considered.

The three readers were ready now, and their oral reading proceeded with the group's complete attention and interest. The planning session, which lasted about ten minutes, certainly succeeded in producing a genuine audience while the preparation time resulted in reading that was as effective as it could be, given the brevity of what had been written. One reader even added sound effects, which he said were meant to make his story "really spooky."

FIGURE 3.6 Oral Reading of One's Own Writing

reason for the oral reading is communication, the only response from a teacher that makes sense is to supply the word quickly so that the reader can continue.

Purpose also provides an answer for a second question, namely, "What should I do when the oral reader misidentifies a word?" If the misidentification distorts or confuses meaning, it should be corrected quickly in a nonpunitive way. Otherwise, a correction is unnecessary. Should it happen that one or more students frequently require help when they read aloud for sharing, insufficient preparation might be indicated. This should be discussed and remedied. It is also possible that the material is too hard, in which case easier text needs to be found.

ORAL READING FOR DIAGNOSIS

Although the usual purpose for reading aloud is sharing, oral reading is sometimes used in school for diagnosis—that is, for helping a teacher learn about a student's particular abilities and shortcomings. Serving that purpose, oral reading has different—in fact, opposite—requirements from what it does when the intent is communication. For diagnosis, a student should *not* have a chance to prepare, as the purpose is to learn what is done in the very act of reading. Because flaws are likely to show up, the reading should also be as private as circumstances permit, preferably with only the teacher listening.

As you will see when Chapter 16 discusses diagnosis, reading done for that purpose sometimes requires oral reading, sometimes silent. When the former is used, the following distinctions need to be kept in mind:

Requirements for Oral Reading

To share: { audience, familiar material,

To diagnose: { privacy, unfamiliar material,

The contrasts highlighted above are stressed now because when round robin reading is used, the requirements noted are not always kept in mind.

DIFFERENCES BETWEEN ORAL AND SILENT READING

Because three differences that set oral and silent reading apart are pertinent for the forthcoming discussion and critique of round robin reading, they are identified now.

Vocalization

The most apparent difference between oral and silent reading is that the former is heard whereas the latter is not. The observable pronunciation of words that is the very essence of oral reading—and of speech—is called *vocalization*.

Vocalization contrasts with *subvocalization,* which is commonly present in silent reading. Subvocalization (also called *inner speech*) is a mental pronunciation of words that is neither heard nor seen.

Whether subvocalizing assists with comprehending is one of the many questions about reading that lacks a carefully documented answer. When Gibson and Levin (10) reviewed existing research, for example, they noted both the difficulties in studying subvocalization and the conflicting findings whenever it was examined. They suggested, nonetheless, that subvocalizing may facilitate the comprehension of difficult material by focusing the reader's attention on meaning.

Frank Smith offers a different hypothesis about why difficult material and an increase in subvocalization often go together (29). He believes that "the explanation is more likely to be that reading a difficult passage automatically reduces speed, and we have a habit of articulating individual words when we read at a speed slow enough for individual words to be enunciated" (p. 200).

Until facts about the relationships among subvocalization, difficult material, and comprehension are available, the position taken here is as follows:

1. Probably everyone subvocalizes too much, even with easy material.
2. Subvocalization not only reduces the speed of silent reading but also is "annoying and difficult to turn off" (10).
3. Because the ability to comprehend at a reasonably fast rate is desirable, anything that fosters needless subvocalization should be avoided.
4. It is possible that a daily use of round robin reading increases subvocalization.

More is said later about the final point.

Eye Movements

How eye movements account for a second difference between oral and silent reading is explained after the movements themselves are described.

Studies of Eye Movements.   As early as the 1920s, a number of facts about the eye behavior of readers were identified with specially designed cameras. Later, computers allowed for the rediscovery of the same facts (23, 24, 32).

Even though it may seem that our eyes move steadily across lines of text when all the words are familiar, this is not the case. Instead, eye behavior during reading is characterized by stop-and-go movements. The active part is called *saccades* (sæcáde); the periods of inactivity, *fixations.* (To understand eye movements, it is essential to keep in mind that an eye fixation is so brief that its duration has to be measured in milliseconds.) Research also shows that "the leaping eye is practically blind" (29). Consequently, "the reading of text occurs only during fixations" (24). What seems like visual continuity, then, is provided by the brain, not the eyes.

A reader's eyes also move backward on occasion. This right-to-left movement, called a *regression,* has a variety of causes. In some instances, readers miss one or more words and have to return to pick them up. At other times, a person might be reading something like the following paragraph. To read it is to identify a different reason for regressions.

The boys' arrows were nearly gone so they sat down on the grass and stopped hunting. Over at the edge of the woods they saw Henry making a bow to a little girl who was coming down the road. She had tears in her dress and also tears in her eyes. She gave Henry a note which he brought over to the group of young hunters. Read to the boys it caused great excitement. After a minute but rapid examination of their weapons they ran down the valley. Does were standing at the end of the lake making an excellent target. (4, p. 87)

As you now know, homographs (identically spelled words with different pronunciations and meanings) also account for regressions. A different but related cause has to do with expectations. Specifically, when text does not conform to the words a reader expects to see, regressive eye movements occur in order to correct what was erroneously anticipated.

Another reason for eye regressions is linked to the need to move from the end of one line to the start of the next. (This essential right-to-left movement is a *return sweep*.) If it happens that the eyes miss what is at the beginning of the new line, the return sweep is likely to be followed by one or more regressions.

One further reason for regressions pertains only to oral reading—specifically, to the *eye-voice span*. Before that is explained, definitions of terms provided thus far are reviewed below.

Eye fixation. Pause in eye movements at which time print is seen. Duration of fixations is so brief it is measured in milliseconds. (1 msec. = 1/1000 of a second.)

Saccade. Movement of eye from one fixation to the next. "The average length of saccades during reading is about 8–10 letter positions.... This is about the size of the region seen during a fixation" (24, p. 163).

Eye regression. Backward (right-to-left) movement caused by such factors as missed words, homographs, concern or confusion about meaning, and incorrect predictions.

Return sweep. The necessary right-to-left eye movement required by the start of each new line of text.

Some of these terms are in Table 3.1, which summarizes data from an eye-movement study (4). The numbers in Table 3.1 show that progress in silent reading

Grade	Average Number of Fixations per Line	Average Duration of Fixation Pauses	Average Number of Regressive Movements per Line
1	18.6	666 msec	5.1
5	6.9	252 msec	1.3
11	5.5	224 msec	0.7

TABLE 3.1   Students' Eye Movements during Silent Reading at Different Grade Levels

is characterized by reduced numbers of fixations, shorter fixations, and fewer regressions. This reference to a developmental pattern, it should be noted, is not meant to suggest that an individual's eye movements are always the same. Difficulty of material and the purpose for reading it are two factors that account for variation.

Eye Movements during Oral and Silent Reading.   The data shown in Table 3.1 were collected while subjects read silently. Had they been reading the same material orally, the numbers would be different except, perhaps, for the first graders. You will be able to predict the differences, once *eye-voice span* is explained.

When we read aloud, it is necessary to pronounce every word. Obviously, this takes much more time than the eye requires to scan the same text. The difference accounts for the *eye-voice span*. This is "the number of words or letter spaces that visual processing is ahead of oral reading" (10, p. 640).

Differences in the rate at which the eye and the voice can deal with text cause a conflict whenever oral reading is occurring. Of necessity, the voice wins out as the eye yields (unconsciously) to the slower pace. While accommodating the voice, however, the eye is still active. As it waits, it wanders and regresses. In this instance, regressions operate to reduce the separation between the eyes and the voice. The eye also fixates longer than would be the case were the reading silent.

All these consequences of the eye's accommodation to the voice are verified when eye-movement records of a person reading the same material orally and then silently are compared. Predictably—at least when the reader is past the initial stage of learning to read—eye movements for oral reading show more and longer fixations and more regressions. Stated differently, the eye movements required for oral reading are *in*efficient for silent reading.

Functions

A third difference between oral and silent reading lies in their respective functions. Specifically, the reason for silent reading is to get or construct an author's message whereas the customary function of oral reading is to communicate to other people. Although an effective oral presentation often indicates that the reader understands the text, comprehension is not an essential requirement. What *is* required are correct pronunciations and phrasing, suitable volume, and appropriate expression. It is important to note that all this can be present when the oral reader does not understand everything the author wrote (8, 18).

IMPLICATIONS OF DIFFERENCES FOR INSTRUCTIONAL PRACTICES

The foregoing sections identified three differences between oral and silent reading having to do with vocalization, eye movements, and functions. Implications of the differences for instructional programs are discussed now in the context of round robin reading, because data from classroom-observation research (2, 6, 7) support the conclusions listed on the next page:

1. Round robin reading consumes a considerable amount of time in primary-grade classrooms. At later levels, it continues to be used but less frequently. When it *is* used with older students, they are usually the poorest readers.
2. Round robin reading in which the entire class participates is common in middle- and upper-grade classrooms during social studies. In this instance, it is viewed as a way to cover the content of textbooks.

In the next sections, round robin reading is critiqued in a framework defined by the differences between oral and silent reading that have been discussed.

Round Robin Reading and Subvocalization

Regardless of the position taken on the function of subvocalization, most reading specialists agree that much of the subvocalizing that goes on in silent reading results in little more than needlessly slow rates—plus annoyance. To be taken seriously, therefore, is the likelihood that the habitual practice of having children follow silently what another person is reading aloud is encouraging the silent followers to pronounce mentally the words they hear. Said differently, a regular use of round robin reading is likely to foster purposeless subvocalization.

Round Robin Reading and Eye Movements

In spite of the persistent use of round robin reading, studying its effects has never been high on any researcher's agenda. One researcher, Luther Gilbert, did look into it and reported his findings in an article entitled, "Effect on Silent Reading of Attempting to Follow Oral Reading" (12).

Gilbert studied children in grades 2 through 6 by photographing their eye movements, first while they read silently and then while they followed silently what another subject was reading aloud. (Gilbert deliberately chose oral readers with varying abilities.) When the two sets of eye-movement records were compared, predictable differences were found. Eye movements for the silent reading that was accompanied by oral reading showed more fixations and regressions than did the silent reading done independently. The fixations were also longer. It was shown, too, that the poorer the quality of the oral reading, the poorer (that is, the less efficient) were the eye movements of the subjects following the material silently. The latter finding prompted Gilbert to write, "The data are unmistakable in condemning the routine practice of requiring silent readers to follow the oral reading of poor and mediocre readers" (12, p. 621). Because observers in classrooms almost never hear excellent oral reading when around-the-group oral reading takes place, Gilbert's findings raise questions about the day-by-day, year-by-year use of round robin reading.

Round Robin Reading in Relation to Function

How the different functions of oral and silent reading figure in a critique of round robin reading can be clarified with a reference to the two ways in which text is commonly dealt with in classrooms. The two ways are depicted in Figure 3.7.

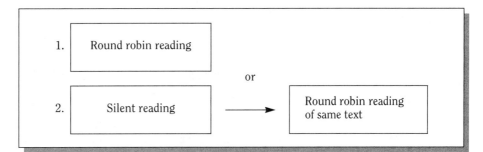

FIGURE 3.7   Common Procedures for Reading Text

If a selection is read only once and round robin reading is used, the motivation for choosing this type of reading must have something to do with promoting comprehension. Why taking-turns-at-oral-reading would be viewed as the best way to achieve that objective is unclear. The reason will be especially hazy to anyone who has listened to the reading; inevitably, it is a halting, listlike rendition of text that bears little relationship to the spoken language with which students are familiar. For that reason, the oral reading may obscure rather than elucidate meaning. Or, as one observer recently commented after being in a classroom in which the poorest readers were doing round robin reading, "What could be worse than having poor readers listen to other poor readers!"

Admittedly, the oral reading is better when the selection was read silently beforehand. Nonetheless, this sequence raises a question about the usual function of oral reading, namely, sharing. If the oral reading *is* done for that purpose, where is the genuine audience, given the fact that everyone in the group has already read the material? Because oral reading done for diagnostic purposes calls for privacy, that function isn't being served either. What we have, then, are more reasons to question any frequent use of round robin reading.

REASONS FOR THE USE OF ROUND ROBIN READING

Preceding sections of the chapter cite reasons for the criticism of round robin reading that started at least as long ago as 1908 (20) and that continues to the present (2, 6, 7). One of the most serious indictments is the misconception it fosters about the nature of reading. That is, by assigning importance to naming words correctly and with expression, round robin reading plays down the need for making semantic connections not only among the words that make up a sentence but also among the sentences that make up a body of text.

This concern, combined with the other negative consequences that are discussed in the chapter, prompt this question: *Why* has its use in classrooms persisted? Explanations from teachers who schedule round robin reading are considered first. Afterward, other possible reasons are identified.

Reasons Cited by Teachers

Why teachers say they have round robin reading is covered below in a reason-response format.

Reason: If I do not have students read aloud, how will I know whether they are remembering the new words?

Response: Learning about any given student's ability with new vocabulary can be achieved during round robin reading only when he has a turn to read aloud. Because the oral reading is usually of a brief passage that may include neither new nor troublesome words, reliable conclusions are ruled out. Teachers do need to know which words are or are not being retained; for that reason, alternative ways of learning about word identification abilities are dealt with in Chapter 6.

Reason: Expression reveals whether the oral reader is comprehending.

Response: This claim is common but unfounded, as an effective oral delivery may be little more than expressive word calling (8, 18). Kenneth Goodman offers other thoughts about expression and comprehension (14). He observes:

> There are periods in the development of reading competence when oral reading becomes very awkward. Readers who have recently become rapid, relatively effective silent readers seem to be distracted and disrupted by the necessity of encoding oral output while they are decoding meaning. Ironically, then, poor oral reading performance may reflect a high degree of reading competence rather than a lack of such competence. (p. 489)

Reason: My students like round robin reading. They object if I do not have it.

Response: Some children do seem to like round robin reading but only until they get their turn to read. After that, off-task behavior is common—which, actually, helps minimize problems related to subvocalization and inefficient eye movements. However, the lack of attention generally means that these individuals are attending to other matters and getting into trouble as a result. Not to be overlooked, either, is the likelihood that some children are intimidated by the need to read aloud, knowing that others will be listening to their mistakes.

Reason: Even though oral reading is not as important as silent reading, I still think children should have a chance to read aloud—especially the young ones. That is why I have round robin reading.

Response: Many teachers seem to think that round robin reading is the only way to allow for oral reading (15). Yet, as earlier sections in the chapter illustrate, many opportunities exist for oral reading that are free of the negative effects associated with the routine use of round robin reading.

Other Possible Reasons for Round Robin Reading

Researchers claim that some teachers use round robin reading as a means for managing or controlling students' behavior (5). This has not been my conclusion during the many times I have seen this combination of oral and silent reading. In fact, it is often the *cause* of behavior problems. I was not surprised, therefore, by the content of a report of an observation in a second grade. The account appears in Figure 3.8 (p. 56).

That round robin reading may be used when behavior problems are unlikely is verified in the account of another class; this one is in Figure 3.9. (The same account verifies that using better material is insufficient to improve reading programs.) My own experiences, along with the report of first graders in Figure 3.9, make it necessary to ask whether the use of round robin reading—at least in some instances— might be the result of not knowing what else to do. An alternative is discussed in the opening section of Chapter 6. At that time, the prereading preparations that make uninterrupted silent reading possible are discussed.

ACCEPTABLE COMBINATIONS OF ORAL AND SILENT READING

With all the criticism that has been heaped on round robin reading, you may have concluded that all combinations of oral and silent reading should be excluded from classrooms. Because that hardly is the intended message, a few descriptions of acceptable combinations bring the chapter to a close.

Read-Along Tapes

Listening centers are fairly common in classrooms; ordinarily, they allow for following a text that is read by a proficient oral reader. Comments about this combination of oral and silent reading follow.

1. For beginning readers who track the text as it is being read, this activity *may* promote faster and more fluent reading. The oral reader will also be demonstrating correct phrasing, which is necessary for comprehension.
2. For more advanced readers, this reading-listening activity could be detrimental by slowing down the rate at which they read silently, because even the best oral reader cannot read at a rate that is possible for silent readers. However, this negative consequence would occur only if a student used tapes all the time—which hardly is the case.
3. For students who do not follow the text, hearing an effective reading of an interesting story may add to their desire to become better readers themselves. Hearing expository text may add to their knowledge of the world.

Plays

Reading plays is another acceptable combination of oral and silent reading. In this case, let's assume that certain students need to improve their oral reading; their teacher decides, therefore, to use a play to help. Because oral reading, not a perfect play, is the concern, the teacher bypasses memorization. Instead, she has members of an instructional group read from a script, which requires one child to read aloud while the others follow the text silently in order to be ready with their parts. For special occasions, the teacher might combine play reading with puppet making. Now, speaking parts for the play are taped by the children, which frees them to give

Last week in class we talked about round robin reading. Many points discussed were exemplified during my observation in a second grade.

A story was read orally by the class as a whole. In fact, it was read four times so that everyone could have a turn. (There were 22 children.) The first few who read did poorly. The material seemed much too difficult for them. Already, others were bored and restless. A big yawn came from the middle of the room; another little girl was doing seatwork behind a propped-up book. Many children were not following the text but, as related in class, this was probably good.

The teacher seemed to emphasize an elocutionary concept of reading. This was suggested by the fact that, after several rounds of poor reading, one girl actually read with expression. The teacher commented immediately, "Good! Now see how she read that?" Throughout the story, the teacher reread lines herself, showing how they *should* have been read. She was obviously disappointed with the lack of expression. Certainly she did not help the students understand that reading is constructing meaning.

In class, it was said that smaller groups are best for holding the attention of all. In the case of the observed activity, the teacher lost the attention of many. Later, when she led the class through the questions that were at the end of the story, she had to show the children where they were supposed to be in several instances. Interestingly, she kept insisting they be quiet, but chose to ignore their inattention. The fact that I was present may have accounted for this.

FIGURE 3.8   Round Robin Reading and Behavior Problems

I was looking forward to today's observation because I had arranged to see a specialized reading teacher. She is responsible for working with small groups of students who are either in the highest or the lowest reading groups in their classrooms. When I arrived, she told me she would be working with first graders who were advanced readers.

The students came in and sat at a small table. Unexpectedly, they began with a round robin reading of *Amelia Bedelia*. It was obvious that these children were able readers, because they read this unprepared selection quite smoothly. The fact that they had already acquired effective decoding skills was apparent; when they came to a word they didn't know, they were able to use phonics to produce or approximate the pronunciation and were then able to say the word correctly. And they did all this quickly.

An exception occurred when one boy came to the word *meringue.* None in the group seemed to know what it was, even after the teacher pronounced "meringue" and briefly explained it.

There was one more instructional opportunity that was bypassed. The book the group was reading is about a housekeeper (Amelia) who takes her boss's cleaning instructions literally and ends up ruining the house. Misunderstood directions included *Draw the drapes when the sun comes in, Put out the lights,* and *Dress the turkey.* The fact that Amelia took everything literally created a funny story. It also provided the perfect time to attend to literal and figurative uses of language and, further, to the fact that words have to be considered in context to know the intended meaning. Unfortunately, nothing like this was done. Instead, all that the "special" session offered these able first graders was round robin reading.

FIGURE 3.9 Why Round Robin Reading?

full attention to manipulating the puppets while the pretaped dialogue runs smoothly in the background. (A reference at the end of the chapter [33] provides directions for making various kinds of puppets: paper bag, stick, sock, finger, fist, and hand.) The point stressed here is that dramatizations—whether simply or elaborately presented—occur infrequently and thus differ in that respect from the round robin reading that has been questioned.

Poems

Like plays, poems were written to be heard. In fact, because they are often composed as much for their sound as for their sense, they are fully appreciated (much as if they were music) only when they *are* heard.

Specialists in children's literature (26) agree that poetry should be read aloud initially by a teacher while students listen. (As recommended in this chapter, they also urge teachers to rehearse.) For a second reading, students can be encouraged to follow along silently because in most instances, the arrangement of words provides a special visual experience. Subsequently, one or more students might also enjoy reading the poem aloud. Whether others listen or choose to follow the text is unimportant. For teachers who may hesitate to use poetry with older students, the poems (and drawings) of Shel Silverstein (27, 28) guarantee an enthusiastic acceptance.

Additional Combinations of Oral and Silent Reading

You might now be wondering, What about day-to-day practices? Should they ever combine oral and silent reading? Surely, but only in certain ways.

To illustrate, let's say that a teacher is working with nine students. The group has just finished reading a selection silently, which might be text the teacher wrote, a chapter in a novel, or a newspaper article. What was read does not matter; what does is how the teacher combines silent and oral reading. (It is possible, of course, that oral reading is not used.) If questions were raised before the silent reading began and some call for a subjective answer ("Which paragraphs include descriptions that make you feel as if you are right at the scene?"), the teacher might have individual students read aloud the passages that succeeded in transplanting them right into the scene of the story or article. But, please note, the others just listen while the paragraphs are read.

It might happen that even factual questions elicit different responses. Should this occur, oral reading again might be required, this time to allow for comparisons and verification. As individual students read aloud, others listen—critically, it is hoped.

At other times, a teacher might choose to have parts of a selection read aloud in order to review something taught earlier. More specifically, if italic print is in a selection to indicate the need to stress certain words, individuals might be asked to read aloud sentences that include italicized words in order to see whether they remember the significance of the special print. If attention has been going to the various ways in which authors of expository text define key words, sentences that provide explanations may also be read aloud.

To sum up, then, certain circumstances do call for combinations of silent and oral reading. Such circumstances, however, are not a daily occurrence, nor are they usually a time to require students to follow silently what another is reading aloud.

SUMMARY

The purpose of Chapter 3 is suggested by its title. It was prepared to help both experienced and prospective teachers make correct decisions about when it is appropriate—even necessary—to have students read aloud and when, on the other hand, silent reading is the medium to use. Circumstances that call for oral reading dominated the discussion, as all the other chapters in this book are primarily concerned with the development of proficient silent reading.

Chapter 3 got under way by citing two important reasons children just beginning to be readers need opportunities to read aloud: to help them understand the connection between spoken words and text and to give them the chance to demonstrate to themselves that they *can* read.

Even though comprehension instruction typically calls for silent reading, times when oral reading must be used were discussed next. This required giving attention to the typographical features of text as well as to the conversations that inevitably occur in stories. How oral reading functions in helping students construct meaning as well as in providing evidence that it was constructed correctly was explained in this section.

After that, the most common and apparent reason for oral reading—namely, sharing—was considered. Requirements for this were identified (preparation and an audience) as were ways to define and promote effectiveness. Examples of classroom activities that include oral reading done for the purpose of communicating brought this section to a close.

The fact that oral reading must also be used for certain kinds of diagnosis was referred to briefly because this topic is discussed in detail in Chapter 16.

Once the various contributions of oral reading were identified, the silent-oral reading combination known as round robin reading received generous attention for two reasons. It consumes large amounts of time in classrooms, and its frequent use can have negative consequences. To prepare for an explanation of likely problems, Chapter 3 discussed differences between oral and silent reading having to do with vocalization, eye movements, and functions. The discussion was intended to show how the habitual use of round robin reading is likely to foster needless subvocalization and inefficient eye movements in students' silent reading. The same discussion also pointed out how round robin reading often confuses the two functions of oral reading: sharing and diagnosis.

Having criticized round robin reading, Chapter 3 concluded with descriptions of acceptable combinations of oral and silent reading. Some of the combinations are likely to occur almost daily; others involve the use of special materials like plays and poems.

REVIEW

1. Four major headings in Chapter 3 are:
   a. Oral Reading for the Beginner
   b. Oral Reading for Comprehension Instruction
   c. Oral Reading for Sharing
   d. Oral Reading for Diagnosis

Summarize the main points made about each topic. Supply examples whenever they help to make a point.

2. Based on Chapter 3, describe times when students should read silently.

3. It seems safe to say that anyone who reads Chapter 3 participated in round robin reading in elementary school. What are *your* recollections? Did you like it? Did you dread it? Why?

4. To help you understand why the habitual use of round robin reading can have negative consequences for participants, Chapter 3 called attention to three differences between oral and silent reading having to do with (a) vocalization, (b) eye movements, and (c) functions. For each, specify the differences.

5. Reexamine the data in Table 3.1. How would the numbers change if subjects read the same text but used oral rather than silent reading? What accounts for the changes?

6. Subvocalization and eye movements are two topics about which teachers ought to be knowledgeable. Neither, however, should be discussed with students. Why not?

7. Viewed from the perspective of the silent followers, describe problems that may develop if round robin reading is used often over a long period of time.

8. Critique round robin reading from the viewpoint of the student doing the oral reading:
   a. when the material was read silently before the start of round robin reading.
   b. when the material was not read ahead of time.

9. Explain the difference between an elocutionary and a cognitive concept of reading.

10. The Preview for Chapter 3 suggests that once you read the chapter, you will see more clearly why the need for teachers to be reflective is underscored repeatedly in this book. Based on your reading of Chapter 3, cite reasons reflection is essential.

REFERENCES

1. Adams, Marilyn; Anderson, Richard C.; and Durkin, Dolores. "Beginning Reading: Theory and Practice." *Language Arts* 55 (January, 1978), 19–25.

2. Allington, Richard. "The Reading Instruction Provided Readers of Differing Reading Abilities." *Elementary School Journal* 83 (May, 1983), 548–559.

3. Artley, A. Sterl. "Good Teachers of Reading—Who Are They?" *Reading Teacher* 29 (October, 1975), 26–31.

4. Buswell, Guy T. *An Experimental Study of the Eye-Voice Span in Reading.* Supplementary Educational Monographs, No. 17. Chicago: University of Chicago Press, 1920.

5. Duffy, Gerald D. "Teacher Effectiveness Research: Implications for the Reading Profession." In M. Kamil (Ed.), *Directions in Reading Research and Instruction.* Washington, D.C.: National Reading Conference, 1981.

6. Durkin, Dolores. "Is There a Match between What Elementary Teachers Do and What Basal Reader Manuals Recommend?" *Reading Teacher* 37 (April, 1984), 734–744.

7. Durkin, Dolores. "A Six-Year Study of Children Who Learned to Read in School at the Age of Four." *Reading Research Quarterly* 10 (1974–75, No. 1), 9–61.

8. Erickson, Sheryl E. *Conference on Studies in Reading.* Washington, D.C.: U.S. Department of Health, Education and Welfare, 1978.

9. Fenderson, Lewis H. "Fighter for Justice." In *Skylines.* Orlando, Fla.: Harcourt Brace Jovanovich Publishers, 1989.

10. Gibson, Eleanor J., and Levin, Harry. *The Psychology of Reading.* Cambridge, Mass: MIT Press, 1975.

11. Giff, Patricia R. "Painting Pictures with Words." In *Skylines.* Orlando, Fla.: Harcourt Brace Jovanovich Publishers, 1989.

12. Gilbert, Luther C. "Effects on Silent Reading of Attempting to Follow Oral Reading." *Elementary School Journal* 40 (April, 1940), 614–621.

13. Glazer, Joan I., and Lamme, Linda L. "Poem Picture Books and Their Uses in the Classroom." *Reading Teacher* 44 (October, 1990), 102–109.

14. Goodman, Kenneth S. "Behind the Eye: What Happens in Reading." In Harry Singer and Robert B. Ruddell (Eds.), *Theoretical Models and Processes of Reading,* 3rd ed. Newark, Del.: International Reading Association, 1986.

15. Green, Frank. "Listening to Children Read: The Empathetic Process." *Reading Teacher* 39 (February, 1986), 536–543.

16. Greer, Gery, and Ruddick, Bob. "Back to the Middle Ages." In *Rare as Hens' Teeth.* Lexington, Mass.: D. C. Heath and Company, 1989.

17. Hayes, Alfred S. *Language and Reading: A Linguist's View.* New York: Harcourt, Brace and World, Inc., 1969.

18. Holmes, Betty C. "The Effect of Four Different Modes of Reading on Comprehension." *Reading Research Quarterly* 20 (Fall, 1985), 575–585.

19. Huck, Charlotte S. *Children's Literature in the Elementary School,* 4th ed. New York: Holt, Rinehart and Winston, 1987.

20. Huey, Edmund B. *The Psychology and Pedagogy of Reading.* New York: Macmillan, 1908.

21. Labbo, Linda D., and Teale, William H. "Cross-Age Reading: A Strategy for Helping Poor Readers." *Reading Teacher* 43 (February, 1990), 362–369.

22. Larrick, Nancy. "Keep a Poem in Your Pocket." In B. E. Cullinan (Ed.), *Children's Literature in the Reading Program.* Newark, Del.: International Reading Association, 1987.

23. McConkie, George W. "Studying the Reader's Perceptual Processes by Computer." Reading Education Report No. 34. Urbana: University of Illinois, Center for the Study of Reading, May, 1982.

24. McConkie, George W.; Hogaboam, Thomas, W.; Lucas, Peter A.; Wolverton, Gary S.; and Zola, David. "Toward the Use of Eye Movements in the Study of Language Processing." *Discourse Processes* 2 (July–September, 1979), 157–177.

25. Rode, Sara S. "Development of Phrase and Clause Boundary Reading in Children." *Reading Research Quarterly* 10 (1974–75, No. 1), 124–142.

26. Shapiro, Sheila. "An Analysis of Poetry Teaching Procedures in Sixth-Grade Basal Manuals." *Reading Research Quarterly* 20 (Spring, 1985), 368–381.

27. Silverstein, Shel. *A Light in the Attic.* New York: Harper and Row Publishers, 1981.

28. Silverstein, Shel. *Where the Sidewalk Ends.* New York: Harper and Row Publishers, 1974.

29. Smith, Frank. *Understanding Reading.* New York: Holt, Rinehart and Winston, 1971.

30. Steiner, Robert; Wiener, Morton; and Cramer, Ward. "Comprehension Training and Identification for Poor and Good Readers." *Journal of Educational Psychology* 62 (December, 1971), 506–513.

31. Sutherland, Zena, and Arbuthnot, May Hill. *Children and Books,* 7th ed. Glenview, Ill.: Scott, Foresman and Company, 1986.

32. Underwood, N. Roderick, and Zola, David. "The Span of Letter Recognition of Good and Poor Readers." *Reading Research Quarterly* 21 (Winter, 1986), 6–19.

33. Weiger, Myra. "Puppetry." *Elementary English* 51 (January, 1974), 55–64.

. . . .

Some topics that literacy teachers at any level need to know about are covered in Part I. For example, the essential nature of the reading process, which provides subject matter for the first chapter, remains unchanged whether students are just learning to read STOP or, on the other hand, whether they are using a variety of reference materials in order to come to terms with the basic nature of electricity. This is why you should not be surprised to find, both in the two chapters that make up Part II and also in later chapters, references to the fundamental importance of experiences and world knowledge for literacy development.

Part II has a narrower focus. The intended audience is kindergarten teachers. Even so, some of the content is equally pertinent for nursery school and Head Start teachers as well as for parents of preschoolers. In fact, references are made in Chapters 4 and 5 both to preschoolers and to children enrolled in prekindergarten classes.

First-grade teachers will find suggestions for their programs, too, as chronological age is hardly the only, or even the most important, factor to keep in mind when decisions are made about suitable objectives and ways to attain them. In fact, taking chronological age too seriously results in a common but questionable practice in our schools: matching instruction to a grade level rather than to the particular students who compose a class.

Anyone familiar with the previous edition of this textbook will find major differences in the two chapters that cover "Literacy at the Beginning" in the present edition and the two that dealt with this topic in its predecessor. One major reason for the differences is the philosophy commonly referred to as "Whole Language" or "Whole Literacy." Although some tenets of whole language have affected instructional materials and procedures at later levels, it seems correct to say that the major influence is seen in kindergartens and first grades.

Some of the influence at the earlier levels originates in the concept "emergent literacy," which is discussed in Chapter 4. Topics associated

Literacy at the Beginning

with emergent literacy are discussed, too. They include print awareness, metalanguage, and invented spelling. The purpose of all these discussions is to allow you to feel at home with these terms when they reappear in Chapter 5. The discussions, therefore, provide background information for Chapter 5.

The central purpose of Chapter 5 is to show with numerous examples how teachers of young children can carry out recommendations that wise educators have always made and that whole language supporters have been reinforcing. Some of the recommendations pertain to meaningful ways to foster literacy development at the very beginning; consequently, you will be reading about shared reading experiences, big books, and predictable text. To provide a setting for all this, classrooms, now viewed as literate environments, are considered first.

Other recommendations and illustrations in Chapter 5 pertain to more traditional but still important concerns—letter names and letter sounds, for example. Whatever the topic, the recommendations are for instruction that is meaningful because it allows children to understand the usefulness of what they are learning for their own reading and writing.

To add to the specific help that Chapter 5 provides, concluding sections focus on a possible schedule for kindergarten. Admittedly, no such thing as one best schedule exists. Nonetheless, this chapter underscores the fact that any schedule that is used, or is even being considered, should allow for matching objectives with children's needs. As you prepare to read the two chapters that make up Part II, keep in mind one thought in the Introduction to *Teaching Them to Read*. It is suggested there that teachers and prospective teachers who know how to acquire information from text *in planful ways* will find it easy to help their students use strategies for achieving the same goal.

Easing Young Children into Literacy

PREVIEW

History tells us that when reading was viewed primarily as a way to learn from the Bible, mothers taught it to their children while they worked in the kitchen. Later, when responsibility for teaching reading shifted to schools, questions about how a school carried out that charge soon followed. When should instruction be initiated? How should beginning reading be taught? Should phonics be introduced immediately, eventually, or ever? Should parents do anything to help preschoolers acquire reading ability? These were the questions asked, and they persist.

The early parts of the forthcoming chapter provide just enough historical material to help you understand the controversial issues and their roots. This material is included not because successful teachers need to be historians; rather, the purpose reflects the truth of the saying that to know the past makes it easier to avoid its mistakes.

Chapter 4 then moves on to underscore the fact that success in acquiring beginning reading ability is a two-sided coin in which both the learner and the instruction play key roles. The more specific point highlighted is that success, or the lack of it, has to do with the relationship between (a) a learner's particular abilities, and (b) the demands made by whatever instruction is available. The significance of this relationship is not always kept in mind in discussions of beginning reading or, for example, of children labeled at risk. In the latter case, discussions are commonly incomplete because of the assumption that it is deficiencies or differences in learners and their families that put them at risk of not succeeding. Keeping the relational aspect of readiness in mind, one can argue that the nature of instructional programs may also put children at risk. The fact that instructional programs can be altered to accommodate children provides one basic assumption for this textbook: Teachers *can* make a difference.

As you continue to make your way through Chapter 4 and approach the end, terms that may be new are introduced—for instance, *emergent literacy, print awareness, metalanguage, invented spelling*. They are discussed and their implications for instruction described not only because they are commonly used terms but also because they are directly related to the topic that is the title of Chapter 4, "Easing Young Children into Literacy."

Over the years, issues about beginning reading have prompted more debate—even rancor—than any aspect of reading (1, 2, 34). The fact that success at the start is *uniquely* important helps explain why this is the case. More specifically, knowing that how children do at the start has considerable impact on later achievement naturally makes everyone eager to promote initial success (21).

At one time, the questions most frequently debated had to do with *when* young children are ready to read, with procedures for determining readiness, and with the best way for schools to help children judged to be "unready" (16). At the core of all this was the basic question, What *is* "readiness?"

In more recent years, questions have been about the meaning of "beginning reading" and about connections between beginning reading and beginning writing. In fact, writing became such a popular topic that literacy now refers to writing as often as it does to reading *and* writing, or to reading only. Without doubt, the most persistent, pervasive, and heated controversy always revolves around phonics: *Should* phonics be taught? If so, *when* should instruction be initiated? *How* should phonics be taught? For *how long* should the instruction continue (7, 8, 34)?

One piece that must be added to the picture drawn thus far has to do with parents of young children and their responsibility vis-a-vis reading. In this case, messages sent by professional educators to parents have ranged all the way from "Hands off!" to "Get involved!"

OLDER QUESTIONS: READINESS FOR READING

The present chapter begins by looking at the older controversy, which centered on young children's readiness to be readers. The motivation for starting this way is that some schools have returned to notions about readiness that began to circulate in the 1920s (15). A reference is made to these schools later. The purpose of the historical material presented now is to discourage current educators from repeating the mistakes of their predecessors.

The account of the earlier decades that follows is brief; a detailed description is available elsewhere (16).

Initial Interpretation of Readiness to Read

The assertion that readiness figures in the acquisition of something new—be it the ability to ride a bicycle or do long division—seems uncontestable. After all, some things *are* prerequisites for accomplishing other things.

Based on the practices of the time, it has to be concluded that professional educators in the early 1900s must have believed that readiness to read exists when children enter first grade. Stated more historically, as soon as the teaching of reading moved out of the kitchen into one-room schoolhouses and from there to buildings organized by grade levels, a close association developed between entrance into first grade and the start of reading instruction. Only rarely was the association questioned (16).

All that changed in the 1920s. To understand why readiness to read began to be linked not to entrance into first grade but to a child's level of maturation and mental age, assumptions that were widely accepted by psychologists in the 1920s need to be reviewed. Once that is done, you can see why expressions like "growing into readiness" were so popular in these earlier times.

Maturation View of Development. Thanks mostly to the influence of psychologist G. Stanley Hall and some of his students—in particular, Arnold Gesell—the view of child development that prevailed in the 1920s went something like this (18, 19, 20):

1. Young children develop in stages that follow one another in a predetermined order.
2. Intelligence, assumed to be genetically determined, affects the rate of development; the environment exerts relatively little influence.
3. Maturation, which occurs automatically with the passing of time, is the key factor in a child's advancement from one stage to another.

Maturation View of Development Applied to Reading. In order to explain why the meaning assigned to "ready to read" changed in the 1920s from an emphasis on school entrance to different considerations, another reference must be made to psychology.

During the 1920s, sometimes called the decade of the testing movement, psychologists exerted great effort to add objectivity to their work (33). One consequence was the appearance of many tests, some for reading. Used in national surveys, reading achievement tests revealed deficiencies among first graders that resulted in a number of retentions. Then, as now, evidence that first graders were having problems with reading caused concern. Then, as now, interest developed in identifying both the reason for and the solution to the problem.

It is likely that multiple factors such as large classes, inadequately prepared teachers, flawed materials, and insufficient attention to individuals accounted for many of the deficiencies that the surveys identified. However, the cause that was named, then quickly and widely accepted, was insufficient readiness on the part of the children when reading instruction began. As you see in the summary in Figure 4.1, the view of child development that Hall and Gesell fostered is pervasive in the proposed description of when children *are* ready to begin to read. (I refer to it as the traditional conception of readiness because, first, it was the initial attempt to formalize the meaning of readiness and, second, it had an effect on schools for an uncommonly long time.) You will also see in Figure 4.1 that the people who proposed or supported the traditional view claimed to identify not only the reason for too little achievement in reading (insufficient readiness) but also the solution (postponed reading instruction).

Mental-Age View of Readiness. Given the interest in objective measurement that characterized the 1920s, contentment with a conception of readiness that attributed it to the attainment of an imprecisely described stage of development was not likely to persist. And it didn't. As early as the 1920s and continuing into the 1930s, researchers attempted to connect readiness to read with a specific mental age (3, 13). Carleton Washburne, a leader of the then popular Progressive Education movement,

Traditional View of Reading Readiness

1. A child's development takes place in stages that follow one another in an inevitable order.

2. Advancement from one stage to the next is the result of maturation (internal neural ripening) that occurs automatically with the passing of time.

3. The ability required to learn to read comes into existence at one of these stages.

4. Reading problems disclosed by surveys suggest that many beginning first graders have not reached that particular stage of development, and thus are not yet ready to learn to read.

5. The solution is to postpone reading instruction so that with the passing of time, the children will become ready.

FIGURE 4.1   Summary: Traditional View of Readiness for Reading

succeeded in winning acceptance of the belief that "ready to read" can be defined as having a mental age of approximately 6.5 years (22). This, he maintained, was evidence of sufficient maturation.

Washburne, superintendent of the highly acclaimed Winnetka (Ill.) school system, showed how seriously he took his own proposal in a 1936 article entitled (in keeping with the prevailing psychological views) "Ripeness." Washburne observed:

> Nowadays each first grade teacher in Winnetka has a chart showing when each of her children will be mentally six-and-a-half, and is careful to avoid any effort to get a child to read before he has reached this stage of mental growth. (35, p. 127)

Evidence of how seriously other educators took the Washburne proposal is in reading methodology textbooks published as many as ten, twenty—even thirty years later. Evidence that some teachers still cling to fragments of the traditional view of readiness is found when classrooms occupied by young children are observed. The report of a class that is reproduced in Figure 4.2 illustrates this. The author of the report also documents that something like tests or checklists are not needed to learn about young children's abilities. Another report of part of what was seen in a nursery school (see Figure 4.3) reinforces the fact that abilities among young children vary—sometimes greatly. Accommodating those differences is as important as it is difficult.

Initial Interpretation of Readiness: An Omission

Whether mental age or maturation is highlighted, the traditional view of readiness has one serious omission. It fails to acknowledge that whether a child is or is not ready to begin to read depends not only on the child but also on the opportunities to learn that are available. Perhaps the omission reflects what seems like a naive belief, namely, that no matter what the instruction, children will succeed if the necessary maturation or mental age is present.

Today I observed a group of 18 three- to five-year-olds, who had 2 teachers. The classroom was furnished with learning centers that lined the walls, leaving a large unused area in the middle. There was no chalkboard and no signs displayed for children to look at or read.

I arrived before the children. After discussing readiness in class, I was interested to learn about the philosophy of the school regarding readiness; so I asked the head teacher whether any time was spent on reading. She said that the children were not of school age, thus were not ready for reading. (This reminded me of the traditional view that children aren't ready to read until they have a mental age of about 6.5 years.) I decided to look for some of the signs of readiness that we discussed in class.

As the children entered, I noticed an obvious affluency about them and even overheard one boy talking about the vacation his family was going to take in Hawaii. Another child came in carrying a well-worn, simply written paperback version of the *Gingerbread Man,* which he read to me after I asked if he knew any of the words. I naturally wondered why the teachers believed that the children weren't ready for reading when at least one child had already begun. (It is possible, of course, that the reading was in fact a memorized story. In any case, the boy said exactly what was printed.)

As the morning continued, I observed four children in the dramatic play center, reading labels on food containers. Although the library center was relatively small and not particularly attractive, five children went to it to look at one or more books during a one-hour period. Other children repeatedly asked the head teacher and assistant to write their names on art work. (Both teachers did so in all capital letters even though lowercase are more common, thus ought to be used.) I observed another child who spotted a friend who had mistakenly gotten a piece of paper on which another child's name was written. He went to the child, showed her the name, and said, "That says 'Carl,' not 'Carol'!"

Repeatedly throughout the morning, I noticed behavioral signs of readiness in the interest displayed in books, in the recognition of names, and in the act of reading itself. The number of times that children displayed either readiness or reading ability during this one observation requires asking, "Why had the teacher said that none were ready?"

FIGURE 4.2 Vestiges of the Traditional View of Readiness

There were 2 adults and 15 four-year-olds in this nursery school. The children were involved with free play when I arrived. The head teacher told me she would be starting a lesson in 5 minutes and suggested that I look at samples of the children's work. While looking, I overheard the following conversation between two girls.

Pointing to a book, one said, "See? This one's mine. It says Amanda. It's mine." Holding up another book, the second child responded, "This one is mine." "No, it's not," the first girl quickly answered. "That's David's. This one is yours. See? This says Katherine." Amanda pointed to several other books on the table and correctly read each child's name. Then Katherine pointed to a name on a book and asked, "David?" "No," Amanda replied. "That's Debbie."

At this point, the head teacher called the 15 children to the front of the room. She began discussing the letters *A, B,* and *C.* She first printed the capital and lowercase forms of each on the board, then said their names. She next asked if anyone's name started with "a big A." Amanda immediately responded, "Mine." The teacher repeated the question for *B,* whereupon one child said, "Anthony Barton." 'Anthony' begins with *A,*" the teacher explained, "but 'Barton' does start with *B.*" The same question was asked for *C;* all the while nothing was written. All the while, too, an increasingly large number of children grew restless. As a result, the aide motioned to certain ones to sit up and reminded others to keep still and listen.

I had to conclude that I was seeing what may have been a waste of everyone's time. It was clear that the children had different abilities, thus needed different kinds of help. Because an aide was available, the accommodation could have been made by dividing the class into groups so that members of each could do something that took advantage of, and extended, their abilities.

FIGURE 4.3   Observing Differences in Ability among Young Children

Both the learner *and* the instructional program are effectively accounted for by David Ausubel in an article about readiness published in 1959 (4). Although Ausubel's interest was not reading, his thoughts about readiness have clear implications for any educator responsible for bringing reading ability into existence. His definition is as follows: Readiness has to do with "the adequacy of existing ability *in relation to* the demands of the learning task" (4, p. 246).

An elaboration of Ausubel's definition is shown in Figure 4.4. (Why experiences, oral vocabularies, and world knowledge are added should now be clear, based on your reading of Chapter 1.) Please examine Figure 4.4 and the commentary about it.

Separation of Readiness from Reading Programs

You can recall from Figure 4.1 that the traditional conception of readiness identified postponing instruction as the solution for reading problems among first graders. Encouragement to delay instruction was logical, given the assumption about the vital role that the passing of time plays in achieving readiness. Acceptance of this assumption meant that what should be done at the start of first grade was a question that soon had to be addressed.

Initially, schools responded in different ways, but it wasn't long before the substitute for reading instruction became more uniform. Specifically, reading readiness workbooks replaced beginning reading textbooks (16). In fact, readiness workbooks—sometimes as many as two or three—soon constituted the initial components in every basal reader series published at the time.

In addition to institutionalizing readiness programs—required of all first graders, ready or not—the workbooks and similar exercises created a distinct separation between preparing children for reading and teaching reading. Said differently, prereading activities were gradually dominated by exercises that had little—sometimes nothing—to do with reading ability or its requirements. Stated still differently, a means (preparing children to be successful with beginning instruction) was turned into an end in itself.

Some of you may recall participating in a readiness program that lasted for a pre-established amount of time at the start of first grade. If you do, you are also likely to remember using workbooks in which you were directed to examine rows of pictures, or geometrical shapes, or various sorts of patterns. The task was to find all the pictures or shapes or patterns that were identical to, or different from, the first one in the row. It is important to note that none of these visual discrimination exercises vanished from classrooms even when researchers repeatedly demonstrated little or no connection between the ability to see similarities and differences in nonverbal graphic displays and the ability to see similarities and differences in letters and words (1, 16).

Other kinds of questions went unheeded, too. In 1969, for example, researchers like Robert Calfee and Richard Venezky (6) openly wondered about matters like these: What is the implication for instruction when children are unable to identify a short-haired dog from among poorly detailed pictures of a Doberman, a Saint Bernard, and a Cocker Spaniel? What is a teacher supposed to do when children fail to

FIGURE 4.4 Commentary   ▶

Learning to identify (and remember) words in their written form is central to the acquisition
of beginning reading ability. One implication of Ausubel's conception of readiness is the need
to provide children with opportunities to learn words in a variety of ways. Specifically, opportunities should be available (a) to learn words as wholes ("Jimmy, this word says 'stop'.");
(b) to learn the sounds that letters record so that sounds can eventually be blended to form
words; and (c) to learn to write words. The variety referred to is *eclectic* methodology. Viewed
from the perspective of Ausubel's conception of readiness, an instructional program characterized by eclectic methodology ensures that each child's abilities are taken advantage of to
the greatest degree possible.

   Another implication of Ausubel's conception is as important now as it would have been
for educators in the 1920s: Altering the *timing* of beginning instruction without ensuring the
availability of high-quality, eclectic instruction is *not* the way to promote maximum success
for a maximum number of young children. This implication needs to be taken seriously by
those who rely on tests of questionable value in order to decide whether a child's admission to
kindergarten ought to be delayed by a year. Ausubel's definition further suggests that anyone
who believes that providing phonics instruction is *the* way to initiate reading ability ought to
reconsider that conclusion.

   The display in Figure 4.4 should remind you that children's oral vocabularies and knowledge of the world—both closely tied to experiences—are the foundation for reading no matter
what method brings reading vocabularies into existence.

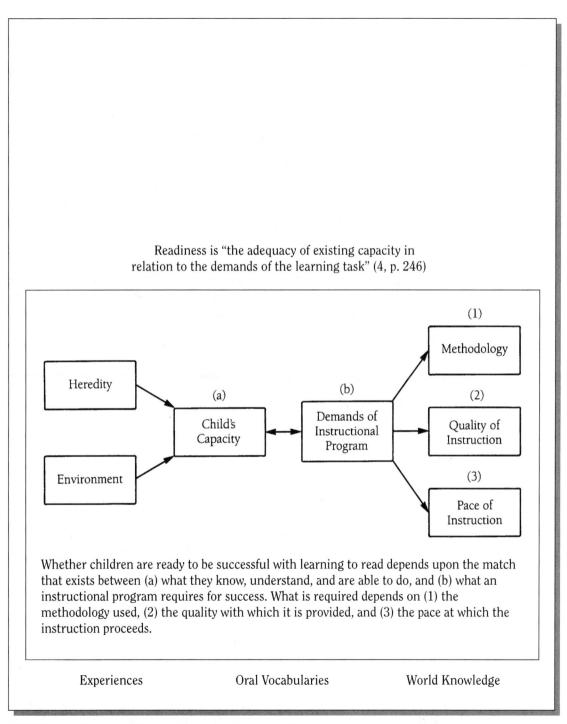

Readiness is "the adequacy of existing capacity in relation to the demands of the learning task" (4, p. 246)

Whether children are ready to be successful with learning to read depends upon the match that exists between (a) what they know, understand, and are able to do, and (b) what an instructional program requires for success. What is required depends on (1) the methodology used, (2) the quality with which it is provided, and (3) the pace at which the instruction proceeds.

Experiences   Oral Vocabularies   World Knowledge

FIGURE 4.4   Variables Affecting Success at the Beginning

select a picture of a jet airplane when the task is to find the vehicle that carries the most people? A more basic question is, What does all this have to do with reading?

Continued Separation of Readiness from Reading

As it turned out, questions and complaints about exercises like those just referred to were less influential in changing the content of readiness workbooks than was the interest that developed in making kindergartens more academic. One consequence of this goal was a gradual shift of the use of readiness workbooks from the start of first grade to kindergarten. Meanwhile, the workbooks themselves moved away from an emphasis on visual discrimination exercises to a generous use of auditory discrimination exercises. Pictured objects were still the focus; now, however, kindergartners were kept occupied naming the objects so that they could decide whether the names began with the same sound or a different sound. Eventually, correspondences between sounds and letters were introduced.

On the surface, the shift in content appeared to bring readiness and reading programs closer together. This was not the case, however, because letters and sounds were connected with names assigned to pictures, not with their use in figuring out what written words say. The focus, therefore, exemplifies *decontextualized instruction*. Applied to reading, this refers to instruction of any kind at any level that fails to make explicit to students the connection between what is being taught and its usefulness for reading.

Decontextualized instruction was too common and obvious to miss when I conducted a study of 42 kindergarten classes in the late 1980s (15). Unexpectedly, it was the fact that the phonics the teachers taught *was* decontextualized that encouraged them to believe that phonics is suitable for kindergarten. Why teaching phonics in ways that fail to clarify its usefulness for figuring out pronunciations made it acceptable is linked to attitudes toward teaching reading. Specifically, when the teachers who had been observed in their classrooms were asked in interviews whether they thought reading should be taught in kindergarten, answers for the most part were negative. This had hardly been predicted, as phonics was never missing from any schedule. The most developmentally oriented of these kindergarten teachers explained their opposition to teaching reading with responses that were reminiscent of the 1920s and 1930s (15). For instance:

> "Reading is a skill that can be taught, but when the child is ready it takes two weeks. At age five, you spend eight months. At age seven, it takes two weeks."
>
> "I believe that if they're ready, they'll read in spite of me."
>
> "Five and a half-year-olds have the ability to move from left to right but not to return. They are visually not ready. If they are not forced, it will happen naturally and more easily."

Why teachers accepted phonics instruction but rejected teaching reading was unclear until one teacher said, "Phonics is not reading instruction because we only teach letters and sounds, not words."

The questionable distinction made by these teachers between teaching phonics and teaching reading reappeared recently when I asked a group of college students majoring in early childhood education to respond in writing to the question, "When do you think children are ready to read?" The question was posed to encourage them to think about the topic before they read about it. The following were typical (and unexpected) responses:

> "Children must first have a foundation in the alphabet. They need to be able to recognize individual letters and associate those letters with a particular sound. Once children have this foundation, they will be ready to read."

> "Children are ready to read once they've learned the alphabet and how each letter has many sounds to it."

> "Children are ready to read when they know the sounds of all the letters and are able to recognize initial and ending sounds."

The responses just cited repeat the views of the kindergarten teachers because they infer that a distinct separation exists between getting children "ready" and teaching beginning reading. That such a separation fails to reflect reality is the position taken by anyone who subscribes to the concept of emergent literacy. That makes emergent literacy an appropriate topic to consider next.

NEWER INTERESTS: EMERGENT LITERACY

Emergent literacy is dealt with here in a way that reaffirms how badly educators in earlier decades applied the concept of readiness to beginning reading. This treatment allows for continuity between previous sections in the chapter and the present section. Although emergent literacy is more of a philosophy than a methodology, it is still considered in a way that suggests desirable practices to use with young children in classrooms. This means the discussion also allows for continuity between the present chapter and the one that comes next.

To introduce the discussion, research that led to widespread interest in early literacy development is reviewed briefly.

Early Studies of Preschool Readers

Even while schools in the United States were still delaying beginning reading instruction beyond the start of first grade, researchers were reporting studies in 1966 in the United States (14), in 1972 in New Zealand (12), and in 1976 in England (10), all telling about children five years of age or younger who were reading. The term *emergent reading* first appeared in the doctoral dissertation by Marie Clay (11).

Early Studies of Preschool Writers

Of relevance, too, is that in the 1970s, two linguists published reports describing preschool children who could write words in ways that demonstrated an understanding of the alphabetic nature of written English even though spellings were not always "correct" (9, 23). More specifically, the writing provided evidence that the children understood that a spoken word is composed of sounds blended together. (Because linguists use the term *phoneme* [phō nēmɇ] to refer to a speech sound, the ability to hear the sounds that make up a word is called *phonemic awareness*.) The young children's writing also showed that they understood that a word is written on the basis of its sounds and, further, that the sounds are represented by letters.

How the children recorded words was eventually referred to as "invented spelling," a description that hardly captures the important understandings that the writing reflects. Figures 4.5 through 4.8 show samples of invented spelling done by kindergartners and first graders.

Considered together, the discovery of early readers *and* early writers promoted a great deal of interest in the development of literacy during the preschool years. This is commonly referred to now as "emergent literacy" (27, 31).

EMERGENT LITERACY: WHAT IS IT?

As mentioned, emergent literacy is more a philosophy and set of beliefs than it is a methodology for teaching beginning reading and writing. In fact, certain supporters say that teaching, as this behavior is usually understood, is unnecessary. Nonetheless, emergent literacy does offer teachers (and parents) of young children some valuable suggestions and guidelines. Before some of the practical aspects are dealt with, the term emergent literacy is explained.

Emergent Literacy: A Set of Beliefs

Proponents of emergent literacy believe that beginning reading and beginning writing are closely related; consequently, they commonly talk and write about written language development. They view reading-writing connections as part of the whole language philosophy in which importance is assigned to making connections.

Some supporters of the emergent literacy concept assign meanings to reading and writing that are not conventional. As William Teale and Elizabeth Sulzby have stated, "we are now 'seeing' reading in toddlers' explorations of picture books and 'seeing' writing in their scribbles" (31).

Whether reading ability and writing ability are assigned conventional or unconventional definitions, agreement exists among emergent literacy advocates that written language abilities develop in young children in ways that parallel the acquisition of oral language. That is why they give considerable attention to social interactions as the means by which growth in written language occurs (30, 32).

For anybody who now wonders what is meant by *social interactions* viewed as a means for gradually cultivating understandings about language, recall a time when you overheard talk between a child and a parent in something like the aisle of a supermarket, which inevitably prompts questions, requests, and the like from children. If the parent felt no need to hurry, you may have heard what was referred to in Chapter 2 as scaffolding. Specifically, you probably heard the parent restating words, clarifying, answering questions, posing other questions, and adding information whenever it seemed necessary. According to the emergent literacy philosophy, these restatements, clarifications, and expansions having to do with print account for the slowly emerging awareness in young children of the functions (usefulness) and forms (e.g., lists, labels, stories) of written text. As you can see in all this, there is a learner and there is a teacher during the interactions; however, now it is the learner who initiates and the teacher who responds.

The emphasis on *emergent* in the emergent literacy philosophy reflects the common-sense fact that literacy is a slow, gradual acquisition. Dorothy Strickland and Lesley Morrow (27) cite the following as "evidence of ongoing literacy development":

- The toddler's insistence on having "the ducky book" and no other.
- The two-year-old's uncanny ability to recognize all the sugar-laden cereals in the supermarket.
- The three-year-old's persistence in writing her own shopping list.

As researchers became increasingly interested in early literacy development, they mapped out certain of its aspects for study. Topics that have relevance for teachers include print awareness, metalanguage, and invented spelling, all of which are to be discussed.

Emergent Literacy: Implications for Schooling

Research on emergent literacy has had many positive effects. To begin, it has clarified that a child hardly becomes ready to read at *a* point in his or her life. By implication, the research further emphasizes that the best way to prepare young children to be readers is to allow for many interactions with meaningful text, not with exercises that focus on geometrical shapes and nonverbal patterns. Nonetheless, Anne Bussis (5) makes an important point when she distinguishes between "knowing about reading" and "being able to read." The point she makes is that emergent literacy research has been generous in providing information and insights about the processes by which young children acquire knowledge about reading; at the same time, she claims, it has not helped very much with the transformation from "knowing about" to "knowing how to do."

Some of the important information provided for what Bussis calls "knowing about reading" refers to topics discussed in subsequent sections of this chapter and referred to again in Chapter 5.

CONVENTIONS OF PRINT

Anyone interested in, or responsible for, *easing* young children into literacy must try to see the world of print from the child's perspective. Doing that makes a person more consciously aware of its conventions. The term *conventions of print* refers to the standard procedures used for recording English. Knowing about them is essential for readers and writers if they ever hope to construct meaning.

As you but not all young children know, standard procedures for writing English include putting words in a row and in a sequence that goes from left to right. Should an author require more than one row, all subsequent rows follow the same pattern. Another standard procedure is to use empty space to show *word boundaries*—that is, to indicate where one word ends and the next begins.

Figure 4.5 and 4.6   Commentary   ▶

A kindergartner did the writing shown in Figure 4.5 soon after her teacher had read a story about sea serpents. The fact that this child wrote a caption for the picture and added her name is not unexpected. Throughout the kindergarten year, either the teacher or a volunteer parent was available to write whatever children requested in ways that allowed them to see their words transformed into print. Afterward, the children were encouraged to read what had been printed.

The kindergartner's writing in Figure 4.6 is part of a response to a suggestion made by her teacher near the end of the year. The class had been talking about summer as a time to vacation, after which the teacher suggested that the children draw a picture of where they would like to go on vacation if they had a choice. The list in Figure 4.6, showing what needed to be taken on one girl's vacation, was on the back of her picture.

Again, the fact that this child listed things to bring on her vacation is not surprising, because the teacher frequently made lists on the board that served as reminders. This point is made because it is the *usefulness* of literacy that prompts some children to try to read and write before they get to school. Usefulness continues to make acquiring literacy meaningful once children enter school.

Another point worth making is that the samples of kindergartners' writing in Figures 4.5 and 4.6 reflect the eclectic methodology used in their classrooms. At times, words were taught, which is reflected in *see, books, paper,* and *dolls*. It is also clear that phonics was taught in a way that made apparent its usefulness for writing as well as for reading. That attention also went to printing instruction is evident, as is the fact that communication is what is valued, not perfectly formed letter

FIGURE 4.5 Early Efforts to Write

Gams
Crds
crlrig Books
Books
Paper
crans
Pers
Traks
Dolls
Paper Dolls

FIGURE 4.6 Useful Writing

FIGURE 4.7   Writing by Two First Graders

My mama and dada tote me how to run.I licked the color green my hol
life. And I got out of dipers. And in 5 yrs I went to prescool. And I
graguwated.

[My momma and daddy taught me how to run. I liked the color green my whole life.
And I got out of diapers. And in five years I went to preschool.
And I graduated.]

Win I was a babe. My mather took me in a strolr. I was

littel. My mather uoost to kere me.

My mather gave me my on toosy.

My ferst werd was dada and momo.

[When I was a baby my mother took me in a stroller. I was little. My mother used to
carry me. My mother gave me my own toys. My first word was dada and mamma.]

When I was a baby and I was toking and

I side mommy and daddy and the uther wrde I

side was no. I gowe teeth. my mom tote me

to coler. and my dad tote me hode my radle

and my tose. my gramol tote me to ride my

triskl. and I growe up to be big and I growe

up and up in tle I was in knagrdne and I

can't wat in tle I'm in frst gade.

[When I was a baby and I was talking and I said mommy and daddy and the other
word I said was no. I grew teeth. My mom taught me to color. And my dad taught
me to hold my rattle and my toys. My grandma taught me to ride my tricycle. And I
grow up to be big and I grow up and up until I was in kindergarten and I can't wait
until I'm in first grade.]

FIGURE 4.8   Autobiographies by First Graders Using Word Processors

These and other characteristics of print suggest that young children must gradually come to understand the conventions that authors follow. What needs to be
known is referred to as *print awareness*. Some of its components are listed in Figure
4.9. Keep in mind that the list is *not* intended to suggest a sequence for attending to
the components.

How much kindergarten children—or those in nursery school—know about the
conventions of print depends directly on previous experiences with text. Children
brought up in highly literate environments in which contacts with text are mediated

> **Print Awareness**
>
> *Child:*
>
> 1. Knows the difference between graphic displays of words and graphic displays made up of nonwords.
> 2. Knows that print is print no matter what medium was used to record it (e.g., pencil, crayon, finger marks in sand).
> 3. Knows that print can appear on different kinds of surfaces (e.g., paper, cloth, metal).
> 4. Knows that print can appear alone or in conjunction with pictures and decorations.
> 5. Understands that print corresponds to speech, word by word.
> 6. Understands the function of empty space in establishing word boundaries.
> 7. Understands that words are read from left to right.
> 8. Understands that lines of text are read from top to bottom.

FIGURE 4.9   Knowing about Important Features of Written English

by helpful adults often arrive in school knowing a great deal about written language. Others, in contrast, can be expected to have minimal amounts of knowledge. The need for teachers to attend to one or more aspects of print awareness with *some* children is the reason for listing the basic elements in Figure 4.9. If you re-examine that list now, you are likely to arrive at a correct conclusion about print awareness: Its various components are not developed one at a time or with one-day lessons. Rather, they are the product of many experiences with meaningful text spread out over time that may also result in some ability to read. Meaningful connected text includes the familiar song shown in Figure 4.10.

METALANGUAGE

As you re-examined the various components of print awareness listed in Figure 4.9, you may have noticed an underlying assumption, namely, that young children un-

> **Happy birthday to you.**
>
> **Happy birthday to you.**
>
> **Happy birthday dear _____.**
>
> **Happy birthday to you.**

FIGURE 4.10   Text Used at the Beginning of the Year in a Kindergarten

derstand the referent for *word*. Often, however, they do not. In fact, research has shown repeatedly that even though young children listen to, and produce, many spoken words themselves, they do not consciously think of the individual words that make up oral language (36). Instead, the whole of an utterance is viewed function-ally—that is, as a means for communicating needs, feelings, requests, or whatever. One consequence is that *word* is a word they may not understand. Yet, when words become objects for study, as they do in both reading and writing, knowing what *word* means is essential.

Words—such as *word*—that enter into literacy instruction are grouped under the heading "metalanguage." *Metalanguage* refers to words that are necessary for dealing with language (metalanguage = language about language). Examples of met-alanguage that literacy teachers use are listed in Figure 4.11.

The fact that teachers unintentionally use metalanguage when children do not yet understand it has been verified during classroom observations. In one kindergar-ten, for example, the teacher wrote *you* and *me* on the board, then asked, "How many words did I just write?" With much enthusiasm a group of children responded, "Five!" (I was impressed with both the quick counting and the confusion about the meaning of *word* and *letter*).

At another time, I had been invited to observe in a classroom occupied by four- and five-year-olds. It was early in the school year, and the teacher was working on visual discrimination. She had placed word cards in the slots of a chart and was asking individuals in a small group to find any two words that were the same. All went well until the teacher pointed to a card displaying *Monday* and asked if anyone could find the same word on the chalkboard. (At the start of the morning, *Monday* and *October* had been written and discussed.) Now, in contrast with the earlier work, nobody could. Upon reflection, the children's failure to respond was no longer unexpected, although at the time it was because of the earlier success. *Monday* had been printed on the board in large, white letters, whereas much smaller letters in black appeared on the card. Clearly, what these children needed to learn was the meaning of "same" and "different" *applied to words*. Eventually, they

---

Some Metalinguistic Terms

1. "word"	7. "sentence"
2. "letter"	8. "period"
3. "beginning of a word"	9. "comma"
4. "end of a word"	10. "question mark"
5. "line"	11. "beginning sound in a word"
6. "beginning of the line"	12. "syllable"

FIGURE 4.11 Language Used to Talk about Language

needed to learn that to all of the following, the same response must be given: gate, GATE, gate, *Gate* and *gate* .

As is true for print awareness, "lessons" are not a suitable means for helping young children add "word" and "same" to their oral vocabularies. Instead, the contacts with meaningful connected text that allow for acquiring print awareness are also productive in clarifying terms that figure in literacy instruction.

This suggestion for instructional programs calls for returning to a distinction referred to earlier:

> Knowing about reading   *vs*   Knowing how to read

Although the distinction shown above does exist, you should now be able to see that what is done to promote an understanding both of the conventions of print and of metalanguage ("knowing about...") may also result in a child's ability to read some words ("knowing how..."). Actual results depend on a number of variables that always include an adult's success in engaging children with text in ways that promote curiosity, understandings, and insights about written language. Not to be forgotten is that the extent to which young children are willing to attend to text depends on the meaning the text has for them. Knowing, for instance, that a display of words has something to do with a trip to the zoo in the near future promotes paying attention.

INVENTED SPELLING

The children's writing shown earlier in Figures 4.5 through 4.7 was done some time ago. (The writing done on word processors is recent.) Older examples were chosen to make the point that invented spelling is not a new accomplishment for young children. What *is* new is the amount of attention invented spelling has received in recent years.

The attention is natural. As the examples in Figures 4.5 through 4.8 demonstrate, there is something inherently appealing about invented spelling. For anyone who takes the time to think through the knowledge that invented spelling reflects, it is also awesome. Still another reason for the widespread interest is that up until the early 1980s, researchers came close to ignoring young children's writing. As a result, little was known about it. This made early writing a very attractive topic to study.

Why it was ignored for so long can be explained by the fact that bringing reading ability into existence was thought to be the school's first responsibility. Only when that was done did attention shift to writing. In fact, only then were children considered to be ready to write. When attention did go to writing, forming letters correctly, copying words, and using standard spelling were the primary concerns.

Clearly, recent studies of emergent literacy have painted a different picture of young children and, as a result, different expectations. Now, one commonly held belief among researchers is supported by whole language proponents; it can be summarized as follows: "The child develops as a *writer/reader.* The notion of reading preceding writing, or vice versa, is a misconception. Listening, speaking, reading, and writing abilities develop concurrently and interrelatedly, rather than sequentially" (31, p. xviii).

Invented Spelling: Origins

Why are children able to invent spellings, even before they start school? To begin, somehow and somewhere they have learned that spoken language is made up of a sequence of sounds. Knowing that letters represent the sounds when spoken language is recorded is another of their remarkable accomplishments.

If children do not yet know which letters stand for which sounds, knowing the names of letters may help. For instance, if a child wants to write "cat," he might start by making the letter *k* because its name and the word "cat" start with the same sound. Thinking about "cat," the same child might also decide that its last sound is spelled with *t* because the word "cat" ends with the sound that starts the name of the letter *t.* With all this in mind, the child writes *kt.*

The fact that the spelling *kt* does not account for the medial sound in "cat" can be explained in two ways. First, medial sounds are difficult to perceive as distinct sounds. Second, the medial sound in cat is unlike the name of any letter. Because this is not the case with the medial sound in a word such as "coat," seeing "coat" spelled *kot* is a reasonable expectation.

Analogies also help. For example, let's say that a kindergarten teacher reads a story and, at some point, shows and talks about words like *wishy* and *washy.* Later, recalling them may help a child who wants to write *once* (as in "Once upon a time…"). Strickland and Morrow (26) refer to one such child who, remembering *wishy* and *washy,* spelled "once" as *wus,* which was later changed to *wuns.* Still later, having seen *once* in a book, the spelling advanced to *wonce.* Eventually, the child "let go of *w*" and used the conventional spelling.

Analogies function in other ways, too. A child who can read *one* may think of that word when he, too, wants to write "once." Consequently, his spelling is *onec.* If, in addition to knowing *one,* he has also learned to read *books* and *paints,* which are labels in his kindergarten classroom, the chosen spelling for "once" might be *ones.*

Later, when some of the sounds that letters represent are known—either because they were taught directly or were gradually learned by the child from experiences with words—the use of letter-sound correspondences figures prominently in invented spelling, especially when teachers demonstrate the value of phonics for both reading and writing.

As the examples of invented spelling in Figures 4.5 through 4.8 illustrate, a young child's efforts to write are characterized by various combinations of (a) words whose spellings have been learned, (b) words whose spellings have been partially learned, (c) words whose spellings are "invented," and (d) words that are recorded with strings of letters bearing no apparent relationship to the word. Stated briefly, these young writers have learned a lot! This explains why invented spelling is not nearly as common among kindergartners, or even first graders, as some individuals mistakenly believe.

Invented Spelling: Problems

Problems connected with the discovery of children's invented spelling are of two kinds. The first is unrealistic expectations on the part of teachers. That is, failing to appreciate all that such spellings require, some teachers mistakenly believe that all—or at least most—young children will turn out to be inventive spellers. Why this hardly is the case is documented in interesting, insightful ways by Judith Schickedanz in *Adam's Righting Revolutions* (25). The book is a detailed account of her son's ups and downs with writing from infancy through grade one. It shows in some detail that invented spelling is neither an easy nor a quick accomplishment.

All the knowledge that invented spelling draws on (combined with the motor control required) has caused researchers who study writing in classrooms to modify original expectations. Elizabeth Sulzby, who has done extensive work in this area, now concludes:

> During kindergarten, the most typical forms of writing used in connected discourse (such as stories or letters) continue to be scribbling, drawing, and nonphonetic letter strings, with fewer children using phonetic (or invented) spelling and conventional orthography (dictionary spelling). (28, p. 72)

Sulzby also notes that, among children who have displayed the ability to engage in invented spelling, the kind of writing they actually use depends on the task. Specifically, a more generous use is made of standard and invented spellings when isolated words or lists are written than when connected text is attempted.

The second problem that has resulted from the widespread interest in invented spelling is a common one in education. I refer to the tendency to turn means into ends in themselves. In the case of invented spelling, the problem is the tendency of some teachers to value invented spelling to such an extent that they seem to forget it is still standard spelling that is the goal. One consequence is the possibility that when children ask, "How do you spell…?" they may be denied help, or simply told, "Spell it the best way you can." Even though the latter suggestion is acceptable when a teacher is busy with other children, it is *un*acceptable when the teacher is free to provide the help requested. The book by Schickedanz referred to earlier (25) provides convincing evidence of the problems that can develop when children are beyond inventing spelling at the same time that their teachers appear to value it more than standard spelling.

Invented Spelling: Contributions

Even though invented spelling *is* only a means to an end (standard spelling), the interest it has generated accounts for a much better attitude toward children's composition than once existed. It has moved attention away from the mechanics of writing to its value as a medium for communicating. Now, instead of attending immediately to how letters are formed and words are spelled, most teachers are considering the child's intended message. Even when spelling *is* the concern, teachers are moving away from looking at what is wrong to highlighting what is right.

Anyone interested in easing young children into literacy by helping them learn *about* reading should also value writing as a helpful way to develop print awareness as well as an understanding of such basic terms as *word*. In fact, because writing involves moving from what is known (how a word is pronounced) to what is unknown (how a word is spelled), learning the referent for *word* may be accomplished more easily for some children in the context of writing than in the context of reading. It is also true that when children write, they soon learn about the need to separate words with empty spaces if they want someone else to know what they wrote. They thus learn quickly the meaning of "beginning of a word" and "end of a word."

Clearly, all of these observations support what is promoted earlier in the chapter: Young children should have a *variety* of opportunities to acquire literacy. To rely on one method or medium only is to deny success to some children.

READING TO CHILDREN

It was said previously that researchers delving into the lives of young children have provided considerable information about helping them *learn about reading*. You can hardly be surprised to hear that reading to young children continues to win accolades not only as a means for helping them learn about reading but also for fostering positive attitudes toward learning to read themselves.

In my own studies of preschool readers (14), subjects inevitably ended up being children who had been read to frequently, starting at an early age. Subsequently, other researchers focused on how parents and other people go about doing the reading (17, 24, 29). Even though this work has not produced evidence of a causal relationship between how the reading is done and a child's literacy development, it is now generally agreed that the reading ought to be *interactive*. That is, instead of being a fairly passive listening experience for children, reading should be a time for them to ask questions, discuss, and make predictions about what might happen next. Previous experiences with storybook reading also allow children to make comparisons and to express likes and dislikes. Meanwhile, they are learning about handling books and about where stories begin and end. And if more than just stories are read, the chance to conclude that books answer questions is made available, too. Learning that some books even tell how to make or do something is another possibility.

As a result of all these contacts with text, it is the unusual child who does not eventually ask, "Where does it say that?" or "What does that word look like?" And so children begin to ease themselves into reading. How teachers can promote interactive reading that is equally productive is discussed in the next chapter, where the focus shifts to classrooms.

SUMMARY

The controversy that beginning reading has always generated is the topic Chapter 4 considered initially. Why the controversy is related to the unique importance assigned to children's success at the beginning was explained.

Chapter 4 then provided some historical perspective. This was done by sketching early notions about the meaning of "ready to read." To provide the perspective, G. Stanley Hall and Arnold Gesell required attention. Their beliefs about the nature of child growth and development helped to form, and win support for, the traditional description of readiness proposed in the late 1920s. In fact, it was the influence of Hall and Gesell that made maturation the key variable. Because assigning importance to maturation inevitably assigns importance to the passing of time, "Wait!" became the key word for anyone worried about the first-grade reading problems that had been identified earlier with national surveys.

Once postponement of instruction was accepted as a way to reduce problems, reading at the start of first grade had to be replaced with something else. The substitution, called readiness programs, was increasingly shaped by the content of reading readiness workbooks. Because so many of their exercises had little relevance for reading, a wide gap soon developed between (a) what was done supposedly to get children ready for reading, and (b) what is actually required to be a reader.

Chapter 4 next pointed out that, during all this time, practically no attention went to the obvious fact that success with beginning reading depends not only on the children but also on the nature and the quality of the instruction available. This two-sided picture was drawn in a definition of readiness that David Ausubel proposed. By defining readiness as "the adequacy of existing ability *in relation to* the demands of the learning task," Ausubel painted a balanced picture.

The concept of emergent reading was discussed next. Because this concept called attention to the gradually evolving nature of reading ability, it succeeded in making three important points. First, it reminded us that readiness does not occur at a given point in time. Second, it emphasized that the seeds for success with reading are planted in the very early experiences that young children have with meaningful text. Third, the same concept succeeded in clarifying that getting children ready is not distinctly different from *easing* them into reading.

Chapter 4 then explained how emergent reading was expanded into emergent literacy when linguists called attention to some preschool children who appeared to have grasped the alphabetic nature of written English. With that knowledge, children were able to engage in what came to be called invented spelling. Why *"invented"* is not the most accurate description and, further, why invented spelling is a difficult accomplishment, was explained with the identification of three understandings reflected in such spelling: (a) that a word is composed of blended sounds; (b) that a word is written on the basis of those sounds; and (c) that the sounds are represented by letters.

The chapter then pointed out that studies of early reading and of early writing promoted attention to two topics that have significance for anyone working with both young children and literacy. The two, print awareness and metalanguage, were discussed next. That the components of neither are taught in lessons but, rather, in conjunction with contacts with meaningful text was one of the major points made.

It should come as no surprise that this chapter entitled "Easing Young Children into Literacy" concluded with a section about reading to children. The fact that this topic is reconsidered in the chapter that follows should not be a surprise, either, for Chapter 5 deals with the school, specifically with "Early Literacy Programs."

REVIEW

1. It has been said that "reading readiness is a good concept that got applied in a bad way" (31, p. xiv). Based on your reading of Chapter 4, explain why this observation is correct (a) when it states that readiness is "a good concept," and (b) when it concludes that it was used "in a bad way" when first applied to children's readiness to begin to read.

2. The descriptions of classrooms in Chapter 4 (see Figures 4.2 and 4.3) demonstrate how much can be learned about young children's literacy development by observing their behavior. Even in grocery stores, behavioral signs of readiness are noticeable. Recently, I was in one such store and observed a girl of about three or four who, penny in hand, walked to a gumball machine. Taped to it was a sheet of paper displaying three hand-printed words: out of order. Upon seeing the sheet, the child turned and asked a passerby, "What does that say?" "It says 'out of order'," the woman answered. "What does that mean?" the little girl inquired. "It means the machine doesn't work. I hope you didn't put your money in." "No," responded the child and walked away. Now, see if you can specify the behavioral signs of readiness that became apparent during the brief conversation just described.

3. David Ausubel, a psychologist, figures prominently in Chapter 4 because of the relevance of his conception of readiness for educators responsible for bringing reading ability into existence. To make sure you understand the relevance, explain the following: Ausubel's definition has relevance for educators because of the explicit attention it gives to the *relational* aspect of readiness.

4. Were you David Ausubel, how would you respond to a kindergarten teacher who made the following request in October. "I teach kindergarten and am required to use the _____ basal reader series.* All the children are doing fine with the exception of two boys. Apparently, they aren't ready to read yet. What readiness materials would you recommend that I use with them?"

5. Describe essential differences between (a) the traditional understanding of readiness for reading, and (b) the concept of emergent literacy.

6. Directing your answer to someone who knows nothing about *print awareness,* explain what it means by referring to its components.

7. Do the same for *metalanguage.*

8. Return to Figure 4.10. Using the text shown:
   a. Specify how it could serve to foster print awareness.
   b. Specify the language about language that could be clarified with the help of the same text.
   c. Name other ways in which this familiar song could be put to good use.

---

*The required series starts instruction by teaching phonics at a fairly brisk pace.

9. Chapter 4 referred to three understandings that are necessary for anyone learning to read and write a language that has an alphabetic writing system. All three are reflected in children's invented spelling. What are the three understandings?

10. *Decontextualized* instruction is something teachers need to avoid.
    a. What *is* decontextualized instruction?
    b. Why did Chapter 4 refer to decontextualized instruction?

REFERENCES

1. Adams, Marilyn J. *Thinking and Learning about Print.* Cambridge, Mass.: The MIT Press, 1990.

2. Adams, M. J.; Allington, R. L.; Chaney, J. H.; Goodman, Y. M.; Kapinus, B. A.; McGee, L. M.; Richgels, D. J.; Schwartz, S. J.; Shannon, P.; Smitten, B.; and Williams, J. P. "Beginning to Read: A Critique by Literacy Professionals and a Response by Marilyn Jager Adams." *Reading Teacher* 44 (February, 1991), 370–395.

3. Arthur, Grace. "A Quantitative Study of the Results of Grouping First-Grade Children According to Mental Age." *Journal of Educational Research* 12 (October, 1925), 173–185.

4. Ausubel, David P. "Viewpoints from Related Disciplines: Human Growth and Development." *Teachers College Record* 60 (February, 1959), 245–254.

5. Bussis, Anne M. "A Review of *Emergent Literacy: Writing and Reading.*" *Journal of Reading Behavior* 20 (1988, No. 2), 181–187.

6. Calfee, Robert C., and Venezky, Richard L. "Component Skills in Beginning Reading." In K. S. Goodman and J. T. Fleming (Eds.), *Psycholinguistics and the Teaching of Reading.* Newark, Del.: International Reading Association, 1969.

7. Carbo, Marie. "Debunking the Great Phonics Myth." *Phi Delta Kappan* 70 (November, 1988), 226–240.

8. Chall, Jeanne S. "Learning to Read: The Great Debate 20 Years Later—A Response to 'Debunking the Great Phonics Myth'." *Phi Delta Kappan* 70 (March, 1989), 521–538.

9. Chomsky, Carol. "Reading, Writing, and Phonology." *Harvard Educational Review* 40 (May, 1970), 287–309.

10. Clarke, Margaret M. *Young Fluent Readers.* London: Heinemann Educational Books, 1976.

11. Clay, Marie M. *Emergent Reading Behaviour.* Unpublished doctoral dissertation, University of Auckland, New Zealand, 1966.

12. Clay, Marie M. *Reading: The Patterning of Complex Behavior.* Exeter, N. H.: Heinemann Books, 1972.

13. Dickson, Virgil E. *Mental Tests and the Classroom Teacher.* New York: World Book Co., 1923.

14. Durkin, Dolores. *Children Who Read Early.* New York: Teachers College Press, Columbia University, 1966.

15. Durkin, Dolores. "A Classroom-Observation Study of Reading Instruction in Kindergarten." *Early Childhood Research Quarterly* 2 (September, 1987), 275–300.

16. Durkin, Dolores. "When Should Children Begin to Read?" In H. M. Robinson (Ed.), *Innovation and Change in Reading Instruction,* Sixty-Seventh Yearbook of the National Society for the Study of Education, Part II. Chicago: University of Chicago Press, 1968.

17. Flood, James. "Parental Styles in Reading Episodes with Young Children." *Reading Teacher* 30 (May, 1977), 864–867.

18. Gesell, Arnold L. *Infancy and Human Growth.* New York: Macmillan, 1925.

19. Gesell, Arnold L. *The Mental Growth of the Preschool Child.* New York: Macmillan, 1925.

20. Hall, G. Stanley. *The Psychology of Adolescence.* New York: D. Appleton, 1904.

21. Juel, Connie. "Learning to Read and Write: A Longitudinal Study of 54 Children from First through Fourth Grades." *Journal of Educational Psychology* 80 (December, 1988), 437–447.

22. Morphett, M. V., and Washburne, C. "When Should Children Begin to Read?" *Elementary School Journal* 31 (March, 1931), 496–503.

23. Read, Charles. *Children's Categorization of Speech Sounds in English*. Urbana, Ill.: National Council of Teachers of English, 1975.

24. Roser, Nancy, and Martinez, Miriam. "Roles Adults Play in Preschoolers' Response to Literature." *Language Arts* 62 (September, 1985), 485–490.

25. Schickedanz, Judith A. *Adam's Righting Revolutions*. Portsmouth, N. H.: Heinemann Educational Books, Inc., 1990.

26. Strickland, Dorothy S., and Morrow, Lesley M. "Developing Skills: An Emergent Literacy Perspective." *Reading Teacher* 43 (October, 1989), 82–83.

27. Strickland, Dorothy S., and Morrow, Lesley M. "New Perspectives on Young Children Learning to Read and Write." *Reading Teacher* 42 (October, 1988), 70–71.

28. Sulzby, Elizabeth; Teale, William H.; and Kamberelis, George. "Emergent Writing in the Classroom: Home and School Connections." In D. S. Strickland and L. M. Morrow (Eds.), *Emerging Literacy: Young Children Learn to Read and Write*. Newark, Del.: International Reading Association, 1989.

29. Teale, William H. "Parents Reading to Their Children: What We Know and Need to Know." *Language Arts* 58 (November/December, 1981), 902–912.

30. Teale, William H. "Toward a Theory of How Children Learn to Read and Write Naturally." *Language Arts* 59 (September, 1982), 555–570.

31. Teale, William H., and Sulzby, Elizabeth. "Emergent Literacy as a Perspective for Examining How Young Children Become Writers and Readers." In W. H. Teale and E. Sulzby (Eds.), *Emergent Literacy*. Norwood, N.J.: Ablex Publishing, 1986.

32. Thomas, Karen F. "Early Reading as a Social Interaction Process." *Language Arts* 62 (September, 1985), 469–475.

33. Thorndike, Robert L., and Hagen, Elizabeth. *Measurement and Evaluation in Psychology and Education*. New York: Wiley, 1969.

34. Turner, Richard L. "The 'Great' Debate—Can Both Carbo and Chall Be Right?" *Phi Delta Kappan* 71 (December, 1989), 276–283.

35. Washburne, Carleton. "Ripeness." *Progressive Education* 13 (February, 1936), 125–130.

36. Yaden, David B. "Reading Research in Metalinguistic Awareness: A Classification of Findings According to Focus and Methodology." In D. B. Yaden and S. Templeton (Eds.), *Metalinguistic Awareness and Beginning Literacy*. Portsmouth, N. H.: Heinemann Educational Books, Inc., 1986.

CHAPTER 5

A Beginning Literacy Program

Most of Chapter 5 is organized around six guidelines thought to be essential for anyone responsible for a beginning literacy program. Before starting Chapter 5, examine the guidelines, which are in the outline.

Chapter 5 discusses each guideline with references to materials and activities that both teachers and prospective teachers should find helpful. The discussions show how a literacy program can integrate all the language arts and, in addition, make generous use of traditional and modern literature.

Toward the end of the chapter all the guidelines are assembled into a whole, with the help of a sample schedule for kindergarten. The schedule, which assumes a half-day program, divides into time for opening activities, small group instruction and review, shared reading experiences, composing, music, art, and storytime.

Like other chapters, Chapter 5 includes reports of classroom observations. One of the best accounts of a kindergarten is written by the teacher herself. Because these accounts are intended to add a note of reality to the content, you are encouraged to read the accounts and the commentaries about them at the time they appear in the chapter. For any readers of Chapter 5 who have not yet taught, the accounts should be especially helpful in allowing for seeing what is recommended or questioned.

• • • • • • •

Hᴏᴡ ᴛᴏ ɢɪᴠᴇ ʏᴏᴜɴɢ ᴄʜɪʟᴅʀᴇɴ the best possible start on their road to literacy is a question that schools usually do not answer in a uniform way. Differences exist not only in the content of programs but also in their length. Although more school systems have half-day than full-day kindergartens (12), others provide classes for four-year-olds. In some places, five-year-olds thought to be unready for a regular kindergarten are assigned to developmental kindergartens. Where the latter do not exist, transitional first grades may be available. These are for children who attended a regular kindergarten but are judged to be unready for the regular first grade. The kindest response to all these practices is to characterize them, first, as a recognition of the major importance of initial success and, second, as well-intentioned but at times misguided efforts to promote achievement at the beginning.

Before guidelines that need to be considered for beginning literacy programs are discussed, findings from the classroom-observation study of 42 kindergartens referred to in the previous chapter are reported and critiqued. The critique should help explain why the guidelines merit attention.

KINDERGARTEN CLASSROOM-OBSERVATION STUDY

As stated in Chapter 4, the maturation view of readiness associated with Arnold Gesell is now enjoying a second round of influence. Evidence of this is the administration of Gesell-like developmental tests in the spring prior to children's entrance into kindergarten, or close to the start of the kindergarten year itself (4). Tests used for screening purposes—including the Gesell School Readiness Test (8)—are heavily weighted with motor tasks (e.g., skipping, walking on a straight line) and visual-motor tasks (e.g., tracing lines and copying patterns). A child's ability to write his or her name, assessed in the context of motor control, is looked at, too. Reasons for the screening, as viewed by the kindergarten teachers in the classroom-observation study, include:

"To see who is developmentally ready"
"To identify those who should stay home for a year"
"To decide who will go to our prekindergarten motor class"
"To spot maturity levels and determine readiness for reading"

Of relevance now is the contradiction inherent in the concern for differences among children that the prekindergarten screening supposedly represents and, on the other hand, the failure to acknowledge differences when the content for kindergarten programs is established. The failure is attested to by the fact that, as Chapter 4 explains, phonics instruction, offered to an entire class, comprised most of what was done with reading in the observed kindergartens.

The various points made thus far can be summarized with a reference to conclusions that Lorrie Shepard reached after reviewing research concerned with the effects of such extras as developmental kindergartens and transitional first grades (19, 20). Shepard and Smith note:

Despite the promises, providing an extra year before first grade does not solve the problems it is intended to solve. Children…show virtually no academic advantage over equally at-risk children who did not have the extra year…. Other alternatives exist…but they are not so popular as simple answers such as a new test or a new grade level…. If one looks at existing research, successful programs are those which responded to individual differences among children. (18, pp. 11–12)

GUIDELINES FOR KINDERGARTEN TEACHERS

Anyone acquainted with kindergartens knows that differences in children's knowledge and abilities at the start of the year are often sizable (5). It is impossible for a textbook like this one, therefore, to prescribe a literacy curriculum that promotes optimum achievement for all five-year-olds. Nonetheless, it can lay out guidelines for kindergarten teachers to consider when they try—as suggested in the passage just quoted—to respond to individual differences.

No matter what the differences may be, kindergarten classrooms—like all others—should exemplify a *literate environment.* The first guideline, therefore, pertains to that.

GUIDELINE NUMBER ONE: PROVIDE A LITERATE ENVIRONMENT

At one time, it was commonly believed that children judged to be unready to learn to read should be kept away from print. It was as if contacts with written language are harmful when made prematurely. Because a trace of these earlier ideas was found by an observer of a developmental kindergarten, this is a suitable time for you to read her report in Figure 5.1 and the commentary about it.

Now that you have read about a *non*example of a literate environment, it is time to discuss examples.

The Nature of Literate Environments

Applied to classrooms, a literate environment is one in which written language, made up of one word or many words, is meaningful and useful. This is why a simple, hand-printed recipe for apple sauce soon to be made is assigned as much value as a handsome bulletin board displaying the book jackets of stories the teacher read to the class when "Growing Up" was the theme that connected activities.

Even though displays of text may be attractive and colorful, their purpose is not to be decorative. Nevertheless, teachers who provide print-rich settings follow the advice of professional decorators who warn, "Too much of a good thing is still too much!" Richness is assessed, therefore, not with the question, "How much?" but with one that asks, "How meaningful?"

When a new school year is beginning, meaningful text includes the children's names, now serving to help take attendance or to show which cubby belongs to which child. Name tags worn by the children help them get acquainted while, at the same time, they show written language. Words like *school, Monday*—if that is the

FIGURE 5.1   Commentary   ▶

Reliable conclusions about the nature and quality of a school program can hardly be reached with one observation; nonetheless, the activities described in Figure 5.1 merit praise. One gets the impression that we are reading about a hard-working teacher doing a fine job with as many as 22 children.

What was *not* seen is the problem. Even though the teacher's stance regarding workbooks is easy to defend, what may have been a deliberate effort to keep written language out of the room is not. Although nobody should either flood classrooms with words or nag children to learn them, keeping kindergartners away from text is not an acceptable alternative.

As the report in Figure 5.1 makes clear, much of what was seen provided opportunities to expose the children to letters and words in meaningful ways. The following, for example, might have been printed had a chalkboard been available:

        cat   hippopotamus
        rat
        hat

The teacher could point to each letter and word while the children sang the song. Afterward, she might have done one or more of the following.

1. Asked the children to count the words as she pointed to them.
2. Asked whether anyone could spell "hippopotamus" now that it can be seen.
3. Drawn a line under the *a* and *t* in *cat, rat,* and *hat* while commenting that the words end with the same two letters.
4. Pointed to all the words in some random order, saying, "Let's see if you can read these words!"

Even if nothing of what is done with the words is retained, the children are still having an opportunity to talk about print and to begin to see what is meant by "word," "end of a word," "letter," "long word," and so forth. Meanwhile, the display of words makes the familiar song more, not less, appealing.

At the start of this morning's observation, the 22 children were in four groups. They were divided, the teacher explained, "according to motor abilities." Those with the teacher were working with textures, feeling various objects and discussing how they felt. The second group was tearing little pieces of sticky paper that the children were attaching to the letters *p, i,* and *g.* Large forms of the three letters had been printed on sheets of paper; each child had a copy. (When I asked a couple of the children what the three letters said, none knew. Nor did any seem to know the names of the letters.) A third group was doing leaf rubbings with crayons, and the final group—the "talented children," according to the teacher— was making puppets.

The next activity included everyone. Because the teacher had been reading different versions of *The Three Little Pigs,* she had prepared a flannelgraph presentation of the story. (Neither the word *pig* nor any other word was displayed.) Once the tale was retold, selected children acted it out and did a wonderful job. All the while I was thinking that the children were as bright and alert as any I have been seeing in so-called regular kindergartens.

Later, during music, songs such as the following were sung: "I spell 'cat', *c, a, t.* I spell 'rat', *r, a, t.* I spell 'hat', *h, a, t.* But I can't spell 'hippopotamus'." I refer to this song because the children knew it so well that I had to wonder why a visual dimension had not been added. It seemed like a perfect time to let the children *see* what they were singing.

This reminds me that the absence of a chalkboard was something that caught my eye almost as soon as I entered the room. The only one available—small in size—was in the play area. Also missing were displays of meaningful print. Two exceptions were the children's names and a calendar. When I was getting ready to leave, the teacher explained that developmental kindergartens like this one are needed because "academics are now begun too soon." She assured me that nobody would ever find a workbook in *her* class.

FIGURE 5.1 A Developmental Kindergarten

day when school starts—and the teacher's name are meaningful when a teacher points to, reads, and talks about them. Because many young children are familiar with calendars, a large one can be hung and discussed as early as the first day of school. Nor is the first day too soon to have a library to which books will gradually be added and, at other times, replaced with others. Highly visible, attractive, accessible—this is what classroom libraries ought to be.

Although libraries are always desirable, other kinds of text *become* desirable through their association with ongoing activities and interests. In spite of the necessary link, the categorization of materials shown in Figure 5.2 should help teachers interested in making their classrooms literate environments.

Making Text Meaningful

It is the exceptional classroom that does not have capital and lowercase letters printed on cards arranged in alphabetical order. Often, in fact, this is standard equipment. One teacher who made the cards more meaningful than is typical waited to display them until most of her kindergartners knew the names of most of the letters. This is what she did.

Throughout November, the class often sang the Alphabet Song while having a midmorning snack. The teacher and the children then talked about the two letters on a card, each shown in its capital and lowercase forms. Once discussed, the card was attached to a wall closer to the eye-level of the children than is commonly seen. Eventually, all the cards were displayed in alphabetical order.

When that was achieved, each child received a copy of the Alphabet Song divided into three pages (see Figure 5.3). After each page and page number were examined, the teacher and children sang the song slowly, all the while tracking the letters on pages one and two. When everyone turned to page three, some children quickly called out "I" and "me," which figured in earlier bulletin-board displays. Taking her cue from them, the teacher printed *I* and *me* on a nearby chalkboard, reread the words, and asked everyone to repeat what they said. Next, she herself slowly sang the Alphabet Song from beginning to end; as she did, the children followed the text. Finally, everybody sang the song, page by page. Before the books were taken home, the children made covers that incorporated letters in one form or another.

Because talk about the weather is as common in kindergartens as it is on the radio, the second example of making text meaningful pertains to weather words. As the illustration is described, you can see how deftly the teacher calls attention to the usefulness of reading and writing. Like other successful teachers, she is consciously aware of objectives:

Objectives:
1. To demonstrate the value of print for preserving information.
2. To underscore the usefulness of the ability to read and write.
3. To provide opportunities to learn to read some words.

Like many kindergartens, the schedule in this one begins with attention to the weather, a topic of interest to young children because it affects their play life. On one Monday morning the teacher comments, "This certainly is a beautiful morning,

Written-Language Displays	*Books*	Commercially published story books Commercially published reference/information books Individual child-authored stories Group-authored stories Individual child-authored information books Group-authored information books
	Communications	Child-authored notes Adult-authored notes Child-authored messages Adult-authored messages Child-authored letters Adult-authored letters
	Lists	**Sign-up**
		Record Songs we know Books we read What we saw on our science walk
		Summary Animals we saw at the zoo Paintings we saw on our museum trip
		Reference Color chart Alphabet chart Sight word list
	Directions	Classroom rules Directions for activities Directions for use of centers Recipes Personal directives (*Example:* Do not move these blocks)
	Schedules	Daily activity schedule Job schedule Monthly objectives Attendance schedule Diary calendar Group rotation schedule Choice-time selection
	Labels	**Organization** Location of centers or activity areas Contents of shelves Containers that hold things
		Identification Labeled color chips Pictures labeled for references (*Example:* This is a...) Captioned art work
	Writing Materials	Paper Crayons Dittos Chalkboard Staples Things to trace Flannel boards Glue Color forms Pens Scissors Plastic letters Pencils Stencils Chalk Markers

FIGURE 5.2   Possible Displays and Writing Materials in a Literate Environment

Source: "The Development of Written Language Awareness: Environmental Aspects and Program Characteristics," Nancy E. Taylor, Irene H. Blum, and David N. Logsdon, *Reading Research Quarterly,* spring 1986, p. 140. Reprinted with permission of Nancy E. Taylor and the International Reading Association.

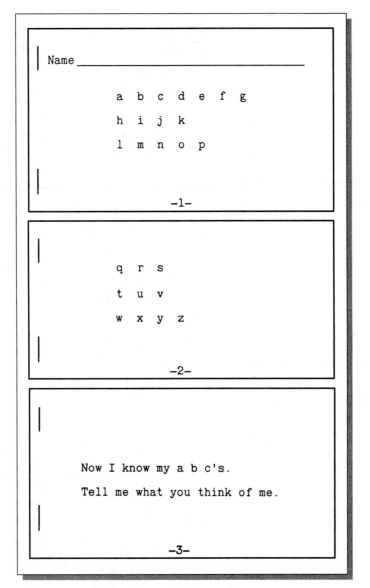

Name _____

    a   b   c   d   e   f   g
    h   i   j   k
    l   m   n   o   p

                    –1–

    q   r   s
    t   u   v
    w   x   y   z

                    –2–

    Now I know my a b c's.
    Tell me what you think of me.

                    –3–

FIGURE 5.3 A Three-Page Alphabet Book

isn't it? Was last Monday as nice as today? Can someone tell us what it was like last Monday?" Responses begin with guessing and end with the conclusion that nobody remembers. Thus it is time for the teacher to propose, "If I write words that tell us about today, then next Monday we can look at what I write, and the words will tell us. We won't have to work so hard trying to remember." A discussion of the current weather then begins and leads to the teacher's printing *sunny* and *clear* at the left side of a wide sheet of paper. By the end of the week, the sheet shows:

Monday	Tuesday	Wednesday	Thursday	Friday
sunny clear	cloudy warm	cold dark windy	rainy windy	sunny clear

A couple of weeks later, this teacher makes another proposal: "We seem to use the same words over and over, don't we? [Points to and reads *sunny, clear,* and *windy.*] If I put all the words on cards, then instead of writing them every day we can just pick out the right cards." Soon, a weather chart with slots for cards is attached to a bulletin board. Meanwhile, all the children work hard at remembering each word so that they will be able to select appropriate descriptions.

GUIDELINE NUMBER TWO: READ TO CHILDREN DAILY

At one time, reading to children was thought of as providing little more than a pleasant pause in the day's activities. Now it is viewed as a vehicle for helping children arrive at an understanding of the nature of "story," for adding to their knowledge of the world, and, as the next section illustrates, for contributing to their understanding both of the conventions of print and of terms that pertain to language. In spite of the potential to be instructive, those who do the reading should not forget that it also is a means for encouraging children to want to be readers themselves. For the children, therefore, being read to should always be an *enjoyable* experience.

Even though enjoyment is a key concern, additional consequences of significant value should not be overlooked. Sometimes, as an incident in a kindergarten demonstrated, nothing special is required to achieve the extras except to read the book. In this case, the teacher read a story about a dog that was listened to with rapt attention. When the story ended, several children commented simultaneously and could not be understood; consequently, the teacher reminded everyone of the need to take turns. Eventually, many took a turn. One child said the animal in the story was like her grandmother's dog. Another said that was impossible because the dog in the story wasn't real. And another referred to the discrepancy between how the story ended and how he thought things would turn out. All in all, it was an excellent discussion that revealed excellent comprehension. That made the teacher's next procedure both unexpected and unnecessary. Perhaps mimicking the practices of a teacher's manual, the teacher posed a series of questions (How many…? What color was…? Where did…? When did…?). By the time the questions ended, a group of squirming five-year-olds had replaced the group of engrossed discussants. Later, the teacher explained the questions with a reference to "helping children with comprehension." Because helping children comprehend what is read *is* important, examples of desirable help follow.

Help with Comprehending: Prereading

One of the most interesting illustrations of an appreciation of the need to prepare children for a story refers not to a teacher but to a girl in third grade who was about to read her revised version of *The Three Pigs* to some kindergartners. (The children's teacher had read the original the day before.) The third grader began by saying that she had revised the story of *The Three Pigs,* after which she explained "revise." She next told her audience about Austria, the setting for her revision. Finally, she explained the meaning of "asthma," an affliction from which the wolf in her version suffered. She then read her illustrated tale to a most attentive audience.

In another room, a teacher prepared for an expository selection, *Look at Your Eyes,* by printing and reading *pupil.* The children provided the familiar meaning; the teacher explained the meaning relevant for the book she was about to read. To help the children understand other information in the book, she showed them how smiling changes the appearance of one's eyes by covering the lower part of her face with paper and asking the children whether they could tell when she was smiling by looking at her eyes. The teacher next had several volunteers show the class, one small group at a time, how the pupil of the eye gets smaller when light—in this case, a flashlight—is directed toward the eye. Somewhat excited, the children nevertheless settled down when the teacher began to read.

Also recognizing the value of prior, relevant knowledge for comprehending, a teacher in another kindergarten reviewed the origins of the three fruit juices that had been discussed thus far (orange, apple, grapefruit). She then said she had found a beautifully illustrated book about another fruit, after which she brought out a pineapple. Once it was felt and discussed, the teacher read the book that told about pineapple trees and where they grow.

Because graphs for other topics had been made earlier, one postreading activity was the preparation of a graph entitled "Our Favorite Juices." Listed at the left-hand side in large letters were *apple, grapefruit, orange,* and *pineapple.* (Responses showed that orange juice was the overwhelming favorite.) The children drew pictures of the sources of the four juices and labeled each with a word selected from the graph.

Help with Comprehending: Postreading

Activities for the book about pineapples effectively demonstrate that plans to help children comprehend need not concentrate on prereading possibilities *or* postreading activities. It is not an either-or consideration. Nonetheless, the present section is confined to postreading possibilities.

The first example is described by the kindergarten teacher who carried out the activities:

Today I read *One Kitten for Kim.* Briefly, the story is about a child whose cat had eight kittens. His parents said he could keep only one and must find homes for the other seven. He succeeds in finding one for each, but ends up with seven other pets because he traded the kittens to get the homes.

After I read the story, I encouraged the children to tell what they thought Kim's parents might say about the new pets. I was hoping the children would conclude that Kim's parents did not want seven new pets anymore than they wanted seven kittens. I was pleased that several children did understand this, even though others did not until we discussed it.

In order to help the children reconstruct the sequence of events, I had them draw pictures of Kim's trip around the neighborhood and the trades he made. Later, we pasted the pictures on a long, narrow sheet of paper and rolled them through our television (a shoebox with an opening). As the pictures appeared, the children retold the story. I took the tale one step further by having the children consider what Kim's parents might do with all the new pets.

I was pleased with the results. The children seemed to understand the subtle humor of the story and enjoyed making the pictures and retelling the events. I felt it was an effective activity for listening comprehension.

This account is useful in making the point that what ought to be done before or after something is read depends not only on the children but also on the nature of the material. Whereas *One Kitten for Kim* provided an appropriate occasion for giving explicit attention to sequence, *Herbie the Hippo,* read to other kindergartners, allowed for attention to the fact that stories that are different on the surface may share the same theme.

Herbie the Hippo is about a baby hippopotamus who wants to be a bird but, as a result of some experiences, learns it is better to be "his own self." Once an open-ended discussion of the story was concluded, the teacher in question inquired of the children, "Have you ever wanted something, didn't get it, and later were glad you didn't get it?" After the children responded, the teacher asked, "Can you remember other stories I've read that told about others—sometimes a person and sometimes an animal—who were like Herbie because they, too, wanted to be somebody else, but then decided it was better to be who they were?" Once the three related stories were recalled and reviewed, the teacher asked, "Can you think of one title that is a good one for all four stories?" (Titles had been discussed earlier.) Eventually, "Be Glad You're You" was selected. The teacher printed it on the board. This was followed by a discussion of why it was the best title.

Postreading discussions can help children recall what was read and also uncover why a book was *not* enjoyed. Having observed a lack of interest on the part of her students, one recently observed second-grade teacher had the courage to use a postreading discussion for the second purpose after she finished reading *Freckle Juice.* The children's complaints included, "It was too long and draggy," "It wasn't very exciting," and "No kid could be that dumb."

The moral of this frank discussion is that teachers need to choose with care what they read. They should keep in mind, for instance, that young children have little patience with excessive detail and slowly moving plots. Like us all, they enjoy suspense—but not too much—and happy endings. Stories of children and animals are usually attractive, as is a book whose theme or content has some connection with themselves. Not to be forgotten, either, is that young children like expository text that satisfies their curiosity.

GUIDELINE NUMBER THREE: PROVIDE EXPERIENCES THAT PROMOTE PRINT AWARENESS AND AN UNDERSTANDING OF METALANGUAGE

The underlying theme of the guidelines offered in this chapter is the importance of developing programs for young children that respond to differences. The fact that kindergartners start the year with an unequal understanding of the conventions of print and of metalanguage is the reason both figure in the third guideline. By reviewing the components of each in Chapter 4 (see Figures 4.9 and 4.11), you can understand why connected text is required whenever one or the other or both are the concern. As you will see when examples of suitable text are discussed, children who come to kindergarten with considerable understanding of the conventions of print and of metalanguage can profit from these experiences. Often, then, an entire class can participate.

Whenever print awareness and metalanguage enter into a teacher's decisions about what to read to children, choices are likely to include poems and nursery rhymes, pattern books that have repeated dialogue and events, alphabet and counting books, and text that describes the children's own experiences. (The latter is referred to as *language experience material.*) Whenever print awareness and metalanguage are of concern, it is also possible that teachers will use big books.

Big Books

Big books are enlarged versions of books that may contain a story, a Mother Goose rhyme, or, perhaps, captions for large, colorful photographs. To be useful, the print must be big enough for children sitting nearby to see *easily.*

The impetus for big books is a recommendation that Don Holdaway made in the late 1970s to use enlarged print in order to allow young children to participate in *shared reading experiences* with either real or pretend reading (11). Holdaway's recommendation was also made for reasons that Ann Dyson has communicated effectively (7). Viewing the acquisition of early literacy as something that confronts children with "a written language puzzle," Dyson correctly points out that "as with most puzzles, children cannot solve it by being given one piece at a time" (7, p. 838). Teachers who agree with this conclusion start with connected text, not with letters and sounds.

It is worth noting that Holdaway's specific recommendation was to print on chart paper enlarged versions of songs, poems, and brief stories containing text that is repeated in a patterned way. This makes the text predictable, thus allowing children to participate actively in the reading. To allow for highly visible print when the text is a book, another of Holdaway's recommendations was to put the pages on transparencies that could be shown with an overhead projector.

As the pedagogical potential of Holdaway's recommendations began to be appreciated, so too did their commercial potential. One consequence is that big books, now available in large numbers, are sometimes flawed. Text that is not worth reading, too many words on a page, print that is too small, poor art work—these common defects make it necessary to choose carefully if it is believed that the use of enlarged text with a group can help realize objectives such as the following.

Reasons to Use Enlarged Text

- To encourage young children to participate when somebody reads to them.
- To allow for experiences with connected text before attention goes to words, letters, and sounds.
- To help children achieve an understanding of what it means to read.

- To teach about the conventions of print.
- To clarify the meanings of words that pertain to written language.

Once again, then, reflective teachers ask, "*Why* am I doing what I'm doing?"

Using Enlarged Text

To show that buying big books is unnecessary, Figures 5.4 and 5.5 show rhymes and songs that teachers can print themselves and use in ways that match children's needs. As you read the commentary about the samples, you can see why it is correct to say that at the same time that young children are learning about reading, they are having the chance to learn to read.

Should a teacher decide to use commercially produced storybooks in enlarged forms, they can serve purposes not possible when text is confined to a poem or song. Placed on something like an easel, big books allow a teacher to demonstrate the mechanics of handling books and to call attention to the beginning of the book, its end, and to numbers on the pages. While examining the cover—after the teacher has read the title and named the author—children might be asked what a story with such a title might be about. Once predictions are made, it is time for the teacher to turn to page one. Sitting to the side of the book allows her to move a hand or pointer under each line. This permits the children to hear and see the text, which establishes the link between the spoken and the written word. The addition of a picture on a page makes it natural to discuss, or raise questions about, the color and details. Pages without illustrations help children understand that it is words, not pictures, that tell the teacher what to say.

If a story has repetitive, predictable text, it inevitably encourages children to share actively in the experience by reading the words themselves. (This is a suitable time to take another look at Figure 3.4, which shows repetitive text for older students. For the young ones, repetitive text presented in a patterned, thus predictable way, includes well-known tales like *The Three Billy Goats Gruff, The Gingerbread Man, The Three Bears,* and *The House That Jack Built.* Not to be overlooked are some of the Dr. Seuss books, including *The Cat in the Hat.*)

Sometimes, a big book is duplicated in a smaller version. Little books permit children to reread (or pretend to read) the tale alone, or to take turns reading it aloud with a partner. At times, a story may lend itself to art projects or even to efforts by some children to do a little composing themselves.

Using Language Experience Material

Teachers interested in helping children understand the conventions of print and metalanguage do not overlook *language experience material*. This is text about the interests or experiences of a group or an individual. It also includes teacher-generated or child-generated material like:

Invitations, thank-you notes, messages for greeting cards, letters to parents, and questions to pose to visitors.
Reactions to pictures, books, or a videotape.
Directions for making something, getting somewhere, or conducting an experiment.

FIGURE 5.4   Commentary   ▶

Text that can be printed large enough for children to see as they sit on the floor close to the stand on which the chart paper is placed begins with "Twinkle, Twinkle, Little Star." If the children already know the text as a song, they can sing it the first time they see it. And while they sing, the teacher will move across each line of text with her hand or a pointer. The written version also permits discussion—for example, of how the sky is different during the day and at night. Depending on the class, a teacher might choose to see whether they know what a diamond is and why a diamond is compared to a star.

"Star Light, Star Bright" illustrates that choices for enlarged text can include selections about the same or a related topic. "Star Light, Star Bright" has the advantage of being brief, which makes it especially suitable for children just becoming aware that speech is segmented into words. The repetitive use of *star, wish* and *I* also allow for attending to the three words with what I heard some children refer to as "peek-a-boo cards." Made of construction paper or cardboard, the cards serve to focus children's attention when a teacher places the opening over a word or phrase embedded in connected text:

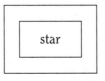

Two other songs that young children often know are also in Figure 5.4. Having sung them, children are ready to see the words. This sequence is helpful for clarifying the connection between spoken and written language. Later, enlarged copies of songs like these can be used by pairs of children. Now, imitating their teacher, they can read and track the lines of text with something like the cardboard tube found inside rolls of paper towels.

All of the examples of text in Figure 5.4 provide teachers with the opportunity to deal with one or more aspects of the conventions of print and to give specific meaning to terms like *word* and *line*.

With the help of the comments made about the songs and rhymes in Figure 5.4, you should now understand why Chapter 4 says that neither print awareness nor metalanguage are topics covered once and for all in a "lesson."

Twinkle, Twinkle, Little Star

Twinkle, twinkle, little star,
How I wonder what you are.
Up above the world so high,
Like a diamond in the sky.
Twinkle, twinkle, little star,
How I wonder what you are.

Star Light, Star Bright

Star light, star bright,
The first star I see tonight.
I wish I may, I wish I might,
Have the wish I wish tonight.

Row, Row, Row Your Boat

Row, row, row your boat
Gently down the stream.
Merrily, merrily, merrily, merrily,
Life is but a dream.

Skipping

Skip, skip,
Skip to my Lou!
Skip, skip,
Skip to my Lou!
Skip, skip
Skip to my Lou!
Skip to my Lou, my darling!

Flies in the buttermilk,
Shoo! Shoo! Shoo!
Flies in the buttermilk,
Shoo! Shoo! Shoo!
Flies in the buttermilk,
Shoo! Shoo! Shoo!
Skip to my Lou, my darling!

FIGURE 5.4   Traditional Songs and Rhymes

FIGURE 5.5   Commentary   ▶

Seeing words they know is a pleasurable experience for young children, for it confirms their ability to read. Once number words are learned, a rhyme like "One, Two, Buckle My Shoe" provides that confirmation. After the text is read several times by the teacher, then reread by the children with as much help is necessary, each of the five pairs of lines can be discussed. The discussion allows for using the text as captions for children's illustrations. If this is done, each child ends up with his or her own 5-page version of "One, Two, Buckle My Shoe."

"Jack and Jill" demonstrates that rhymes may provide perfect opportunities to call attention to words that begin with the same letter. Because of a recent observation in a kindergarten in which four children had given names beginning with *J,* I can picture a helpful list like the following:

Jack

Jill

Jared

Jeffrey

Josh

Jason

Meaningful words such as children's names also provide an opportunity to talk about the fact that words that begin with the same letter often start with the same sound. (Having everyone read aloud a list of familiar names helps to verify this.) Meanwhile, at least some children in the group are beginning to understand descriptions like "the beginning of a word" and "the first letter in a word." Some may even be starting to understand that a word is made up of more than one sound. They are on their way, therefore, to acquiring phonemic awareness.

Two words in "I Know a Little Girl" are underlined in Figure 5.5 to suggest that this rhyme can be used to demonstrate that stressing certain words makes oral reading more effective. Later, more concentrated attention goes to underlining as a possible signal to stress a word. (This is discussed in Chapter 3.)

"Winter Wind" is in Figure 5.5 because I recently heard a kindergarten teacher read a simple but highly informative account of how certain birds, including robins, manage to survive cold winters. "Winter Wind" is a suitable follow-up to the expository text.

One, Two, Buckle My Shoe

One, two,
Buckle my shoe.
Three, four,
Close the door.
Five, six,
Pick up sticks.
Seven, eight,
Close the gate.
Nine, ten,
A big fat hen.

Jack and Jill

Jack and Jill went up the hill
To fetch a pail of water.
Jack fell down and broke his crown
And Jill came tumbling after.

I Know a Little Girl

I know a little girl,
Who has a little curl,
Right in the middle of her
forehead.
When she is good, she is
very, very good.
But when she is bad, she is
horrid!

Winter Wind

The north wind doth blow
And we shall have snow.
And what shall poor Robin do
then?
Poor thing!

He'll sit in the barn,
And keep himself warm,
And hide his head under his wing.
Poor thing!

FIGURE 5.5　Mother Goose Rhymes

Two questions teachers often ask about language experience material are stated and answered below:

1. *Should language experience material be used with an entire class?* Ideal use involves one child, which means that classrooms in which teacher aides or parent volunteers are present should offer numerous opportunities for highly personal uses of language experience material. Reality being what it is, unassisted teachers usually work with small groups because the whole class should participate only when an experience is of interest to everyone. The text in Figure 5.6, for example, was composed by a whole class with the help of the teacher's questions about what had been done and seen. The more detailed attention that went to the text later involved only seven of the most advanced children.

2. *How does a teacher decide when to use the children's words, when to modify them, and when to do most of the composing herself?* This question calls for another reference to the dependent relationship between objectives and teaching procedures. More specifically, some reasons to use language experience material (e.g., to show the connection between oral and written language) make it essential to write exactly what children say. Different objectives, however, do not. If what children say, for instance, is not spoken in sentences and one preestablished objective for the material is to teach that a period indicates the end of a sentence, a teacher needs to compose sentences based on the fragments.

To explain further the effect of objectives on the development and use of experience-based text, one more example is offered. It describes a kindergarten teacher attempting to achieve the following objectives:

Objectives:
1. To teach what is meant by *word.*
2. To teach the function of empty space in establishing word boundaries.

Yesterday was Tuesday. We went for a walk to
Hessel Park. We saw squirrels eating acorns
that had fallen to the ground. They held them
in their hands like people   The leaves are
turning colors. We played in the park and got
hot. Mrs. Urbank got red in the face from
running.

FIGURE 5.6   Recollections of a Walk to a Park

After lunch, a magician put on a show for kindergarten and first-grade children. Subsequently, one kindergarten teacher wisely took advantage of the special event to attend to the objectives just named. Following is the conversation that took place after the children made spontaneous comments about the show. (In this case, the interest of all the children in the topic allowed for a whole-class activity.)

Teacher:	To make sure we don't forget all the things we saw the magician do, let's write them here [pointing to the chalkboard]. Who wants to tell us one thing the magician did?
Kevin:	He pulled a rabbit out of a hat!
Teacher:	He sure did. Let me write what you said, Kevin. Say it one more time.
Kevin:	He pulled a rabbit out of a hat.
Teacher:	Who remembers something else that the magician did? Margie, what did you see him do?
Margie:	Pick a black ace out of a deck of cards.
Teacher:	Yes, he did that, too. Let's see now. Kevin said, "He pulled a rabbit out of a hat." What do you want to say?

Soon the chalkboard displayed the account shown in Figure 5.7.

To realize the two preestablished objectives, procedures similar to the following should be used. They are listed now to reinforce a principle emphasized before: *How* anything ought to be done depends on *why* it is being done.

To teach the meaning of "word" and the use of empty space to show word boundaries, a teacher can:

1. Say aloud each word as it is written. This permits children to watch talk become print.
2. Read the entire account *in a natural speaking fashion,* pointing to each word as it is identified.
3. Suggest to the children that they might like to read the text. (As the children "read," the teacher reads along with them, all the while moving her hand under each line.)
4. Point to and read words that appear more than once. If the children are interested, let them "read" these words again.

He pulled a rabbit out of a hat.

He pulled an ace out of a deck of cards.

He threw up lots of balls and always caught them.

FIGURE 5.7   Kindergartners' Account of an Experience

5. Make a comment like, "There are so many words up here!" Then count them, pointing to each one. Show how a space separates one word from another. Next, have the children count the words. Point to each as it is counted.
6. Reread the entire account. Encourage the children to read along.

In addition to specifying what a word is and indicating the function of space to show word boundaries, the procedures just described (a) demonstrated how words are read from left to right; (b) showed that identical words have the same spelling; (c) gave the children a chance to pretend they can read; and (d) gave them the opportunity to learn some words. If the group had been fairly small, or if the help of an aide was available, the teacher might have asked each child for her or his favorite words. Named words could have been quickly printed on small cards to be taken home to be read to parents and anyone else willing to listen. The cards can also be used to get personal collections of words started.

GUIDELINE NUMBER FOUR: TEACH WORDS IN MEANINGFUL SETTINGS

Kindergartners who work and play in literate environments inevitably learn to read some words. Typically, the first words learned are their own names and those of classmates. Why learning these words early *is* typical is no mystery. The fact that the names are meaningful, constantly available, and named often makes them memorable. The same facts explain why so many kindergartners learn words such as *Monday, September, cloudy, two,* and *green.* In the case of words like those just referred to, the activities of which they are a part—taking attendance, talking about the date and weather, counting objects, naming colors in pictures—provide a context that makes the words interesting as well as meaningful. The activities also allow for seeing the words repeatedly but not in routine, monotonous ways.

Connected text can make the same contribution, as Figures 5.4 and 5.5 demonstrate. This is an appropriate time, therefore, to return to those samples of rhymes and songs. Consider them now as a means for getting reading vocabularies started.

The specifics of what teachers can do to ensure that words *are* learned and that reading vocabularies do keep growing is the subject of Chapter 6, "Whole Word Methodology." For now, the important point is this: Young children should have numerous experiences with connected text that are mediated by adults in ways that lead to the start of reading vocabularies. A number of examples of teachers working with text in ways that can realize that end have been described. One more follows. This example, which focuses on "Jack and Jill," was seen in a kindergarten.

Initially, an enlarged version of "Jack and Jill" was used to foster print awareness and to specify the meaning of "word" and "letter." Later, each line of the rhyme was printed on a strip of tagboard. With the help of the children, the strips were placed in the pockets of a chart in correct order. Still later, the teacher cut each strip into separate words, shuffled the cards, and asked the children to name as many of the words as they could. Eventually, the words were printed on still smaller cards, which were placed in envelopes marked *Jack and Jill.* Individuals or pairs worked with each set of cards to reassemble the rhyme. For less able children, each line was kept intact in order to simplify the reassembling process. Meanwhile, everybody was making additions to their reading vocabularies.

GUIDELINE NUMBER FIVE: TEACH LETTER NAMES AND SOUNDS IN THE CONTEXT OF WORDS

Just as words take on meaning from the text in which they are embedded, letters and sounds become meaningful in the setting of words. One use of *Jack and Jill,* you recall, makes this point. (See the Commentary about Figure 5.5.)

Even though an alphabetic writing system connects sounds with letters, teaching letter names should precede work with sounds. In fact, attention should not go to the sound that a letter represents until the letter can be named instantaneously. The need for children to be able to name letters automatically is underscored in the book *Thinking and Learning about Print* (1), which gives a detailed account of research with beginning reading. Author Marilyn Adams makes the point about automaticity this way: "A child who can recognize most letters with thorough confidence will have an easier time learning about letter sounds and word spellings than a child who still has to work at remembering what is what" (p. 79). Reflecting these recommendations, the following discussion of letter names and letter sounds separates the two.

Names of Letters

Like parents, some teachers seem to believe that "knowing the alphabet"—equated with reciting letter names in correct order—contributes to a child's success with learning to read. In fact, however, this ability contributes more to parents' pride than to their children's acquisition of reading ability. Only when the need arises to arrange things in a systematic, retrievable way—labeled pictures, for instance—does it help to know alphabetic order. Nonetheless, it has to be acknowledged that children who know something like the Alphabet Song do have the impression of having heard the name before when, at some point, a teacher shows a letter and assigns it a name. Only in this limited way does "knowing the alphabet" help.

What helps children remember the names of letters is interest. This explains why a child named Jon quickly learns to name *j, o,* and *n,* and why a girl whose name is Sue learns the names of *s, u,* and *e* equally fast. This suggests that teachers should attend to the name of a letter when it is of interest. Following a story about a zebra in a zoo, for example, is a suitable time to show and name *Z* and *z.*

Why teachers must consider factors other than interest can be explained with the suggestion just made. The letter *z* may be of special interest after hearing about a zebra in a zoo; however, knowing its name is not nearly as useful as knowing the names of letters that appear frequently in words. Frequency of use, therefore, must also affect letter names taught and practiced.

The third factor that needs to be taken into account is the shapes of letters. Specifically, if the shape of one letter—for instance, *d*—is similar to the shape of another—for instance, *b*—the names of the two should not be featured in close proximity. Adams makes the same suggestion when she states that "to minimize confusion between visually similar letters…it is best to separate their introduction in time such that the first is thoroughly learned before the second is presented" (1, p. 442). A point to keep in mind is that confusable letters such as *b* and *d*, or *g* and *q*, cause fewer problems when encountered in words than when seen alone.

To sum up, then, three factors need to be considered when decisions are made about a sequence for teaching letter names: interest, frequency of use, and confusability. Making careful selections, encouraging children's attention when a letter is named, and providing ample practice in naming letters all foster automatic responses.

One more point needs to be made. It can be introduced with the question, "What descriptions should be used for letters—big, little, lowercase, uppercase, capital?" Keeping certain letters in mind (e.g., *B, b, H, h*) eliminates "big" and "little" as accurate descriptions. My preference is "capital," as opposed to "uppercase," because children's familiarity with "capital" is useful later when capitalization gets attention. The recommendation, therefore, is to use "capital" ("This is a capital *A*.") and "lowercase" ("This is a lowercase *a*."). The experience of developing a language arts curriculum for four-year-olds showed that the two terms present no problems for young children (6).

Printing Letters

To learn to associate a letter with its name requires attending to the shape of the letter. This is why many teachers choose to connect learning letter names and learning to print. (Printing is also called *manuscript writing*.)

Requirements for initiating help with printing begin with teachers: They should know how to print correctly *and* quickly. Here, "correctly" is not meant to suggest there is only one right way to form each letter. Instead, the intention is to emphasize the importance of consistency. One model should be selected, therefore, and used regularly. (An example of a model is in Figure 5.8.)

Requirements for children start with opportunities to use paper, pencils, and crayons before any serious efforts are made to print. Drawing and scribbling, in fact, commonly precede printing. When printing instruction does begin, unlined paper should be used because it makes fewer demands of neophyte printers. It goes without saying that a teacher's expectations should keep the age of the children in mind as well as the fact that what lands on paper will vary. Typical differences are illustrated in Figure 5.9.

Children who arrive in school able to print commonly use capital letters, probably because of their prominence in environmental text. Illustrations of early writing in Glenda Bissex's detailed account of her young son's literacy development show not only his generous use of capital letters but also his understanding of the functions of print (2). To get his mother's attention, for example, he once delivered the message, R U DF (Are you deaf?).

The fact that kindergartners require help in learning that shapes as different as *A* and *a* are the same letter needs to be kept in mind. Here, the observations of one teacher are pertinent. They have to do with her resolve to match instruction with needs.

> Today, while a parent volunteer was in my classroom, I took one child at a time to a
> nearby room to learn which letters he or she could name. I heard comments like the

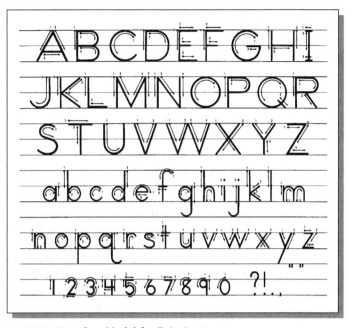

FIGURE 5.8 One Model for Printing

following more than once. Thomas was struggling with capital *H* so I asked, "Where have you seen this letter before?" (At the beginning of the year, he wrote his name in capital letters.) Thomas answered, "It used to be in my name, but it isn't anymore." I found his response interesting, because we've been working during the past couple of weeks on printing first names using a capital letter at the beginning only.

Sounds for Letters

As with letter names, learning letter sounds is more meaningful for children when a letter and its sound are in familiar words. To illustrate, having children read aloud

FIGURE 5.9 Printing at Midyear in One Kindergarten

known words such as the following helps them begin to understand that *s* often stands for /s/.*

> six
> seven
> sun
> sand

Words like those below show that the sound is the same whether a letter is printed in its lowercase or capital form.

> turkey   Tom
> two   Tanya
> ten

Decisions for beginning instruction about letter-sound correspondences should reflect certain facts, one of which was just identified: Learning about letters and sounds is meaningful when they are in words children can read. Another fact has also been emphasized, namely, knowing about the *usefulness* of letter-sound relationships promotes both interest and retention. Teachers who keep this fact in mind avoid decontextualized instruction by making comments like:

> Now that you know that *f* stands for /f/, you also know how words that start with the letter *f* sound at the beginning. For example, even if you don't know this word [writes *fast* on the chalkboard], you do know that it starts with the sound /f/. Does anybody know this word? Can anyone read it?…No?…It says "fast." What does it say?…Let's say "fast" again, and you'll hear that it starts with /f/ because that's the sound that goes with the letter *f*. Let's say this word together.

Another fact for teachers to keep in mind is that consonant letters are more consistent than vowel letters in the sounds they record. This suggests to teach frequently occurring consonant sounds before any vowel sounds receive attention.

That the easiest sound to extract from a word is the sound in initial position is another fact worth remembering. This one accounts for the wisdom of using words like *two* and *ten,* not *nut* and *ant,* when the concern is to connect *t* and /t/. A postscript needed here is the reminder that initial sounds are the easiest to perceive as distinct sounds *when words are not overly long.* This means that when it is time to attend to the short sound for *e,* a word like *elf* is an appropriate illustration whereas *elephant* is not. In fact, by the time a child says or thinks "elephant," the initial sound may be forgotten.

A more detailed discussion of phonics instruction is in Chapter 9. The facts and procedures included here can be summarized as follows.

Early Work with Letter-Sound Correspondences

1. Attend to the sound that a letter represents only if the name of the letter is known at the level of automaticity.

---

*Slash marks indicate the reference is to a speech sound. Consequently, *s* refers to a letter, whereas /s/ refers to the beginning sound of *six.*

2. Sounds for consonant letters that occur frequently in words provide subject matter for initial instruction.
3. To illustrate a letter-sound correspondence, use short words in which the letter and sound are in initial position.
4. During instruction, demonstrate the connection between knowing letter-sound relationships and figuring out what written words say.

Even though the last statement is about reading, Chapter 4 explains how knowing letter names and sounds enters into invented spelling. Because the next and final guideline pertains to writing, this is an appropriate time to reread the section in Chapter 4 called "Invented Spelling: Origins." It also is an appropriate time to read about some activities in a kindergarten described by the teacher who planned them. Her report is in Figure 5.10.

GUIDELINE NUMBER SIX: ENCOURAGE CHILDREN TO COMPOSE

As Chapter 4 explains, encouraging young children to print—much less to compose—was once thought to be appropriate only if done after they had begun to read. Studies of preschool readers that made me question this conventional wisdom are referred to now because the findings are relevant for teachers of young children.

Preschool Pencil-and-Paper Kids

At a time when it was assumed that children first learn to listen, then to speak, then to read, and *then* to write, I conducted two long-term studies of children who had begun to read prior to attending school (3). Carried out in states as far apart as California and New York, the research revealed striking similarities in the two groups of subjects. Similarities included having (a) homes that were literate environments, (b) parents who themselves read and who read frequently to their children, and (c) parents who enjoyed having a family and thus spent considerable time with the children.

Even though similarities did dominate, one difference was unexpected: Some of the children, appropriately called pencil-and-paper kids by the mother of one, had been more interested in writing than in reading and, in fact, became early readers mostly by reading what they themselves had written. According to the parents, the origin of the interest in writing was the opportunity to watch others write. Influential materials included a large assortment of alphabet books and small chalkboards that had the alphabet displayed at the top.

One other difference is important to note in a textbook intended for teachers. It is the fact that siblings reacted differently to the opportunities to acquire literacy. One family with three children is useful in pointing out differences that are especially relevant for teachers. In this case, the boy in my study was the youngest child. Asked to describe the route followed in his becoming an early reader, the mother began by contrasting him with his two sisters. The first daughter showed no preschool interest in learning to read but did well when instruction began in first grade. (She attended school when reading was kept out of kindergarten.) Learning to read

FIGURE 5.10   Commentary   ▶

Separate discussions of letter names, letter sounds, and printing are limited by their failure to show interconnections. The limitation is the reason this teacher's report appears in the chapter now. Her description of a highly productive experience succeeds in demonstrating how many of the recommendations made in this and other chapters fit together. To illustrate, the activities attended to two important contributors to comprehension, word meanings and world knowledge. They also reflected the need to help children experience the usefulness of being able to read and write.

Another contribution made by this teacher's work is pertinent for anyone who automatically assigns phonics to a skill-and-drill category and assumes that it requires constant use of exercise sheets. The account in Figure 5.10 should encourage them to rethink those conclusions.

Considering the perceptiveness of the teacher who wrote the account, it is possible that food containers will soon be added to the text that makes her classroom a literacy-rich setting. Here, however, a word of caution is in order. She and other teachers who make use of this type of environmental text must be sure that children distinguish between the words that tell what is—or was—inside a container and all the other marks and colors that are merely decorative. Calling attention to the words can serve other purposes as well. For example, the words can be counted and spelled. Distinctions can be made between capital and lowercase letters. The words might even allow for giving attention to word meanings with the help of categories like "liquid" and "solid" or, perhaps, "fruit" and "vegetable."

As with all text, once this environmental print loses its appeal, a replacement is called for. This reflects another recommendation made earlier: Text in classrooms should reflect current activities and interests.

I like to take each class to a local grocery store because it adds to the children's experiences and language. The manager and I talk briefly before each trip so that he'll know what I'm trying to accomplish. I'm getting ready now for a unit on fruits and vegetables, so we'll spend extra time in the produce section.

To prepare for the trip, we made a shopping list on the board. (Tomorrow we'll have a fruit and vegetable tasting party, so we need to buy the food.) We also talked about the reasons why people make lists.

At the store, we started with the produce department. The children quickly named familiar fruits and vegetables; the manager and I identified others. We talked about where some of the products came from and compared colors, sizes, shapes, and tastes.

Other parts of the guided tour included the preparation and storage rooms. A meat cutter demonstrated his work with sausage, hamburger, and porkchops. In the "deli," the children were shown how doughnuts are filled and how bread and meat are sliced. They also sampled cold meats and pumpernickel bread. (They had a lot of fun saying— or trying to say—"pumpernickel.") As we walked up and down the aisles, the children spontaneously read a number of labels and signs.

We completed the tour by purchasing fruits and vegetables. Before leaving, the manager gave each child an apple. Thanks to him, other employees, and the two parents who came with us, the trip was a success.

The first thing we did when we returned to school was to write a thank you note to the manager, Mr. Crang. One of the parents typed the note and made copies for the children. Each signed his or her name and added a picture. All the notes were put into a large envelope, which I promised to mail.

Earlier, when we had made cookies, I talked about *c* and the sound it has at the beginning of *cookie.* I also called attention to *color,* because it's displayed in the room, and to *Cathy,* because that is one girl's name. Now, using *Crang* to start with, I decided to see how much the children remembered about this sound for *c.* Comments about the manager's name, which I wrote on the board, were enough to generate from the children *cabbage, coconut, Coca Cola, cake, cookies, carrots,* and *casing.* (The latter was a word the children heard when we watched sausage being made.)

Because everyone was a little tired by now, I suggested spending the rest of the morning looking at books, coloring, writing, working with puzzles, or playing quiet table games. I was surprised—and pleased—by the number of choices that related to our trip to the store. Quickly, a number of the children were drawing pictures and writing words that reflected an experience that all had enjoyed.

FIGURE 5.10 Literacy Experiences for Kindergartners

became attractive to the second daughter only when her sister started to do some. Unlike her younger brother—he was the one characterized as a paper-and-pencil kid—the second daughter showed no interest in writing but, like her brother, read before starting school.

The point to be emphasized now is that just as differences exist among siblings, so, too, do differences characterize kindergartners. Even though all will want to participate in the precursors of conventional writing—scribbling and drawing—kindergarten teachers should not expect everyone to have equal interest in composing and, certainly, not equal ability to do some.

Getting Writing Started

When children entering kindergarten are asked to write their names, all will generally put something on paper. Typically, results range all the way from nearly perfect letters sequenced correctly to aimless, random marks. In between is writing in which some of the marks resemble letters. If a teacher wants children to continue writing, her acceptance of all these signatures must also characterize her response to later efforts to compose. That is, she should see herself not in the role of evaluator but, instead, in the role of audience and, at times, respondent. In the latter case, she may choose to write a note in response to a child's note to her.

To encourage young children to want to write, opportunities to do some should be available from the beginning. Starting any later gives children the chance to learn that, first, one right way to write exists, and, second, they are unable to do it. Before inhibition takes over, therefore, the recommendation from emergent writing researchers is to say to children something like, "Do it your own way. It doesn't have to be like grown-up writing" (23). In a kindergarten writing program developed in Texas, Miriam Martinez and William Teale encouraged early efforts by showing the children writing samples done by other kindergartners (15). They made sure that the samples included scribbles and drawings, random strings of letters, and some invented spelling. The availability of writing materials (e.g., paper, envelopes, index cards, pencils, crayons, chalk and small chalkboards, plastic letters) provides an incentive to write, too.

Children accustomed to storybook reading by adults often move easily into producing their own stories with scribble writing. For those who have participated in shared reading experiences similar to those discussed earlier in this chapter, scribbling in a left-to-right, top-to-bottom sequence is common.

Like other authors, children do their best when they write with an audience in mind. This suggests that when they do write something like a story, they should have the chance to read it to another child and, whenever possible, to the teacher, an aide, or a parent volunteer. Displaying children's writing on a bulletin board, or hanging it from a clothesline, provides even more reasons to be an author.

While children continue to compose stories with scribbles and drawings, it is not atypical for some to begin using conventional writing when the reason to do it requires little more than a word or two. This is why labels are often the first words written with conventional letters and standard spellings.

Children's own names are labels (10), which are soon written to show possessions (box of crayons) and productions (picture of a sea serpent). When teachers routinely make lists on the board to serve as reminders—for instance, the morning's schedule—nobody should be surprised if kindergartners make lists, too.

Sometimes, children who are unwilling to do their own writing like to copy words displayed in a room. (Recall the earlier reference to the teacher who had children copy labels from a graph about four fruits.) Whether accurate or not, the copying—like all other efforts—should be accepted and praised on the assumption it is the best the child can do.

Eventually, just about all kindergartners begin to show in their writing—whether limited or extensive in length—not only recognizable letters but also evidence of knowing some letter sounds. (Proximity to young writers often allows for hearing them sound out words.) They are on their way, therefore, not only to conventional writing but also to integrating what they are learning about reading and about writing.

PUTTING IT ALL TOGETHER

Sketching a typical kindergarten schedule and program is impossible because of the variation that exists. Even so, it still seems necessary to conclude the chapter with a synthesis. This is done with the use of a schedule that is amplified with commentary, mostly about objectives and materials. The schedule selected is for half-day programs, as they are still more common than full-day kindergartens (12).

Deliberately, the schedule and commentary lean toward the conservative side so that teachers who have failed to keep up with the many developments in the area of literacy do not view the illustrative program as being out of reach. For those who do keep abreast of current thinking, the hope for the forthcoming sections is that they will be of interest—even of help—at least intermittently.

To prepare for the final part of the chapter, the six guidelines that organize earlier parts can be reviewed by examining the outline for Chapter 5.

A SAMPLE SCHEDULE

The schedule that will be used to tie things together is shown below.

8:30	Attendance, date, weather, current interests
8:45	Small group instruction
9:10	Small group instruction
9:35	Music
9:55	Bathroom, recess, snack
10:30	Shared reading experiences/Composing
11:00	Art
11:30	Storytime
11:50	Preparation for home

As with any schedule, the one used here would never be allowed to take charge, at least not with a Teacher A. Schedules are meant to assist, not to constrain. This means that the need exists in kindergartens for flexible structure—or is it structured flexibility? Either way, schedules should reflect the class they are intended to serve. With young children, flexibility is especially necessary because what takes a long time to do at first is done fairly quickly as time moves along. As it does, schedules should be adjusted not only to accommodate this change but also to reflect new interests.

POSSIBLE CONTENT AND MATERIALS

It is a generally desirable practice to start a new day with quiet activities that involve the entire class. This is reflected in the sample schedule.

Opening Session

The focus now is the block of time shown below.

8:30–8:45 Attendance, date, weather, current interests

Children's names, combined with calendars and the weather, provide continuous opportunities not only for children to talk about their interests but also for teachers to initiate literacy. Because children's fondness for their own names never wanes, written names can be used to attend to objectives related to:

Names of letters
Spacing between words
Capitalization
Printing
Letter-sound correspondences
Alphabetical order

Using cards on which first names are printed (approximately 5 × 12 inches), children learn early to take attendance by placing their card in a pocket chart. One positive by-product of children's involvement with attendance taking—in addition to saving a teacher's time—is a heightened awareness of who is absent. As a result, an absentee's return to school will be greeted with enthusiasm, a response likely to contribute to that child's positive feelings about school (6). Once children are writing their names, a sign-in sheet can be kept close to where the children enter the classroom.

Discussions of calendars, large enough that numbers and words are easily seen, inevitably include birthdays. A display such as the one in Figure 5.11 can be placed on a bulletin board. As Figure 5.11 shows, names of the children are written in large print on whichever train car displays the month in which their birthday occurs. (Notice that the engine is at the left, thus encouraging left-to-right scanning.) By the time the train is taken down—nothing should be displayed so long that it becomes neither eye- nor mind-catching—some children will be able to read all the words shown; others will know considerably fewer. The more important point is that

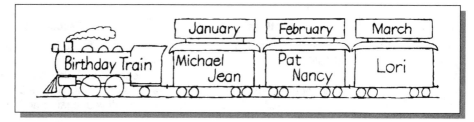

FIGURE 5.11　Personalizing Learning to Read

all children have had the opportunity to learn words in a meaningful context that is of personal interest.

Weather is another topic rich in opportunities for expanding literacy. How one teacher worked with weather-related words was described earlier. A bulletin-board display entitled "April Showers" was used in another room. In this case, blue construction paper covered the board to which were attached clouds (gray) and raindrops (white). Words suggested by the children when they discussed activities suitable for rainy days (e.g., *read, write, draw, color, play a game*) were printed on the raindrops. Some children illustrated an activity, after which they copied the appropriate word to serve as a description.

How another teacher used the four seasons is described in Figure 5.12. This account shows that work with topics such as weather or seasons is not necessarily confined to a given period or to one type of activity. More specifically, attention to seasons may originate with a calendar but may also expand to include a walk in the neighborhood, attention to colors and counting, and even the use of a simple time line. How topics expand but still connect was illustrated earlier when the trip to Mr. Crang's supermarket was described.

Small-Group Instruction

Working with the entire class is a relatively common practice among kindergarten teachers even when differences among the children are so great as to be obvious almost immediately to anyone observing (4, 5). To make sure that at least part of a program recognizes differences in a planned way, it is recommended that time be allotted to small-group instruction.

8:45–9:10	Small-group instruction
9:10–9:35	Small-group instruction

Further comments about small-group instruction follow:

1. Every child in a kindergarten is ready to acquire literacy to some degree.
2. Because children entering kindergarten vary considerably in what they know, understand, and can do, instruction ought to be offered to subgroups of children organized on the basis of needs. Because of time restrictions, subgroups may

Objectives	Procedures
To teach the meaning of "fall" and "autumn." To introduce sequence of seasons.*	1. Used first day of autumn to introduce <u>fall</u>. Printed on board and pronounced it. Named other seasons too. Also talked about different meanings of <u>fall</u> with help of sentences like, "Don't fall off your chair" and "Try not to fall when you play."
	2. On the following day, introduced <u>autumn</u> as a word that can be used in place of <u>fall</u>. Read a story about the fall as a time of changing colors in leaves.
	3. The next day took children to the park to collect leaves. Upon return to school, used them to remention <u>fall</u> and <u>autumn</u> and to provide practice in counting and naming colors.
	4. A week later, read story about squirrels gathering nuts to prepare for winter. (Also showed children some nuts.) Used story to review <u>fall</u> and <u>autumn</u> and to introduce the fall season as one that is followed by winter and preceded by summer. Showed sequence of four seasons with time line.

*The teacher chose the second objective because of an answer from one of her more sophisticated kindergartners. Asked, "When does spring come?" the child responded, "In the fall."

FIGURE 5.12   Preplanned Instruction Related to the Seasons

have to be limited to two. Membership in each group will vary from day to day depending on objectives.

3. Even if differences were not as pronounced as they typically are, working with less than an entire class would still be recommended as a way to maximize children's attention to whatever requires attention.

4. Subject matter should be presented in ways that link it with children's everyday experiences. Instruction with numbers, for instance, should make generous use of clocks, TV schedules, calendars, license plates, birthday cards, rulers, telephone books, store catalogs, menus, and telephones. To do otherwise, one author warns, is to make "reading and writing in the kitchen with a parent" so at odds with "school reading and writing" that the child will conclude that the two are essentially different (22).

5. Whenever possible, teachers should also work with individuals or small groups to provide extra help or extra challenge. When an aide is available, such extras ought to be the rule, not the exception.

Possible topics for instruction designed to accommodate differences include:

- Names of colors, numbers, letters, shapes
- Counting
- Words that name colors, shapes, numbers
- Words related to weather, size, feelings
- Words highlighted in a book read earlier by the teacher or during a shared reading experience
- Words that relate to ongoing activities, current interests, or themes being featured
- Printing, starting with letters in the children's names
- Letter-sound correspondences

Time spent with less than an entire class also allows for the preparations that are essential for children's writing—whether done with scribbles, invented spellings, conventional spellings, or some combination of all three. Once a topic is selected, warm-up sessions might include (a) reading an article or brief book that deals with the topic, (b) questions and discussion to get members of the group thinking about their own writing, and (c) listing words suggested by the children that pertain to the topic.

Periods scheduled for small-group instruction may concentrate on review with children who are unable to profit as much as others from the opportunities to learn that occur daily. In sections that follow, which describe other parts of the sample schedule, you can see more clearly likely times when some children may require concentrated, slow-paced help to supplement earlier, less structured experiences with text.

Music

The placement of music in the sample schedule reflects the need to follow work periods with both relaxation and movement. Or, as Linda Lamme states, "singing and chanting help to make work light" (13, p. 297).

9:35–9:55 Music

As has been demonstrated, songs have much potential for literacy development. Even though the fun and freedom of music should never be stifled with nagging efforts to include reading and writing, occasions do arise when attention to written language adds to the music as well as to children's literacy. A much enlarged copy of a page from a song book, displayed for all to see, can show how notes tell singers when to go up and down with their voice and also how the written words tell what to sing.

If attention is going to musical instruments, perhaps with the help of recordings, a bulletin-board display of labeled pictures showing a variety of instruments adds specificity as well as interest to the information provided. Appropriate to refer to here is an article by Frances Smardo (21) that tells of a field trip taken by children to hear a symphony orchestra. "Back at school, their teacher read them *The Philharmonic Gets Dressed* by Karla Kuskin, which humorously explains how the 105 men and women in the orchestra get ready for a concert and travel into town with their bulky instruments" (p. 700).

As young children learn songs, additional ways to feature written language are possible. In one about four farm animals, with a verse for each, a picture of the appropriate animal can be shown each time a new verse is begun. Later, when the song is repeated, the teacher can show the same pictures, this time with identifying labels. After the procedure has been used on a number of occasions, the teacher might next hold up cards on which only an animal's name is written, asking, "Who can tell me what this animal is?" And then, "Let's sing that verse."

With other songs, one word might be highlighted. A song about children's games, for instance, provides an opportunity to call attention to *games*. (It might also be a time to compare *games* and *game* on the chalkboard.) The song "Getting to Know You" can lead to attention to *you*.

On days when children are unusually restless, music functions well in providing for movement as well as for attention to certain words. Such days might be the time to have children (accompanied by suitable music) tiptoe, walk slowly, walk quickly, clap loudly, and clap softly. All these directions can be printed on signs, which are held up by the teacher or a child. It might also be an opportunity—depending on the children—for looking at, and talking about, words composed of two words (*tiptoe, raindrop, chalkboard*). Or it might be the time to discuss the meaning of *opposite* applied to words like *slowly* and *quickly, loudly* and *softly*. Were this done, reading *Push, Pull, Empty, Full* by Tana Hoban would be an excellent complementary activity. Using large photographs of objects, animals, and people (e.g., gumball machine, turtle, and human hands and feet), the author of this book helps pinpoint the meaning of such descriptions as *many* and *few, together* and *apart, heavy* and *light*. Reading the book leads naturally to drawings made by the children on which they can print antonyms to serve as captions.

Having considered possibilities for literacy development inherent in music, this is an appropriate time to look in on a kindergarten during the time set aside for music. This description of a classroom is in Figure 5.13.

Having read the report in Figure 5.13, you know that the observer's account is incomplete. Her report was interrupted to allow *you* to finish it. Even though what the observed teacher did may have been just right for the day when the observation took place, consider now what else might have been done—as the author of the report writes—"to add to the children's abilities with language."

Art

The sample schedule suggests about thirty minutes for shared reading experiences or composing. Because the two were dealt with earlier, let's go on to the next item in the schedule.

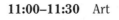

11:00–11:30   Art

When children are encouraged to write "in their own way," pictures will be used to convey some or even all the ideas they want to communicate. Some kindergarten

During my observation this week, I saw several unused opportunities to use music to add to children's abilities with language.

This kindergarten teacher began by calling the children to the carpeted area in front of the piano. She waited until everyone was settled before starting the first song, "Where is Thumbkin?" The teacher encouraged the children to join in when she sang the first verse. It was clear that it had been sung before because they sang along enthusiastically while doing the appropriate hand movements. The class next sang about five little ducks who wander away from their mother, one by one. The song had repetitive language and was very predictable. The children knew it well and sang it especially loud on the "quack quack" part when the mother duck called her ducklings back. Everyone—including the teacher—was having a good time.

Following the two songs, the teacher went to the record player and put on a Hap Palmer movement song called "Shake My Sillies Out." The children automatically stood and carried out the actions that the song suggested: shaking their sillies out, clapping their hands, stamping their feet, and swaying their bodies. The teacher modeled the movements so that any child needing help could watch her. Following all this, the teacher asked the children to sit with their hands in their laps, which settled them on the carpet again. She said it was time for some quiet music, after which several lullabies were played. As they were, the teacher quietly told a few students at a time to get their coats and bags to get ready to go home.

I felt this teacher was very much in tune with characteristics of young children. She provided just the right music after they had been sitting for a while. However, it could also be said that she bypassed opportunities to do more than just sing. For example,...

FIGURE 5.13 Music in a Kindergarten

teachers, in fact, have eliminated art as a special period on the assumption that children will become artists when it is appropriate to assume that role. Nonetheless, because other kindergartens still allot time for art, let me deal with it now in a framework that views art as having—like music—potential for literacy development.

Painting at easels is an activity still found in just about all kindergartens. Equally common is the chance for children to learn that mixing one color of paint with another makes a third color. A summary of these experiences makes a meaningful addition to literate environments. (See Figure 5.14.)

With children's art, bulletin-board displays can add a personal touch to a classroom. In one, the children drew self-portraits with their signatures serving as labels. Soon, pictures were on a bulletin board arranged under the question, "Who Are You?" Later, when attention was going to numbers, the children drew pictures of their homes, with addresses now serving as labels. They, too, went on the board, arranged under the title, "Where Do You Live?" The positive feature of titles like these is the chance they give teachers to talk about titles, the use of capital letters in titles, and the function of question marks. Helpful, too, are the repeated contacts they permit children to have with hard-to-remember but important words like *who, where,* and *are.*

Time set aside for art also allows for illustrating covers for books produced by individuals, small groups, or an entire class. In one kindergarten, many such books resulted from protracted attention to the theme "Water." During the course of a week, for instance, the teacher planned "experiments" with water, all summarized on a chalkboard with the help of the class. Afterward, each child received a typed copy. (Two summaries are in Figure 5.15.) On Friday, the children used the time scheduled for art to design covers for their water books.

Storytime

In addition to allotting time to shared reading experiences, the sample schedule ended the day with storytime. Because reading to children was featured in an earlier segment of the chapter, all that is said now is that storytime should always be special even if this requires reducing the time spent on other activities. To make it special, some teachers choose an author whose books are favorites and read them for a

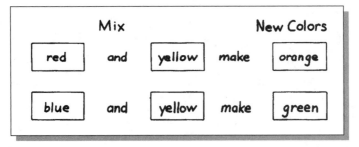

FIGURE 5.14   A Bulletin-Board Display

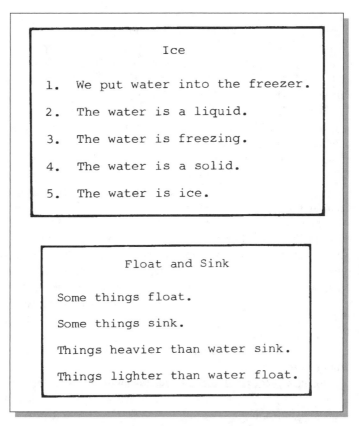

FIGURE 5.15 Summaries of Water Experiments

while. Then another author is chosen. Other teachers make sure that if children express curiosity about something, it is satisfied with the books they read. Still others choose themes like "Animals" as a way to unify activities. In these cases, the theme guides their selections not only of books but also of projects that might include making posters or even murals.

SUMMARY

How schools acknowledge differences among five-year-olds with provisions like developmental kindergartens and transitional first grades was the initial topic considered in Chapter 5. The next section contrasted these accommodations with the fact that too many kindergartens concentrate on one kind of instruction—for instance, phonics—offered to an entire class. The contrast was intended to underscore the contradiction that is inherent in the "special provisions" and the uniform instruction. The contradiction may have reminded you of a statement in the previous chapter when the implications of David Ausubel's conception of readiness were the concern: "Altering the timing of beginning instruction without ensuring the availability of high quality, eclectic instruction is *not* the way to promote maximum success for a maximum number of children."

To promote maximum success, six guidelines were offered in Chapter 5 to help anyone responsible for assembling a beginning literacy program. The first recognized the benefits of providing kindergartners with a literate environment dominated by text that reflects current activities and interests. The second guideline, "Read to children daily," should have come as no surprise, given the points made in Chapter 4 about the importance of reading to young children in ways that encourage them to interact with the text.

The third guideline also reflects a point made in the previous chapter, namely, that some young children arrive in school knowing very little either about the conventions of print or the meaning of terms that figure in literacy instruction. Because remedying these deficiencies requires the use of connected text, big books and language experience materials were featured in the discussion of this third guideline.

Connected text continued to be the focus when the next guideline was offered. This one suggested: Teach words in meaningful settings. "Settings" such as poems and rhymes were the focus now, because these kinds of repetitive text provide both the setting that makes individual words meaningful and the repetition that makes them memorable.

Just as the fourth guideline urged teachers to call attention to individual words in the setting of connected text, the fifth one recommended making letter names and sounds meaningful by dealing with them in the setting of words. Why the name of a letter should be known at the level of automaticity before its sound receives attention was explained. Afterward, specific factors were named that should enter into decisions about a sequence for teaching letter names and sounds.

The sixth guideline, "Encourage children to compose," reflects research done with emergent literacy. Using findings from studies of children who learned to read prior to attending school, this section of the chapter did not overlook the need for teachers to keep in mind that some kindergartners will have little interest, and even less ability, in composing. In fact, to expect all children to compose is no more reasonable than to expect all to learn letter-sound correspondences when they are taught in a decontextualized way to an entire class. Individual differences, then, are the norm and not the exception.

To show how the six guidelines interconnect in practice, Chapter 5 next featured a sample schedule, while emphasizing that schedules are meant to serve, not constrain, instructional programs. The schedule allowed for calling attention to the many ways in which literacy development can be promoted in kindergartners. One part of the schedule, called "small-group instruction," was identified as a means for accommodating differences among the members of a class. At times they call for challenge; at other times, for a slower pace that includes ample amounts of review.

REVIEW

1. In Chapter 5, the end of one account of a classroom was omitted (see Figure 5.13). The omission was designed to encourage you to think of how the observed teacher might have used the songs and recordings described in the report to advance her student's literacy development. Now, identify specific ways in which the music could have been used to serve that goal.

2. **a.** Explain the following, which reflects some of the recommendations that Chapter 5 makes.

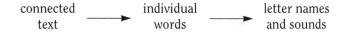

   connected text   ⟶   individual words   ⟶   letter names and sounds

   b. The use of the arrows might be misleading. That is, they may mistakingly suggest a linear progression when, in fact, progression that moves back and forth among connected text, individual words, and letter names and sounds is the progression that ought to characterize what is done to develop beginning literacy. With specific examples, explain this back-and-forth progression.

3. Effects of the *commercialization of instruction* were referred to in the previous chapter when reading readiness programs were the topic. It was necessary in Chapter 5 to refer to the effects again in the discussion of big books.
   a. Based on the discussions of readiness programs and big books, explain what is meant by the commercialization of instruction.
   b. Teacher B was introduced in Chapter 2. What is the connection between the commercialization of instruction and Teacher B?

4. Any teacher or prospective teacher who wants to be better than a Teacher B needs to know which factors to consider when making decisions about a sequence for teaching the names of letters. Chapter 5 named three. What are the three factors?

5. Chapter 5 urges teachers to be sure that children know the name of a letter at the level of automaticity before they teach a sound that the letter represents.
   a. Does this recommendation mean that children need to be able to name all 26 letters before instruction about letter-sound correspondences begins? If yes, why? If no, why not?
   b. *Why* do children need to be able to name a letter without thinking before they are helped to learn about a sound that goes with the letter?
   c. Many commercially prepared materials teach the sounds that letters stand for by dealing with the letters in alphabetic order. Name all the reasons this practice is questionable.
   d. Many commercially prepared materials use *big* and *small* to make distinctions between what Chapter 5 refers to as capital and lowercase letters. Why are the descriptions *big* and *small* unsuitable?
   e. Why does Chapter 5 recommend using the terms *capital* and *lowercase*?

6. Like the previous chapter, Chapter 5 states that invented spelling may enter into young children's efforts to compose, especially when teachers encourage them to write what they want to say, not what they think they can spell. All this reminds me of a child's poster that I saw hanging next to the door of a second grade. The poster was entitled "Watch Were Your Going!" What do you think about this second-grader's spelling? Were you the child's teacher, would you display the poster in the hall?

7. Young children enjoy music and art. Describe two ways in which music can make a contribution to one or more of the language arts (listening, speaking, reading, writing). Do the same for art.

8. If you are familiar with kindergartens, contrast what you have seen with any part of Chapter 5.

REFERENCES

1. Adams, Marilyn J. *Thinking and Learning about Print*. Cambridge, Mass.: The MIT Press, 1990.
2. Bissex, Glenda L. *GNYS AT WRK: A Child Learns to Write and Read*. Cambridge, Mass.: Harvard University Press, 1980.
3. Durkin, Dolores. *Children Who Read Early*. New York: Teachers College Press, Columbia University, 1966.
4. Durkin, Dolores. "A Classroom-Observation Study of Reading Instruction in Kindergarten." *Early Childhood Research Quarterly* 2 (September, 1987), 275–300.
5. Durkin, Dolores. *Curriculum Reform: Teaching Reading in Kindergarten* (Technical Report No. 465). Urbana-Champaign: University of Illinois, Center for the Study of Reading, 1989.
6. Durkin, Dolores. "A Language Arts Program for Pre-First Grade Children: Two-Year Achievement Report." *Reading Research Quarterly* 5 (Summer, 1970), 534–565.
7. Dyson, Anne H. "Reading, Writing, and Language: Young Children Solving the Written Language Puzzle," *Language Arts* 59 (November/December, 1982), 829–839.
8. Gesell Institute of Child Development. *School Readiness Test*. Lumberville, Penn., 1978.
9. Goodall, Marilyn. "Can Four Year Olds 'Read' Words in the Environment?" *Reading Teacher* (February, 1984), 478–482.

10. Goodman, Kenneth, and Goodman, Yetta. "Reading and Writing Relationships: Pragmatic Functions." *Language Arts* 60 (May, 1983), 590–599.
11. Holdaway, Don. *The Foundations of Literacy*. New York: Scholastic, 1979.
12. Karweit, Nancy. "Quality and Quantity of Learning Time in Preprimary Programs. *Elementary School Journal* 89 (November, 1988), 119–132.
13. Lamme, Linda L. "Exploring the World of Music through Picture Books." *Reading Teacher* 44 (December, 1990), 294–300.
14. McGee, Lea M., and Richgels, Donald J. *Literacy's Beginnings*. Boston, Mass.: Allyn and Bacon, 1990.
15. Martinez, Miriam, and Teale, William H. "The Ins and Outs of a Kindergarten Writing Program." *Reading Teacher* 40 (January, 1987), 444–451.
16. Morrow, Lesley M., and Rand, Muriel K. "Promoting Literacy during Play by Designing Early Childhood Classroom Environments." *Reading Teacher* 44 (February, 1991), 396–402.
17. Neuman, Susan B., and Roskos, Kathy. "Play, Print, and Purpose: Enriching Play Environments for Literacy Development." *Reading Teacher* 44 (November, 1990), 214–221.
18. Shepard, Lorrie A. "School Readiness and Kindergarten Retention: A Policy Analysis." Paper presented at the American Educational Research Association annual meeting, San Francisco, 1986.

19. Shepard, Lorrie A., and Smith, Mary Lee. "Escalating Academic Demand in Kindergarten: Counterproductive Policies." *Elementary School Journal* 89 (November, 1988), 135–146.

20. Shepard, Lorrie A., and Smith, Mary Lee. "Synthesis of Research on School Readiness and Kindergarten Retention." *Educational Leadership* 44 (November, 1986), 78–86.

21. Smardo, Frances A. "Using Children's Literature As a Prelude or Finale to Music Experiences with Young Children." *Reading Teacher* 37 (April, 1984), 700–705.

22. Spencer, Margaret. "Emergent Literacies: A Site for Analysis." *Language Arts* 63 (September, 1986), 442–452.

23. Sulzby, Elizabeth; Teale, William H.; and Kamberelis, George. "Emergent Writing in the Classroom: Home and School Connections." In D. S. Strickland and L. M. Morrow (Eds.), *Emergent Literacy: Young Children Learn to Read and Write*. Newark, Del.: International Reading Association, 1989.

Even though most of our reading is of connected text, the ability to identify individual words is not insignificant. In fact—as we all have experienced—sometimes, when certain words are unknown, they keep us from understanding the text in which they occur.

All the words we can identify in their written form make up our *reading vocabularies*. How teachers at all grade levels can ensure that students' reading vocabularies are continuously enlarged is the concern of the chapters in Part III.

The five chapters make an important assumption. As they discuss how students can be helped to acquire sizable reading vocabularies, they assume that the students know the meanings of the words. This assumption was also made in previous chapters. To illustrate, when Chapter 5 described how children learn to read words like *sunny* and *windy* in conjunction with efforts to keep track of the weather, the implicit assumption was that they knew the meaning of sunny and windy. Stated differently, it was taken for granted that the two words were in the children's *oral vocabularies*. The concern of the teacher, therefore, was confined to selecting procedures to help them learn the written forms.

Assuming that meanings are familiar is not the same as saying that developing oral vocabularies is of no concern to teachers responsible for advancing reading abilities. Actually, because they are of *paramount* importance for reading, and thus for teachers, an entire chapter—Chapter 11—is devoted exclusively to that topic.

Given the significance, you might now be wondering, Why the delay? Postponing attention to oral vocabularies reflects the conviction that Part III shows so clearly the dependence of reading on oral vocabularies that when they are considered in Chapter 11, they receive the attention they deserve. In a way, then, the chapters in Part III are preparations for the later chapter. But now it is time to look more closely at Chapters 6 through 10.

The content of these chapters reflects how students acquire reading vocabularies. The words they learn initially are usually some that were named as wholes. This was often done directly. ("Sarah, do you see that sign? It's the name of our street. It says 'Kirby'.") Other words may have been named indirectly. (A colored photograph of an apple with *apple* printed beneath suggests a connection between the name of the fruit and the label.) Either way, it is correct to say that certain words are in a student's reading vocabulary because at some point they were named as wholes. And this continues to be the case. In a fourth

Developing Reading Vocabularies

grade, for instance, *ocean, island, isthmus,* and *tomb* are in the students' reading vocabularies because, prior to starting a chapter in a social studies textbook, their teacher named each as a whole. In another classroom, *muscle, tendon,* and *sinew* are among the words the students can read because the teacher wrote and named them after showing a film that explained their meanings. How whole word methodology functions at all grade levels, therefore, is the concern of Chapter 6.

It is fortunate that the words students know sometimes help them deal with others they do not know. Take Sarah—the child referred to above—as an example. Should she want or need to read *Our house is on the corner of Kirby and Prospect,* her ability to identify all the words but the last one may be enough to allow her to make an inference about the last word. Using known words to get help with unknown words in the same context is referred to as using contextual cues. Teaching students how to use these cues provides subject matter for Chapter 7.

Chapters 8 through 10 deal with two other parts of the cueing system of English. Chapters 8 and 9 are concerned with graphophonic cues—that is, with the help available to readers because of the connection between the spelling of a word (*grapho*) and its pronunciation (*phonic*). Chapter 8 covers what needs to be taught to allow students to take advantage of these connections; the chapter that follows explains *how* it can be taught to make it maximally useful with unfamiliar words.

When words that students need to know are composed of more than a root—words like *careless, rewrite,* and *untraceable,* for example—structural cues take on significance. Now it is necessary to teach about word structure by attending to roots, prefixes, and suffixes. How to teach students about these parts of words so they can use them to figure out unknown derived and inflected words is dealt with in Chapter 10.

Having learned from all the chapters in Part III that reading vocabularies cannot exceed oral vocabularies, you will be ready for Part IV, which starts with attention to ways for making students' oral vocabularies increasingly large and rich.

CHAPTER 6

Whole Word Methodology

Aware of the multiple problems that can accrue from the routine use of round robin reading, teachers should be eager to replace it with something better. Viewed from the students' perspective, a desirable alternative is *uninterrupted silent reading of appropriately difficult material for which adequate preparations have been made.*

As the description indicates, this recommended option assigns certain responsibilities to teachers. The one on preparations divides into three parts:

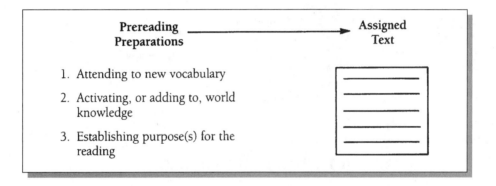

Our own reading experiences make it clear that knowing every word in a selection is not usually required for comprehending it. The same experiences also tell us, however, that not knowing too many words makes comprehension an impossible achievement. A teacher's concern about words in a piece of text that are likely to be unfamiliar, therefore, is well grounded.

What needs to be done to ensure that such words make their way into students' reading vocabularies is the subject of Chapter 6. As its title suggests, the specific focus is the use of whole word methodology to realize that objective.

The times when a new word ought to be named as a whole is the first topic considered. When a new word can be presented alone and, on the other hand, when it needs to be shown with other words are the next two questions that Chapter 6 answers. Because learning new words requires practice, that topic is discussed, too. Not overlooked in the discussion is that reading extended pieces of text—books and magazine articles, for instance—is a very productive kind of practice. This recognizes that children do learn to read by reading.

• • • • • • •

NAMING UNKNOWN WORDS AS WHOLES, viewed as the initial step in getting the words into students' reading vocabularies, is the subject of this chapter. Because attention is on the whole of a word, it is called whole word methodology. At one time, this way of teaching words was commonly referred to as the *look-say method* in order to contrast it with other methods—for instance, phonics—that call attention to parts of words. The fact that whole word methodology is also called the *sight method* leads some persons to conclude erroneously that a "sight word" is one that was initially introduced with whole word methodology. To make sure you do not make the same mistake, let me underscore now that "sight" pertains *not* to how a word was taught but to the fact that it is known at the level of automaticity—that is, is known "on sight."

Regardless of the label, whole word methodology is simply a matter of naming words. Because anyone who can read is able do this, some explanation does seem necessary as to why an entire chapter is devoted to whole word instruction.

One reason is that naming a word only once rarely leads to permanent retention by students. Because nothing less than permanent recall should be the goal of school instruction, it is imperative that professional teachers know how to foster retention. That explains why the chapter considers such topics as practice and cues.

Because students must be able to read many more words than those they happen to inquire about, the professional teacher also needs to know which words to select for whole word methodology. When it ought to be used, therefore, is the first question addressed.

WHEN TO USE WHOLE WORD METHODOLOGY

Whether teachers should name unknown words as wholes is affected by two considerations. The first has to do with their students, specifically with what they know that can help them deal with unknown words themselves. This consideration means that when children are first starting to be readers, whole word methodology is used all the time because no alternative exists. There is no alternative because, first, beginners lack *decoding* ability. (Decoding is using a word's spelling to achieve its pronunciation.) Because beginners know so few words, using known words to get help with an unknown word is also out of their reach. This limitation, then, is the second reason why whole word instruction is used routinely at first.

Once reading vocabularies are larger—thanks to the use of whole word methodology plus practice—and, in addition, students have acquired some ability in decoding, the correspondence between the spelling and the pronunciation of a new word becomes a key consideration. Now, new words with spellings that suggest their pronunciation (e.g., *pun, sleet, alto*) are left to students to decode on their own. When this is not the case (e.g., *eye, quay, aisle*), whole word methodology comes back into play.

All that has now been said can be summed up as follows: As students learn more and more, whole word methodology is used less and less. The desirability of this reflects the desirability of enabling students to acquire independence in coping with unknown or forgotten words.

GUIDELINES FOR USING WHOLE WORD METHODOLOGY

How teachers should proceed when they decide to name words directly is considered next.

Teaching Function Words: Guidelines

When teachers working with beginning readers make a conscious effort to select words for instruction that are both meaningful and of interest, it still does not take long before it is necessary to get into children's reading vocabularies words that are neither meaningful in and of themselves nor of interest. I refer to some like *the, and, of,* and *is.* Words like these are called *function words.* They include prepositions, conjunctions, auxiliary verbs, pronouns, articles, and the various forms of the verb *to be.* Function words require attention fairly early because they specify relationships among the components of a sentence. They thus allow for phrases, clauses, compound subjects, compound verbs, and compound sentences. For instance:

Mike drove <u>into</u> snow <u>at</u> work.
Mike, <u>who</u> drove into the snow, went home early.
Mike <u>and</u> Tom drove into a pile of snow.
Mike drove into snow <u>and</u> got very angry.

Because function words hold the structure of text together, they are sometimes referred to as *structure words.* Examples of function (or structure) words commonly found in easy text have been cited. Function words that are in more difficult text are illustrated below:

The men were afraid. They <u>nevertheless</u> kept walking.
The sun was too hot. <u>Therefore</u>, they went home.
You may go out. Be back by nine o'clock, <u>however</u>.
Mr. Stevens waited for his son. <u>Meanwhile</u>, he watched the crowd.

The important point for teachers to keep in mind is this: *Whenever a function word is taught, it should be introduced in the context of other words that are known.* Short contexts are sufficient for some function words. For instance, if *pen* and *pencil* are known, a suitable context for *or* is *pen or pencil.* Other function words that serve as cohesive ties and link sentences together require longer contexts. A function word such as *anyhow* requires something like *I know you're angry. Count to ten anyhow.* Either way, a context must be used so that the function word is meaningful.

To expand the meaning that you may now be assigning to *context,* let me describe a context that a very effective first-grade teacher was observed using on the day she worked to get *and* into her students' reading vocabularies.

She started by praising the members of an instructional group for all the color words they had learned. While the children recalled the colors, she wrote (and read) the names of the colors in a way that allowed for extra space between each one and that stretched the words across the chalkboard—to the great delight of the onlookers. The teacher then started to reread the words, this time saying "and" between the first and second colors. Immediately she stopped to observe, "Oh, oh. I put in a word that isn't here. Did anyone hear the word I said that isn't on the board?" Immediately the children responded, "And!" The teacher continued, "If I'm going to say 'and', I had better write it. Watch me write 'and'." Each time it was written between two color words, the children named, spelled, and renamed it. Finally, the entire line of words was read with both enthusiasm and pride.

Now it was time for more practice that made use of cards prepared ahead of time. They displayed contexts like the following.

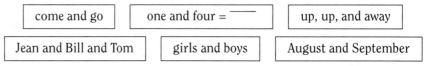

| come and go | one and four = ‾‾‾‾ | up, up, and away |
| Jean and Bill and Tom | girls and boys | August and September |

At the end, *and* was printed alone, then read, spelled, and reread. And so a very interesting presentation of an uninteresting word came to a close.

What happens when first-grade teachers (and all others) do *not* give sufficient attention to function words is pinpointed in an account of an observation in a second grade. The account is in Figure 6.1.

Teaching Content Words: Guidelines

Content words, which are nouns, verbs, adjectives, and adverbs, differ from function words because they have meaning in and of themselves. Whenever content words are taught with whole word methodology, teachers need to decide which ones require a context and which do not. Most do not. Certain types, however, always require a context. They are homonyms, homographs, and homophones. The three are defined and illustrated below.

Homonyms are words that are spelled the same but that have different meanings. The fact that readers must rely on contexts to decide which meaning to assign to a homonym is generously illustrated below with the help of the homonym *hand*.

> I've hurt my <u>hand</u>.
> One <u>hand</u> is missing from the clock.
> Please <u>hand</u> me the scissors.
> She makes all that pottery by <u>hand</u>.
> They're always ready to lend a helping <u>hand</u>.
> You have to learn some things first <u>hand</u>.
> He got a big <u>hand</u> after his talk.
> They lead a <u>hand</u>-to-mouth existence.
> He rules his family with a heavy <u>hand</u>.

Homographs are words that are spelled the same but that have different pronunciations and meanings. That contexts determine, in this case, both pronunciation and meaning can be illustrated with pairs of sentences:

> They live <u>close</u> to us.
> Please <u>close</u> the door.
>
> The <u>wind</u> is noisy tonight.
> Did you remember to <u>wind</u> the clock?

When I observed this week in a second grade, I was reminded of the discussion we had in class about the critical importance of large reading vocabularies that include function words.

Almost as soon as I entered the room, the teacher asked me to listen to several children read in order to see whether they remembered the new words in a story they had read earlier. Without waiting for an answer, she gave me a copy of the words she wanted checked.

The first child, a boy by the name of Dwayne, brought his chair close to mine in a corner of the room. After spending a short time to get acquainted, he opened a basal to read. Because his reading group had read the story at least once before, he seemed a little bored to have to read it again, but read it he did.

What I especially noticed as Dwayne read reinforced the fact that a function-word vocabulary is of great importance for comprehending. Dwayne was able to read all but one of the ten new words listed, including *helicopter;* but he stumbled over, or missed, an average of 5 to 9 function words per page. Partly because he had read the story before, but mostly as a result of his inability to name function words readily, the story must have been little more than a word-naming exercise. Dwayne became tired very soon and seemed to miss the basic point of the story as he read things like "They found the helicopter in the building" when the text stated *They found the helicopter on the building.*

When the children left for music, I discussed my findings with the teacher. To my surprise, her response to my reference to the function words was that children "should know them when they get to second grade," and that all she had time to do is "let them practice the words in the stories they read." I was disappointed with the lack of concern about constantly recurring words and came away realizing their importance more than ever before. It makes me wonder to what extent the comprehension problems of older students result from deficiencies with basic words. Like a snowball rolling down a hill, problems with function words expand when teachers don't recognize their importance.

Later, I couldn't help but wish that I had been able to use phrase and sentence cards with Dwayne so that comparisons could be made for words like *in* and *on* and all the others he misnamed.

FIGURE 6.1   Function Words and Comprehension

He had <u>tears</u> in his eyes as he read the lines.
The <u>tears</u> in their clothing suggested they had fought.

The young <u>does</u> ran through the forest.
Sally <u>does</u> that constantly.

Homophones are words that are pronounced the same but that have different spellings and meanings. This is illustrated below.

If I could, I <u>would</u> go with you.
The <u>wood</u> is finally burning.

He can tell a great tall <u>tale.</u>
The dog's <u>tail</u> wagged and wagged.

I'll <u>meet</u> you tonight at eight.
This <u>meat</u> is too tough to chew.
They'll have to <u>mete</u> out the water carefully.

On the assumption that you have fixed in your mind the meaning of homonym, homograph, and homophone, I want to add a comment about homophones. Even though homonyms and homographs *always* need a context either to define their meaning or to determine their pronunciation, this is not the case for homophones. Once students have learned to read a homophone—for instance, *tale*—its spelling is enough to suggest its meaning. Said differently, students who are able to read *tale* and *tail* need no further help than the spellings in order to know which word refers to a story and which is something that certain animals have.

Reasons to Know Guidelines

At this point some of you may be thinking, Why all the fuss about contexts? Reasons for the "fuss" are two in number. The first has to do with the significance of meaning for reading whether the focus is one word or many words. Specifically, to avoid asking students to learn what is essentially meaningless ("This word says 'although'.") and, further, to avoid causing confusion about meaning ("This word is 'note'."), teachers need to decide ahead of time which new words are text-dependent and which are not.

The second reason for the detailed coverage has to do with efficiency. Specifically, when the manuals in a basal reader series provide suggestions for dealing with new vocabulary, they commonly show all the words in sentences—needed or not (8). Because using contexts takes time, using them when it is unnecessary wastes time. For that reason, a Teacher A who is using a manual divides new vocabulary into words that require a context and words that do not. The guidelines that have been discussed provide Teacher A with a strategy—that is, with a plan for making the distinction.

Why teachers who are attempting to use a literature-based reading program also need to know how to work with words not in their students' reading vocabularies is demonstrated in the account of a classroom in Figure 2.5. This is a suitable time, therefore, to reread that earlier report.

USING WHOLE WORD METHODOLOGY: AN ILLUSTRATION

More teachers than not use basal readers some of the time. Therefore, an illustration of how whole word instruction might proceed focuses on a third-grade teacher who is preparing a group of ten students to read a basal story. Before the instruction is described, some preliminary comments are in order.

Preliminary Comments

Reading done in classrooms in which round robin reading is not used often divides as follows:

Shared Reading

Teacher and students read a short selection together. Often, the purpose is enjoyment.

Independent Reading

Students read on their own something they themselves may have selected. Self-selected or not, the text is easy enough for them to comprehend without help.

Guided Reading

Students read something that they can deal with on their own, if adequate preparations were made.

The third-grade instruction described pertains to a basal selection that ten students would not be able to read were preparations omitted. In this case, the preparation is focusing on new vocabulary; nonetheless, you can see how the teacher also imparts background information. This suggests that even though "attend to new vocabulary" and "activate relevant world knowledge" are cited in the Preview as separate, prereading responsibilities, the two commonly overlap.

As you read through the lesson, you can see exactly how the teacher uses whole word methodology to teach four of the eleven words cited in the basal reader manual as being new. For reasons referred to earlier, the teacher decided that the students should be able to deal with the remaining words as they encounter them in the story. (After the group has read the story silently, independently, and without interruptions, the teacher will check to see whether her conclusion about the words is correct.)

Whenever it happens that the words requiring prereading help from a teacher are excessive in number, only those that relate to central ideas in the selection should receive attention. If, for example, one new word is *fuchsia* and it is used in a reference to a shrub, it might be eliminated from prereading preparations for two reasons. First, the shrub has nothing to do with key ideas in the selection. Second, *fuchsia* is an uncommon word.

One final note. If an excessive number of words requiring prereading attention is the rule and not the exception, it is possible that overly difficult material is being used. If this *is* the case, the solution is not to spend more time on preparations; rather, it is to use easier material.

Illustrative Instruction

The concern of the instruction that follows is four new words: *hummingbird, honey, experiment,* and *touch.* The lesson is presented here in the form of a dialogue in order to make the description maximally specific.

With the group sitting close to a chalkboard somewhat removed from the other students, the teacher starts with *hummingbird* because this bird is central to the plot of the story.

Teacher:	It takes a lot of letters to name the most important character in the story you'll be reading today. I'll write just three of them. [Prints *hum.*] How do you pronounce this word?
Group:	Hum.
Teacher:	I'll add more letters. [Adds *ming.*] Now what do all these letters say?
Group:	Humming.
Teacher:	Right. What does "humming" mean, Billy?
Billy:	Humming is like singing, but there aren't any words. You don't have to open your mouth either.
Teacher:	I have to add one more part to this word so that you'll know whom you'll be reading about. [Adds *bird.*] Today the story is about what?
Group:	A hummingbird.
Teacher:	Right you are. I've never seen a hummingbird around here. They're tiny birds, and they make a humming noise. That's how they got their name. Let me show you some pictures of hummingbirds. The ones in your reader are very small.

The teacher proceeds to show colorful pictures, which elicit comments from some members of the group. The teacher then continues:

Teacher:	Let's take a look at some other words. The story you'll be reading is about a hummingbird, but it's also about [teacher finishes by printing *honey* on the board]. Who knows this word?... Nobody? I bet you'll know if I write something else. [Adds to board so that it shows *bee and honey.*]
Michael:	I know. Honey!
Teacher:	Yes, I thought you'd think of honey if I wrote *bee.* [Erases *bee* and *and.*] Have any of you ever eaten honey?
Mary Ann:	My mother puts it on toast, but it makes me sick.
Trish:	Sometimes my mother puts it in carrots when she's cooking.
Teacher:	Yes, honey is sweet, so it's good on toast and in carrots. Some recommend using it instead of sugar.
Mary Ann:	It's too sweet and sticky. It makes me sick.
Teacher:	Mary Ann, when you read the story you'll have to see whether the hummingbird agrees with you. When all of you read the story you'll find a fairly long word, and I'm not sure you'll know what it means so we had better look at that, too. [Writes *experiment.*] What is this word?

Billy: It says "ex" at the beginning and "ment" at the end, but I don't know the rest of it. I don't think I've ever seen that word before.

Teacher: Maybe not. Scientists use it a lot. Does anyone know what it is?... No? It says "experiment." What is it?

Group: Experiment.

Teacher: Rob, you didn't look at *experiment*. You'll never remember it if you don't look at it when you say it. Let's all look at this word. (Teacher points to *experiment*.) What is it everyone?

Group: Experiment.

Teacher: What does "experiment" mean? Does anyone know what an experiment is?

Billy: It's when you try something, and you have to be careful because it might blow up. The other night on television, two guys did an experiment and it almost killed them.

Teacher: That was one kind of experiment, Billy. Not all experiments are dangerous. In fact, I'm carrying on an experiment right now at home. I have two plants that are the same. I'm watering one every week and the other about every ten days. I'm trying to learn which amount of water is better. It's not dangerous, but it's an experiment because I'm trying to learn something by doing different things and then looking at the results. That's what the story is about. Someone is trying to find out something about hummingbirds. And it has to do with honey.

Trish: I bet I know what happens. Some bees sting the hummingbird because they both want honey.

Teacher: I can't tell you because then there wouldn't be any mystery. Before you find out what does happen, there's one more word I want you to look at because you might have trouble figuring it out. [Prints *touch*.] Can anyone read this? Jim?

Jim: Touch? [Pronounces it to rhyme with *couch*.]

Teacher: Jim, have you ever heard a word that sounds like "touch?" [Repeats Jim's pronunciation.]

Jim: I don't think so. I guess I don't know what it is.

Teacher: Let's see if you do now. [Writes *touch football*.] Jim, think about what I just wrote. What does this word [points to *touch*] say?

Jim: Touch. Touch football.

Teacher: Yes, in this case *touch* means a kind of football game in which you touch rather than tackle the players. [Erases *football*.] In the story about a hummingbird, it will just mean to touch something—the way I'm touching Mary Ann's shoulder. Jim, I think I know why you first thought this word said "touch" [pronounces it to rhyme with *couch*]. With this word [writes *couch* directly under *touch*], we do say "couch." We give that /ou/ sound to the digraph *ou*. But in "touch," the vowel sound is /ŭ/. All this shows the importance of asking—what question should you always ask after you think you've figured out a new word?

Group: Does it make sense?

Teacher: Correct. The reason I wrote *touch football* is to show you how words you can read help with words you're not sure of. There are other words in the story about the hummingbird that are new, but the way they're spelled should tell you what they say. Be sure to read all the other words in the sentence. They'll help, too. To make sure you don't have problems with the words we've been talking about now, let's read them a few more times. Please look at each word when you say it. I'll point to them quickly to see if you can read them quickly.

After the story is read silently, the teacher shows the group phrase and sentence cards, each containing at least one of the seven new words that were not taught before the reading began. Exactly how members of the group decided what they said is discussed. Sentences using the words that had been pretaught are shown next. By having individuals read the cards aloud after the group has had time to read them silently first, the teacher learns which, if any, of the eleven new words are causing problems and require further attention.

Comments about the Instruction

Much that contributes to the successful use of whole word instruction is exemplified in the lesson just portrayed, not the least of which is the inclusion of practice. In fact, the teacher demonstrated one important postreading responsibility: Check up on new words, whether they were or were not pretaught.

The same teacher knew enough to use what is known (touch football) to help with what is not known (the word *touch*). In the process, she demonstrated with both touch football and the association between bees and honey how known words can help with other words that are not known.

Recognizing the primary importance of meaning, the teacher made sure that *experiment* was understood, because this word is important in the story. Wisely, her example showed that experiments are not confined to scientists' laboratories.

Not to be overlooked is this third-grade teacher's adherence to the dictum: Be sure students look at a new word *when* it is named. To encourage students to attend to the words receiving attention was the reason other words were erased once they served their purpose.

A Final Comment

One objective of this chapter is to encourage use of uninterrupted silent reading, made possible with adequate preparations. How one third-grade teacher prepared students by attending to new words was just described. To provide a contrast, I want to refer again to round robin reading, in particular, to another possible consequence that is not desirable. The drawback is identified with a reference to a second grade in which the observed teacher was overseeing round robin reading in which ten students were the participants. Pertinent to the present discussion is what happened while one member of the group was reading aloud.

When he was first asked to read, he immediately had difficulty with *toward;* consequently, he looked up to the teacher for help. She told him what it said, and he continued. A few lines later he encountered *toward* again, still could not read it, and looked up to the teacher once more to get help. Soon it was another child's turn to read; however, had the first one continued and come across *toward* again, it is safe to predict that he still would not know it. Why not? Each time the teacher named it, he was looking at her, not at *toward*.

Because of what has been seen in many classrooms, the following guideline clearly merits your attention: *Encourage students to look at an unknown word at the time it is being named.* Implied in this guideline are two others:

1. New words should not be presented to as many as an entire class.
2. Whole word instruction should not begin until everyone appears to be paying attention.

ANOTHER WAY TO ENLARGE READING VOCABULARIES

Sometimes, new words have meanings that are connected. Whenever this is so, the possibility exists to organize them into *semantic categories* or, as they are sometimes called, *conceptual sets* (14). I use the word "possibility" because nothing is so good that it ought to be done all the time. Done too often, even the best procedures become routine and are not likely to win the attention of students. And, as has been emphasized, attention is critical for developing reading vocabularies.

Generally, conceptually related words are more common in expository material than in text that relates a story. An article about a certain country, for instance, is likely to include vocabulary that can be grouped under such headings as Location, History, Population, Resources, and Occupations. Nonetheless, the webbing in Figure 6.2 shows how it functions with fiction (3).

Whenever various kinds of displays are printed on chart paper and kept, they are useful not only in introducing new words in ways that make it easier for students to remember them but also in reviewing the words after the text is read. Sometimes, the same display offers prompts for retelling the content of a selection.

[handwritten margin note: homophone (hear)]

WORD PRACTICE

Naming and renaming a word, hopefully in ways that are not too tedious, are the essence of word practice. The discussion of practice that follows looks at its purpose and provides guidelines for making practice productive. Afterward, examples of word practice are described.

Purpose of Practice

Like practice of any kind, the goal of word practice is proficiency. Its specific goal is a maximally large sight vocabulary. A *sight vocabulary,* you will recall, consists of all the words that an individual can read on sight—that is, automatically.

Why word practice is discussed in some detail reflects two facts. First, it is a requirement for automatic identifications. Second, in spite of its importance, word

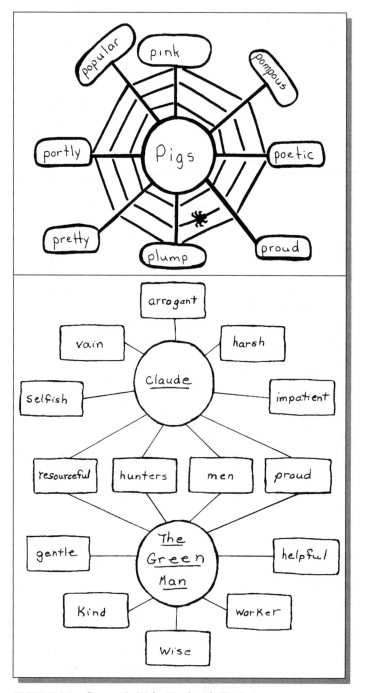

FIGURE 6.2 Semantic Webs Used with Fiction

Source: Webbing with Literature, by Karen D'Angelo Bromley, © 1991 by Allyn and Bacon. Used by permission of Suzanne S. French and Lisa Milano.

practice is often allocated insufficient time in classrooms, especially beyond the third-grade level (7, 9). Frank Green describes the consequences somewhat dramatically when he observes, "Reading is often a trial, with each word a problem-solving crisis" (10, p. 536).

Why word practice is sometimes neglected is puzzling, given the fact that both research (2, 12) and our own experiences confirm that the ability to identify most words that appear in a body of text is essential for comprehending it. (Knowing the words is also essential for developing self-confidence as a reader.) The same two sources tell us, too, that the faster such identifications are made, the easier it is to comprehend. All this, plus the role that practice plays, is depicted in Figure 6.3.

To supplement the message inherent in Figure 6.3, let me add the following observation:

> Human attention is limited. To understand connected text, our attention cannot be directed to individual words and letters. In reading as in listening, the process of individual word perception must proceed with relative automaticity, and such automaticity is afforded only through practice. (1, p. 283)

Based on the discussion of comprehension in Chapter 1, you also know that automatic identifications are no guarantee of successful comprehension. Signs like the following make that point:

> No shoes.   No shirt.   No service.

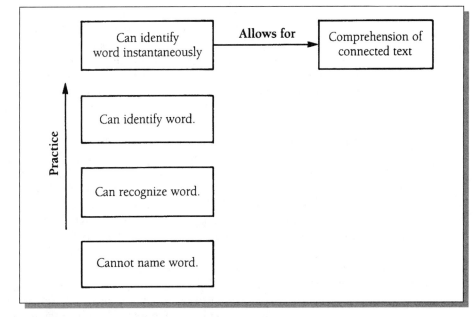

FIGURE 6.3   Origins of Sight Vocabularies

Attached to the door of a restaurant, this warning is useful in demonstrating that comprehending, in this case, requires the ability not only to identify the six words but also to link them into a cause-effect relationship. Nonetheless, knowing the six words is the foundation for concluding that in this restaurant, the effect of not wearing shoes or a shirt is not having food or drink served.

Guidelines for Practice

The ability to identify words at the level of automaticity is the purpose of practice; nonetheless, much of the practice suggested in commercially prepared materials such as teacher's manuals focuses on word recognition, not word identification. To make sure that practice *is* dealing with identifications, it is essential for teachers to know the difference between identification and recognition.

Identification vs. Recognition. *Identification* refers to the ability to name a stimulus directly (e.g., *five, 5*) without any external prompt. *Recognition,* on the other hand, is the ability to name the stimulus with a prompt.

It is safe to claim that everyone reading this book has experienced considerable amounts of word recognition practice because it has been common in commercial materials for a long time—and still is. To be more specific, you can recall, I am sure, workbook pages composed of lists of words in boxes:

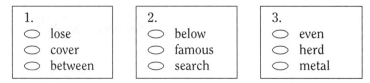

Reading from the basal manual, a teacher was apt to say something like: "Find box number one. Look at all the words in that box. Find the word *cover* and draw a line under it." To provide practice in taking tests, more recent versions of the same exercise are likely to have directions that state: "Find the word *cover*. With your pencil, fill in the oval in front of the word *cover.*" Whether students are underlining or filling in ovals, the exercise deals with word recognition, because a word is named not independently by the student but with the aid of a prompt. In this case, the teacher offers the prompt when she says the target word.

Teachers in the habit of asking, *"Why* am I doing what I'm doing?" may choose to use workbook pages like the one just described but change the task to word identification by having students produce, not choose, words. This can be done by asking individuals to read aloud all the words in a box.

When time is not available for listening to individual responses, written procedures can be substituted. Possibilities are illustrated in Figure 6.4. In addition to providing practice with procedural text, the examples show how written assignments can call attention to meaning at the same time that they allow for practice with word identification.

In addition to making certain that practice is with word identification, not word recognition, teachers need to be sure that they are not inadvertently using irrelevant

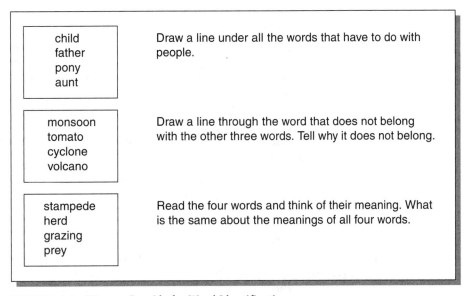

child father pony aunt	Draw a line under all the words that have to do with people.
monsoon tomato cyclone volcano	Draw a line through the word that does not belong with the other three words. Tell why it does not belong.
stampede herd grazing prey	Read the four words and think of their meaning. What is the same about the meanings of all four words.

FIGURE 6.4 Ways to Provide for Word Identification

cues. To explain the meaning of this guideline, relevant and irrelevant cues are both explained.

Cues. Applied to word learning, a *cue* is what a learner uses to establish a connection between a given word (stimulus) and what it says (response). Or, stated differently, one or more features of a written word are selected to help remember it. If that prompt fixes the correct response permanently, it is a *relevant* cue. If it offers only temporary assistance and eventually fosters confusion and erroneous responses, it is *irrelevant*. With classroom illustrations, let me cite examples of the latter.

An abundant use of irrelevant cues occurred in a first grade near the beginning of the year when the teacher was reviewing color words. As she wrote each word on the board, she used a different colored piece of chalk. The word *blue,* for instance, was written with blue chalk, *yellow,* with yellow chalk, and so on. Predictably, when she finished writing the words, the children had no difficulty remembering them. Equally predictable is that those who did not know the words before this colorful review would not know them any better when they appeared later in books or written with white chalk or black ink. Why? The teacher used an irrelevant cue (color) to help establish connections between visual stimuli (words) and correct responses to them.

More recently, another misuse of color was seen in a workbook. Described as providing practice in reading two new words, the page listed sentences that included one or both. Unexpectedly, each time one of the words appeared, it was printed in red. Whenever the other word showed up in a sentence, the print was blue. All that the children needed to do, therefore, was to attach a response to a color.

A student teacher used another kind of irrelevant cue to help the children she was working with remember *peak* and *gully.* She began by printing *peak* at the top of the chalkboard and *gully* at the bottom. Then, as she named and explained the words, she assured the group that they would have no trouble remembering the words because of where she had placed them—and they didn't, as long as *peak* was at the top and *gully* was at the bottom.

I had assumed that another irrelevant cue—word contour—had been permanently abandoned; however, I recently saw a spelling workbook that made liberal use of the configuration of words. The problem with explicit attention to contour is made clear below and is the reason configuration is an irrelevant cue.

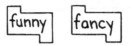

You may now be wondering, What is left for examples of relevant cues? To respond, let me first remind you of the meaning of relevant cue: permanent features that distinguish words. One permanent feature of a written word is the sequence of its letters. (The fact that sequence *is* a distinctive feature is made apparent in words like *tap, pat,* and *apt.*) Because of the significance of letter sequence, some teachers have children spell words when they are being taught. Name, spell, and rename are the requests these teachers make if their students can name letters automatically but have limited knowledge of letter-sound correspondences.

In an alphabetic writing system, letter-sound correspondences are a second kind of relevant cue—something that ought to have been used to help the students referred to earlier learn *peak* and *gully.* The third type originates in the structure of words. That is why instruction for roots, prefixes, and suffixes is said to focus on structural cues.

It should be noted that students' knowledge of graphophonic and structural cues reduces substantially the number of times they have to name a word before it becomes part of their sight vocabularies.

Examples of Practice

To discourage you from thinking that word practice is confined to naming words on cards as quickly as a teacher can show them, I want to start the examples of practice with some that a fifth-grade teacher provided. Her report of what she did in her first year of teaching fifth grade is in Figure 6.5. Earlier, she had taught third grade for two years. Although the teacher views the work she describes in the report as an effort to eliminate round robin reading, you will see that it allows for word practice, too.

The introductory comments in this discussion of samples of word practice are not intended to discourage word-card practice. (You may recall that the third-grade teacher who prepared students for the story about the hummingbird used sentence cards to check up on new vocabulary after the reading was done.) The purpose of the comments was simply to show that practice comes in many forms.

One fourth-grade teacher uses cards for practice effectively and efficiently. Typically, she has two reading groups, each of which uses a basal reader some of the

After considering all the problems associated with round robin reading, I am now trying to find purposeful and enjoyable alternatives for students to read orally. One activity that many enjoy is reading plays. Unlike the round robin reading I used to have, reading plays is something we do occasionally.

It just so happens that the novel one group is currently reading (*The War with Grandpa*) has frequent dialogues that lend themselves to oral reading. Periodically, I have students assume the roles of characters engaged in a conversation. Today, for instance, two students read a conversation between the young boy and his grandfather while I served as narrator. At times, the conversation becomes quite emotional and heated because the two are talking about what it means to be at war.

Typically, this group reads one chapter of a book at a time. Today, after the chapter was discussed, I asked them to return to the conversation referred to above so that they could read that part one more time. I then asked the boys in the group if any would like to be the grandfather and the boy so that we'd be able to hear exactly how the conversation sounded. Two quickly volunteered. (Sometimes I ask for volunteers; sometimes I assign parts.) While the two read their parts and I read mine, others in the group just listened. For whatever reason, the two boys asked if they could read the dialogue "one more time." During the second reading, they added their own touches to show the emotional nature of the conversation. The others listened as attentively the second time as they had the first. These positive reactions are wonderful, but I am making sure that I do not overuse this kind of oral reading.

The current experiences with oral reading are very different from the round robin reading I used to take for granted. To begin, the initial reading is always silent and is done without interruptions. Second, when oral reading *is* used, it has a purpose. Today, for example, the purpose was to communicate the emotional nature of a conversation. Third, when the oral reading takes place, students not participating merely listen. Now, there is no worry about extraneous things like making sure they have the place if asked to read aloud.

I think I can honestly say that the oral reading being done now adds to both the students' enjoyment and their comprehension of whatever it is they're reading.

FIGURE 6.5 One Kind of Word Practice

time. The systematic attention she gives to practice concentrates on basal reader vocabulary. For each reader used, this is what she does.

After teaching the words in a basal selection that require prereading attention, she prints them and others that she did not preteach on cards. All the cards are filed in alphabetical order and are not used until a Unit in the basal reader is finished. (A Unit is made up of four or five selections.) At that time, vocabulary review begins. The first kind focuses on combinations of cards that might show something like the following. (Cards are placed in a card holder.)

forlorn personality	enormous appetite
uncommonly helpless	shrill siren
piteously inferior	discouragingly endangered

The task for the instructional group is to name the combined words. Then, to show that the meaning is understood, a volunteer uses the words in a sentence.

Once this review ends, the cards are left on a table along with larger cards on which labels like *Nouns* and *Adjectives* are printed. Whenever time permits, members of the instructional group can work at the table to organize the word cards according to grammatical function. Eventually, each group of words is printed on chart paper to allow for more review.

Sometimes, students also arrange words according to meanings. One such cluster is shown below. Again, the clusters provide for review.

Noise			
crunch	whine	rustle	shriek
bleat	chirp	slam	whimper
crackle	mutter	growl	thud

Aware that she spends more time on word practice than is typical, this teacher explains her efforts as follows:

> I view all the plans I make for reviewing vocabulary as a means for allowing my students to *enjoy* the books they choose to read on their own. They do have large vocabularies. The work does pay off.

You may have noticed that the teachers referred to in the examples of word practice thus far work at levels beyond the primary grades. The choice is deliberate because, as stated earlier, word practice is sometimes neglected at the higher levels in spite of the fundamental importance of sight vocabularies for comprehending connected text.

Lest primary-grade teachers feel left out, Figure 6.6 lists ways in which teachers of younger children used bulletin-board displays for word practice.

LEARNING TO READ BY READING

Why a chapter concerned with developing reading vocabularies ends with a section called "Learning to Read by Reading" can be explained with a conclusion reached by

Hallowe'en
Every day starting on October 1, a paper ghost is added to a bulletin board. Appearing on each is a word selected by the children as being especially difficult. Daily, all the ghosts on the board are read until thirty-one have accumulated by the time Hallowe'en arrives.

Autumn
Prompted by the plentiful supply of apples available, a teacher attached a large paper tree to a board. She also cut out red paper apples on which words in need of practice are printed along with other words to provide a context (e.g., *far away*). Whenever a child reads an apple correctly, the teacher attaches it to the tree. At the end, the apples are picked, allowing the group to review all the words. Using the same procedure, this teacher uses a pine tree and ornaments in December. (Other possibilities: cornucopia and fruit, net and fish, mailbox and envelopes, jar and cookies.)

Questions/Answers
Phrase cards on a board allow a teacher to ask questions and children to respond by reading the cards. If the teacher asks, "When you're crossing the street, where should you *not* go?" the card displaying *between cars* provides the answer.

Jack and the Beanstalk
To highlight a much-enjoyed story, one teacher put a tall, thick stalk (green paper rolled tightly) on a board, attached to which were long leaves on which phrases had been printed. Also on the board were paper figures of both Jack and the giant. Children take turns being one or the other. With the selected figure in hand, the climb is attempted. Misread words bring the child crashing to the ground, after which another child has a chance to attempt the climb. Successful climbers get to keep a figure temporarily.

FIGURE 6.6 Interesting Word Practice

Keith Stanovich (13). After reviewing research concerned with factors that promote or impede the acquisition of literacy, Stanovich writes: "Many things that facilitate further growth in reading comprehension ability—general knowledge, vocabulary, syntactic knowledge—are developed by reading itself" (p. 364).

A detail that needs to be added to Stanovich's conclusion is that students do learn to read by reading if most of the words in the text are in their sight vocabularies. This permits them to use known words to resolve problems with unknown words. Encountering and recognizing the latter more than once constitute practice, which elevates word recognition to the level of word identification.

The multiple benefits that derive from reading independent-level material—in addition to enlarging reading vocabularies—are sufficiently important to merit special attention:

Benefits of Reading Independent-Level Material
1. Allows for the consolidation and realistic use of what has been taught.
2. Moves attention away from individual words to the meaning of connected text.
3. Fosters good habits insofar as rate is concerned.
4. Adds to the reader's knowledge of the world.
5. Promotes self-confidence and, with it, a greater interest in reading.

Just because students *can* read does not mean they *will* read. Procedures that some teachers have used to motivate reading are described below.

- Whenever students show special interest in a topic, our school librarian and I seek out books that pertain to it. Together, we usually succeed in finding material written at a level that each child can handle. Initially, I meet with the group of interested children to discuss the topic, to distribute books, and to set a date for a subsequent meeting. Often, postreading discussions are as mature as any that adults might have. One bonus feature is the opportunity that the discussions give to less able readers to make significant contributions for, very often, the content of their books is just as informative as that found in more difficult sources.

- Because my contacts with students are often impersonal, I meet as often as I can with individuals, ostensibly to discuss what they have been reading on their own. At such times, I am more eager to learn how children feel about reading than to assess abilities or deficiencies. These meetings give me a chance to recommend books or to find some that match expressed interests. I especially try to find out the questions that are important to students and then try to locate books that might offer answers.

- If children enjoyed a book, they may, if they wish, tell in writing why they enjoyed it. Recommendations are displayed on a board to assist anyone who is looking for a book. If multiple copies of a really good book are available, I feel no compunction about asking certain students to read it. We first meet as a group so that I can introduce the book and set a date for getting reactions. When we meet again, I am ready with questions, but I ask them only if something is needed to get a discussion started. If the children appear to have enjoyed a book, I am also ready to show others by the same author or similar books by different authors.

- Many of the new informational books—even those written at fairly simple levels—are more interesting than textbooks. Students like them better, too. That's why I encourage groups to do extra reading on topics that originate in social studies and science texts. With the supplementary reading, we often get contradictory information, which results in lively discussions and, very often, in further reading.

- Sometime each year I suggest the possibility of looking for interesting new words in self-selected books. To fan some interest, I couple the suggestion with a few examples I've come across in my own reading. (I always go out of my way to let students know that I am an avid reader.) At some designated date, interested students and I get together to discuss our findings.

- By the time children get to third grade, some are effective oral readers. With guidance from me or the school librarian, they select books that kindergartners and first graders will enjoy. After reading the books silently, they read them aloud to small groups of younger children.
- Whenever parents or other adults in the community have interesting hobbies, I invite them to tell my students about them. I then try to find books that relate to the hobbies. Parents who have traveled and have taken slides also speak to us. Again, I work with our librarian to find books about the places each person has been to.
- Into some of the library books in my room I tuck cards that make a request. (Students call them the "Would you" cards.) One is: "Would you pretend that you're the author of this book as you read it? When you're finished, be ready to tell which parts of the book were hardest to write." A card in another book might ask, "Would you get a friend to read this book when you're finished? Together, the two of you can make a mobile whose parts will show drawings of characters or scenes or happenings in the book. Later, you can use the mobile to tell others about the story."

References at the end of the chapter offer additional suggestions for promoting interest in reading books (5, 11). Others tell of books that children especially enjoy (4) and name some that are easy to read (6).

SUMMARY

That round robin reading, with all of its negative consequences, ought to be replaced with something better was an underlying theme of Chapter 6. The replacement suggested was uninterrupted silent reading.

To allow for this when the difficulty of text exceeds what students can manage on their own, teachers have to assume responsibility for certain prereading preparations. One kind of preparation has to do with new vocabulary. Naming new words as wholes, commonly referred to as *whole word methodology,* was the topic of Chapter 6.

Why whole word methodology has to be used with beginners was explained with a reference to their inability to use the cueing system of English to deal with words themselves. That is why Chapter 6 stated that, even though whole word methodology is never laid aside permanently, its use should decrease as students' knowledge increases. The details of whole word instruction were then explained.

When new words need to be presented in contexts was the first question considered. The answer required dividing vocabulary into function words and content words. Because function words depend on other words for their meaning, the recommendation was to present all function words in the company of other words that are familiar. Because content words known as homonyms, homographs, and homophones are also text-dependent words, the same recommendation was made for them.

On the assumption that a picture *is* better than a thousand words, Chapter 6 sketched a picture of whole word methodology with the help of a dialogue that took place in a third grade when the teacher was attending to new vocabulary. The lesson was then analyzed in order to specify its positive features.

Following the analysis, it was said that whenever all or some of the words that students need to learn have connected meanings, they should receive attention together. The fact that making the connections explicit helps students remember the words was the reason for this suggestion. Making words memorable is important because it reduces the amount of practice required to get the words into students' reading vocabularies.

Some amount of practice, Chapter 6 pointed out, is necessary—except for such special words as the children's own names. The significance of practice for moving written words out of the category "unknown" and into the category "known on sight" accounts for the detailed discussion of practice.

This discussion began by clarifying the difference between word recognition and word identification. It was necessary to do that because practically all the suggestions that commercially prepared materials make for practice deal with recognizing words. This is a serious flaw, because word identification—quick identification—is necessary for comprehending connected text. The distinctions made next between relevant and irrelevant cues served a similar purpose: to keep teachers from providing word practice that, in the long run, is nonproductive. To keep teaching from being nonproductive, one guideline was especially emphasized: Make sure students look at a word *when* it is named.

Even though the focus of Chapter 6 was on preparations required for text that is too difficult for students to read on their own, it closed by attending to other reading that can be done without help. This was an appropriate ending because one benefit of independent-level reading is the opportunities it provides for enlarging reading vocabularies. This explains why the final section is called "Learning to Read by Reading."

REVIEW

1. Chapter 6 recommends teaching together words that are related. Now, to review terms used in Chapter 6, explain each term in the two charts shown on p. 159 in a way that makes implied relationships explicit.

2. Use illustrative words to explain the following:
   Presenting all new words in contexts wastes time. On the other hand, merely to list them in a column and name them shows disregard for text-dependent words.

3. Attending to new vocabulary and activating (or adding to) relevant world knowledge were cited in the Preface for Chapter 6 as separate prereading responsibilities for teachers. Yet in the chapter itself, a statement was made that the two often overlap. What does this mean? Use an example to make your explanation clear.

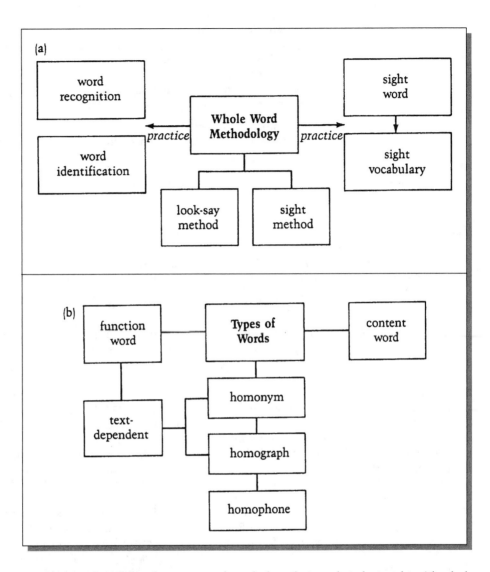

4. Chapter 6 said that the amount of vocabulary that needs to be taught with whole word instruction may be excessive at times.
   a. What is meant by "excessive?"
   b. If the number of words requiring prereading attention with whole word methodology *is* excessive, how can a teacher eliminate some?

5. Relying on irrelevant cues to help students remember new words makes practice nonproductive.
   a. Define "irrelevant cue."
   b. Explain why the use of irrelevant cues makes practice ineffective in the long run.

    c. Chapter 6 made two references to color serving as an irrelevant cue. Is the following assignment another example of turning the use of color into an irrelevant cue? Explain your response.

        An assignment sheet shows a list of sentences, each containing a word that names a color. Directions ask children to read each sentence and underline the color word with a crayon of the same color.

6. You were reminded in Chapter 6 that:

    Those who presuppose that students will be able to comprehend connected text as long as they can read all the words do not understand the comprehension process.

    How *did* Chapter 6 remind you of this statement?

REFERENCES

1. Adams, Marilyn J. *Thinking and Learning about Print*. Cambridge, Mass.: The MIT Press, 1990.
2. Adams, Marilyn J., and Huggins, A. W. F. "The Growth of Children's Sight Vocabulary: A Quick Test with Educational and Theoretical Implications." *Reading Research Quarterly* 20 (Spring, 1985), 262–281.
3. Bromley, Karen D. *Webbing with Literature*. Boston: Allyn and Bacon, 1991.
4. Children's Book Council and IRA. "Children's Choices for 1991." *Reading Teacher* 45 (October, 1991), 128–139.
5. Cullinan, Bernice E. (Ed.) *Children's Literature in the Reading Program*. Newark, Del.: International Reading Association, 1987.
6. Cunningham, Pat. "Books for Beginners." *Reading Teacher* 34 (May, 1981), 952–954.
7. Durkin, Dolores. "Is There a Match between What Elementary Teachers Do and What Basal Reader Manuals Recommend? *Reading Teacher* 37 (April, 1984), 734–744.
8. Durkin, Dolores. "Phonics Instruction in New Basal Reader Programs." Technical Report No. 496. Urbana: University of Illinois, Center for the Study of Reading, 1990.
9. Durkin, Dolores. "What Classroom Observations Reveal about Reading Comprehension Instruction." *Reading Research Quarterly* 14 (1978–1979), 481–533.
10. Green, Frank. "Listening to Children Read: The Empathetic Process." *Reading Teacher* 39 (February, 1986), 536–543.
11. O'Masta, Gail A., and Wolf, James M. "Encouraging Independent Reading through the Reading Millionaires Project." *Reading Teacher* 44 (May, 1991), 656–662.
12. Perfetti, Charles A., and Lesgold, A. M. "Coding and Comprehension in Skilled Reading and Implications for Reading Instruction." In L. B. Resnick and P. Weaver (Eds.), *Theory and Practice of Early Reading*. Hillsdale, N.J.: Erlbaum, 1979.
13. Stanovich, Keith E. "Mathew Effects in Reading: Some Consequences of Individual Differences in the Acquisition of Literacy." *Reading Research Quarterly* 21 (Fall, 1986), 360–406.
14. Wixson, Karen K. "Vocabulary Instruction and Children's Comprehension of Basal Series." *Reading Research Quarterly* 21 (Summer, 1986), 317–329.

Contextual Cues

Verbal contexts, the focus of Chapter 7, consist of known words, some of which were learned with whole word instruction. (That is why whole word methodology is discussed first.) The more specific focus is the use of known words to recognize unknown words.

Anyone who read the previous chapter encountered *context* frequently. For example, early in Chapter 6 it is suggested that, "Whenever a function word is taught with whole word methodology, it should be introduced in the context of other words that are known." If *pie* and *cake* are words students can read, an illustration of the suggestion is the use of *pie or cake* to introduce *or*. "Context," then, refers to parts of writing that precede or follow, and are connected with, a particular word.

More directly related to Chapter 7 is the use of contexts by the third-grade teacher, also referred to in the previous chapter. To help her students decide what *honey* and *touch* said, she showed *bee and honey* and *touch football*. This use of contexts has a direct connection with Chapter 7, because the two contexts enabled the students to recognize words that were familiar orally but not visually. The prompts that derive from known words are referred to as *contextual cues*.

Like subsequent chapters that deal with the use of relevant cues to recognize words, Chapter 7 shows teachers and prospective teachers how to help students acquire independence in coping with words not in their reading vocabularies. It is assumed that such words *are* in the students' oral vocabularies. Thus, their meanings are familiar even though their visual forms are not. (How to use contexts for help with meanings is explained in Chapter 11.)

As you make your way through Chapter 7, you may be surprised to learn that work with contextual cues can get started even before children are able to read. This is possible because spoken language provides listeners with contextual cues to the same degree that written material makes them available to readers. This means that Chapter 7 has content that is relevant for teachers who work with nonreaders as well as for teachers whose students are quite proficient.

To see how proficient you are in using contextual cues, try filling in the blanks in the second question in the Review section for Chapter 7. Once you have read the chapter, try this cloze exercise again to see how much you've learned.

THE THIRD-GRADE TEACHER DESCRIBED IN CHAPTER **6** used contextual cues so effectively to provide help with *honey* and *touch* that her work is referred to now to make some introductory comments. They are intended to provide a framework for your study of Chapter 7.

INTRODUCTORY COMMENTS

The teacher's use of *bee and honey* is considered first in order to make three of her assumptions explicit. The context *touch football* is dealt with next to make one additional point.

To begin, the teacher in question assumed that the students were familiar with honey even though they could not read *honey* when she wrote it on the board. The teacher further assumed that their knowledge of honey associated it with bees. One more assumption, therefore, was that the students' ability to read the words *bee* and *and* would prompt them to think "honey" when they saw it in the context *bee and honey*. And that is exactly what happened.

The same teacher's use of *touch football* assumed not only that this game was familiar because the students had played, watched, or heard about it but also that the word *touch* had been used to refer to the game. This is an important point because, conceivably, children can play touch football without having heard its name. For them, writing *football* after *touch* adds nothing to their ability to recognize *touch*.

With the help of these comments, you should now understand that even though contextual cues are said to be rooted in words that can be read, complementary sources of help are experiences, oral vocabulary, and world knowledge. To be kept in mind, too, is that the use of all this results in recognizing, not identifying, a word. As the previous chapter states more than once, progressing from recognition to identification requires practice.

This reminder relates directly to the subject of the present chapter because contextual cues exist in a body of text only when most of its words can be identified. One might question the contention, for example, that a sentence like the following, in which three of the five words are unknown, is a context:

A ____ ____ at ____.

To ensure that students have ample opportunities to use contexts is one reason excessively difficult material should never be assigned. Such opportunities are important because knowing how to use contextual cues for help with unfamiliar words reduces a student's dependence on a more able reader or, for instance, on a dictionary.

KINDS OF CONTEXTUAL CUES

Having considered key ideas about contextual cues, it is now time to look at the two ways known words do help with other words that cannot be recognized.

One way lies in the order in which known words occur. This explains the description *syntactic cue* for one kind of contextual help. Because the second source of help lies in the meaning of the words that are known, it is assigned the description *semantic cue*. The fact that two topics cannot be discussed simultaneously explains why syntactic cues and semantic cues are dealt with separately even though readers use the two jointly.

Syntactic Cues

Syntactic cues are available because English is a *positional language*. In a positional language, the order or sequence of words affects meaning. You can see the effect in contrasting sentences like:

> They painted the house yellow.
> They painted the yellow house.

That words are sequenced only in certain patterned ways reinforces the fact that English is a positional language. Results when a pattern is not adhered to is illustrated below.

> They house the yellow painted

When word order is considered, the focus is usually a sentence. Exactly how the words in a sentence are ordered is referred to as its *syntax*. That is why the help for an unknown word that derives from the sequence of the words known is called a syntactic cue.

With all this in mind, let's return to the sentence noted earlier in which three of the five words were said to be unfamiliar to a reader:

> A _____ _____ at _____.

Anyone acquainted with English syntax knows that the last word has to be a noun. Because this is a sentence, it must have a verb; however, verbs do not follow an article such as *A*. From this it can be inferred that the verb precedes *at*. Because articles like *A* signal that a singular noun is forthcoming, the name of something follows *A*. Thanks to all these syntactic cues, it is reasonable to conclude that the sentence could be something like:

> A friend smiled at mother.

Word order allows for inferences about the grammatical function of an unknown word even when that word is embedded in a context that is less than a sentence. This is illustrated next:

> these _____   beyond the _____
> an _____   a very scornful _____
> mother and _____ hydrangeas or _____

All the examples noted above allow for nothing but nouns in the blanks. The first and last illustrations call for plural nouns; the second piece of text, in spite of the brevity, confines the omitted noun to one that is singular with a spelling that starts with a vowel.

Admittedly, knowing that a word is a noun—or a verb or an adjective or whatever—does not provide direct help for recognizing the word. Nonetheless, the constraints that originate in syntactic cues serve a reader well by eliminating possibilities. When constraints that reflect syntax are combined with constraints originating in semantic cues, even more words can be eliminated as a reader wonders, "What *is* that word?"

Semantic Cues

Like all languages, English makes sense. Consequently, when a word that is not in an individual's reading vocabulary appears in connected text, the collective meaning of the known words places constraints on what the unknown word can be. That collective meaning is the source of semantic cues. (Semantics, from which "semantic cue" derives, is a branch of linguistics concerned with the study of meaning.)

How semantic cues increase the constraints that syntactic cues provide is illustrated in the sentence below, in which the blank represents the unknown word.

The children are playing _____ the park.

The syntax of the sentence suggests that the unknown word is a preposition; however, the collective meaning of the known words indicates that only certain prepositions are semantically acceptable. Replacing the blank with prepositions like *at, in, outside,* or *beyond,* for example, makes sense whereas replacements such as *into, on,* or *between* do not. The conclusion, then, is that slots in sentences are constrained both syntactically and semantically.

It should be noted both here and for children that semantic cues, unlike syntactic cues, are not confined to the sentence in which the unfamiliar word is found. This is the case because connected text is composed of sentences that are linked semantically. For instance:

This room is hot. Turn on the _____ .

The syntax of the second sentence shown above confines the unknown word to the category "noun." In contrast, semantic cues in the same sentence are much less restrictive. *Faucet, radio, television, light, engine,* and *music* are some nouns that make sense. When the meaning of the previous sentence is taken into account, however, the additional constraints prompt readers to think "fan."

Why it is wise for readers not only to keep previous sentence(s) in mind but also to read ahead when a word causes problems is demonstrated next:

The _____ in the pot is wet. Don't water that plant.
When you feed the dog, be _____ . He bites.
I don't use _____ in tea. It makes it too sweet.

The last context is useful for reviewing the fact that contextual help is dependent on a reader's experiences and the knowledge they yield. A more specific point for teachers to keep in mind is that individual experiences make the notion "meaningful" somewhat subjective. This was brought out during a visit to a classroom. Reading aloud, one boy said, "The men went into the horse" in response to the sentence *The men went into the house.* Because the teacher had been stressing that reading must make sense, she naturally asked, "Kevin, does it make sense to say that men went into a horse?" "Yes," responded Kevin without hesitation. "Once on TV, I saw men marching into a wooden horse to hide there."

The moral of this story pertains not only to the significance of experiences but also to the need for readers to consider graphophonic cues as well as cues originating in a context. After all, *house* is not "horse" no matter what a child's experiences may have included. As shown in the following sections, the combined use of contextual and minimal graphophonic cues can be featured early.

SPOKEN CONTEXTS

Even though young children are not consciously aware that making sense is the essence of language, they display an intuitive knowledge when they speak. It is their tacit knowledge that makes attention to contextual cues possible even before children are able to do any reading.

How one kindergarten teacher who knows the value of contextual cues for readers worked with a group of eight is depicted below. The procedure was planned to the extent that the teacher knew she would remind the children of the detective in the story read the previous day and that she would use this to encourage a discussion that allowed for the use of spoken contexts.

Teacher:	Does anyone know what a detective is?
Vincent:	I do. He catches robbers.
Maria:	Sometimes he gets shot, too.
Teacher:	Yes, that's true. How is a detective able to catch a robber, Vincent?
Vincent:	If somebody knows him, they can tell the police.
Teacher:	But what if nobody does? Maybe he's wearing a mask, and nobody knows who he is. What then? Might he do something in the store he's robbing that will help a detective find him?
Joan:	The other night on television a robber had wet shoes and left puddles in the store. That's how come he was caught.
Teacher:	What do we call something like puddles—or maybe fingerprints? What do you call what a detective uses to catch a thief?
Peter:	I know. They're clues. He uses clues.
Teacher:	Good for you. Has anyone else heard the word "clue" before?
Michael:	I have. I have a detective game at home.
Teacher:	Good detectives know how to use clues, don't they?
Maria:	They use them to find people who kill people, too.
Teacher:	Yes, they do. Today I want to find out if *you* are good detectives. I'm going to give you a clue by saying something. I won't say everything, though. I'll leave out a word at the end; but if you listen, you'll be able to tell me the word I'm thinking of but don't say. Listen now. See if you can tell me the word at the end that I don't say. In our room, we have fifteen girls and only nine—who can finish it?
Group:	Boys!
Teacher:	Say, you really *are* good detectives. You certainly know how to use clues. I'll have to make it a little harder. This time if you think you know the word I don't say, raise your hand. Here goes. When we draw pictures, we use crayons or _____.

Correctly, the kindergarten teacher referred to above started with brief sentences that had familiar content. She used "clue" rather than "cue" because the former word has meaning for children. She also provided maximum contextual help by omitting a word at the end of the sentences.

On another day, both to shift the position of the omitted word and to vary how a discussion is carried on, the same teacher might deal with contextual cues by commenting as follows:

> Sometimes, parents know so much about us that it seems they know what we're thinking even before we say it. They can almost read our minds, can't they? Let's see whether you can read *my* mind. I'll say something, but I'll leave out one word. I'll think of the word but won't say it. When I come to the word that I'm thinking of, I'll raise my hand. Every Monday morning at ten, Mrs. _____ comes to our room for art. What word did I leave out?

To provide still more variety, pictures can be used. In this case, pictures easily seen are placed on a chalkboard ledge or mounted on chart paper and numbered. In the first instance, children point to a picture and name it as a way of completing a sentence spoken by the teacher. In the second case—and this procedure moves more briskly—a child names the number of the picture, then names the picture itself.

Samples of spoken sentences that a teacher might use in conjunction with pictures are listed below.

1. To keep us dry, we can carry an _____. (picture of an umbrella)
2. My favorite pet is a _____. (pictures of a dog, a cat, and a bird)
3. The children in the park are _____. (picture of children on swings)

The last two sentences allow for calling attention to the guideline used for evaluating children's responses: Any response is acceptable as long as it is syntactically and semantically consistent with the rest of the context. In the third example above, acceptable responses include "swinging," "having fun," and "playing."

Another way to use spoken contexts is described by a kindergarten teacher in Figure 7.1. Her report illustrates a reflective teacher.

Even though this section highlights early use of contextual cues with spoken language, the fact that most kindergartners can read some words should not be overlooked. After all, even limited reading vocabularies are sufficient to make available to children opportunities to arrange words in a meaningful order. Known words can be printed on small cards so children can put them together—perhaps on the floor—in ways that convey meaning:

Recently, I have been working with rhymes. This morning I decided to extend their use to give attention to spoken contexts. Using spoken contexts was not something I had done before.

After quickly reviewing what rhymes are, I talked about the meaning of "riddle." I explained that a riddle is like a mystery because one can find the answer by paying attention to all the clues. I next told the group that I was going to say some riddles, all of which were about animals they knew. I reminded them that in order to answer a riddle, they needed to listen carefully to all the clues.

Because the children like cats, I began with the following:

> Soft paws.
> Sharp claws.
> Thick fur.
> Loud purr.
> What is that?
> Yes, a…

It became clear almost immediately that I had forgotten to remind the children that everyone must wait with their answer until I got to the end of the riddle. That there was no need to shout out answers had to be discussed, too. Once we talked about appropriate behavior, five more riddles were used. (I learned that by lowering my voice, the children quickly followed suit.)

The chapter on contextual cues motivated me to experiment with the activity just described. It does make sense to provide practice with spoken contexts before children are doing much reading.

After reflecting on what I had done, I thought of several ways in which it could have been done better. Although I did talk about the meaning of "rhyme" and "riddle," I failed to write the words on the board. By writing one directly under the other, I could have highlighted the similarity at the beginning of the words.

The next time I do this, I think I will add a labeled picture of an animal, following each solved riddle. Exposing the children to the words may be enough for some to remember them. In addition, the labeled pictures might provide a starting point for the children's own writing.

FIGURE 7.1   A Kindergarten Teacher's Use of Spoken Contexts

SPOKEN CONTEXTS AND MINIMAL GRAPHOPHONIC CUES

To change the use of spoken contexts into a procedure that is more like reading, teachers combine spoken contexts with minimal graphophonic cues as soon as it is possible to do so. (Graphophonic cues, as you recall, are the prompts found in the spellings of words that help readers arrive at their pronunciations. "Minimal graphophonic cues" refers to the use of an initial consonant letter—along with a spoken context—to suggest a word that starts with that letter.) Now, the constraints placed on an unspoken word come from two sources: (a) the words that make up the context, and (b) the sound suggested by a letter.

One teacher's early use of spoken contexts plus minimal graphophonic cues is portrayed below. She confines the discussion to the letter *t*. Later, a variety of consonant letters can be used.

Teacher: [Holds up card showing *t*.] We've just been talking about the sound that goes with this letter. Again, tell me some words that begin with that sound.

Danny: *Tell* starts with it.

Kim: So does *two* and *ten* and *tall*.

Teacher: Well, you certainly know lots of words that begin with the sound that goes with *t*. I wonder, though, if you can think of one certain word that starts with *t*. I'll think of it but won't say it. See if you can tell me what it is. Listen. Right now we have two pets in our room. One is a _____. Which of our pets am I thinking of?... How did you know I was thinking of the turtle?... Why did you know I *wasn't* thinking of the gerbil? What if we had a tiger for a pet? Might I have been thinking of that?

Letter cards similar to the one for *t* can also be used with riddles: "Who can think of something that starts with this letter—think of its sound—and that we wear on our hands?" Because some children remember words with minimal amounts of practice, it is sometimes advisable to print on the board whatever words are suggested by contextual cues and an initial letter—*mittens,* for example. ("Sometimes" is added to remake the point that nothing is so desirable that it should be done all the time.) Teachers may be pleasantly surprised at the number of words children remember as a result of casual but meaningful opportunities to see what specified words look like.

Letting children see the words they name allowed one teacher to deal with an unexpected response in very appropriate ways. At the time, she was using the unfinished spoken sentence "My little kitten is _____," plus a card displaying *s*. The first three responses from the children were "soft," "silky," and "sick." The next was "for sale," spoken by a child who, as speakers do, gave considerably less stress to "for" than to "sale." Visibly surprised at first, the teacher quickly recovered and turned to the chalkboard. After she printed *for sale,* the board displayed:

soft   for sale
silky
sick

While pointing to *sale,* the teacher said to the child, "Yes, 'sale' does begin with *s* and it does make sense to say—although I'll never sell her—'My little kitten is for sale'."

Erasing all the words, the teacher next wrote and read *For Sale.* She continued: "I wrote Timmy's answer again—these two words say "For Sale"—because sometime you'll see these two words on a sign in front of a house. If you're outside and see these words on a sign, what will they tell you?" Once the informative digression ended, the teacher and children returned to finishing unspoken sentences with words starting with a specified letter.

I chose to describe this teacher not only because she was using spoken contexts and minimal graphophonic cues but also because she was wise enough both to show the word-by-word connection between spoken and written language and to call attention to environmental text. She thus illustrated what is referred to in Chapter 2 as "unplanned, intentional instruction."

WRITTEN CONTEXTS: A STRATEGY FOR READERS

Work done with unfinished spoken sentences, plus a letter, does relate to reading but in a limited way. Admittedly, when teachers write the children's responses to verify that their suggestions begin with the designated letter, the connection is enlarged somewhat. Nonetheless, students need to be shown as soon as possible, and in explicit ways, the role that written contexts play in providing readers with a strategy for recognizing words that are visually unfamiliar.

Written Contexts: Instruction

Some teachers initiate attention to the use of written contexts when students misread a word or simply do not know the word. Others start in a way that is illustrated below. The teacher is speaking to an instructional group:

> We all know that when people read, they sometimes come across words they don't know or have forgotten. There are a couple of ways in which readers can help themselves whenever that happens. I want to talk now about one way. It's as simple as using the words you can read to help you with the ones you can't read. To demonstrate how this works, I'm going to show you a sentence on this card. [*The boy almost _____ on the bone.*] Let's pretend that a word you can't read is where the blank is. Since you know the other words, let's read them together. Clap when you get to the blank, and then read the rest of the sentence.

In this case, one student immediately volunteers, "I know what the word is. It's 'choked' because once I almost choked on some fish bones." In response the teacher says, "That's just the word I wrote on this card. Everyone, please look at this word. What is it?"

Once *choked* is read by all, the teacher prints it in the blank and asks the group to reread the sentence. She then continues:

> Travis suspected the missing word was "choked" for two reasons. To begin, the words I wrote suggested it might be "choked" because it makes sense to say that a

person almost choked on a bone. For Travis, the right word came to mind quickly because he remembered when he himself almost choked. So he did what we all should do when we come across a word we don't know: Read the words you *can* read to see whether they remind you of anything you know. Let's try more sentences. By the way, can anyone think of a word besides "choke" that also makes sense in this sentence?

When one student offers "coughed," the teacher rereads the sentence on the card, replacing "choked" with "coughed." Then she comments:

A bone certainly might make a boy—or anyone—cough, but I think if it did, we'd say something like "The bone got stuck in the boy's mouth and made him cough." I don't think we'd say that he coughed *on* the bone. I believe "choked" is about the only word that fits where this blank is—although, come to think of it, a word like "gagged" fits, too. *I* usually say that somebody choked on a bone, but "gagged" makes sense, too.

The teacher continues with additional sentences—they are also printed on cards to keep things moving—in order to reinforce that decisions about the word that fits in a blank are helped by reading all the other words and thinking about their collective meaning. The last two sentences are from the basal reader selection that the group will read next. Naming the source is something this teacher makes sure she does, because it clarifies the usefulness for reading of what is being done.

Written Contexts: Practice

Opportunities for practice in using contexts are available whenever students read connected text. Some teachers like to use written practice, which can take a variety of forms, all calling for writing words in blanks:

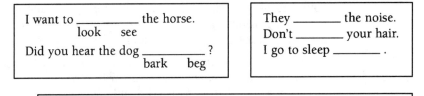

With written practice like that shown above, it is important for teachers to keep two points in mind. First and foremost, *be sure students understand that a blank space is presumed to be a word that is visually unfamiliar and that the purpose of the practice is to show how words that are known in their written form often help readers with others that are not.* Second, allow time whenever possible for students to explain how they decided on the word to put in a blank. Discussions are helpful because they give teachers the chance to examine the thought processes students are using. In addition, the thoughts described by one student may help others. Even thoughts that lead a student astray can be enlightening.

Written Contexts: More Advanced Practice

Filling in blanks with words that are acceptable syntactically and semantically is something you probably experienced in taking comprehension tests. It is usually referred to as the *cloze* procedure. *Cloze* comes from the word *closure,* a term associated with Gestalt psychologists, who maintain that human behavior is motivated by the need for wholeness or completeness.

The relevant point now is that cloze procedures can be used not only to assess comprehension but also to provide practice in using contextual cues. Specifically, if students will be reading an expository selection about how birds keep warm in the winter, they can be asked to fill in the blanks in a paragraph like the one below after the reading is done. In this case, an added bonus is practice with new words in the selection.

If you live where it's cold, you won't see many _____ in winter. Most _____ south. The ones who stay have ways to keep _____. To begin, birds can lower their body _____. This _____ the amount of heat they need to stay _____. Birds also _____ to make more heat in their bodies. To save the heat they have, they grow more _____. The ones that really keep them warm are called _____. To _____ themselves from the cold _____, they _____ on the inside branches of _____ trees. That is why you don't _____ many birds during the _____.

Once students begin to receive instruction about grammar, cloze exercises can focus on whatever part of speech is being taught. Sentences like the following, for example, highlight nouns:

The _____ in the _____ will soon arrive.
These old _____ aren't of _____ anymore.
Chuck and his _____ went _____ early.

Written Contexts: Concluding Comments

While observing in a classroom recently, I had the opportunity to ask three third-graders what they were doing in their workbooks. (They were filling in blanks in sentences with words that were listed at the top of the page.) None was able to offer any better explanation than "Writing words." Asking "*Why* are you writing words?" resulted in silence. This experience suggests the need to reinforce some points made earlier.

First, as soon as written contexts are used, students should be helped to understand that blanks in sentences symbolize unknown words. Second, how words they know help in coping with words they do not know should be clarified. To do this, students should have the chance to explain why they wrote (or chose) the words they did. Finally, as often as possible, attention to contextual cues should use text taken from selections that students have read or will read. That a given selection *is* the source of the text should be made clear. This is helpful in specifying the connection between (a) what is being taught and practiced, and (b) how to be a better reader.

A report by a second-grade teacher who followed the guidelines just outlined appears in Figure 7.2.

In my first entry, I explained that I listen to children read individually in a private area of the room as often as I can. When doing this recently, I noticed that many of them were stopping when they came to an unknown word and immediately began using phonics rather than reading the rest of the sentence first. Failure to read to the end of the sentence indicates they are not using contextual cues. I would not be overly concerned if their decoding skills were fast and efficient; but the majority of children are slow at decoding and, as a consequence, have comprehension problems. Following is a discussion of a lesson designed to help certain students become aware of the help that contextual cues give, and to provide practice.

Sentences written on strips were prepared ahead of time. Each had a blank where a word was omitted. The sentence offered both syntactic and semantic cues. I put many of the blanks near the beginning of the sentence so that I could stress the importance of reading the latter part of the sentence to find help. When I introduced the lesson to children identified as needing help, I did not use the words "syntactic" and "semantic" because, as pointed out in class, terms like these can be confusing. Nor did I use words like "noun" or "verb" because these children do not have adequate understanding of the parts of speech. Instead, I simply explained that the words near an unknown word often give clues about the unknown word, and all good detectives use them.

The sentence strips were placed in a word chart, one at a time. As suggested in class, this procedure maximizes attention to whatever requires attention. The children were directed to read a sentence silently and to think of a word that made sense in the blank. All answers that made sense were accepted. I then pointed out that when reading, unknown words are like the blanks and the sentence can give clues about what that word may be.

To provide additional practice, the children played a board game that required them to draw a card showing an incomplete sentence. If the child named a word that made sense, he moved the number of spaces rolled on the dice. The first one to the finish line won. The children seemed to enjoy the game.

The main benefit I derived from our class discussion of contextual cues was a realization of the importance of explaining and showing children the relationship between instruction and use of what they are learning when they are reading. In other words, children should realize that all practice is a means to an end.

FIGURE 7.2   Making Connections between Practice and Reading

WRITTEN CONTEXTS AND GRAPHOPHONIC CUES

If texts were always composed so that contextual cues could be counted on to suggest any word that is unknown, graphophonic cues would be relatively unimportant. This hardly is the case, however. Even when text *is* generous with contextual help, the number of unknown words may be sufficiently large as to obscure it. This indicates that not too much time should be spent on working with written contexts before graphophonic cues are added.

If students are as yet unable to decode the whole of words, partial spellings can be used. When they are, the text in which they appear needs to be sufficiently helpful to make the partial spellings sufficient. As was the case when spoken contexts were the concern, minimal graphophonic cues—now used with written contexts—are considered initially.

Written Contexts and Minimal Graphophonic Cues

To show students, first, how contextual cues suggest possibilities when a word is unknown and, second, how graphophonic cues restrict those possibilities are the two objectives of concern now. Both enter directly into the work of one teacher, which is described next.

I've written a sentence on the board and, as you can see, one word is missing. [*On Saturday we're going to* _____ *our car.*] Who wants to say what the missing word might be?... Okay. Josh thinks it's "sell." Does anyone think it might be something else?... There have been four more very good suggestions. "Buy," "trade," "wash," and "clean" are all acceptable because they make sense. However, the letter with which the missing word begins is on the back of this card. What letter is this?... Since it's *s*, what is the missing word?... Yes, of the words named, only "sell" starts with *s*.

To discourage her students from concluding that one letter is enough to decide what a word is, the teacher now adds *w* to the sentence on the board:

On Saturday we're going to w_____ our car.

The teacher continues:

Because I added *w*, I bet you're all thinking "wash." Right?... I thought so. Let me show you what the word *really* is.

The teacher now adds *a* and *x* after *w* and continues the discussion:

Now that I've written the whole word, you know the plans are to wax, not wash, the car. I did this to show you that one letter may not be enough to tell you what a word is. You usually have to use more than one. In fact, sometimes all the letters have to be used. That's why I'm helping you learn about letters and the sounds they stand for.

At another time, the same teacher may choose to give attention to the value of minimal graphophonic cues (plus contexts) when she is helping students learn new words in a basal selection about to be assigned. For illustrative purposes, the ensuing modeling by the teacher covers just two words, *forest* and *roar*. (You can recall from Chapter 2 that modeling by a teacher is displaying, or thinking aloud, processes that can be used to solve a problem or reach a goal.) Sentences taken from the basal selection are on the board. The fact that they are in the selection is made clear.

> All the animals lived in a f_____.
> The lion said, "I will r_____ so loud all will hear me."

The teacher begins:

As I said earlier, the story you'll be reading is about animals. I think you'll know all the animal names—like "lion," for instance—but you might not be able to read some other words. Let me tell you how I'd go about figuring them out if I didn't know them. I'll start with this first sentence. It's in the story. The word I don't know starts with *f*. This is the way I'd think. First I'd read the words I know. "All the animals lived in a." Oh, it's probably "forest." All the animals lived in a forest. That makes sense. They also live in jungles and zoos but neither of those words start with *f*. Now I'll do the next sentence. It's in the story, too. "The lion said, 'I will (blank) so loud all will hear me'." It could be "yell" because yelling is noisy, but "yell" doesn't begin with *r*. Let's see. What do lions do that's loud and starts with *r*? Oh, sure. Roar. Lions roar. "The lion said, 'I will roar so loud all will hear me'."

Written Contexts and Additional Graphophonic Cues

The teacher referred to next is reminding students about the common need to rely on more than an initial letter (plus the context) to decide what a word is. The following sentence is on the chalkboard:

> The water was d_____.

The teacher starts:

"We've been talking about the fact that by using words we know and the sound that a beginning letter stands for, we can sometimes decide what a new word is. With this sentence on the board, we're going to pretend it ends with a word we don't know. As you can see, the word starts with *d*. It's a word that tells about the water. What do you suppose it is if it begins with *d*?" [Given the purpose of the lesson—to demonstrate the need to rely on more than the first letter—the teacher has in mind a number of suitable words starting with *d*.] The first volunteer suggests "dirty." "Yes," responds the teacher, "we've all seen dirty water, but the word in the sentence ends with *k*. [Adds *k* at the end.] If the word starts with *d* and ends in *k*, can it be 'dirty'?" Although the children agree it cannot, none is able to think of a word that starts with *d*, ends with *k*, and makes sense. Consequently, the teacher adds a sentence to the board:

> There were no lights. The water was d_____k.

Several children simultaneously call out "dark." This is followed by a discussion of the fact that help for a word can often be found in other sentences and that such help, plus some of the letters in the unknown word, are sometimes sufficient for deciding what the word is.

Other sentences useful for the same purpose are shown below. The third piece of text is used if the initial and final letters are insufficient to suggest "bank."

1. They got into the b_____ and left fast.
2. They got into the b_____k and left fast.
3. The robbers came at about six o'clock.
   They got into the b_____k and left fast.

Written Contexts and Initial Syllables

Words are decoded syllable by syllable. That is why single-syllable words have been featured in illustrative lessons (e.g., *sell, wash, wax, dark, bank*). Once students (a) know that decoding focuses on syllables and (b) have the ability to blend sounds to produce syllables, attention to contextual and graphophonic cues can focus on the helpfulness of an initial syllable in deciding what an unknown word is. (How to divide unknown words into syllables is explained in the next chapter.) Just how helpful initial syllables are is demonstrated in the following text.

You can use a pen or pen_____. Don't hur_____ with your work. Turn in a good pa_____. In fact, make it ex_____ good today.,

Why the use of initial syllables is featured has to do with an important fact: *The faster an unknown word is recognized, the less is it likely to disrupt comprehension* (1). Admittedly, knowing the initial syllable in an unfamiliar word is not always sufficient to infer what the word is even when contextual cues are also considered. Nevertheless, they are helpful often enough to warrant attention.

A lesson in which a teacher is focusing on the use of contexts and initial syllables might proceed as follows. In this case, the instruction starts after the teacher has demonstrated procedures for using the complete spelling of *cactus* to arrive at its pronunciation.

Teacher: It took a fair amount of time to get *cactus* figured out, and that's okay if it's necessary. However, if *cactus* is in a story that takes place in a desert, you might not need to work on it all, letter by letter and sound by sound. Let's say, for instance, that a sentence in the story is "I only saw one cactus plant." Now, knowing how the first syllable is pronounced might be enough to suggest the word is "cactus," especially since it's followed by the word "plant." After all, in a desert the most common plant is a cactus. I've written some sentences on these cards. They're in the next story you'll be reading, so let's see if you can figure out some of the new words if I just write the first syllable. Again, be sure to read all the words in the sentence before you decide what the word is when I write its first syllable. And don't forget to use what you know. Remember that it was knowing about plants in deserts that helped with "cactus."

Some of the new words in the basal story (*silver, mountain, escape, tiny*), placed in the sentences in which they occur but with only their initial syllables printed, are:

The spider spun a sil_____ web.
It's on the other side of the moun_____.
They tried to es_____ by running.
All they needed was a ti_____ bit of sun.

The teacher shows the first sentence card [*The spider spun a sil_____ web.*] and says:

Teacher: Please read this sentence to yourselves. Who can pronounce the first syllable in the word that goes here [points to *sil_____*]?

Michael: I know what the whole word is. It's "silly."

Teacher: "Silly" *does* begin with *s, i, l*. Michael, how do you pronounce a syllable spelled *s, i, l*?

Michael: "Sil."

Teacher: That's correct. One vowel but not at the end. "Sil" *is* the first syllable in this word, and "silly" starts with that syllable. "The spider spun a silly web." Does everyone think "silly" is the word that tells about the web?

Mary Pat: I'm not sure "silly" makes sense. At least *I* don't think webs are silly looking.

Adam: I was thinking of "silver." I usually think of webs as being white, but silver is really a better way to talk about the color.

Teacher: Any other thoughts about this word?... None? I'll finish printing the word, as both "silly" and "silver" describe something and both start with the syllable "sil." [Adds *ver.*]

Adam: I thought I might be right.

Teacher: Michael pronounced the first syllable correctly but, usually, spider webs are quite beautiful and perfect, especially when you remember how quickly they're made. Let's all take a look at the word. What is it?

Group: Silver.

Teacher: Please read the whole sentence together, because it's one you'll see when you read the story later.

Group: The spider spun a silver web.

Teacher: Here's another sentence you'll find. Again, I only printed the first syllable of the new word. [Shows card that displays *It's on the other side of the moun_____.*] Please read this sentence to yourselves to see what the last word might be.

Adam: I think I know this word, too. It's "mountain."

Teacher: Pronounce *m, o, u, n* for us, Adam.

Adam: Moun.

Teacher: Correct. "Mountain" begins that way, and it makes sense to say that something is on the other side of the mountain. How about another word that makes sense and starts with the syllable "moun?" Any suggestions?... The only other word that *I* can think of that starts this way and has more than one syllable is "mounted," as in "They mounted the horses." But that certainly doesn't make any sense here. I'll finish printing this new word. [Adds *t, a, i, n.*]

Adam: I'm right again!

Teacher:	Yes, Adam. You've been correct twice because you thought of the pronunciation of the first syllable and then of a word that starts that way that makes sense in the sentence. That's what everybody should do when they come across a new word. If it has more than one syllable, think about the pronunciation of the first syllable and then think of a word you know that starts that way and fits with all the other words. Let's take another look at this new word. [Points to *mountain.*] Tracy, you don't seem to be looking where I'm pointing. Everybody, what is this word?
Group:	Mountain.
Teacher:	Please read the sentence together.
Group:	It's on the other side of the mountain.
Teacher:	You'll have to read the story to find out what it is that's on the other side of the mountain.
Tracy:	I bet it's a wild animal or something like that.
Teacher:	You'll just have to wait to find out, Tracy. By the way, Tracy, what is this word? [Points to *mountain.*]
Tracy:	Mountain.
Teacher:	Good. Okay, everybody, please read this sentence again.
Group:	It's on the other side of the mountain.

Using the same procedures, the teacher attends to *escape* and *tiny*.

Written Contexts and Graphophonic Cues: Concluding Comments

The underlying theme of this section of the chapter is *balance*. The specific theme is the value of using in a balanced way both contextual and graphophonic cues to help with words that are visually unfamiliar. Stanovich makes the same point when he states that "contextual and graphophonic information should be used in an integrated manner" (5, p. 369).

Because reading is a sense-making process, "What makes sense?" is a question of central importance when contextual and graphophonic cues are used. In fact, "What word would make sense here?" is the first question a reader needs to consider when encountering a new word. After a decision is made about the word, the question is altered to ask, "Does *this* word make sense here?"

Even though graphophonic cues are the subject of the next chapter, they are considered now because using them in conjunction with contextual cues reduces the time it takes to recognize a word. As explained, speed is important because the more time spent on a word, the more likely will the pause interfere with comprehension.

How the present chapter went about covering contexts is summarized in Figure 7.3.

WRITTEN CONTEXTS, NEW VOCABULARY, AND INDEPENDENT READING

Like all the chapters that make up Part III, an underlying concern of the present one is the alternative proposed earlier for round robin reading: well-prepared, uninter-

Spoken Context
1. Spoken sentence with omitted word at the end.
2. Spoken sentence with omitted word anyplace in the context.

Spoken Context and Minimal Graphophonic Cues
3. Spoken sentence with omitted word whose beginning letter is named or shown.

Written Context
4. Written sentence with omitted word. Children select suitable word from listed possibilities.
5. Written sentence with omitted word. children fill in the blank with a suitable word.

Written Context and partial Graphophonic Cues
6. Written sentence with initial letter of target word supplied.
7. Written sentence with initial and final letters of target word supplied.
8. Written sentence with first syllable of target word supplied.

FIGURE 7.3   Progression in Using Contextual Cues

rupted silent reading of appropriately difficult text. Like the other chapters, Chapter 7 has something to say about preparations having to do with words in the text thought to be new. (Please return to the Preview for Chapter 6 to take another look at the three components of prereading preparations.)

The previous chapter is concerned with new words that are taught with whole word instruction. That chapter recommends that if the words are excessive in number, those most important for understanding the text should be selected for prereading help.

The present chapter identifies another way for teachers to reduce the number of words requiring attention: If any of the new words appear *initially* in a selection in helpful contexts, do not preteach them. Instead, give students the opportunity to use what they have been learning about contextual help. Once the selection has been read, time should be taken to see whether the students were in fact able to use the help provided by known words. Whenever possible, they should also be encouraged to tell how they went about reaching conclusions about the words.

Teachers who follow these recommendations not only show students the value of what they have been learning but also add to their ability to deal with unfamiliar words on their own.

MORE EXTENSIVE CONTEXTS

Thus far, "context" has been confined to limited amounts of text—in some instances, to just a few words. This should not obscure the fact that larger pieces of discourse are contexts, which also offer readers help with new or forgotten words. A story, for instance, usually takes place in a certain setting and has particular kinds of characters, both of which may allow readers to anticipate certain words. By anticipating them, readers are in a better position to recognize them. Knowing this, teachers may at times choose to raise questions before a story is read not only to cover background information but also to call attention to words that may or may not be in the students' reading vocabularies.

Let's take a story about hiking in the mountains to show how this might be done. To prepare students who live far from mountains to read the story, a teacher can begin by saying: "Because the story you'll be reading next is about a boy who took a three-day hike in the mountains with his dad, I was wondering whether any of you have done that or have seen mountain hikers on TV or in a movie." This introductory comment could lead to a discussion that reveals the need to clarify the difference between a hazardous type of mountain climbing and the recreational activity of hiking in the mountains. As soon as it seems timely to do so, the discussion might be structured with questions designed to highlight certain words. Two sample questions and the vocabulary in the story that prompted them are listed below:

> In the city, we usually walk on sidewalks. Where do people walk when they are in the mountains or the woods? (*trail*)

> Because the two people you'll be reading about spend two nights where there are no hotels or motels, what will they have to have? (*tent, sleeping bag, flashlight, fire*)

Teachers who pose questions to call attention to certain words and who keep that purpose in mind accept reasonable answers but also make sure that preselected words are eventually mentioned even if they themselves have to name them. To illustrate, if the first question listed above brings responses like "on a dirt road" and "on a path," both are accepted. Afterward, a teacher can add, "The word the author of the story uses is 'trail' [which is written on the board]. The author talks about the boy and his dad following a trail, which, of course, is a path. What is this word on the board?"

Attending to vocabulary in the way just described should not be done all the time. Nor is the procedure sufficient to put words into students' sight vocabularies; practice is required for that. Even so, it does allow for meaningful attention to new words and for establishing an appropriate mental set for the reading about to be done.

SUMMARY

Accomplished readers have learned how to resolve the various kinds of problems they encounter in their efforts to construct the meaning of text. As other authors have said, proficient readers know "how to think their way through a problem situation..." (2, p. 417). That is, they need to become strategic readers who have plans for coping with problems (4). The "plan" that Chapter 7 dealt with was: Use words you can read to help recognize others that are visually unfamiliar.

As Chapter 7 showed, using known words to prompt thoughts about other words can get started before children are able to do any reading. This possibility was discussed under the heading "Spoken Contexts." Because it is now common for young children to know some consonant sounds, using spoken contexts, plus letter-sound relationships, was explained and illustrated, too.

Soon, Chapter 7 shifted the focus to written contexts, as they are directly pertinent for readers. The fact that the known words that bring written contexts into existence help in two different ways was clarified. This called for a discussion of syntactic cues and semantic cues. Although the help that the former provide is confined to a sentence, the latter are not similarly restricted.

Even though syntactic and semantic cues were discussed in separate sections of the chapter, readers use the two jointly. In fact, superior readers use the two kinds of cues not only together but also so automatically that they are not even aware—most of the time—of relying on this help.

Calling attention to contextual cues makes sense for students when they have the opportunity to experience their helpfulness with new or forgotten words. That is why the chapter's treatment of instruction with contextual cues was linked with something the students would soon be reading.

The usefulness of syntactic and semantic cues is the reason teachers should examine the contexts in which new words occur in text that will be assigned reading. As Chapter 7 explained, any such word that appears initially in a helpful context should not be among those that receive prereading attention. Adherence to this guideline not only reduces the number of new words requiring attention, it also allows students to appreciate the value of what they have been learning about contextual help. In the end, experiences like this help students move toward becoming strategic readers.

REVIEW

1. Using the following as prompts in the order indicated, construct a brief summary of Chapter 7.
   a. contextual cues
   b. word recognition
   c. syntactic cues
   d. positional language
   e. semantic cues
   f. modeling
   g. strategic reading
   h. alternative to round robin reading

2. To achieve a more specific review of the content of Chapter 7, fill in the blanks below.
   English is a (a) _____ language in which word order is critical for determining (b) _____ . The arrangement of words that makes up a sentence is referred to as its (c) _____ ; consequently, when the position of an unknown word in a sentence helps to recognize it, that help is called a (d) ____ cue. Syntactic cues offer assistance by establishing the (e) _____ (f) ____ of an unknown word. For instance, in the sentence "Many ____ were in the room," syntax signals that the omitted word is a (g) ____ (h) ____ functioning as the subject of the sentence.

Just as language as a whole makes sense, so, too, do individual phrases and sentences. The sense, or meaning, communicated by phrases and sentences offers a second type of contextual help. Because it has to do with meaning, it is called a (i) _____ cue. The sentence "Many _____ were in the room" provides minimal semantic help; one like "The swing went up and _____ " provides (j) _____ semantic help.

Because the (k) _____ use of syntactic and semantic cues often provides considerable assistance with new or forgotten words, students should be encouraged to think about them whenever they have a problem with a word. Sometimes—as in "The swing went up and _____ "—contextual cues will provide so much help that just about all words except one can be (l) _____ from consideration. Most of the time, however, contextual cues will have to be used in conjunction with the help that derives from the (m) _____ of the unknown word. That is why beginning instruction in (n) _____ goes along with early work with contexts.

3. Four points about contextual cues were made at the start of Chapter 7:
   a. The availability of contextual cues is affected by the reader's world knowledge.
   b. Contextual cues help only with words that are in the reader's oral vocabulary.
   c. The use of contextual cues allows for word recognition, not word identification.
   d. Contexts exist only when an individual can read most of the words in a selection.

   Explain the meaning of each statement. Include examples in your explanations that are different from any in Chapter 7.

4. Chapter 7 stated and restated that students should understand what blanks in text symbolize whenever blanks are used in work done with contextual cues.
   a. What *do* the blanks symbolize?
   b. Why is it essential for students to know what they represent?

5. In the illustrations it provided, how did Chapter 7 adhere to the advice: Do not teach anything unless and until it is useful?

REFERENCES

1. Adams, Marilyn J., and Huggins, A. W. F. "The Growth of Children's Sight Vocabulary: A Quick Test with Educational and Theoretical Implications." *Reading Research Quarterly* 20 (Spring, 1985), 262–281.
2. Duffy, Gerald G., and Roehler, Laura R. "Teaching Reading Skills as Strategies." *Reading Teacher* 40 (January, 1987), 414–418.
3. Durkin, Dolores. *Strategies for Identifying Words* (2nd ed.). Boston: Allyn and Bacon, 1981.
4. Paris, Scott; Lipson, Marge; and Wixson, Karen. "Becoming a Strategic Reader." *Contemporary Educational Psychology* 8 (July, 1983), 293–316.
5. Stanovich, Keith. "Matthew Effects in Reading: Some Consequences of Individual Differences in the Acquisition of Literacy." *Reading Research Quarterly* 21 (Fall, 1986), 360–406.

Graphophonic Cues: Content

Anyone who looked at the Table of Contents for this book may have wondered why two chapters deal with graphophonic cues whereas contextual and structural cues are each covered with one. Two facts account for the two-chapter coverage.

The first is that some teachers have inadequate knowledge of what is commonly referred to as "phonics." Admittedly, sufficient knowledge is no guarantee that phonics will be taught in ways that make it useful. Still, it would be difficult to believe that insufficiently knowledgeable teachers and effective instruction go together.

The second fact has to do with commercial materials, which are more plentiful for phonics than for any other part of an instructional program. The relevant point now is their flaws. Even in newer materials, shortcomings include incorrect use of terms, misinformation, and instruction that bears little or no relationship to the texts students are reading (3). In and of themselves, such flaws are regrettable. The fact that some teachers use the commercial materials makes them even more regrettable. With all this in mind, the goal of Chapter 8 is to help teachers and prospective teachers acquire enough knowledge so they can replace suggestions in flawed materials with better instruction.

Persons already knowledgeable about subject matter for phonics instruction may wish to skim Chapter 8 as a review. Others who know less and want to learn more should allow time to *study* the chapter. To assist with this, Chapter 8 does several things. To begin, it moves at a pace slow enough to accommodate anyone whose knowledge of phonics is fairly limited. To avoid making the content overly dense, whatever is discussed is complemented with illustrations. As in all the chapters, key terms appear in italic print and are defined. Sometimes, they are redefined later. Finally, once a topic is covered, you are referred to one or more related questions in the Review section of Chapter 8. This allows for self-testing and, perhaps, for the realization that one or more sections need to be reread.

Sometimes, individuals who know almost nothing about phonics experience frustration with Chapter 8, expressed with questions like, "If *I'm* having so much trouble learning all this, how can we expect kids to learn it?" Kids learn it not only because of effective instruction but also because they have the chance to learn the subject matter in Chapter 8 over several years. This allows for slow-paced instruction, review, and numerous opportunities to use what is taught. The moral of the story is that the amount of time and attention required for Chapter 8 depends on your prior knowledge of the topics covered.

• • • • • •

IT MIGHT BE HELPFUL TO BEGIN THIS CHAPTER with a few comments about phonics and the whole language philosophy. The need for comments at the start derives from widespread misunderstandings.

PHONICS AND WHOLE LANGUAGE

In an article entitled "Myths of Whole Language" (5), two Canadian educators closely associated with the whole language movement identify and discuss misconceptions that they have met "head on" in both Canada and the United States. The authors, Judith Newman and Susan Church, list *You don't teach phonics in whole language* as one misconception. (The "grand myth," they claim is: *There is one right way to do whole language.*)

Based on this article and on other writings by whole language proponents, the most important points to emphasize about phonics vis-à-vis whole language have already been made. For instance:

- Children's earliest experiences with reading in school should be with meaningful pieces of connected text, not with letter-sound relationships.
- Children of all ages should be helped to understand the value for reading of the information and strategies they are acquiring.
- Children should have prompt opportunities to use in their reading what they are learning.

To avoid dwelling on previously made recommendations, let me instead quote from the part of the Newman and Church article that deals with phonics:

> No one can read without taking into account the graphophonic cues of written language. As readers all of us use information about the way words are written to help us make sense of what we're reading. But these cues aren't the only cues readers use. We use a variety of other language cues: cues about meaning (semantic cues) and cues about the structure of a particular text passage (syntactic cues). We use pictorial cues when they're available, we bring our general knowledge about the subject into play, and we bring all our previous experiences with reading and writing to bear when we read. Whole language teachers do teach phonics but not as something separate from actual reading and writing. (5, pp. 20–21)

A message that permeates the previous chapter directly reflects the passage just quoted: In order to recognize as quickly as possible words that are visually unfamiliar, readers should use contextual and graphophonic cues together. This statement both identifies and implies common characteristics of the two kinds of cues. What they share is made explicit below.

Contextual and graphophonic cues:
- Are used as a strategy for recognizing words that are familiar orally but not visually.
- Are used in the framework of, What word makes sense?
- Are used to increase a reader's ability to cope with unknown words independently.

Even though a balanced use of contextual and graphophonic cues marks the behavior of accomplished readers, this chapter focuses on graphophonic cues only.

Its specific focus is the subject matter that should be taught to maximize students' abilities to use a word's spelling to arrive at its pronunciation. Spellings can serve this purpose because English has an alphabetic writing system.

ALPHABETIC WRITING

As explained in Chapter 5, letters stand for speech sounds in alphabetic writing. This accounts for the availability of graphophonic cues, which are prompts that readers use to move from spellings to pronunciations. The use of graphophonic cues is called *decoding*. A less common term is *deciphering*.

Regularly and Irregularly Spelled Words

If only because of the variation in the sounds that vowel letters represent, it cannot be said that words have a one-to-one correspondence between the letters that make up their spelling and the sounds that make up their pronunciation. It *can* be said, however, that many words *are* regularly spelled. As used here, a *regularly spelled word* is one whose pronunciation can be predicted from its spelling, because the spelling adheres to one or more patterns. (It is the patterns that are verbalized in the generalizations considered later.) Regularly spelled words include *me, met, meat, meet,* and *mete.* Examples of regularly spelled words composed of more than one syllable are *alto, mascot, candle, illustrate, volcano, imbue, hectic, torpedo,* and *vortex.* The generous number of regularly spelled words just cited is meant to raise a question about a suggestion commonly made by both manuals and teachers in third grade and beyond, when certain words in a selection are likely to be unfamiliar. I refer to the advice, "Look them up in the glossary (dictionary)." Admittedly, nobody supports teaching phonics forever. At the same time, to teach it and then not use what was taught is equally questionable.

Terminology for Letters and Sounds

Because the decoding process moves from letters to sounds, some terms needed to discuss decoding pertain to letters whereas the referents for others are speech sounds. Readers start with spellings; the discussion of terms, therefore, also begins with those pertaining to letters.

Letters.* Although the terms *consonant* and *vowel* are used by phoneticians to make distinctions among speech sounds, both terms are commonly used by the nonspecialist to refer to letters. The simplest way to identify the consonants is to say they are all the letters in the alphabet with the exception of *a, e, i, o,* and *u,* which are vowels. *Y* and *w* are unique; they function as both consonants and vowels.

The term *cluster* refers to certain consonants that often appear in succession in syllables. The consonants *s* and *t* in *sty,* for instance, are a cluster.

The word *sty* was chosen to illustrate a cluster in order to allow for a comparison of the terms *cluster* and *digraph.* A digraph is a pair of letters—in this case, two

---

* Because of the influence of linguistics on phonics instruction during the last 1960s and into the 1970s, letters are sometimes referred to as *graphemes* (grăˊ-fēmə). The same influence accounts for the use of *phonemes* (fōˊ nēmə) for speech sounds.

consonants *or* two vowels—that stands for one sound. The word *shy,* therefore, has two sounds; the word *sty,* three sounds. The important message for decoders is this: Deal with a digraph as a unit—that is, as if the pair of letters were one letter. This is not the case with clusters; each letter in the pair stands for one sound.

Figure 8.1 can help you contrast clusters and digraphs. In Figure 8.1, *y* and *w* are part of four vowel digraphs: *ew, aw, ow,* and *oy.*

Phonogram also refers to letters. (The term *graphemic base* may be used, too.) In this case, the referent is a series of letters, starting with a vowel, that appears at the end of syllables and words. Examples of phonograms are *-ight, -ug, -ell,* and *-ack.* Some phonograms are words in themselves—for instance, *-ill, -all, -in,* and *-at.*

To sum up, then, *consonant, vowel, cluster, digraph,* and *phonogram* all refer to letters. Terms that refer to speech sounds are considered next.

Sounds.   Because syllables are central to the decoding process, they are defined first. A *syllable* is a vowel sound to which consonant sounds are commonly added. The nucleus of a syllable, therefore, is a vowel sound. That is why it is said that there are as many syllables in a word as there are vowel sounds.

Two descriptions used for vowel sounds are *long* and *short.* Below, the underlined letters in the words listed first stand for long sounds; those in the second column, for short sounds.

Words with Long Vowel Sounds	Words with Short Vowel Sounds
age	at
eat	end
ice	if
ode	odd
use	us
cool	cook

Clusters

bl	(blow)	fl	(fly)	sc	(score)	st	(storm)
br	(brag)	fr	(free)	sk	(sky)	sw	(swing)
cl	(clean)	gl	(globe)	sl	(sled)	tr	(trace)
cr	(crop)	gr	(grass)	sm	(smell)	tw	(twist)
dr	(drum)	pl	(plum)	sn	(snip)	scr	(script)
dw	(dwell)	pr	(pray)	sp	(space)	str	(straw)

Consonant Digraphs

sh	(she)	ph	(phone)
ch	(chill, chef)	ng	(sing)
th	(the, thin)	gh	(rough)

Vowel Digraphs

oo	(cool, cook)
ew	(crew)
aw, au	(auto, awl)
ou, ow	(out, owl)
oi, oy	(oil, oyster)

FIGURE 8.1   Some Terms for Letters

When vowel sounds are first taught, some teachers use diacritical marks to help children remember decisions that have been made about vowels. Marks indicating a long vowel sound, a short vowel sound, and a so-called silent vowel are shown below.

āg¢   ăt   cōol   cŏŏk

Any page in a dictionary shows how often the *schwa* sound—symbolized by /ə/—occurs in unstressed syllables. In the words below, each underscored letter stands for the schwa sound, which is similar to a de-emphasized short *u* sound:

ród<u>e</u>nt   <u>a</u>róm<u>a</u>   c<u>e</u>mént   <u>o</u>ffénse   ácc<u>i</u>d<u>e</u>nt

Two terms used to describe sounds that *c* and *g* stand for are *hard* and *soft*. The hard sounds occur initially in *cat* and *go*; the soft sounds, in *cent* and *gym*.

Voiced and *voiceless* consonant sounds are referred to now only to make the point that the digraph *th* stands for the voiced sound in *the* and the voiceless sound in *thin*. Unlike commercially prepared materials, teachers should not mix the two sounds when attention first goes to *th*. Initially, words like *the, there, them,* and *this* are suitable illustrations, first, because they start with the same (voiced) sound and, second, because they are common words.

Blend is another term that refers to speech sounds. As the word suggests, a blend is a synthesis of sounds. Clusters, you may remember, stand for blends of two sounds (e.g., /st/) or of three sounds (e.g., /spr/). The vowel digraphs *oi, oy, ou,* and *ow* each stand for a close blend of two sounds—so close, in fact, that each of the four should be taught as a digraph that represents one sound. The blend that each of these vowel digraphs records is called a *diphthong*. The reason for mentioning this now is that commercial materials sometimes use diphthong, almost always incorrectly (3).

Two consonant letters, *x* and *q*, also stand for blends. In a word such as *box*, the blend that *x* records is /ks/. In *exact*, *x* stands for /gz/. The letter *q*, as all "Scrabble" players know, is always followed by *u*. Students should be taught to think of *qu*, therefore, as if it were one letter—a consonant. The blend /kw/ is recorded by *qu* in a word such as *queen*.

To sum up, then, the following terms pertain to speech sounds: *syllable, long, short, schwa, hard, soft, blend,* and *diphthong*.

Review

This is a good time to review the terminology that has been defined, because subsequent parts of this chapter, and all of Chapter 9, assume the terms are familiar. Suggestions for review follow.

1. Reread what has been said in the chapter thus far.
2. Examine the definitions in Figure 8.2. (More terms are defined in Figure 8.2 than have been discussed.)
3. See whether you can define, and give illustrations of, the following terms: *blend, cluster, consonant, consonant digraph, hard sounds for c and g, long vowel*

Blend.   A synthesis of speech sounds. The two sounds recorded by *fr* in *free* are a blend.

Cluster.   Two or three consonants that occur as adjacent letters in syllables. Each stands for a sound. The letters *fr* in *free* are a cluster.

Consonant.   Refers to all the letters except *a, e, i, o,* and *u.* The letters *y* and *w* function as both consonants and vowels.

Digraph.   A pair of vowels or consonants that stands for a sound unlike the sound associated with either letter making up the pair. The letters *au* in *auto* are a digraph. The letters *th* in *bath* are also a digraph.

Diphthong.   A close blend of two vowel sounds. The letters *oi* in *oil* record a diphthong. The blend is so close that diphthongs are treated in phonics instruction as if the reference is to a single sound. *Oil,* therefore, is said to be composed of two sounds.

Grapheme.   A linguistic term for *letter.* Commercial materials waver between *grapheme* and *letter,* depending on what is perceived to be in current use.

Graphemic base.   A series of letters beginning with a vowel that often constitutes the final part of a syllable or word. In *tell* and *fell, -ell* is a graphemic base.

Hard sound.   Traditionally used in phonics to refer to the sounds recorded by *c* and *g* in *call* and *go.*

Long vowel sound.   The vowel sounds in *aim, eel, ice, old, use,* and *pool* are traditionally referred to in phonics as long.

Phoneme.   A linguistic term for speech sound.

Phonemic awareness.   Ability to hear that syllables and words are composed of blended phonemes.

Phonics.   A body of information about connections between letters and speech sounds designed to help readers figure out the pronunciation of words unknown in their written form.

Phonogram.   A series of letters beginning with a vowel that often constitutes the final part of a syllable or word. In *nine* and *fine, -ine* is a phonogram. Commercial materials use phonogram or graphemic base depending on what is perceived to be in current use.

Regularly spelled word.   One whose pronunciation can be predicted from generalizations taught in phonics.

Schwa sound.   An unstressed, deemphasized sound closely resembling the short sound for *u.* It appears commonly in unstressed syllables and is symbolized by /ə/.

Short vowel sound.   The vowel sounds in *at, end, if, odd, us,* and *book* are traditionally referred to in phonics as short.

FIGURE 8.2   Terms for Phonics Instruction

> **Soft sound.**   Traditionally used in phonics to refer to the sounds recorded by *c* and *g* in *cent* and *gem*.
>
> **Syllable.**   A vowel sound that is usually combined with one or more consonant sounds. The letters *pa* and *per* in *paper* both record syllables.
>
> **Vowel.**   Refers to the letters *a, e, i, o,* and *u.* The letter *w,* and more often the letter *y,* also function as vowels.

FIGURE 8.2   (cont.)

sounds, phonogram, schwa sound, short vowel sounds, soft sounds for c and g, syllable, vowel, vowel digraph.
4. Answer the Review questions 1 through 6 at the end of the chapter.

GENERALIZATIONS FOR DECODING

Even though the spelling and pronunciation of English words do not have a letter-by-letter, sound-by-sound correspondence, spellings and pronunciations do adhere to certain patterns. These patterns make it possible for readers to decode unfamiliar words.

The decoding that is the focus of this chapter concentrates on roots, specifically on the syllables that compose root words. In fact, all the generalizations stated in subsequent sections of the chapter assume the syllable to be the unit of pronunciation. That explains why the generalizations stated initially have as their objective the division of roots into syllables.

Whether the goal of a generalization is to help with syllabication or with the pronunciation of a syllable, each statement is about *visual cues*. Visual cues are letters and their sequence. In fact, this is what spelling patterns are: letters appearing in certain sequences in syllables. The spelling patterns of *me, met, meet, meat,* and *mete* make these words regularly spelled and readily decodable. As the five words suggest, the number and placement of vowels in a syllable are at the core of spelling patterns.

One final comment: Even though students have no need to state generalizations, teachers do. This requirement does not mean that each generalization must be stated in one certain way, although each statement must include essential details. Instead, the requirement is a recognition that teachers must be able to verbalize generalizations if they are to help students understand them. The essential ability for students, on the other hand, has to do with *using* generalizations. Ronald Wardhaugh, a linguist, explains what is and is not necessary this way:

> He [the child] may not be able to verbalize the rule any more than he could tell you how he ties his shoelaces; but just as he can demonstrate that he knows the rules for tying shoelaces by tying shoelaces, so he can demonstrate his knowledge of the rules

for pronouncing *c* by reading *city* and *cat* correctly. His knowledge of the rules is demonstrated by his performance and it is unnecessary for him to learn to verbalize a statement about what he has learned, that is, about what he knows. (8, p. 136)

RESULTS OF USING GENERALIZATIONS

Applying generalizations to an unknown word that is regularly spelled should result in its pronunciation. To be kept in mind, however, is that the pronunciation allows a reader to access the meaning only when the word is in the reader's oral vocabulary. Some of you, for instance, may have concluded earlier that the word *mete* rhymes with *Pete* but did not know its meaning. That made the pronunciation useless for reading. More than 30 years ago, Roger Brown, another linguist, made the same observation:

> The usefulness of being able to sound a new word depends on the state of the reader's speaking vocabulary. If the word that is unfamiliar in printed form is also unfamiliar in spoken form the reader who can sound it out will not understand the word any better than the reader who cannot sound it.... The real advantage in being able to sound a word that is unfamiliar in print, only appears when the word is familiar in speech. The child's letter-by-letter pronunciation, put together by spelling recipe, will, with the aid of context, call to mind the spoken form. There will be a click of recognition, pronunciation will smooth out, and meaning will transfer to the printed form. (2, p. 69)

"Smoothing out" pronunciations is often required when the word causing problems has more than one syllable. Take the word *pendulum* as an example. Readers who have heard—perhaps even used—the spoken version of "pendulum" can easily achieve the pronunciation when the use of generalizations results in "pĕn-dū-lŭm." Not to be forgotten is contextual help. Finding *lawyer* in a context, a reader who is familiar with the word in its spoken form will experience that click of recognition with the decoded pronunciation "law-yer."

As shown repeatedly in the previous chapter, the combination of oral vocabularies and contexts even allows readers to deal successfully with irregularly spelled words. Some like *pint* and *yacht,* for instance, may not be a problem in such helpful contexts as *He needed only a pint of paint for the door* and *The yacht moved smoothly through the water.*

Not to be overlooked is that the purpose for reading sometimes makes it necessary to know neither the pronunciation nor the exact meaning of a word. If one is reading a novel, for instance, and a character's dress is described as being brown, beige, and black, then inferring from the context that the referent for *beige* is a color is sufficient. On the other hand, if the purpose is to follow directions like *Draw a pattern using only brown, beige, and black,* the requirement is different. Now, the color to which *beige* refers has to be known even though its pronunciation is still unnecessary.

None of this is meant to suggest that pronunciations are of slight significance. After all, Chapters 8 and 9 are part of this book because figuring out the pronunciation of a visually unfamiliar word signals its meaning—*if* the word is in the reader's oral vocabulary. In other words, "reading depends on spellings, speech sounds, *and* meaning" (1, p. 291).

MODELING USE OF GENERALIZATIONS

Because modeling is an especially suitable teaching procedure for the various aspects of decoding, one think-aloud is portrayed before the chapter states and discusses generalizations. The example is intended to show how generalizations function.

The think-aloud is about *flee,* embedded in the sentence *They had to flee from the storm.* Following is what a teacher might say to a group of students to let them hear her thoughts while she goes about figuring out the pronunciation of *flee.*

> This word tells what they had to do. Evidently the storm made them do it. It's not "run" because it doesn't start with *r.* Luckily, it has only one syllable because it has only one vowel sound. I know that because of the two *e*'s. Because they're not a digraph, the first probably stands for its long sound and the second *e* is silent. I know the sounds for *f* and *l,* so I'm ready to blend all this together: $\bar{e} \rightarrow$ flē. Oh, "flee." It *is* something like "run." "They had to flee from the storm." That makes sense.

It should be noted that the attempt to describe how decoding *flee* proceeds does not assume that thoughts occurring virtually simultaneously can be described. All that is offered is a rough approximation of how one decoder figures out the pronunciation. Acknowledged, too, is that the decoding could have made use of a known word (e.g., *tree*), plus a substitution of two initial sounds, to arrive quickly at the pronunciation of *flee.* This point is made because correct *and* quick decoding is essential for the comprehension of connected text.

STATEMENTS OF GENERALIZATIONS

Because syllables are the focus when decoders select appropriate generalizations dealing with sounds, the first group of generalizations that are stated describes ways to divide an unknown word into syllables using the sequence of letters that are the word's spelling.

Generalizations for Dividing Unknown Words into Syllables

It must be recognized, first of all, that where one syllable in a spoken word ends and the next begins is often debatable. Again, let me quote a linguist to make this point more explicit:

> Although the number of syllables in an English utterance can be fairly easily determined, the precise point at which one syllable may be said to end and another begin is often impossible to determine.... The result is that the syllable divisions recorded in a written text are made according to convention and are essentially arbitrary. (7, p. 786)

Why decoders need to make "arbitrary" divisions can be explained with the help of some words, starting with *awful* and *away*. In *awful, a* and *w* function as a digraph because they are successive letters in a syllable. In *away,* each letter functions independently because *a* is in one syllable and *w* is in another.

Later in this chapter you learn about (or review) *r*-controlled vowel sounds. The referent is the sounds that a vowel followed by *r* in the same syllable represent. This pattern is significant for decoders, as it affects the sounds recorded by vowels in words like *her* and *dirt*. Contrast, however, these two words with others such as *erase* and *irate*. Because of syllabication—*e/rase* and *i/rate*—no *r*-controlled vowel sound occurs in either *erase* or *irate* because, in both instances, the vowel is in one syllable and the *r* is in another.

The gist of all this is as follows: The precise point at which one syllable in a spoken word ends and the next begins *is* arbitrary. Still, to be maximally successful, decoders need to syllabicate unknown words before they think about sounds.

The four generalizations for dividing unknown roots into syllables are in Figure 8.3. Please study any that are unfamiliar. The commentary about the generalizations is intended to make helpful observations.

Sometimes, commercially prepared materials collapse statements of generalizations like those listed in Figure 8.3 into abbreviated spelling patterns. When they do, C is used to represent consonants; V is used for vowels. The statements in Figure 8.3, therefore, would be abbreviated as follows.

Syllabication

Spelling Pattern		*Examples*
1. VCCV	[VC CV]	album, accent, kindergarten, panther
2. VCV	[V CV]	oval, flavor, isolate, author
3. Vxv	[Vx V]	exact, Texas, maximum, axis
4. Cle	[-Cle]	bugle, scramble, possible, article

Two points about abbreviated descriptions of spelling patterns need to be made. First, the information in the abbreviated forms is too compact for some students to understand. Second, the abbreviated descriptions are meaningful for other students only after they have had experiences in applying statements of generalizations to unfamiliar words. Teacher As who use manuals some of the time keep these two points in mind.

All teachers should know that another generalization could have been added to the four in Figure 8.3; in fact, its relevance for syllabicating unfamiliar words has already been demonstrated. I refer to this statement: *Every syllable must have a vowel sound.* This is the feature of English that tells readers, based on quick visual inspections, that words like *string, slump, crawl,* and *thrush* have one syllable. The same generalization informed the teacher who decoded *flee* that it, too, had one syllable (flēe). The generalization also explains why decoders know it is time to quit after they divide *album, accent,* and *panther* into two syllables.

Before proceeding, you may want to test yourself on stating and using generalizations to divide words into syllables; question 7 in the Review at the end of the chapter allows for this.

Generalizations for Vowel Sounds

The fact that every syllable must have a vowel sound means that every syllable has one or more vowel letters. Notice all the vowels, for example, in the one-syllable words shown below.

squeeze   voice   sleeve   plaque

The inevitability of having one or more vowel letters in every syllable may be thought of as unfortunate, given the fact that the sounds that vowels represent vary much more than do consonant letters. The fortunate part of the picture is that much of the variation follows patterns, which are described in generalizations. Because terms related to vowel sounds—for instance, long and short—are used in statements of generalizations, this is the time to review the two kinds of vowel sounds. All are illustrated earlier in the subsection of the chapter called "Sounds."

Generalizations also refer to so-called "silent" letters—that is, to vowels that do not add a sound to a syllable. As a reader, you know that final *e*s are commonly silent *e*s. This is reflected in the words below, which also serve to review diacritical marks:

ăt   měn   hĭm   ŏdd   ŭs

āt¢   mē∌n   hī   ōd¢   ūs¢

All the words above are regularly spelled. "Regularly spelled," as explained earlier, describes a word in which each letter in each syllable—or pairs of letters if a digraph—stands for the sound predicted by a generalization. In such words, silent letters are also predictable, based on a generalization.

The five generalizations that help decoders deal with the vowel letters in unfamiliar words are listed in Figure 8.4. It may be helpful to use the Commentary facing Figure 8.4 to move down the list.

Like the generalizations for dividing words into syllables, those about vowel sounds can be abbreviated as here:

Vowel Sounds

Spelling Pattern	*Examples*
1. (C)VC	act, bunch, dim, rancid
2. (C)V	able, she, radon, alto
3. (C)VV(C)	aid, tea, coax, eel
4. (C)VCe	ode, safe, ozone, cite
5. (C)VCCe	hinge, dunce, solve, elapse

The C enclosed in parentheses may have raised a question. Some Cs are noted that way because the consonant is not an essential part of the spelling pattern. Words like *act* and *bunch* are useful in illustrating the meaning of (C)VC. Both words have a single vowel that is followed by one or more consonant letters. These two features are the essence of the pattern described with (C)VC. Whether the single vowel is, or is not, preceded in the syllable by one or more consonants is inconsequential.

FIGURE 8.3   Commentary   ▶

Having examined each of the four generalizations, you should now be able to see that all describe visual cues. The cues, in this case, are letters (consonants and vowels) and their arrangement or sequence in the whole of a word. Let's relook at each generalization listed.

1. The words *album, accent,* and *panther* required one application of the generalization. (*Kindergarten* required its use three times.) Knowing that every syllable must have a vowel sound, a decoder should conclude that *album, accent,* and *panther* can have no more than two syllables each. This illustrates that knowing when to quit is important. It is also necessary to remember that digraphs function as if the pair of letters is only one letter. More specifically, *th* in *panther* should be treated as one consonant. In *panther,* then, the two consonants to which the generalization refers are *n* and *th.*
2. *Author* has two digraphs. In *author,* the one consonant referred to in the generalization is *th;* the vowel that precedes it is *au.*
3. The third generalization describes an exception to the second one. To illustrate, *oval* and *exit* both have a consonant that is preceded and followed by vowels. However, because *x* is the consonant in *exit,* the syllable division is different. This is illustrated below.

oval	o val
exit	ex it

4. Students should be encouraged to examine the whole of a word in a left-to-right progression before making decisions about syllables. Even so, knowing that a root word ends with a consonant followed by the letters *le* is relevant, for the three letters constitute a syllable. The pronunciation of all such final syllables is a blend of the sound of the consonant, the schwa sound, and the sound for *l.* The final syllable in *bugle,* therefore, is /gəl/. All such syllables are unstressed (búgle); hearing the schwa sound in the final syllable of words like *bugle* and *scramble,* therefore, is not unexpected.

1. When two consonants are between two vowels (*window*) a syllable division usually occurs between the consonants (*win dow*). For example:

album	accent	kindergarten	panther
al bum	ac cent	kin der gar ten	pan ther

2. When one consonant is between two vowels (*pilot*), a syllable division usually occurs between the first vowel and the consonant (*pi lot*). For example:

oval	flavor	isolate	author
o val	fla vor	i so late	au thor

3. When *x* is the consonant that is between two vowels (*exit*), *x* and the preceding vowel are in the same syllable (*ex it*). For example:

exact	Texas	maximum	axis
ex act	Tex as	max i mum	ax is

4. When a word ends in a consonant followed by *le* (*idle*), the consonant plus *le* are the final syllable (*i dle*). For example:

bugle	scramble	possible	article
bu gle	scram ble	pos si ble	ar ti cle

FIGURE 8.3   Generalizations for Syllabication

FIGURE 8.4   Commentary   ▶

1. Notice that the first generalization is relevant for any syllable in which there is *one vowel* that *does not occur at the end.* It applies, therefore, to words like *act* and *dim.* The same generalization describes all the syllables in *ethnic (eth nic), album (al bum), campus (cam pus),* and *rancid (ran cid).*

2. A comparison of the first two generalizations underscores the significance of both the number of vowels *and* their placement in the syllable. The significance is highlighted in contrasts like the following:

no	she	hi	so
not	shed	him	sob

3. Notice the reference to vowel digraphs in the third generalization. This serves as a reminder that the generalization does not refer to words like *void* and *Paul* or to the final syllables in *decoy* and *cocoon.* Here, it is important to note a unique characteristic of the digraph *ow.* Sometimes, as in *plow* and *chowder,* it functions as a digraph. At other times, it exemplifies the third generalization in Figure 8.4. This is true of words such as *snow* and *window.* (The variation is one of many reasons flexibility in using generalizations is underscored and illustrated when the next chapter discusses instruction.)

4. The frequency of final, silent *es* is known to us all. Less well known is the significance of the number of consonants that separates the first vowel in the syllable and the final *e.* The fourth generalization pinpoints the significance for the sound of the first vowel when one consonant is between the two vowels.

5. The fifth generalization pinpoints the significance for the first vowel when it is separated from the final *e* by two consonants. Again, contrasting words like the following highlight conclusions reached in the fourth and fifth generalizations about the sound for the first vowel.

sole	sine	mine
solve	since	mince

A syllable is the focus of all the generalizations that follow. Use of the generalizations does not begin, therefore, until decisions have been made about syllables in the word. The details in each generalization pertain to the visual features of a syllable that offer suggestions for the sound that a vowel is likely to represent.

1. When one vowel is in a syllable and is not the final letter (*ramp, cactus*), that vowel generally stands for its short sound. For example:

act	plot	ethnic	campus
dim	bunch	album	rancid

2. When one vowel is in a syllable and is the final letter (*so, veto*), that vowel generally stands for its long sound. For example:

she	halo	radon	alto
go	silo	siphon	limbo

3. When two successive vowels, which are not digraphs, are in a syllable (*eat, maintain*), the first vowel generally stands for its long sound and the second is silent. For example:

aid	tea	waif	reason
eel	coax	eagle	pertain

4. When two vowels are in a syllable, one of which is final *e*, and the two are separated by one consonant (*ade, stroke*), the first vowel generally stands for its long sound and the final *e* is silent. For example:

ode	cite	cascade	abuse
safe	mete	surprise	ozone

5. When two vowels are in a syllable, one of which is final *e*, and the two are separated by two consonants (*else, solve*), the first vowel generally stands for its short sound and the final *e* is silent. For example:

since	hinge	elapse	revolve
dunce	fudge	impulse	indulge

FIGURE 8.4 Generalizations for Vowel Sounds

If you now think you understand the five generalizations about vowel sounds and can state in some form the essential details for each, try answering question 8 in the Review section at the end of the chapter.

Before other generalizations are introduced into the discussion, comments about *r*-controlled vowel sounds are in order because they are in words used to illustrate generalizations—specifically, kind<u>er</u>g<u>ar</u>ten, panth<u>er</u>, flav<u>or</u>, auth<u>or</u>, <u>ar</u>ticle, p<u>er</u>tain, and s<u>ur</u>prise.

The first point is that the letters that account for an *r*-controlled vowel sound are a vowel and an *r* that follows the vowel in the same syllable. This means that an *r*-controlled vowel sound is in each of the two syllables that make up the word *order*. It also means that words such as *roam* and *rest* do not have *r*-controlled vowel sounds.

The second point meriting attention is that a vowel plus *r* stand for a blend of two sounds. In the word *order,* for example, *or* stands for the blend /or/, and *er* stands for the blend /er/.

The third point has to do with instruction. Specifically, it is the blend that is pronounced for students, not the sound for each letter in the pair. This procedure is followed because it is almost impossible to hear the blend as two distinct sounds.

The blends that all the vowels plus *r* commonly stand for are shown at the top of Figure 8.5. The fact that *ar* and *or* stand for additional blends is shown, too.

Decoders also need to be on the lookout for syllables in which a vowel is followed by *re*. The blends that vowels plus *re* stand for can be identified in the words listed below. They are contrasted with other words to help you distinguish between blends recorded by a vowel plus *r* and blends that are represented by a vowel plus *re*.

car	her	fir	for	cur
care	here	fire	fore	cure

Contrasts like those above also help children make the necessary distinctions.

Even more words in which a vowel is followed by *re* in the same syllable are shown below.

mare	sincere	dire	snore	pure
square	ampere	umpire	pinafore	obscure

```
/er/*      /or/*     /ar/*
her        nor       arm
fir
fur


/er/       /or/
cedar      war
worth
```
*Common blends for letters listed.

FIGURE 8.5   *R*-Controlled Vowel Sounds

Generalizations for Y

It was said earlier that *y* and *w* function as both consonants and vowels. Serving as vowels, they are part of the vowel digraphs *aw, ew, ow,* and *oy.* Even though the four digraphs may suggest that *w* functions as a vowel more often than does *y,* that is not the case. In fact, *w* is a vowel only in the three digraphs just cited. As is also true of *y, w* is a consonant whenever it occurs in initial position. Words in which *w* and *y* serve as consonants are cited below. Four of the eight words were selected in order to emphasize that initial position refers to the beginning of a syllable, not to the beginning of a word. Once again, then, the significance of syllables for decoding is illustrated.

Consonant Sounds for W and Y

wave	await	yard	beyond
wind	beware	yellow	canyon

The significance of syllables is very pronounced when readers come across an unfamiliar word, notice that it has a *y,* but—because they are unable to read the word—do not know whether *y* is functioning as a consonant or vowel. Let me show ways for resolving the dilemma with more think alouds. Let's assume that one word causing problems is *nylon.*

Let's see. I wonder whether *y* is a consonant or vowel. To be a consonant, it has to be in initial position. But it can hardly start a syllable in this word because that would leave *n* all by itself. That's not possible because every syllable has to have a vowel sound. Apparently, *y* is a vowel. Because it is, the word divides into syllables between *y* and *l* because of the VCV pattern for syllabication.

Another think aloud follows. In this instance, the troublesome word is *olympic.*

I wonder if *y* is a consonant or vowel. If it's a consonant, that would mean there are three consonants in a row. Considering the sound for *y* when it *is* a consonant, I don't think it's possible to pronounce those three letters. If *y* is a vowel, then the first syllable in this word is *o,* the second is spelled *l, y, m,* and the third is what's left—*p, i,* and *c.*

Once readers decide that *y* in an unknown word serves as a vowel, they next consider whether it represents /ĭ/, /ē/, or /ī/. Three generalizations suggest which is likely to be the correct sound.

Because *olympic* was just scanned by a decoder, let's start with the following generalization:

> When *y* is in medial position in a syllable that has no other vowel letter (*gym, system*), it stands for the short sound of *i.* For example:
>
> | | | | |
> |---|---|---|---|
> | myth | hymn | symbol | hypnosis |
> | cyst | lymph | crystal | olympic |

Dividing the four multisyllabic words shown above into syllables reveals why the generalization is applicable:

sym bol   crys tal   hyp no sis   o lym pic

Before the next generalization for *y* is stated, one comment is in order. It is the reminder that all the generalizations in this chapter pertain to root words—that is, to words like *hurry* and *candy* but not to others such as *curly* and *windy*. The last two words are excluded because they are derivatives in which *y* is a suffix. Here, the concern is for multisyllabic roots. A generalization about them follows:

> When *y* is the last letter in a multisyllabic word and it is preceded by a consonant (*pony, penny*), it usually records the long sound of *e*. For example:
>
> | bunny | hurry | artery | lady |
> |-------|-------|--------|------|
> | candy | fancy | dignity | autopsy |

Why the generalization above specifies that a consonant precedes the *y* can be explained with words in which a vowel precedes *y*:

galley	abbey	chimney	array
[gal lēy̆]	[ab bēy̆]	[chim nēy̆]	[ar rāy̆]

As the diacritical marks suggest, decoding the final syllables in words like these requires the use of a generalization stated earlier: When two successive vowels that are not digraphs occur in a syllable, the first commonly stands for its long sound and the second is silent.

The third generalization for *y* serving as a vowel provides information by eliminating the spelling patterns described in the first two generalizations. Consequently, it is time to list all three generalizations together. This is done in Figure 8.6.

Now that the three vowel sounds for *y* have been discussed, you should be ready to respond to question 9 in the Review section of the chapter.

Generalizations for C and G

Generalizations taught and used long before students ever encounter words like *dynamo*, *artery*, and *crystal* pertain to sounds for *c* and *g*. Earlier in the chapter, their hard and soft sounds are identified.

Hard Sounds		**Soft Sounds**	
c̲up	sac̲	c̲ent	ic̲e
g̲ap	bug̲	g̲ym	ag̲e

Words that include the hard sounds for *c* and *g* appear in easier text, which means that those two sounds are taught first. Once students know about the two sounds for each letter, the generalizations in Figure 8.7 require attention.

One final point needs to be made about *g*, when it is followed by *u* in a syllable. Based on a generalization already stated, the expected initial sound in words like

1. When *y* is in medial position in a syllable that has no vowel letter, it stands for the short sound of *i*, as in *hymn*.
2. When *y* is the final letter in a multisyllabic word and is preceded by a consonant, it usually stands for the long sound of *e*, as in *trophy*.
3. Otherwise, *y* stands for the long sound of *i*. For example:

dye	cry	nylon	dynamo	cycle
type	shy	gyrate	thyroid	hyphen

Commentary:

Examining the illustrative words for the third generalization stated above shows that none has a spelling pattern that is featured in the other two. The fact that *dye* and *type* have a vowel in addition to the *y* eliminates the first generalization. *Cry* and *shy* could not have more than one syllable, which makes the second generalization irrelevant. When the other words used to illustrate the third generalization are divided into syllables, it can be seen that they do not fit the other patterns either:

nylon	gyrate	dynamo	cycle	hyphen
ny lon	gy rate	dy na mo	cy cle	hy phen

FIGURE 8.6   Generalizations for *Y*

gum and *gull* is the hard sound for *g*. But, what about words such as *guess* and *guide*? The following generalization describes them:

When *gu* occurs in a syllable that includes a vowel other than *u*, *gu* functions as a single consonant and records the hard sound for *g*. For example:

guest	guard	guilt	guide	vague	brogue

1. When *c* or *g* are followed in a syllable by *e*, *i*, or *y* (*cent, cite, cyst; gem, gin, gym*), they usually record their soft sounds. For example:

cedar	city	cynic
gentle	giraffe	gypsy

2. When *c* and *g* are not followed in a syllable by *e*, *i*, or *y*, or are the final letters in syllables, they stand for their hard sounds. For example:

cab	coal	cute	fact	picnic
game	golf	gust	green	maggot

FIGURE 8.7   Generalizations for *C* and *G*

A comment about *vague* and *brogue* is in order. Words do not end in the letter *u*; therefore, when *gu* records the final sound in a word, as it does in *vague* and *brogue*, the hard sound for *g* is still spelled *gu,* which is followed by silent *e.*

Now, having considered two consonants, *c* and *g,* that show more variation in the sounds they represent than is true of most consonants, you might want to look at the last question in the Review section. It deals with both *c* and *g.*

SUMMARY

To ensure that teachers and prospective teachers are prepared to offer instruction that maximizes for students the help with unfamiliar words that is rooted in graphophonic cues, Chapter 8 covered information about (a) letter-sound correspondences, and (b) factors that affect them. Because all the observations—called generalizations in the chapter—about the two topics focus on syllables, those parts of words received generous attention. Why unfamiliar words do need to be syllabicated before a decoder's thoughts turn to pronunciation was illustrated and reillustrated throughout Chapter 8. That is why the first group of generalizations were about the use of spelling patterns to divide unknown words into syllables.

Teachers have to use certain terms while providing phonics instruction and when they encourage students to use what they are learning. All these terms, therefore, were defined and explained with examples. The terms divided into those that refer to letters and those that are about speech sounds. To make definitions readily retrievable, Figure 8.2 provided a glossary.

Because the sounds that vowel letters record show much more variation than is characteristic of consonant letters, the second set of generalizations in Chapter 8 had to do with the visual cues in syllables that guide decoders in their decisions about the sounds to assign to vowels. Here and elsewhere in the chapter, visual cues were defined as letters *and* their sequence in a syllable. They thus refer to spelling patterns.

The fact that *y* serves as a vowel with considerable frequency was the next topic addressed. When *y* serves as a consonant and when decoders need to think of *y* as a vowel were explained. The three vowel sounds that *y* represents were identified as /ĭ/, /ē/, and /ī/. When each sound is likely to be the one to use for *y* was described with generalizations. Again, they focused on spelling patterns.

The fact that certain consonant letters do vary in the sounds they represent accounted for other content in Chapter 8. Fortunately for decoders, some of these letters—for instance, *x* and *q*(u)—appear infrequently in words. Others—notably *c* and *g*—are fairly common. That is why the multiple sounds for *c* and *g* were identified and why generalizations about the likely occurrence of each sound were stated.

Now that Chapter 8 has dealt with *what* is taught to maximize the help with words that derives from their spelling, Chapter 9 covers how to instruct about graphophonic cues.

REVIEW

1. Because every syllable has a vowel sound, it is important to know the fifteen vowel sounds referred to in Chapter 8.
   a. Name 15 words that illustrate the fifteen sounds.
   b. Name the letter(s) in each that records the vowel sound.

2. Vowel sounds divide between those called long and those called short. Name six words that illustrate the six long vowel sounds; then name six other words that illustrate the short vowel sounds.

3. Eight pairs of vowels are digraphs.
   a. Spell the eight.
   b. Pronounce the vowel sound for each digraph.

4. Because vowel sounds in unstressed syllables are often reduced to the schwa sound, it is necessary for teachers to know when this happens. In the words listed below, (a) mark the syllable in each that is stressed, and (b) draw a line under any vowel letter that records the schwa sound.

   platoon   infidel   ostracize   maintain   semantic   count   vista

5. Arrange the words listed alphabetically below into four groups labeled "Hard Sound for *C*," "Hard Sound for *G*," "Soft Sound for *C*," and "Soft Sound for *G*."

city	grunt	ignite	ounce
collapse	guest	indulge	page
cymbal	gypsy	innocent	plague
ginger	hectic	object	sac

6. Some successive consonants in syllables are clusters; others are digraphs.
   a. Define *cluster* and *digraph*.
   b. In the words below, underline all the pairs of consonants that are digraphs.

perch	hyphen	photo	ounce	ranch
smash	string	indent	waist	object

7. As Chapter 8 stated a number of times, the focus of generalizations that describe likely sounds for letters assumes the syllable is the unit of pronunciation. This explains why a consideration of syllables is the first step in decoding an unknown word.
   a. Based on the generalizations for syllabication stated in Chapter 8, use a slash mark (/) to indicate the syllable divisions in the ten pseudowords shown below.

ximdle	shigur	cuxot	voog	quawz
vipho	gebthor	hoyk	dowx	ciftaung

   b. For each of the ten pseudowords, state the generalization(s) used to divide it into syllables.

8. Soon after Chapter 8 got under way, it was said that *me, meat, meet, mete,* and *met* are regularly spelled. By adding *mince,* the six words illustrate the five generalizations about vowel sounds discussed in the chapter. For each of the six words, state the generalization that provides information about the sound for every vowel.

9. Chapter 8 explained that like *w,* the letter *y* functions as both consonant and vowel. *Y* functions sufficiently often as a vowel that generalizations describe features of syllables and words that suggest likely sounds for *y.* In order to review the generalizations, cite which one(s) help with the sound to assign to all the *y*'s in the pseudowords shown below. (Divide the words into syllables first.)

chaylar tylm yund

hoyk gysan rincy

10. As the underlined letters emphasize, all the spellings for the six words shown below include *c*s and *g*s. For each underlined letter, explain why it stands for the sound it records. (Remember: Like all the generalizations about letter-sound relationships and the factors that affect them, generalizations about *c* and *g* focus on syllables. To start, therefore, consider each of the six words in relation to syllables.)

giganti<u>c</u> <u>c</u>an<u>c</u>el sta<u>c</u>k fu<u>g</u>ue oun<u>c</u>e <u>g</u>inger

REFERENCES

1. Adams, Marilyn J. *Beginning to Read: Thinking and Learning about Print.* Cambridge, Mass.: The MIT Press, 1990.
2. Brown, Roger. *Words and Things.* New York: Free Press, 1958.
3. Durkin, Dolores. "Phonics Instruction in New Basal Reader Programs." Technical Report No. 496. Urbana: University of Illinois, Center for the Study of Reading, 1990.
4. Durkin, Dolores. *Strategies for Identifying Words* (2nd ed.). Boston: Allyn and Bacon, 1981.
5. Newman, Judith M., and Church, Susan M. "Myths of Whole Language." *Reading Teacher* (September, 1990), 20–26.
6. Venezky, Richard L. "English Orthography: Its Graphical Structure and Its Relation to Sound." *Reading Research Quarterly* 2 (Spring, 1967), 75–105.
7. Wardhaugh, Ronald. "Syl-lab-i-ca-tion." *Elementary English* 43 (November, 1966), 785–788.
8. Wardhaugh, Ronald. *Reading: A Linguistic Perspective.* New York: Harcourt, Brace and World, 1969.

Graphophonic Cues: Instruction

This chapter continues to pursue the interest of previous chapters in Part III. It shows how students' reading vocabularies can be increased. Increasing these vocabularies is a serious responsibility for teachers at all grade levels, given that unknown words can disrupt the comprehension process. Not to be forgotten is that the inability to identify words is a frustrating experience for readers, especially when the text is something they *want* to read.

Like Chapter 7, which covers contextual cues, Chapter 9 deals with the cueing system of written English. Its specific concern is how to teach students ways to use spellings to reach conclusions about pronunciations. To this, two caveats must be added. First, pronunciations without meanings are useless for reading. Second, using relevant cues such as spellings to make decisions about unfamiliar words leads to recognition, not identification. To move from recognizing a word to identifying it, practice is essential. Fortunately, a knowledge of letter-sound correspondences reduces the amount of practice required.

In order to achieve its overall objectives, Chapter 9 does the following. It begins by reminding you that new vocabulary must receive attention to enable students to do assigned reading independently. It also reminds you that new words with regular spellings can be eliminated from prereading preparations if students are able decoders. The rest of Chapter 9 explains what teachers can do to teach decoding so that it eventually becomes highly proficient—that is, correct *and* fast.

As a way of organizing the content, requirements of decoding are divided into (a) need to know, and (b) need to be able to do. What students need to know is covered in the previous chapter. In Chapter 9, how to teach what they need to know is illustrated with a number of lessons that include teacher-student dialogues. The assumption is that specifically described lessons are more instructive than are lists of do's and don't's, especially for anyone who has not yet taught. Comments about the lessons are intended to make them more illuminating.

To teach the doing part of decoding—for instance, adding, substituting, and blending sounds—modeling by teachers is highly recommended. That is why Chapter 9 also presents lessons through the vehicle of think-alouds. These illustrations of modeling are another reflection of the dictum, "Don't just talk about it—show it!"

Aʟʟ ᴛʜᴇ ᴘʀᴏʙʟᴇᴍs ᴀssᴏᴄɪᴀᴛᴇᴅ ᴡɪᴛʜ ʀᴏᴜɴᴅ ʀᴏʙɪɴ ʀᴇᴀᴅɪɴɢ accounted for the earlier recommendation to replace it with *independent, uninterrupted silent reading of appropriately difficult material*. At the time the recommendation was offered, prereading preparations that make independent reading possible were described. (See the Preview for Chapter 6.) Teaching new vocabulary is part of those preparations.

Subsequently, two other recommendations were made. Chapter 6 said whenever words thought to be new are excessive in number, prereading preparations should concentrate on the words necessary for comprehending the text. It also said that if words expected to cause problems are routinely large in number, excessively difficult material is probably the cause.

Later, when Chapter 7 discussed contextual cues, another recommendation was made. This one suggested examining the contexts in which new vocabulary appears in a selection for the first time. The purpose of this recommendation is to eliminate any word students can cope with on their own, thanks to help from a context. Adherence to the recommendation not only reduces the time required for prereading preparations; it also gives students meaningful opportunities to apply what they are learning.

Now that you are knowledgeable about the information a word's spelling provides, you should be able to predict the next recommendation: Eliminate from prereading preparations any new word that is regularly spelled. "Regularly spelled," as you recall, refers to words whose spellings adhere to patterns that make it possible to reach conclusions about how to pronounce them. Features of spelling patterns are described in generalizations in the previous chapter.

To sum up, then, three recommendations have been made for dealing with new vocabulary. First, omit any word that is regularly spelled. (Remember that we are assuming meanings are known.) Second, examine the contexts in which the remaining words occur initially. The availability of contextual help is likely to eliminate even more new words. (Remember that contextual cues combined with graphophonic cues often allow for dealing successfully with irregularly spelled words.) Third, if the new words that remain are excessive in number, attend only to those that are essential for understanding the text to be read.

Ideally, all the decisions just referred to would be made by individuals who prepare manuals that accompany materials like basal readers and content subject textbooks. That is not the case, however. The following, for example, are said in one fourth-grade basal manual to be new vocabulary in a selection. (The fact that only root words have been considered thus far accounts for the second column.)

New Vocabulary	Roots
braggart	brag
eloquent	eloquent
humble	humble
impressed	impress
landlord	land, lord
prosperous	prosper
scoundrel	scoundrel
tenant	tenant

Underlined roots are regularly spelled and need not be pretaught. For now, the relevant point is that the manual makes no distinctions among the eight new words. Again, therefore, teachers are needed who can make knowledgeable decisions for instruction.

INSTRUCTION: SOME QUESTIONS

To ensure that students are eventually able to deal with regularly spelled words—and with irregularly spelled words in helpful contexts—instruction about letter-sound correspondences and factors that affect them is essential. Before examples of instruction are provided, two questions need to be answered:

1. What should be taught when?
2. What kinds of teaching procedures should be used?

The question about sequence is answered first.

Sequence to Follow

The importance of giving students opportunities to experience the value for their reading of what they are learning has been underscored many times. Acceptance of the importance means that *usefulness* ought to determine when the various pieces and parts of decoding instruction receive attention. To be underscored here is that children learn and remember what they find useful.

In spite of this, as Chapter 4 points out, commercially prepared materials commonly determine what is taught, starting as early as kindergarten (3). This is the practice even though dependence on something like a basal manual has been the subject of criticism for a very long time (6, 7). More recently, whole language supporters have been unanimous in their complaints about phonics instruction that shows little or no connection with the texts students need or want to read (9).

Admittedly, opportunities for children to use what is taught at the very beginning are considerably less than they are when more subject matter has been covered. Even at the beginning, however, the promise of future opportunities merits explicit attention. Knowing the correspondence between *p* and /p/, for instance, children should be helped to see that such knowledge will eventually assist them in reading (and writing) words like *puppy, play,* and *paper,* all of which can be printed on a chalkboard and read by a teacher.

As Chapter 5 explains, letter-sound instruction should start with consonants. When each consonant sound is taught should be affected by the words children are learning with whole word methodology and, in addition, by the frequency of their appearance in words. The latter criterion explains why *t, n,* and *s* merit early attention and why letters like *z, q(u), x,* and *j* do not.

Similarity of sounds is another factor that must be taken into account if confusion about sounds is to be minimized. This criterion suggests that if the correspondence between *t* and /t/ is taught, subsequent instruction should *not* focus on the sound that *d* represents, because /d/ and /t/ are similar. Or, to cite another illustration, if children are learning that *p* stands for /p/, the correspondence between *b* and /b/ should not be taught next. To do that invites confusion.

At some point, the long and short vowel sounds require attention. Although the long sounds for *a, e, i, o,* and *u* are easier to learn, they are less useful to know. The second characteristic is the reason the short sounds should be introduced first.

Once children know some vowel sounds, they are ready to understand and then apply generalizations that describe when the various sounds are likely to occur. At this point, single-syllable words should be used both to illustrate the content of the generalizations and for practice in applying the content. Now, application requires other work with blending sounds to produce syllables.

Eventually, students must be able to cope on their own with multisyllabic words. They thus need to learn generalizations that help in getting unfamiliar words divided into syllables. This is the time, too, for offering help in putting syllables together in order to end up with a word.

Meanwhile, instruction with letter-sound correspondences continues. Now the concern is consonant and vowel digraphs and single consonants that occur infrequently in words. All the while, instructional time continues to go to blending sounds, ultimately reaching the point when flexible application of what has been taught is the key concern.

The critical importance of flexibility suggests adding the reminder that concern for phonics instruction should not be so great as to obscure the fact that the purpose of decoding unknown words is to make sense of connected text. Viewed from that perspective, the need for readers to use all available cues comes to the forefront. So, too, does the requirement of providing contexts when students are learning to use what they know about (a) dividing unknown words into syllables, (b) letter-sound correspondences, and (c) factors that affect correspondences.

Teaching Procedures to Use

Whenever phonics instruction is considered, a distinction must be made between what successful decoders *know,* and what successful decoders *do.* This distinction is necessary because it allows for decisions about the kind of teaching that is appropriate. Specifically, if a letter-sound correspondence is the concern, productive instruction is likely to be some combination of explanations, descriptions, examples, and questions. On the other hand, if blending sounds to produce a syllable is the goal, the instruction that has the best chance of succeeding is modeling—that is, verbalizing and acting out a particular strategy, in this case for blending.

Because of the importance of the distinctions just made, the sample lessons that follow refer to teachers who are helping students *know* something. Subsequent sections focus on sample lessons for helping students *do* something.

WHAT DECODERS NEED TO KNOW

Because letter-sound instruction should begin with consonants, the first illustrative lesson focuses on teaching about the correspondence between *s* and /s/. Starting this way allows for attending to a notorious problem related to consonant sounds.

Teaching Consonant Sounds

The problem is that consonant sounds—in particular, stop sounds—are noticeably distorted when produced apart from words. Try saying the following sounds aloud. As you do, you will find yourself adding to each something that approximates a short *u* sound.

Stop Sounds

/b/	/p/
/d/	/t/
/g/	/k/

Why speech sounds are altered when produced alone is explained well by Stott (10):

> It is part of the very essence of language that sounds are uttered in very rapid sequences which become words. Each sound has such a fleeting existence that it is not truly reproducible outside the context of a word. Wresting it out of its natural place makes it something different, altering its length and the amount of breath put into it, and sometimes making it into a syllable by the addition of another sound. (p. 11)

It is not necessary to be a phonetician to understand, and agree with, Stott's observations. However, all one has to do is try to teach a sound to realize that some children *require* explicit identifications. That is, they need teachers who make statements like: "All these words begin with *f,* so they all begin with the same sound—with the sound that *f* stands for. The sound for *f* is /f/. You'll hear /f/ at the beginning of each of these words when I read them again. Listen: *first, fall, fun, fence*...".

The distortion of consonant sounds when produced outside the context of a word is one reason some individuals support *implicit* instruction. This type of teaching expects children to be able to extract a given sound from a spoken word, or, more commonly, from several spoken words. In the case of the example just referred to, the underlying assumption of implicit instruction is that children *can* hear /f/ as a distinct sound when they listen to *first, fall, fun,* and *fence.* This is the case even though the little research done on this topic supports a point made above: Children are not always able to perceive the separate sounds that make up words (1, 2).

A second reason offered in support of implicit instruction is that it fosters independent learning. That is, as children have experiences listening for a certain sound and associating it with a given letter, they are engaging in an activity that encourages them to make additional letter-sound associations on their own. Although this is highly desirable, nothing in the research literature provides evidence for such a consequence.

Having said all this, the question now is, How *should* letter-sound correspondences be taught?

When it is kept in mind that learning about letter-sound correspondences is a means to an end, the guideline to follow is as simple as: Use whatever works. When the importance of making initial instruction meaningful is also kept in mind, another guideline surfaces: Use words children can read so that the part of the words being singled out will be better understood, as will the nature of alphabetic writing. All this can be summarized as follows:

> At the very beginning, use known words (e.g., *to, take, turn, toy*) to call attention to the connection between a given letter (*t*) and a given sound (/t/). If children are able to extract that sound from the words, fine. If not, identify the sound for them. Once children seem to understand how spellings and pronunciations are linked, it is time for explicit instruction in which sounds are directly identified. This will be easier for many students; it also allows for covering content faster.

To clarify the summary statement, a sample lesson follows, which deals with a consonant sound. A second lesson focuses on the sound that a consonant digraph represents.

Sample Lessons: Consonant Sounds

Some preliminary comments are in order before the first lesson is described.

To begin, the teacher's goals are twofold: (a) to help an instructional group begin to understand alphabetic writing and (b) to teach that *s* stands for /s/. Words beginning with *s* that the children learned from the teacher's use of whole word methodology illustrate the sound.

In the lesson itself, the children demonstrate their ability to perceive /s/ in the illustrative words by naming additional words that begin with /s/. For that reason, the teacher does not say /s/ directly. The lesson, therefore, exemplifies implicit instruction. Had the children shown no evidence of having heard /s/ in the illustrative words, the teacher would have said something like: "The sound that *s* stands for in all these words is /s/. What sound does *s* stand for?...Listen for that sound at the beginning of all these words...". In this case, the instruction is explicit.

One further point needs to be made. Because the children are just beginning to learn that letters stand for sounds, the value for reading of knowing that *s* records /s/ is not referred to until the end of the lesson.

The lesson as a dialogue follows.

Teacher: Some words you know are on the board. [The words *saw, six,* and *some* are printed in a column to make apparent that all start with *s*.] What's the same about all these words?... Kathryn?

Kathryn: They all have *s* at the first.

Teacher: Yes, the first letter in each is *s*. Please read these words, everybody.

Group: Saw, six, some.

Teacher: Did anyone *hear* something that's the same about all these words when you said them?...No?...Let's read them again. See if you hear the same sound at the beginning of all these words. Please read them and listen for the sound that all of them start with.

Group: Saw, six, some.

Teacher: All the words you just read start with the same sound because they all start with *s*. Listen for the sound that *s* makes in all these words. Please read them again to listen for the sound for *s*.

Group: Saw, six, some.

Teacher: Can anyone think of another word that starts with the sound you hear at the beginning of "saw," "six," and "some"?

David: "Say" starts that way.

Teacher: Yes, David, it does. "Saw," "say." I'll write "say" under "some." [Prints *say* under *some*.] Now there are four words that start with the same letter and the same sound. Please read them.

Group: Saw, six, some, say.

Teacher: How about one more word that starts with the sound you hear at the beginning of "saw" and "six."

Amy: "Cynthia" starts that way.

Teacher: Yes, it does. "Saw," "Cynthia." But, Amy, there's something different about "Cynthia." You'll see the difference when I write it. (Prints *Cynthia* apart from the other words.) "Cynthia" begins with the sound we're talking about, but it doesn't start with *s*. With what letter does it begin?

Group: *C.*

Teacher: Yes, "Cynthia" is a girl's name that starts with *c*. Later, we'll talk about other words like *Cynthia*. For now, let's stay with words that start with *s* and that begin with the sound you hear at the beginning of "saw." Can anyone think of another word that starts the way "saw" begins? (Teacher erases *Cynthia*.)

Fran: "Sucker" is another word, and so is "soup."

Teacher: Fran, you certainly know lots of words that start with the sound that's at the beginning of "saw."

Bonnie: I know one, too. "Soap."

Teacher: Wait a minute now until I get all these words on the board. [Adds *sucker, soup,* and *soap* to the column.] Wow! We have seven words that start with the sound of *s*. Listen. I'll read them all so that you can hear that sound. If you want, read the words with me. Let's go. "Saw," "six," "some," "say," "sucker," "soup," "soap." Try to remember the sound that *s* makes. That way, when you see a word you can't read and it starts with *s*, at least you'll know the first sound. I'm going to write some words I don't think you know. Then I'll read them. When I do, you'll hear that they all begin with the same sound—with the sound that goes with the letter *s*. [Prints *sox, sun,* and *silly*.] With what letter do all these words start?

Group: *S.*

Teacher: Because each word begins with *s*, each one starts with the sound that goes with *s*. You'll hear that sound at the beginning when I tell you what these words are. Listen. "Sox," "sun," "silly."

Later, teachers who subscribe to *text-driven* instruction teach a less common sound for *s* when the texts that students are reading include words like *resort* and *exercise*. They use the presence of such words as a signal to contrast familiar words like *bus* and *has*—both of which may have been taught much earlier with whole word methodology—to call attention to the fact that *s* may record /z/ except when *s* is the first letter in a word. Aware of the multiple sounds, students should be helped to use /s/ first and to try /z/ next if the more common sound does not result in a recognizable word. Words in which *s* stands for /z/ include, in addition to *resort* and *exercise,* others such as *husband, reason,* and *phrase.*

The next lesson to be described has as its objective teaching the sound that the digraph *sh* represents. An observation that this second teacher makes reflects two statements made earlier in the book that merit being repeated. First, as is true of contextual and structural cues, using graphophonic cues allows only for recognizing unfamiliar words. Practice is necessary to achieve the ability to identify them. Second, less practice is required to realize that goal when readers know letter-sound correspondences.

The lesson for *sh* exemplifies explicit instruction because the teacher states directly the sound that the digraph represents. It also illustrates the close link that ought to exist between instruction and students' current needs.

Teacher: You know a lot about the sounds that letters stand for, and you've learned that knowing about sounds helps with words you can't at first read. Knowing about sounds also helps you remember new words so that you'll know them the next time you see the words. In the story you'll be reading today, some of the words start with *sh.* (Prints *sh* on the board.) One of these words is a new one. The others are words you should know. In any case, I want to say something special about *sh.* You know the sound that *s* usually stands for. You hear it at the beginning of words like these. [Prints *sun* and *seven.*] Please read these two words.

Group: Sun, seven.

Teacher: You also know the sound for *h.* I'll write some words that start with *h.* (Prints *here* and *how.*) Read these words.

Group: Here, how.

Teacher: The point I want to make is that when *s* and *h* are together in a syllable as they are in words like "shut" and "show" [prints the known words *shut* and *show*], the two letters have a special sound that isn't like the sound for *s* or like the sound for *h.* The sound that *sh* makes in words is one we sometimes use when we want somebody to be quiet. The sound that *sh* makes is /sh/. What's the sound for *sh?*

Group: /sh/.

Teacher: Correct. Please read these two words now [points to *shut* and *show*] and listen for the beginning sound in each.

Group: Shut, show.

Teacher: You know other words that *end* with /sh/. I'll write some. Don't say anything, please, until I finish writing. [Prints *wish, push,* and *dash.*] Please wait until I call on you. [Points to *wish.*] What's this word, Carol?

Carol: Wish.

Teacher: Read this word for us, Tom. [Points to *push.*]

Tom: It says "push."

Teacher: How about this word? [Points to *dash.*] Who can tell us what it says? Jerry.

Jerry:	Dash.
Teacher:	The story you'll be reading later is about a little girl who is very sick. A new word tells what she has. This is the word. [Prints *rash*.] What word that we just read is very much like this new one? Look at the three words here that end with *sh*. Which one is like the new word?
Margie:	Dash. The new word is "rash," like what I had when I had the measles.
Teacher:	You're right, Margie. It says "rash." Everyone, what does it say?
Group:	Rash.
Sue:	I don't think the girl in the story has measles because when I had measles, I didn't get very sick.
Margie:	When *I* had measles, I had a very bad case and was *really* sick.
Teacher:	You'll just have to wait to find out what the sick girl in the story has. Right now, I want you to look at another new word. This one starts with *sh*, so you should know its beginning sound. [Prints *shock*.] Can someone read this word?...It starts with /sh/ and ends with /k/. Can anyone read it now?
Gary:	Shucks?
Teacher:	Not quite, Gary, but you're close. I'll write *shucks* under the new word. [Prints *shucks* directly under *shock*.]
Margie:	I know it. It says "shock."
Teacher:	Correct. What is this word, everyone?
Group:	Shock.
Teacher:	What does "shock" mean? Gary?
Gary:	It means what you get from electricity.
Teacher:	That *is* one meaning. *Shock* has another meaning in the story. This is the sentence in which you'll first see *shock*. It should help with the meaning. When I write the sentence, you'll see that the new word has *ed* at the end. [Prints *Her mother was shocked when she got the news about Nancy.*] First, let's have Gary read the sentence.
Gary:	"Her mother was shocked when she got the news about Nancy."
Teacher:	Nancy is the name of the girl in the story who's sick. With the help of this sentence, can someone explain what *shocked* means?
Tom:	It means the mother is crying and stuff like that because she thinks her daughter is dying.
Teacher:	Well, we don't know for sure, Tom, if Nancy is dying, but what you said about "shocked" is correct. The mother is surprised at something she hears about Nancy and maybe she does cry. Mostly, "shocked" means "surprised," because something happens when you don't expect it to happen or you're surprised because somebody says something that you just didn't expect to hear. Since the word in the story is *shocked,* let me write that. [Erases *shucks* and prints *shocked* directly under *shock* so that one root word is directly under the other. Points to *shock*.] Please look at this word, everyone. What is it?
Group:	Shock.
Teacher:	When *ed* is added to *shock,* what does it say?

Group: Shocked.

Teacher: Yes, "shocked." It begins with the letters *sh* and with the sound—what sound do *shock* and *shocked* begin with, everybody?

Group: /sh/.

Teacher: Yes. Remember that when *s* is followed by *h*, the two letters together stand for one sound. *S* and *h* stand for /sh/. Listen for that sound while you read all the words on the board together.

Teaching Generalizations

As the previous chapter points out, some generalizations for decoding provide help with vowel sounds. One such generalization is the concern of the next lesson: A single vowel in final position usually stands for its long sound. This generalization was originally listed in Figure 8.4. Words used at the time to illustrate the content include *she, halo, radon, siphon,* and *alto.*

The lesson about this generalization, as well as the lesson described afterward, demonstrate how known words are used to teach and how unknown words are featured when it is time for students to apply what they learned. The two lessons are presented in a format designed to highlight the importance of teachers' making sure that students are ready to achieve a selected objective. Prerequisites, therefore, are identified.

Sample Lesson: Generalization for Vowel Sounds

Prerequisites.   Students (a) know the long and short vowel sounds, (b) know what a syllable is, (c) understand the meaning of "final position," and (d) understand that "final position" refers to the placement of a letter in a syllable.

Teaching the Lesson.   After reviewing the long and short vowel sounds, the teacher prints five familiar words on the board and asks the group to read them.

> me
> no
> she
> go
> hi

Once the words are read, the teacher probes: "How many vowels are in *me*?...Which of its sounds does *e* stand for in *me,* the long or the short?" After asking similar questions about the remaining words, the teacher calls the students' attention to the placement of the single vowel by asking, "Where is the one vowel in all these words?"

To synthesize the relevant details, the teacher continues, "You've told me three things that are the same about all these words. You said they have one vowel, the vowel is at the end, and it stands for its long sound. Now, when you see a word that you can't read and it has one vowel letter that's at the end, you'll know that it will have its long sound—or at least most of the time the vowel will stand for its long sound. I'm going to write all those things on the board to help you remember them." As the teacher prints, she reads:

1. one vowel letter
2. at the end
3. long sound

To show how this pertains to words in the selection that the children just read, the teacher goes through the three pieces of information with them. As they do this, words that entered into the lesson are found (*she* and *me*) as well as two other words that did not (*he, so*). The teacher also discusses a word in the selection in which a single, final vowel does not have the long sound (*to*). This is done to emphasize that words must make sense—that calling *to* "toe" does not make any sense in *They ran to the house.*

The generalization taught in this lesson is reviewed and then applied the next day when *silo, acorn, stable,* and *pony* are among the new words introduced in preparation for reading a story that takes place on a farm.

Sample Lesson: Generalization for Syllabication

To help students understand how to use a spelling pattern to divide unknown words into syllables is the reason for the next lesson. To achieve that objective, the following generalization is taught: When a word has one consonant and there is a vowel before and after it, the first vowel is in one syllable and the consonant and the vowel that follows it are in another syllable. This generalization is listed in the previous chapter in Figure 8.3. Words used at the time to illustrate the content were *oval, flavor, isolate,* and *author.*

Prerequisites.   Students (a) know what is meant by "consonant," "vowel," and "syllable," and (b) understand the significance of syllables for decoding.

Teaching the Lesson.   The teacher starts by commenting, "Three of the new words in what you'll be reading today about pollution are the same in the sense that all have a vowel followed by a consonant followed by a vowel. To help you remember that, I'll use some shorthand. I'll write three letters for vowel, consonant, and vowel."

VCV

"I'll come back to these letters later because you can use them to get the three new words divided into syllables so that you can figure out what they say. Right now, I'm going to show you words you know that also have a vowel followed by a consonant followed by a vowel. I've printed them on this chart. Please don't read them aloud yet."

music
open
paper
final

"Okay. You've had a chance to look at these words. Please read them together.... I'm going to ask how many syllables are in each word, so, keeping that question in mind, please read the words again.... How many syllables does each of these words have?...Correct. Two. The first word is "music." Who can spell the first syllable? Raise your hands, please. Emily.... Right. The letters *m* and *u* make up the first syllable. That means *s, i, c* is the second syllable. I'm going to use a slash mark to show where the first syllable ends and the second begins."

Eventually the chart shows:

music	mu/sic
open	o/pen
paper	pa/per
final	fi/nal

"Please look at the four words in this column where I've shown the syllables. Look at the first syllable in these four words. What kind of a letter is at the end?... Fine. The first syllable in all four words ends with a vowel. I have another question. Look at the words again. What kind of a letter starts the second syllable in all of them?... Right again. The second syllable starts with a consonant. Now my question is, 'What kind of a letter comes after the consonant?'... That's right. In every case, a vowel comes after the consonant. Let me draw a line under all these letters."

m<u>u/s</u>ic

<u>o</u>/pen

p<u>a/per</u>

f<u>i/na</u>l

"In each word, I underlined a vowel followed by a consonant followed by a vowel. That's why I wrote VCV on the board earlier. When a word has this series of letters, the first syllable ends with the first vowel. See? This is exactly what happens in 'music,' 'open,' 'paper,' and 'final.' In 'music,' the vowel letter *u* ends the first syllable and *s* and *i* are in the second syllable."

After giving similar attention to the three remaining words, the teacher says, "Let me put all this together. As I do, I'll point to certain parts of each of the four words. Please look at them so that you'll see where I'm pointing. This is what you need to remember. When a word has a vowel followed by a consonant followed by a vowel, the first syllable ends after the first vowel. Let me go back to my shorthand over here. I'll show where that syllable break comes."

VCV

V CV

"Please use these letters to answer my next questions. They're about three *new* words that you'll see later when you read the article about pollution. Even if you can't read them now, you *should* know where they divide into syllables. I've written the new words here. Look at them, please."

emit

radon

ozone

"The first word is spelled *e, m, i, t*. Do you see anything about these letters that's the same as the letters in words like *music* and *open*?... That's absolutely right. This new word has a vowel, *e,* followed by a consonant, *m,* followed by a vowel, *i.* What did we say about words like this?... Yes, the first syllable ends with the first vowel, in this case with *e*...".

Similar procedures are used with *radon* and *ozone.* The instruction part of the lesson thus ends with two lists:

emit	e/mit
radon	ra/don
ozone	o/zone

After the words are divided into syllables and the generalization for syllabication is restated, attention shifts to how the words are pronounced and to what they mean. How they might be related to pollution is considered next.

This is an appropriate place to insert an observation about words with the spelling pattern discussed in the lesson just described. Let me introduce it by calling your attention to the following words, in particular, to the vowel sound in the first syllable of each:

ō/val	sī/lent	lē/gal	bā/con
bŏ/dy	lĭ/zard	lĕ/mon	wă/gon

As expected, all the words in the top row have a long vowel sound in the first syllable. Unexpectedly, all the words in the second row have a short vowel sound in the first syllable. The point to be made is that words like those in the second row are sufficiently common that teachers should, at some point, call students' attention to them. Again, it is a case of trying the expected sound first, then replacing it with the unexpected sound if use of the first one does not produce a recognizable word.

This might also be an appropriate time to insert the reminder that words such as *body* rarely occur alone. When they are found in the company of known words, substituting one vowel sound for another may not be necessary because of the contextual help. Recently, for example, I was looking at a story in a third-grade basal reader that told about life in the early West. One adventure occurred because a rainstorm left a creek gushing. The following sentence shows how a context offers help with *body:* "The creek was not playing. It grabbed her body and pulled it under the board."

WHAT DECODERS NEED TO DO

The lessons described thus far deal with some things that decoders need to know. The same lessons also imply the need for students to be able to *do* something with what they know. For instance, in order to recognize the new word *shout* as quickly as possible, students have to be able to blend /sh/ and the known word *out.* Or, to cite other illustrations, they have to be able to blend /s/ and /ī/ and, on another occasion, /s/ and /ā/ in order to achieve, in these cases, pronunciations for the initial syllables in new words like *silent* and *saber.*

At its simplest level, blending is adding a sound to the initial or final parts of known words:

	out	eat	in	arm
	shout	seat	thin	charm

ten	see	tea	ran
tent	seed	team	ranch

Later, initial and final additions work together, as illustrated below.

can	or	in	car	ran	an
scan	for	pin	scar	ranch	and
scant	fort	pinch	scarf	branch	stand

How the sounds that make up a known word can be blended with other sounds to produce a different word is the focus of the lesson described next. The blending that is done is viewed as a way to speed up the decoding process.

Sample Lesson: Adding Final Sounds to Known Words

In the lesson that follows, the teacher starts by reviewing the sound that *t* records and having the children read known words that are on the board written in a row rather than a column: *ten, for, an, car.* The teacher then proceeds by demonstrating blending with the expectation that the demonstration will begin to clarify the nature of blending sufficiently well that the children will eventually be able to do it themselves.

Teacher: Please read this first word again.
Group: Ten.
Teacher: This morning, I'm going to show you how you can use the word *ten,* plus the sound for *t,* to learn a new word. The new word I'm thinking of is spelled *t, e, n*—just like the word *ten*—but this word has *t* at the end. It looks like this. [Prints *tent* directly under *ten.*] This is what I do to learn what this second word is. [Points to *tent.*] I say "ten" and then add /t/. Listen as I do that. "Ten," "tent."
Steve: I know what a tent is. You use a tent at night when you camp outside.
Teacher: Yes, a tent is like a home away from home. Now, Steve, you not only know what a tent is but you also know what the word that says "tent" looks like. Okay, everybody. Look up here, please. Read these two words again.
Group: Ten, tent.
Teacher: Read them one more time to make sure you hear yourself adding /t/ to the word "ten."
Group: Ten, tent.

The lesson deals in a similar way with *for* and *fort, an* and *ant,* and *car* and *cart.* A visual complement is on the board:

ten	for	an	car
tent	fort	ant	cart

Depending on how the first lesson goes, a subsequent one might attend to pairs of known and unknown words in ways that focus on adding a variety of final letters and sounds. For example:

see	her	far	four	too	pin
seed	herd	farm	fourth	tooth	pinch

Lessons that deal with adding sounds to the *initial* part of known words proceed in a similar fashion. Words that might figure in such lessons are illustrated below:

at	end	cat	it	arm	air
fat	bend	scat	fit	charm	hair

low	cab	tack	lump	rug	our
blow	scab	stack	slump	shrug	scour

Blending Sounds to Produce Syllables

Once students have been helped to add sounds both to the beginning and to the end of known words, they are ready to learn how to blend sounds to achieve the pronunciation of an unknown word (e.g., *shirk, acquire*) when (a) the new word does not remind them of any word they know, and (b) the new word is in an insufficiently helpful context. These details are specified immediately in order to underscore that blending sound-by-sound to achieve a pronunciation is a slow process that readers should use only when no alternative exists and the word appears to be important. This identifies the need for teachers to help students know *why* they are learning something, *when* they are to use what they are learning, and *how* they are to go about using it.

Having circumscribed the use of sound-by-sound blending, it is important to note that commercially prepared materials commonly omit attention to all blending (5). The assumption seems to be that if students know all the sounds that compose a syllable, they will be able to pronounce the syllable (4). (This assumption would not be supported by anyone who visits classrooms regularly.) To illustrate, in one basal series, teachers are told to have the children notice the vowel letter in the new word *such*. Even though blending has not received attention, the next recommendation is: Have the pupils pronounce *such*.

So that *you* can understand what students need to do in order to decode a one-syllable word like *such* when a word like *much* is not in their reading vocabulary or it does not come to mind, the following guidelines are offered.

Blending Sounds to Produce Syllables

1. The first job with an unfamiliar word is to consider its syllables, because the syllable is the unit of analysis for applying generalizations. With *such,* one vowel indicates one syllable.
2. Thoughts now turn to the likely sounds for *s, u,* and *ch.*
3. Once decisions are made about the sounds, it is time to blend them into a syllable, in this case into a word. Because consonant sounds are distorted when produced apart from words, the recommended sequence for blending begins with the first vowel in the syllable, progresses by adding preceding consonant sounds,

and concludes by following the sequence of the remaining letters. All this is demonstrated below:

4. Returning to the context, the decoder decides whether the word generated is correct, that is, is a recognizable word that makes sense in the context *Such a day!*

One postscript to the above is this: Had the unknown word been *each,* the same steps are taken to decode it. However, because *each* starts with a vowel, the blending procedure reflects the sequence of the letters:

ē̸ach

ē̸a̸

ē̸ach

To clarify still further the recommended sequence for blending sounds, more examples are shown here.

lăp	ăct	sō̸ap	mēt̸e	voic̸e	shawl
ă	ă	ō̸a	ē	oi	aw
lă	ăc	sō̸a	mē	voi	shaw
lăp	ăct	sō̸ap	mēt̸e	voic̸e	shawl

brŭsh	rōom	turn	ouch	hŭnt	āc̸e
ŭ	ōo	ur	ou	ŭ	ā
brŭ	rōo	tur	ouch	hŭ	āc̸e
brŭsh	rōom	turn		hŭn	
				hŭnt	

The examples of blending procedures listed above should make apparent the relationship between blending and earlier lessons both for adding final sounds to known words (*ten* → *tent*) and for adding initial sounds to known words (*at* → *fat*).

Sample Lessons: Blending

To show how blending sounds to generate syllables can be taught, only the modeling part of lessons is described. The first illustrative lesson is for students who can add sounds to known words and who are now ready to use that ability to blend sounds to decode *un*known words. For the think aloud that follows, the unknown word is *owl* embedded in the context *You can hear an owl, but you can't see one in the dark.*

> This is the name of something that makes noise. The *o* and *w* act like one vowel, so there's only one syllable. Let's see. I'll try the sound for *ow* that's like the sound for *ou*. Then I'll add the sound that *l* stands for. That would be *ow → owl*. Oh sure. It's "owl." I thought you could see an owl's eyes in the dark, but maybe not.

As part of a lesson with another group, a teacher models how to decode *ramp*, found in the sentence *In place of stairs, a ramp was used to get into the new house.* In this case, a known word (*am*) is useful because all its letters are in the same syllable.

> There's only one vowel, so this word has one syllable. I know *am*. If I add the sound for *r* at the beginning, it'll be *ram*. Now I'll add the sound for *p* and that gives me *ramp*. I know what that is. It's a board. Lots of buildings have ramps now for people who can't use stairs. In this case, I guess they're using the ramp because there aren't any stairs yet.

The next example of modeling focuses on a multisyllabic word, *umpire*, found in *An umpire is not always liked.* As is true of the previous illustrations of modeling, this example is offered to students as a complement to what is written on the board. By the time the teacher's think aloud ends, the chalkboard displays the following:

An <u>umpire</u> is not always liked.			
umpire	ŭm	fire	úm píŕe
um / pire	ŭ → ŭm	pire	úm pire

The think aloud itself follows.

> This word is the name of something that isn't liked all the time. That doesn't help very much. There's *m* and *p* with vowels before and after. I'll divide between them. One vowel not at the end. I'll try the short sound for *u*. I know the sound for *m*, so that's ŭ → ŭm. I can't think of any word that starts with "um." I had better look at the second syllable. Oh, that looks like *fire*. Maybe it says "pire." Umpíre. Oh, úmpíre. An umpire is not always liked. Boy, that's for sure.

The modeling just portrayed allows for making two points about decoding words composed of more than one syllable:

1. After a word is divided into syllables with the help of visual cues, the pronunciation of one or more of them may result from a simple substitution—for instance, *fire → pire*. (Some decoders might have used another substitution for the first syllable in *umpire: am → um.*)
2. The pronunciation of each syllable, plus contextual cues, may be enough to bring to mind a word that is known in its spoken form. That is helpful, because the decoding process tends to make each syllable sound like a separate word (*úm píŕe*). Knowing the spoken form, the reader also knows which syllable is stressed.

Focus for the Decoder	Concern of the Decoder
Context	1. What makes sense?
Word	2. Syllabication
Each syllable	3. Letter-sound correspondence 4. Blending
Word	5. Stressed syllable?
Context	6. Does this word fit the context?

FIGURE 9.1   A Strategy for Decoding

To allow for attention to other reminders, further work with a multisyllabic word is covered with a detailed explanation rather than with modeling. The unknown word is *infect,* and it is the only unfamiliar word in the sentence, *I don't want to infect you with my cold.*

As always, the decoder's first consideration is the context. This one indicates the troublesome word is a verb and is related to having a cold. It's something that the person with the cold doesn't want to do to somebody else.

The next focus is the word's spelling to see what it suggests for syllabication. Consideration of all the letters and their sequence suggests a division between *n* and *f* (*in fect*). The two vowels indicate that two syllables are the maximum number.

Having considered syllables, the decoder's next job is to deal with the pronunciation of each one. With *infect,* the word *in* provides the pronunciation of the first syllable directly. The presence of one vowel in the second syllable, which is not in final position, suggests trying a short sound for *e.* The *c* probably stands for its hard sound because it is followed by a consonant. With all this in mind, the decoder proceeds to blend sounds to learn the pronunciation of the second syllable: $ĕ \rightarrow fĕ \rightarrow fĕc \rightarrow fĕct$.

Having arrived at possible pronunciations for the two syllables, the decoder is ready to consider which syllable is stressed. If *infect* is familiar orally, the sounds derived from the analysis (ĭn fĕct) suggest both the pronunciation (ɪnfĕct) and meaning. The achieved pronunciation is also a word that makes sense in the context.

What has been described in some detail is summarized in Figure 9.1. Portrayed there is an outline of a strategy for decoding—that is, a systematic plan for coping with words that are unfamiliar visually (8).

Initially, teachers need to model use of the strategy. After a sufficient number of think alouds, students—with a teacher's assistance—can do the modeling. To help, the steps listed in Figure 9.1 can be printed on a large chart. Eventually, students will be able to use the strategy themselves. All this is summarized below.

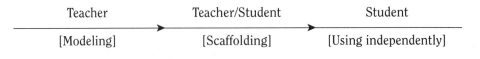

Teacher	Teacher/Student	Student
[Modeling]	[Scaffolding]	[Using independently]

Flexible Decoding

Assuming the word causing problems for a reader is regularly spelled and is familiar orally, the strategy depicted in Figure 9.1 is highly successful in achieving correct pronunciations. Irregularly spelled words, on the other hand, require a *fix-up* strategy. That is, decoders must have a plan for using alternative sounds when predicted sounds result either in an unsuitable word or in a nonword. That is why proficient decoding can be characterized as problem solving that proceeds with a systematic plan to achieve a solution that may be realized directly and quickly, or only after trial-and-error efforts.

To illustrate both direct success and trial-and-error efforts, let's say that the first time students see *flood* in print, it is in a very helpful context: *The rain keeps coming. It will flood all the basements.* In this case, the sounds that *f, l,* and *d* record, plus the students' ability to blend, plus their knowledge of basements and the fact that some get flooded when heavy rain persists, are likely to be sufficient to allow for a correct conclusion about the pronunciation of *flood* even though the double-*o* represents neither the long sound (cōol) nor the short sound (cŏok).

Let's consider a different situation in which *flood* appears in a less revealing context: *Nobody wants to think about a flood.* In this instance, a reader should conclude from the context that the unknown word is the name of something. However, because many nouns make sense, the spelling of *flood* assumes importance. Noting *oo,* the reader should first try "flōod," then "flŏod." Both should also be abandoned because neither produces a real word. What to do?

With one reader, trying the incorrect sounds for *oo* may be enough to suggest the correct one. With another, a trial-and-error process may be required in which other vowel sounds are used until something clicks—that is, until a recognizable, sensible word results. More specifically, the second reader tries "flŏd," "flăd," "flĕd" (a real word but not one that fits the context), "flĭd," and finally "flŭd." (Trying short vowel sounds first makes sense because of the absence of a final *e.*)

The message inherent in these illustrations is that successful decoders work differently but always with flexibility. The message for teachers is that flexible procedures do not just happen; they require instruction, modeling, and practice.

Substituting Sounds

As pointed out earlier, the ability to blend sounds to reveal the pronunciation of an unknown word (*ā → āc¢*) has its roots in the ability to add sounds to known words (*it → kit; hum → hump*). On the other hand, the ability to try alternative sounds when the predicted one is nonproductive (*flăd, flĕd, flĭd, flŏd, flŭd*) is an extension of the ability to substitute sounds in known words. Types of possible substitutions are specified in Figure 9.2.

As is true of adding sounds, the only way to teach students how to substitute sounds is by demonstrating the process. Done often enough, demonstrations are usually effective.

Sample Lessons: Flexible Use of Sounds

Except for single-syllable, regularly spelled words (e.g., *nap, cool, dire, lymph*), the result of decoding is best described as an estimate of a word's pronunciation. When

	Known Word	Unknown Word	Substitution
	make	cake	initial consonant
	ice	ace	initial vowel
	arm	art	final consonant
	he	hi	final vowel
	act	ant	medial consonant
	bench	bunch	medial vowel

FIGURE 9.2   Substituting Sounds

the word is multisyllabic and regularly spelled, the estimate is close enough to the correct pronunciation that all that may be required is an adjustment in stress (e.g., *tóx ic → tóx íc; món sóon → mon sóon; í cón → í con*). At times, an adjustment also includes use of the schwa sound (e.g., *cár pét → cár pət; á wáy → ə wáy; ám bú lánce → ăm bu lənce*). These adjustments are easy to make when the words are in the reader's oral vocabulary; they are even easier when contextual cues are available.

Oral vocabularies and contexts also help with irregularly spelled words, as demonstrated earlier with *flood*. That example of decoding also brought to the forefront the importance of a reader's ability to replace predicted sounds with others. Because such replacements involve doing something, students' ability to make them is achieved most readily when teachers model replacements. How teachers can do that is illustrated next. In this lesson, the unknown irregularly spelled word is *prove*, which is in the sentence *That doesn't prove a thing.*

> The sentence tells me the word I can't read is a verb, but that's about it. I had better take a look at the spelling. I can't think of any word that makes sense that starts with *pr*. Let's see. This word ends with *ve*. That means that /v/ is the last sound, that the *e* is silent, and that the word has only one syllable. I'm glad of that. Now for the *o*. *O* probably stands for its long sound because of the final *e*. I'll try blending all this, starting with *o*: ō → prō → prōv̸e. *Prōv̸e*? I've never even heard of a word like that. I'll try the short *o* sound: prŏv̸e. That's no better. I guess I had better keep trying other sounds for *o*. With that final *e*, I'll start with the long sounds: prāv̸e, prēv̸e, prīv̸e,…gosh, I can't even pronounce it with a long *u* sound. I'll try the long sound for *oo*; prōōv̸e. Oh, sure, It's *prove*. Why didn't I think of that earlier? That doesn't prove a thing.

Subsequent to modeling like that illustrated above, the teacher might want to remind students that vowel sounds are often problems, which is why she concentrated on *o*. She might also review that /v/ in final position is recorded with *ve*. At this point, familiar words like *cave* and *dive* should be written. Finally, the teacher might want to remind the students that trying out different sounds for *o* is similar to what they did earlier when they made substitutions like:

sit	shall	must	dime	like	luck
sat	shell	mast	dome	lake	lock
set		mist			

To emphasize that vowel sounds are not always the source of problems, the same teacher might work next on *giddy* embedded in the sentence *The children were too giddy to hear what the man said.* The modeling for *giddy* is illustrated next.

The children were too something to hear what the man said. *Noisy* makes sense, but that starts with *n*. I better check the spelling. A *y* at the end is a vowel, so that's two consonants with a vowel before and after. It probably has two syllables. I'll divide between the *d*'s. The first syllable is like *kid*, so that's *jĭd*. The *y* stands for a long *e* sound. That means the second syllable is *dē*. *Jĭddy. Jĭddy?* That's a funny word. Maybe it isn't even a word. What's the problem now? Maybe *g* stands for its hard sound. That makes the first syllable say "gĭd." *Gĭddý* Oh, *gíddy*. The children were too giddy to hear what the man said. They were probably bouncing around so much they couldn't hear anything.

In this instance, the teacher might choose to show the connection between what she did with *g* and what the students did earlier when they substituted consonant sounds:

ride	back	seat	number	simple
hide	pack	heat	lumber	dimple
side	sack	meat		pimple
wide	lack	beat		
tide		bleat		

Making explicit the connection between what students know and what appears to be new is helpful not only in simplifying and clarifying what is new but also in adding to students' confidence in being successful with a new task.

SUMMARY

The focus of Chapter 9 was decoding instruction. Before any instruction was described, the chapter responded to two questions. One had to do with a sequence for teaching about letter-sound correspondences and the factors that affect them. Especially emphasized in the answer is the need to consider *usefulness*. The point made is that it is senseless to burden students with instruction if what is taught cannot be applied in their reading fairly quickly. Text-driven instruction, therefore, was central when lessons were portrayed.

The second question was about the kinds of teaching procedures that are most likely to be effective. Here, a distinction was made between what decoders need to know and what they need to be able to do. When need-to-know is the concern, the recommendation was to use some combination of explanations, examples, and questions. Allowing for application was not overlooked. All these ingredients showed up when lessons were described by means of teacher-student dialogues.

When need-to-be-able-to-do is the concern, modeling by teachers was endorsed. It was also used many times in the chapter to explain how students can be helped to add, substitute, and blend sounds in order to resolve problems with words. Also pointed out is that the failure of commercially prepared manuals to attend to these abilities makes it incumbent on teachers to ensure that students get the help they need. Because manuals omit attention to decoding starting in about grade three and send students off to glossaries and dictionaries, Teacher As are also needed to encourage correct, efficient, and continuous use of what was taught earlier.

Underlying all the content of Chapter 9 was the assumption that students can learn to estimate the pronunciation of a word from its spelling. When the word is familiar orally, moving from an approximately correct pronunciation to the correct one is relatively easy, especially for readers who use spellings in conjunction with contextual cues. Adopting a problem-to-be-solved stance, the same readers learn to deal successfully even with irregularly spelled words.

Toward the end, Chapter 9 summed up much of what had been discussed earlier with an outline of a strategy for using graphophonic and contextual cues jointly. The recommendation to teachers was to model the strategy so that, eventually, students can assume responsibility for dealing with troublesome words on their own.

REVIEW

1. Explain the statement below. Then respond to the questions posed.
   a. The use of phonics allows only for word recognition. Practice is required to achieve the ability to identify the decoded word.
   b. Because decoded words need to be practiced, why bother teaching phonics? Why not reserve instructional time for whole word methodology and practice?

2. Chapter 9 recommends that known words should be used for instruction and that unknown words should be featured when the objective is to provide opportunities to apply what has been taught. Explain the reasons for the two recommendations.

3. Let's say you are teaching the correspondence between *k* and /k/. After printing and reading words that begin with this letter and sound, you ask for additional examples. One student suggests *king,* after which another immediately offers *queen.* Why might *queen* have come to mind? How would you respond to the child who suggests *queen*?

4. Whenever students have to stop reading to decode a word that seems important, they should reread the sentence in which the word is embedded once the decoding is done. Why is the rereading important?

5. Using examples, explain each of the two following statements:
   a. Adding sounds to the beginning and end of words is preparation for blending sounds to produce syllables (or words).
   b. Substituting sounds in words is preparation for using with flexibility what has been taught about letter-sound correspondences and the factors that affect them.

6. Chapter 9 recommends modeling—that is, think alouds—when the objective of a lesson is to teach students how to do something. With that in mind, let's assume that *group* is unknown and appears in the sentence *Schools group students by their ages.* Demonstrate a think aloud for decoding *group.*

7. The point has been made several times that decoding needs to be both correct *and* fast. Why is fast decoding essential?

REFERENCES

1. Adams, Marilyn J. *Beginning to Read: Thinking and Learning about Print.* Cambridge, Mass.: The MIT Press, 1990.

2. Commission on Reading. *Becoming a Nation of Readers.* Washington, D.C.: National Institute of Education, 1985.

3. Durkin, Dolores. "A Classroom-Observation Study of Reading Instruction in Kindergarten." *Early Childhood Research Quarterly* 2 (September, 1987), 275–300.

4. Durkin, Dolores. "The Decoding Ability of Elementary School Students." Reading Education Report No. 49. Urbana: University of Illinois, Center for the Study of Reading, 1984.

5. Durkin, Dolores. "Phonics Instruction in New Basal Reader Programs." Technical Report No. 496. Urbana: University of Illinois, Center for the Study of Reading, 1990.

6. Durkin, Dolores. "Phonics: Instruction That Needs to Be Improved." *Reading Teacher* 28 (November, 1974), 152–156.

7. Durkin, Dolores. "Some Questions about Questionable Instructional Materials." *Reading Teacher* 28 (October, 1974), 13–17.

8. Durkin, Dolores. *Strategies for Identifying Words.* Boston: Allyn and Bacon, 1981.

9. Newman, Judith M., and Church, Susan M. "Myths of Whole Language." *Reading Teacher* 44 (September, 1990), 20–26.

10. Stott, D. H. Manual for "Programmed Reading Kits 1 and 2." Toronto: Gage Educational Publishing Limited, 1970.

Structural Cues

Helping students learn how to cope with unknown words is significant for two reasons. First, independence makes a substantial contribution to students' progress in learning to read. Second, it has a pronounced effect on whether they *want* to read.

In spite of the significance of independence, the fact that many students need help with solving the mysteries of unfamiliar words becomes apparent whenever classrooms are visited. Because oral reading is common, it is impossible *not* to notice the large number who seem unable to take advantage of the cueing system of English when they come across words not in their reading vocabulary (4). Seeing these students repeatedly accounts for the attention that previous chapters give to contextual and graphophonic cues. It also is the reason for the inclusion of Chapter 10, which, as the title indicates, deals with another cue—word structure.

As made explicit earlier, using graphophonic cues is concerned with roots, thus with words like *circle, stress, alloy, illustrate,* and *opaque.* Using structural cues, on the other hand, is for deciphering words that are more complex in their composition—such as *unsuccessfully, penniless, prereading, maltreatment,* and *coexistence.* By the time you finish reading about words like these in Chapter 10, you will understand an observation that Lee Deighton made more than thirty years ago: "Frequently, polysyllables composed by adding one suffix to another frightens the developing reader out of all proportion to their real difficulty" (1, p. 29).

To show how students can be helped to use a systematic plan for dealing with *unhappy* and *spotless* and, later, with *forewarned* and *homelessness* is the goal of Chapter 10. To attain it, the chapter identifies what needs to be accomplished each time a prefix or suffix is taught. The objectives are illustrated whenever think-alouds portray the use of relevant cues, including cues rooted in a word's structure.

The teaching described in Chapter 10 divides between lessons that deal with what students need to know and with what they need to be able to do. What they need to do with words like *indefensible* and *counteraction* is outlined and illustrated.

Throughout your reading of Chapter 10, it is important to keep in mind that able readers use contextual cues along with structural cues. The former makes the use of structural cues not only easier but also something that can be done quickly.

• • • • • • •

Lᴵᴷᴇ ᴛʜᴇ ᴘʀᴇᴠɪᴏᴜs ᴄʜᴀᴘᴛᴇʀ, this one is about decoding. It not only continues the discussion, however, but it also enlarges the focus. It does this by dealing with letters that are prompts for meaning as well as pronunciation. Specifically, Chapter 10 recognizes that letters like *mis-* and *re-* help readers not only to pronounce words such as *misteach* and *reteach* but also to unravel their meaning (7, 8). The chapter further acknowledges that letters like *-er* and *-s* offer cues for the pronunciation and meaning of words such as *teacher* and *teachers*.

Words like *teach, misteach, reteach, teacher,* and *teachers* are useful in explaining word structure as well as terms used in instruction. They illustrate, first of all, that English words divide into families, members of which have the same origin. In the case of the family just referred to, the origin, namely, *teach,* is a self-sustaining root. In a family made up of members like *spectator, inspect, spectacles,* and *spectacular,* the origin is not an English word. Either way, the existence of families accounts for the fact that words have a structure. In some instances, the structure is simple. That is, the word is a root (*teach*). In other instances, the structure is more complex because it is composed of a root plus one or more affixes (*reteach, unteachable, reteaching, teacher, teachers, teaches*).

All this can be summed up by saying that whereas the previous chapter deals with self-sustaining roots, the present one is concerned with self-sustaining roots to which one or more affixes (prefixes and suffixes) are added. The goal of Chapter 10, therefore, is to show how teachers can help students from the earliest grades onward to acquire a strategy for coping with words like *burned, wishes, playful, retie, mismanagement,* and *unconquerable*. To be noted is that a knowledge of prefixes and suffixes is beneficial only when readers know the meaning of the roots to which they are affixed. Said differently, if *untie* is unfamiliar, of what value is it to know all about the prefix *un-* if the meaning of *tie* is not known?

AN INTRODUCTION

Chapter 10 starts with background information that provides a framework for the more detailed content covered later. The framework is assembled in three ways. Initially, a decoder's efforts with *flawlessly* are described. Starting the chapter this way shows how contextual, structural, and graphophonic cues function together. The second type of background information is the identification of goals for lessons with affixes. Here, the purpose is to outline the kind of instruction that gives students a strategy for dealing with both the pronunciation and the meaning of words like *flawlessly*. After that, the focus shifts to the question, When do I do all this teaching?

COMBINED USE OF ALL CUES

The purpose of the think-aloud that follows is to model how contextual, structural, and graphophonic cues work together to help decoders with unfamiliar words. Here, the word is *flawlessly,* found in the sentence *All the children danced flawlessly.*

Let's see now. It tells how the kids danced, so this word is an adverb (contextual cue). The *l* and *y* must be an inflection (structural cue). It's pronounced "lē." Maybe *l, e, s, s* is another suffix, like in *careless* (structural cue). I remember when we learned that. It's pronounced with the schwa sound. That leaves *f, l, a,* and *w*. That must be the root. The *a* and *w* act like one vowel, so that means one syllable (graphophonic cue). *F* and *l* are a cluster and I know the blend they stand for (graphophonic cue). I better put all these sounds together to see what the root is: aw → flaw. That's something that's wrong with something (oral vocabulary). With -*less* added to it, though, it means without flaws (structural cue). Oh, I see. There was nothing wrong with the kids' dancing (contextual cue). It must have been pretty good. All the children danced flawlessly.

It is acknowledged that the think-aloud just described is a contrived portrayal of mental activities that is designed to make explicit how three types of cues function together. In reality, proficient decoders are not as concerned about pronunciation as is the decoder depicted above. This is the case because meaning is what counts and because comprehension requires readers to keep moving. It is likely, too, that when *flaw* is sorted out as the root, blending the three sounds proceeds more quickly than the contrived description suggests. It is even possible that *flaw* is recognized, once it is mentally separated from the two suffixes.

What is not contrived is the dependence of decoding on oral vocabularies. Worthy of explicit attention is that knowing the meaning of *flaw* contributed to the decoder's success in two ways. It helped with the root itself, and it also allowed for use of the decoder's knowledge of the suffix -*less*. As explained, it is of little value to know that the suffix -*less* means "without" unless it is affixed to a root whose meaning is known.

As the think-aloud demonstrates, the possibility that an unknown word has an affix needs to be considered early in the decoding process. *Not* to do this may obscure structural units (prefix, root, suffix). This consequence is specified below with the help of the derivatives *redraw* and *disable:*

Structural Divisions		**Phonological Divisions**	
redraw	disable	redraw	disable
re draw	dis able	red raw	di sa ble

As the examples show, using generalizations that apply to roots (phonological divisions) when, in fact, the unknown word is more complex, may result in erroneous pronunciations. More important, meaning is disregarded by the failure to keep structural units intact.

All this suggests the need for a revised strategy for decoding when derived and inflected words become common in the materials students are reading. The strategy that incorporates early attention to affixes is shown in Figure 10.1. It is contrasted with the strategy demonstrated in the previous chapter, when the focus was unknown root words.

Having seen the significance of structural units for both meaning and pronunciations, you might now wonder why this book deals with phonological units first.

At the beginning...
Contextual cues
   Looking for syntactic and semantic help.
Graphophonic cues
   Looking at letters and their sequence in the syllable(s) of a root in
   order to decode the root.
Contextual cues
   Checking to see whether the conclusion about the root makes sense.

Later on, when inflected and derived words become common in selections that
students are expected to read...
Contextual cues
Structural cues
   Looking for one or more letters that suggest one or more affixes.
Graphophonic cues
Structural cues
Contextual cues

FIGURE 10.1   Sequences for Decoding Unknown Words

The sequence reflects the fact that the majority of words that beginning readers
learn are roots. Other words are inflected in simple ways—for example, *girls, talking, rides, played.* At this early stage, words like *girls* and *talking* are taught with
whole word methodology; attention does not go to inflections. Later, however, the
same words can serve as illustrations when it is time to give explicit attention to the
inflections *-s, -ing,* and *-ed.*

More is said later about decoding derived and inflected words. Now the question
is, What should be the outcomes of instruction with affixes?

OBJECTIVES OF INSTRUCTION

Before the necessary outcomes of instruction are identified, it is helpful to make
certain that terms pertaining to word structure are understood. These terms are
listed and defined in Figure 10.2. The list begins with terms discussed earlier in the
chapter.

Now that you have reviewed terminology, it is time to attend to the objectives
that ought to be realized with instruction about a prefix or suffix. They are listed
below; comments about each objective follow the list.

Instructional Objectives
Students:
1. Know the spelling and pronunciation of whatever affix is being taught.
2. Understand how that affix affects the meaning of roots.
3. Can transfer all this to a new derived or inflected word.

Word Family. Words having the same origin (e.g., *read, reader, readable, reread,* and so forth).

Root. The origin of a word family. A root (e.g., *teach*) cannot be reduced (e.g., *teach* to *each*) and still remain a member of the family. Sometimes, *stem* or *base* is used instead of *root.*

Prefix. A unit of one or more letters placed before a root that alters its meaning (e.g., *re*tie, *fore*tell, and *a*moral).

Suffix. A unit of one or more letters placed at the end of a root.

Derivational Suffix. A unit of one or more letters placed at the end of a root that alters its meaning (e.g., care*ful* and care*less*).

Derived Word. Composed of a root and a prefix (*re*act); a root and a derivational suffix (act*or*); or a root, a prefix, and a derivational suffix (*re*act*or*).

Inflectional Suffix. A unit of one or more letters placed at the end of a root for grammatical purposes (e.g., want*s*, box*es*, tall*er*, slow*ly*). Sometimes called *inflection.*

Inflected Word. Composed of a root to which an inflectional suffix is added (e.g., do*ing*, girl*s*, and rich*es*).

Affix. Refers to a prefix, a derivational suffix, or an inflectional suffix.

FIGURE 10.2   Terms for Word Structure

Knowing the spelling is essential because this enables a decoder to spot in an unfamiliar word what may be a prefix or suffix. Even though affixes are almost always regularly spelled, knowing how to pronounce them as a unit speeds up decoding.

The second objective listed specifies the major reason attention goes to affixes. The third one reflects the fact that the essence of instruction worth offering is its transfer value. That is, what is taught serves readers when they are on their own and encounter words that are related to those used for instruction.

SCHEDULING INSTRUCTION

The following sections answer the question, When should instruction about structural units be offered? Later, descriptions of lessons embellish the answer. As you read the next sections, keep in mind that what is said about scheduling instruction for structural cues applies equally to scheduling instruction for letter-sound correspondences and the factors that affect them.

In Connection with Assigned Reading

Attention has been called several times to the prereading preparations that enable students to do assigned reading independently. One part of the preparations is the attention given new vocabulary. Based on previous recommendations, you should now be able to predict another one: New words that are derived or inflected do not have to be pretaught if students are prepared to decode them themselves.

The point to be emphasized now is that time spent with vocabulary also allows for teaching or reviewing subject matter related to word structure. To illustrate, if one new word is *flawlessly,* it might be used to review the suffixes *-ly* and *-less;* or it might allow for reviewing the strategy for decoding outlined earlier in Figure 10.1. If attention has not yet gone to the fact that, unlike prefixes, more than one suffix can be affixed to a root, *flawlessly* can also be used to discuss inflected derivatives.

At an earlier grade level, a teacher may decide to use the new word *playful* to initiate instruction for *-ful.* This is a wise decision if one or more other new words have the same suffix, or if *-ful* can be affixed to roots the children know—*color, house,* and *care.* Such teaching is desirable, as it makes apparent the usefulness of knowing about the suffix *-ful.*

At Other Times

If all instruction for affixes were offered in conjunction with preparations for assigned reading, the time spent on new words could be sufficiently long as to reduce interest in doing the reading. That is why some instruction for affixes should be offered apart from assigned reading. At such times, it is still important to use derived or inflected words in newspapers, magazines, environmental text, and other sources that have the affix being taught. To illustrate, let's say it is time for students to know that the suffix *-y* changes nouns into words that describe. Attending to all the goals identified for lessons with affixes can be accomplished with words learned earlier to describe the weather: *windy, rainy, snowy.* Cereal boxes that highlight *crunchy* and *healthy* provide more examples. So, too, does a box of cookies that describes them as *crispy* and *chewy.*

Text seen on a grocery bag would be helpful for teaching the suffix *-able,* for it displayed *recyclable, reusable, degradable,* and *renewable.* The title of a brochure in a doctor's waiting room ("Diabetes Is Treatable but Not Curable") could add to the illustrations. Or, if radon is a topic being discussed, it is a perfect time to call attention to the suffix *-less* with the help of words that describe radon: *odorless* and *colorless.*

The point of these examples is that words in environmental text not only add interest to instruction, they also demonstrate that what is taught has relevance that exceeds the classroom. Not to be overlooked is that, eventually, affixes taught apart from assigned reading will be useful when attention goes to new words in selections assigned at some subsequent date.

BEGINNING INSTRUCTION

On the assumption that a framework for thinking about instruction with word structure has been established, it is time to consider teaching affixes. As you know from the list of terms in Figure 10.2, affixes are of three kinds: prefixes, inflectional suffixes, and derivational suffixes. The three types are illustrated next:

Prefix	**Inflected Suffix**	**Derivational Suffix**
<u>re</u>name	name<u>s</u>	name<u>less</u>

Because there *are* three kinds of affixes, it is also time to inquire, Which of the three should be taught first?

Usefulness merits immediate consideration. Even a quick look at easy material shows that inflected words like *played* and *colors* appear earlier than do derived words like *playful* and *colorless*. Inflected words also show up before derivatives like *replay* and *miscolor*. A sensible conclusion, then, is that lessons about word structure should be initiated with common inflectional suffixes such as *-s, -ing,* and *-ed*.

Instruction with an Inflectional Suffix

Plural nouns occur early in written material; consequently, the first lesson described is for the inflection *-s,* also referred to as a *plural marker* when affixed to nouns. The teacher begins by calling the children's attention to two words they know:

brown cat

After the children read *brown cat* aloud, the teacher says (as she holds up a picture of two brown cats), "If I want to talk about these two brown cats, I can't say 'brown cat'. Instead, what do I need to say so that you'll know I have a picture of more than one brown cat?…That's right. I say 'brown cats', not 'brown cat'. Let me show you what 'brown cats' looks like":

brown cat
brown cats

"What did I add to 'cat' to make it say 'cats'?…Yes, I added *s* at the end. Now let me see if I can fool you. This is the sign you see every day near the box of pencils. (Shows card on which *pencils* is printed.) What is this word?…Right. It's 'pencils'. Who can tell me—now think—who can tell me what to do to this word to make it say 'pencil'?…Correct. If I take away *s,* it just says 'pencil'. It needs to be 'pencils' on the card because there's more than one pencil in the box. I'll print both words on the board. Watch as I write them."

pencil
pencils

"Please read these two words…. Good. I'm going to write other words you know, starting with this one."

The teacher quickly prints *pet,* has the children read it, comments about their having two pets in the room, then prints *pets* making certain that the roots are lined up. This makes apparent the similarity but also the difference. After the children read *pets,* other familiar roots—considered one at a time—are written to which *-s* is added:

pet	top	girl	boy	hat	boat	car	room	dog
pets	tops	girls	boys	hats	boats	cars	rooms	dogs

At the end, the teacher reviews that adding *-s* to the end of words like *cat* and *top* makes them mean more than one.

Eventually, other ways to form plurals are taught when words such as *boxes, ponies,* and *loaves* appear in text. (If children are not ready to learn about the plural form for a word like *pony,* then *ponies* is taught as a whole word. It is useful later to illustrate how plurals are formed when the root ends in *y.*) Meanwhile, the instruction that focused on the plural marker *-s* allows for written practice that attends to both structural and contextual cues. For instance:

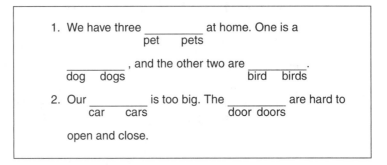

With practice like that shown above, the correct word is written in the blank rather than circled or underlined, because the writing fosters attention to the details of words.

Other Instruction with an Inflectional Suffix

A lesson for the inflectional suffix *-ed,* which is referred to as a *past-tense marker,* is described next. The following sentence is on the board:

Today we will play.

Once the instructional group reads the sentence aloud, the teacher inquires, "Did any of you play yesterday?" Responses are positive and include descriptions of a variety of activities. The teacher then comments, "I'm going to write a sentence that tells that you played yesterday."

Today we will play.
Yesterday we

After printing *we,* the teacher stops to ask, "Should I write 'play' again? Do we say 'Yesterday we play', or do we say something else? Today we will play. Yesterday we…What should I write here?" After the children tell her, the board shows:

Today we will play.   play
Yesterday we played too.   played

Once both the sentences and *play* and *played* are read aloud, the teacher suggests, "Please look at this word [pointing to *played*]. What did I add to the end of *play* to make it say *played*?…Yes, I added *e, d.* When I did that, I showed you played yesterday, not today. I'm going to add *e, d* to other words you know." At the end, the board displays the following words, each of which is used by a child in a sentence to verify that the past-tense meaning is understood.

play	talk	jump	call	work	walk
played	talked	jumped	called	worked	walked

In the lesson just described, the teacher deliberately avoided using *wanted,* a word taught earlier with whole word methodology. However, children must eventually learn the following generalization for the past-tense marker *-ed*. When they are ready to learn it, *wanted* can help illustrate the generalization.

When *-ed* is added to a verb ending in *t* or *d* (*count, add*), it is a syllable pronounced /əd/. Otherwise (*march, clean*), *-ed* adds a sound but not a syllable. For example:

wanted	needed	played	wished
painted	landed	helped	called

In time, students learn other ways to indicate past tense (*make, made; say, said; am, was; write, wrote*). But this information is acquired gradually as the need for it arises. Eventually, too, other inflectional suffixes are taught—for instance, small*er*, small*est*, quick*er*, quick*ly*.

Nonstandard Speakers and Inflectional Suffixes

In the lessons described thus far, inflections have been linked to oral language ("If we want to tell about something that happened yesterday, what do we have to say?…Yes, we'd say 'played', not 'play'."). When children's speech is standard English, the connection is helpful; when it is not, references to oral language may cause problems. With that possibility in mind, teachers should adhere to the following guideline: Whereas references to spoken language ought to be made when standard speakers are being instructed, a similar reference may confuse nonstandard speakers, who do not always pronounce inflections like *-ed* when they talk. For such speakers, therefore, instruction ought to be a direct telling process in which it is advisable to make statements like: "When you're reading about something that has already happened—maybe it happened yesterday or last week or even last year—you'll often find the letters *e, d* at the end of the word. That's why I put *e* and *d* at the end of *play*. I wanted to show that you did that yesterday. You played on Thursday. Let's look at some other words that tell about things that have already happened." One at a time, sentence cards are placed in a chart pocket to allow for reading and discussion:

> Last night I burned my finger.
> I walked in the park yesterday.
> This morning I asked my mom for a dime.

Teachers also need to keep in mind that how students respond aloud to an inflected word like *burned* (whether with "burn" or "burned") is less important than is their understanding of the grammatical significance of *-ed* (or of whatever the inflection might be). The fact that understanding is the key issue reflects a point emphasized very early in this book, namely, the primary concern of reading instruction lies with comprehension, not with what students say when they read aloud.

Samples of nonstandard deviations that have relevance for instruction with inflections are listed next (2, 6).

Written Language	Nonstandard Speech
I dropped it.	"I drop it."
He looks.	"He look."
She is coming.	"She is come."
They let us do it.	"They lets us do it."
He started crying.	"He stard cryin'."
Joe's bike.	"Joe bike."

LATER INSTRUCTION

Very few visits to classrooms are required to learn that derivatives like *unattainable, worthlessness, impracticality,* and *counteraction* present middle- and upper-grade students with a major challenge unless they have a systematic plan for unraveling pronunciations and meanings (4). Because derived words are composed of a prefix and a root (*miscount*), or a root and a derivational suffix (*spoonful*), or a prefix and a root and a derivational suffix (*prepayable*), this is the time to examine the prefixes and derivational suffixes listed in Table 10.1.

With derived words as the focus, it is also time to ask, Should prefixes or derivational suffixes be taught first? A general guideline is to start with some derivational suffixes for the following reason. Adding letters to the end of a known root leaves the root more visible than when letters are affixed to the beginning. Specifically, if students can read *act,* they are more likely to see what they know in *actor* than in *react.* Such a guideline is not intended to discourage teaching the prefix *dis-* if it happens that two new words in assigned reading are *disagree* and *disapprove.*

Instruction with a Derivational Suffix

Like all instruction for word structure, known roots are a starting point in lessons for derivational suffixes. As stated earlier, three objectives need to be achieved. If the concern is the derivational suffix *-less,* students should end up:

1. Knowing the spelling and pronunciation of *-less.*
2. Understanding its effect on the meaning of roots.
3. Able to deal with *-less* when it is in a derived word they have not seen previously.

Let's now examine how the objectives are realized. In this case, the proximity of Thanksgiving accounts for a discussion of everyone's blessings, one of which is having a home. This allows for attention to *home* (which is on the chalkboard) and to the fact that many more people are without homes than is often thought to be the case.

The teacher continues by stating there are different ways to say that many people do not have homes. First she writes:

Prefix	Meaning	Example	Suffix	Meaning	Example
ir-	not	irregular	-er	one who;	teacher
il-		illegal	-or	doer of action	actor
im-		impatient	-eer		auctioneer
in-		inactive	-less	without	spotless
a-		atypical	-able	capable of being	readable
non-		nonhuman	-ful	full; character-	careful
un-	opposite of	unlock, unkind	-y	ized by	oily
			-ous		dangerous
dis-	not	disobey	-ful	amount that fills	cupful
	remove	disarm	-ic (ical)	connected with	poetic, historical
re-	again	remake	-ist		humorist
	back	recall	-ness	state of	softness
mis-	wrongly	miscount	-hood		childhood
pre-	before	preschool	-ship		friendship
fore-	before	forewarn	-ance		tolerance
	in front	foreward	-ence		dependence
co-	with	co-author	-tion (ation)		action, starvation
counter-	against	counteract	-ment		enjoyment
anti-		antiwar	-ward	in the direction of	homeward
under-	below	underage	-age	act of	marriage
semi-	half	semicircle		amount of	mileage
	partly	semitropical		home of	orphanage
	coming twice	semiannual	-ee	object of action	employee

TABLE 10.1 Common Prefixes and Derivational Suffixes

Many people do not have a home.

Once the students read the sentence together, the teacher says, "The same thing can be said this way," after which she adds to the board:

Many people are without a home.

The students read both sentences; the teacher then prints a third, which she herself reads:

Many people are homeless.

After underlining *home* in *homeless,* the teacher states: "This part of the word is 'home'. When I add *l, e, s, s* to 'home', the word is 'homeless'. It means 'without a home'. 'Homeless' is a short way to say 'without a home'." The teacher then prints:

homeless = without a home

After rereading *homeless,* the teacher continues, "When I add *l, e, s, s* to the end of a word like 'home', I say it so fast that it sounds like 'luss' instead of 'less'. Listen. 'Homeless. Many people are homeless'." (If students know about the schwa sound, this is a time to refer to the occurrence of /ə/ in *-less.*)

Before the teacher attends to other roots to which *-less* will be added, she encourages further discussion of homeless people and of how grateful everyone should be to have a home. At what seems like an appropriate time, the group's attention is called back to *homeless*—to how the word is pronounced and to what it means. Subsequently, additional known roots are read both alone and with *-less* affixed to them:

mother	tree	shoe	head	tie	spot
motherless	treeless	shoeless	headless	tieless	spotless

For all these words, the semantic effect of *-less* is stressed.

As subsequent lessons concentrate on additional suffixes, they offer students considerable help with word meanings. Soon, for instance, attention to antonyms in a form such as the following is possible:

careless	useless	painless	helpless	colorless	joyless
careful	useful	painful	helpful	colorful	joyful

Systematic and frequent attention to derivatives is especially important for the following reason. Although derivatives appear regularly in written material, they are much less common in spoken language. This discrepancy is illustrated below. For each example, the first sentence typifies what might be found in print; the sentence in the parentheses illustrates how the same thought might be expressed in speech.

The remains of that ship are unsalvageable.
(They'll never be able to save what's left of that ship.)

Reasonless fear kept her awake.
(She was afraid for no reason, and it kept her awake.)

The handwriting was indecipherable.
(You couldn't even read the handwriting.)

Humorlessness characterizes the man.
(The man has no sense of humor.)

Their tastes are indistinguishable.
(They have the very same tastes.)

He shows unquenchable optimism no matter what happens.
(He's always optimistic no matter what happens.)

The differences illustrated above mean that students' oral language may not help very much with the derivatives they inevitably find in text as it becomes increasingly difficult. Therefore, the differences also mean that students can be *expected* to have problems with derivatives unless they have a systematic plan for unraveling their pronunciation and, more important, their meaning. To ensure that students *are* equipped with a strategy, two kinds of instruction are necessary. The first is like what has been illustrated: teaching students about affixes and how they affect root words. The second kind of instruction focuses on how to use this information to decipher derivatives. The first kind of instruction is described below; the second kind receives attention next.

Instruction with Prefixes

Earlier, a recommendation took the form of a general guideline: Teach some derivational suffixes before shifting attention to prefixes. The recommendation reflects the fact that seeing the known root in a word like *actor* is easier than seeing it in *react.*

As pointed out when the advice is offered, it is not meant to discourage teaching the prefix *dis-* if new words in a selection include *disagree* and *disapprove.* Nor is the recommendation intended to convey the message that large numbers of derivational suffixes should be introduced before lessons with prefixes start. Why some derivational suffixes are *not* covered first is suggested in the entries in Table 10.1; they show that the meanings of a number of derivational suffixes are abstract. This abstract quality makes it difficult to explain them to students. Here I have in mind suffixes like those in soft*ness* and enjoy*ment,* defined as indicating "state of." The difficulty explains why instruction with some derivational suffixes should be followed by attention to common, easily understood prefixes.

At one time, prefixes stood out in text because hyphens separated them from roots. Because this use of hyphens has practically disappeared, increased attention must go to prefixes to ensure that students recognize them in unfamiliar derivatives. How a lesson with a prefix might progress is described next.

While discussing the traits of a character in a story, *happy* is used. Afterward, the teacher returns to this adjective to teach the prefix *un-* by saying, "The word *happy* reminds me of another word. The word I'm thinking of is interesting because it has *happy* in it, yet it means just the opposite. It means 'not happy'. Can anyone tell me the word I'm thinking of?"*

If nobody can, the teacher answers her own question. Keeping in mind the objectives of lessons for affixes, she pronounces *un-* and talks about its effect on the meaning of descriptive words like *happy.* Using other adjectives in the students' reading vocabulary, she provides more illustrations. To highlight what is common and what is different, pairs are written as follows:

| happy | tidy | hurt | even | fair |
| unhappy | untidy | unhurt | uneven | unfair |

At another time, the same teacher demonstrates that *un-* affixed to verbs means "to do the opposite" (*unbend, unwrap, untie, unlock*). This difference in meaning is important to keep in mind, as commercial materials do not always make the distinction (3). That is, some restrict the meaning to "not," which is correct for adjectives but not for verbs.

Sometimes, too, students need to learn that *un-* at the beginning of a word may be part of another prefix (*under*ground, *under*fed) or an integral part of a root (*uncle, unit*). Because of the tendency to overgeneralize—in this case, to think that *u* and *n* at the beginning of a word are always a prefix—teachers should model trial-and-error procedures similar to the one in the think-aloud that follows. The word in question is *unite* in the sentence *The people need to unite if they expect to win.*

---

*Once, another teacher phrased her comments differently: "I'm thinking of a word that means just the opposite of 'happy'. Can anybody tell me what it might be?" One child responded "Sad." In this case, the response should—and did—tell the teacher about an important omission in her request.

This word tells what the people have to do to win. The *u* and *n* are a prefix, and there's nothing at the end that looks like a suffix. That means *i, t, e* is the root. That would be pronounced "īt̸." I don't think there is such a word. At least I never heard of a word that sounds like that. Maybe *u* and *n* aren't a prefix. That would make the whole thing the root. If it is, there are two syllables: *u* and *n, i, t, e*. Oh, sure. *Unite*. You have to stick together to win. The people need to unite if they expect to win.

The thoughts described above reemphasize the relevance of oral vocabulary for decoding, for it was competence in oral language that led to the rejection of *ite* as a root and of *un* as a prefix. The decoder's oral vocabulary also established the correctness of "unite."

To promote equally correct conclusions by students, teachers should select words that appear to have prefixes and suffixes but in fact do not and then model decoding procedures similar to the one just portrayed. (Examples of such words are *pres*to, *rem*nant, *anti*que, const*able*, *razor*, and dig*est*.) By doing this on a number of occasions, teachers provide a model that permits students to use what they have heard and observed.

SPELLING GENERALIZATIONS AND WORD STRUCTURE

It is not overly difficult to sort out suffixes, whether inflectional or derivational, when the spelling of the root is unchanged. Seeing suffixes in *worthless, harmful, curbs,* and *arches,* for instance, is fairly easy for anyone familiar with the four suffixes. In contrast, sorting out the root in words like *making* and *penniless* can be a problem. To enable students to resolve problems resulting from altered spellings of roots, teachers should spend time on what are usually thought of as spelling generalizations. (See Figure 10.3.) If they are to function for readers, the connection between the content of the generalizations and sorting out structural units must be made explicit.

Let's consider one spelling generalization now:

When a root ends with a silent *e*, the *e* is commonly dropped when a suffix beginning with a vowel is added. For example:

bake	fine	cube	bride	solve
baker	finest	cubed	bridal	solvable

After reading the generalization, your first thought may have been, But how will students *know* that the roots in unfamiliar words like *baker* and *finest* end with a silent *e*? The answer is, They won't. Nonetheless, they will be correct more often than not if they are familiar with both the suffixes -*er* and -*est* and the generalization above and then assume that the two roots end with *e*. Making this assumption, they may recognize the roots. If not, each root is readily decodable.

When a root ends in silent *e,* the *e* is usually dropped when a suffix beginning with a vowel is added. For example:

bake	starve	cube	bride	strange
baker	starvation	cubist	bridal	strangest

When a root ends in a consonant followed by *y,* the *y* is changed to *i* before most suffixes are added. For example:

cry	pony	duty	merry	melody	history
cried	ponies	dutiful	merrily	melodious	historical

When a root ends in a consonant that is preceded by a single vowel, the consonant is usually doubled before a suffix is added.* For example:

rob	mud	chop	run	forget
robbed	muddy	chopping	runner	forgettable

The plural of nouns ending in *f* is formed by changing *f* to *v* and adding *es.* For example:

elf	leaf	calf	loaf	self
elves	leaves	calves	loaves	selves

*The doubled consonant is useful in signaling information about the sound of the previous vowel. Contrasts like the following illustrate the usefulness:

dinner	tapped	hopping	holly
diner	taped	hoping	holy

FIGURE 10.3 Spelling Generalizations

As spelling generalizations are being taught, they should figure in work that concentrates on uncovering roots in derived and inflected words, as this is what readers need to do. For example:

merrily	= merry	+ ly	merriment	= merry	+ ment
miner	= mine	+ er	graduation	= graduate	+ ion
staring	= stare	+ ing	melodious	= melody	+ ous
witty	= wit	+ y	wiry	= wire	+ y
wisest	= wise	+ est	enviable	= envy	+ able

Because the need to sort out roots usually occurs with words in contexts, exercises like the following ought to be common. In this case, students provide what appears in brackets.

I work puzzles <u>easily</u>.	[easy	+ ly]
The kittens ate <u>hungrily</u> from the bowl.	hungry	+ ly]
Everyone danced <u>happily</u> around the room.	[happy	+ ly]
<u>Angrily</u>, the man pounded on the door.	[angry	+ ly]

Contexts can also be used to review statements of spelling generalizations:

She <u>slammed</u> the door.   I like the <u>coziness</u> of this room.
Don't be so <u>nosy</u>.   He <u>regretted</u> doing that.
He is the <u>tiniest</u> of all.   Their <u>facial</u> expressions were
interesting.

DECODING DERIVED AND INFLECTED WORDS

The ability to sort out roots in the ways just referred to is not accidental. It is, instead, the product of instruction and practice designed to provide a systematic plan for dismantling and reassembling the structural units of formidable-looking words like *unenviable, foretelling,* and *lawlessness* (5). Steps for executing such a plan are listed in Figure 10.4. How the strategy, plus a spelling generalization, function with the three words is also shown.

In order to see more clearly how students might use the strategy outlined in Figure 10.4 (initially on paper, later mentally), let's get inside the head of a student to examine his thoughts. He is having trouble with *unenviable* in the context *They had the unenviable job of having to do it twice.* You can see that this decoder follows the sequence shown earlier in Figure 10.1:

1. Contextual cues
2. Structural cues
3. Graphophonic cues
4. Structural cues
5. Contextual cues

These are the decoder's thoughts:

> This word says something about the job they had to do two times. The *u* and *n* could be a prefix. I had better take a look at the end. If *a, b, l* and *e* are a suffix, that could mean the *i* is really *y.* If it is, the root is just those four letters: *e, n, v, y.* Oh, sure, *envy.* That means you want something. Maybe somebody has something and you wish you had it. But the prefix makes it mean just the opposite. You don't want it. Let's see. *Unenviable.* That means you don't want their job. That makes sense. Who would want to have to get into that icy water twice? They had the unenviable job of having to do it twice.

This is an appropriate time to return to the earlier description of how *flawlessly* was decoded. It is near the start of Chapter 10. It also is an appropriate time to read an account of the efforts of a learning disability teacher to give her students a strategy for dealing with words that are more complex than a root. The account is in Figure 10.5.

**A Strategy for Decoding
Derived and Inflected Words**

1. Lay aside the prefix first.

2. Lay aside each suffix, one at a time.

3. If the root is unfamiliar, decode it.

4. Put back the suffix immediately next to the root.

5. If there is a second suffix, add that next.

6. Add the prefix last.

Applying the Strategy

unenviable	foretelling	lawlessness
enviable	telling	lawless
envy	tell	law
enviable	telling	lawless
unenviable	foretelling	lawlessness

Commentary: The importance of keeping intact roots that are part of derived and inflected words is underscored early in Chapter 10. Doing that acknowledges the significance of meaning for reading. In addition to keeping all structural units intact, the recommended strategy keeps before the decoder real words at all points in the dismantling and reassembling processes. Specifically, the sequence reflects the fact that prefixes are sometimes affixed to inflected and derived words (*definable—indefinable; wanted—unwanted*) but not to their roots (*define—indefine; want—unwant*).

FIGURE 10.4   Decoding Inflected and Derived Words

A particular section in the chapter on structural analysis caught my attention. It dealt with the problem readers have with strung-out words. Several of my intermediate students tend to get overly excited when they encounter such words. They panic even when the base and affixes are familiar ones. ("Panic" is a good description of what happens. Students seem to forget what they know when the words are longer than two syllables.) For these reasons, I chose to teach another lesson dealing with affixes.

During a recent reading assignment, my students had trouble reading *unopened.* I copied the sentence from their book and underlined *unopened.* Using the sequence suggested in the chapter, I wrote *unopened, opened, open, opened,* and *unopened.* (The words were in a column with the common root lined up.) I modeled the decoding procedure, calling attention to each step.

Since the group is familiar with the terms *base, prefix,* and *suffix,* I brought out a chart listing the six steps that are in the chapter. We discussed each one. I gave the students a chance to practice other strung-out words with known bases. I didn't want the connection between the exercise and real reading to go unnoticed, so I said that the words came from the reader they use in their classroom.

We did several words on the board together; then I gave out a worksheet with more examples. The six steps were typed at the top of the page for reference. One student had difficulty with the assignment. It was obvious he needed more instruction. I will work with him later individually.

To conclude the lesson, we played a game. Each player received four cards with inflected words like *opened, wanted, liked.* The students took turns selecting prefix cards from the deck. The object was to match cards to form a more complex word. To receive credit, the student had to pronounce and give a meaning for the new word. The first player to match four cards correctly won.

Chris was allowed to play even though he had difficulty earlier. Excluding him from the game would have hurt his feelings. He was able to play with some assistance from me. I will have plenty of time to help him tomorrow, since he meets with me for 30 minutes of one-on-one instruction before the other two join us.

As for the other two, they really caught on to the process. They were successful in reducing the word to the base and rebuilding it to its derived form. They even conquered challenge words like *unmanageable* and *co-authored.* Quite a feat for these children.

The lesson, I thought, turned out to be very beneficial. Not only did Kenny and Charles move a step closer to independence, but the lesson also helped pinpoint a problem Chris is having with decoding.

FIGURE 10.5   A Report by a Learning Disability Teacher

DECISIONS ABOUT NEW VOCABULARY

Before Chapter 10 ends, a synthesis of recommendations made in Chapters 6 through 10 for new vocabulary might be helpful. To accomplish that, let's consider the question, How does a teacher decide what to do with vocabulary thought to be new in text about to be assigned? To respond, five factors need to be kept in mind.

Factors Affecting Decisions about a New Word
1. Words in students' oral vocabularies.
2. Context in which the new word appears.
3. Spelling and pronunciation of the new word.
4. Students' ability to use contextual, graphophonic, and structural cues.
5. Words in students' reading vocabularies.

By now, the significance of oral vocabularies should be so apparent as to make additional comments unnecessary. Even though the relevance of the other factors listed above should be equally clear, their significance is further clarified with illustrations. This seems necessary, given the fact that frequently used materials like basal reader manuals typically provide poor suggestions for dealing with new words.

When children are just beginning to learn to read, the lack of decoding ability requires that each new word be identified—unless a word is in a context that is so rich with cues that only one word is possible. A second reason for the frequent use of whole word methodology at the start is that a number of the words required to construct sentences (e.g., *was, of, the, to*) have irregular spellings, making decoding ability (assuming some exists) nonproductive. To be noted, however, is that as children acquire decoding ability, they will be able to figure out the pronunciation of some irregularly spelled words (e.g., *would, should*) with help that derives from words learned earlier with whole word methodology (e.g., *could*).

Implied in all this is that unknown words ought to be named for students only when no alternative exists. This is most important for ensuring that students develop maximum independence. Whether an alternative exists depends on the five factors listed earlier.

What has now been said offers the following guidelines for teachers:

1. Examine new words in the selection to be assigned and the contexts in which they occur initially in order to eliminate any that students ought to be able to handle alone because of (a) the words they know, and (b) their ability to use contextual, structural, and graphophonic cues.
2. Use whole word methodology with the remaining words. If any is a derived or an inflected word, present the root first. For instance, if *imperfectly* requires attention because students do not have sufficient ability in using structural cues, show the word first as a root, then in the more complex form:

perfect
perfectly
imperfectly

3. Once the assigned reading is done, attention should go to the new words whether they were or were not pretaught. This helps the teacher know whether further practice with the words is necessary or, perhaps, whether more help is needed for using the cueing system of English.

SUMMARY

As the synthesis just presented indicated, the ability to use structural cues contributes to students' ability to deal with new words on their own. How to use them and what needs to be taught to make their use possible were both covered in Chapter 10.

The chapter began by explaining the nature of derived and inflected words. At this point, terms related to word structure were defined. The objectives that need to be achieved whenever instruction focuses on a prefix or suffix were then named.

When to provide instruction was considered next. One suggestion was to offer instruction when new words in assigned reading include one or more derived or inflected words. To avoid spending excessive time on prereading preparations, the second suggestion was to offer additional instruction at some other time. That words in authentic text—including environmental text—should be used in these lessons was emphasized.

Chapter 10 then considered factors that need to be taken into account in order to decide whether prefixes or suffixes should be taught first. Usefulness was the criterion that put inflectional suffixes at the top of the list. Accommodations that are necessary when inflectional suffixes are taught to children whose speech is nonstandard English were described. Other recommendations were to teach some derivational suffixes before attention to common prefixes begins. For all such instruction, illustrative words should be some that are in text that students need or want to read. This makes explicit the value of what is being taught.

Attention also went to spelling generalizations, now viewed as offering decoders help whenever the spelling of a root is altered in derived or inflected words. The point was made that the relevance of these generalizations for reading must be demonstrated.

The final section of Chapter 10 focused on how to help students use what they know about prefixes and suffixes in order to decipher derived and inflected words. A systematic strategy for achieving that goal was outlined and modeled.

Even though few generalizations are included in Chapter 10, they, plus the generalizations covered earlier in Chapter 8, are grouped together in the summary that follows.

Generalizations for Decoding: A Summary

Syllabication

Structural Divisions:

Most prefixes and suffixes are syllables (*un lock; care less; play ing*).

When the suffix -ed is added to a verb ending in *d* or *t*, it is a syllable (*need ed, dent ed*). Otherwise, it adds a sound to the verb but not a syllable (*marched, pulled*).

When the suffix -ion is added to a root ending in *t*, the letters *tion* form a syllable (*act, ac tion*).

Phonological Divisions:

When two consonants are preceded and followed by vowels, a syllabic division usually occurs between the consonants (*win dow*).

When a vowel precedes and follows a consonant, a syllabic division usually occurs after the first vowel (*si lent*).

When *x* is preceded and followed by a vowel, the first vowel and *x* are in the same syllable (*tax i*).

When a root ends in a consonant followed by *le*, the consonant and *le* are the final syllable (*pur ple*).

For purposes of syllabication, consonant digraphs and vowel digraphs function as if they were single letters (*ath lete; au thor*).

Vowel Sounds

When a syllable has one vowel and it is in final position, it commonly stands for its long sound (*silo*).

When a syllable has one vowel and it is not in final position, it commonly stands for its short sound (*album*).

When a syllable has two vowels, the long sound of the first is common (*meet, mete*).

When a syllable has two vowels, one of which is final *e* and the two are separated by two or more consonants, the short sound of the first vowel is common (*pulse*).

Vowel sounds in unstressed syllables are often reduced to the schwa sound (*rándom*).

The digraph *oo* has both a long and a short sound (*cool, cook*).

The digraph *ow* stands for the long *o* sound (*own*), and for the sound in the initial position in *owl*.

When a vowel is followed by *r* in a syllable, three different sounds are possible (*art, her, for*).

When a vowel is followed by *re* in a syllable, five different sounds are possible (*care, mere, hire, bore, pure*).

Y Functioning as a Vowel

When *y* is in medial position in a syllable that has no vowel, it commonly stands for the short *i* sound (*myth*).

When *y* stands for the final sound in a multisyllable word, it usually records the long *e* sound (*fancy*).

Otherwise, *y* is likely to stand for the long *i* sound (*try, style, cycle*).

Consonant Sounds

When *c* and *g* are followed in a syllable by *e, i,* or *y,* they commonly stand for their soft sounds (*cell, cigar, cyst; gem, gin, gypsy*). Otherwise, the hard sounds are common (*can, talc, act; glad, pig, wagon*).

The letter *s* stands for either /s/ or /z/ (*see, has*).

The digraph *th* records a voiced and a voiceless sound (*the, thin*).

The digraph *ch* commonly records the sound heard initially in *chop*. It may also stand for the sounds heard initially in *chef* and *chord*.

Together, *q* and *u* stand for either /kw/ or /k/ (*quit, plaque*).

The letter *x* stands for /z/, /ks/ or/gz/ (*xylophone, sox, exact*).

REVIEW

1. Define the terms listed below. Include at least two examples of each term in the definitions.

   a. word family   **c.** prefix   **e.** inflectional suffix

   b. root   **d.** derivational suffix   **f.** structural unit

2. The objectives that every lesson dealing with an affix needs to realize are specified in Chapter 10.

   a. State the objectives.

   b. What should students know and be able to do when a lesson for the prefix *mis-* concludes?

   c. Name derivatives that can be used either to help with the instruction for *mis-* or to allow for application.

3. From your study of Chapter 10, you should be able to explain the following statement. Support your explanation with examples different from those in the chapter.

   In decoding, structural units are considered first, then phonological divisions. The structural units take precedence over the phonological units because of the fundamental importance of meaning.

4. What are *structural* divisions in the following words?

   a. imperfectly   **d.** readable   **g.** miscounted
   b. goldfish   **e.** showy   **h.** meaningful
   c. syllable   **f.** reappointment   **i.** fabrics

5. If students have problems with derivatives, teachers should be prepared to decompose and reassemble the structural parts in a way that helps with both the pronunciation and the meaning. Guidelines for doing that are provided in Chapter 10.

   a. State the sequence for dismantling and synthesizing structural units.
   b. Keeping the sequence in mind, show on paper (as you might list on a chalkboard) the steps for dismantling and reassembling the structural units in the words below.

   resprinkled   unforgettable   momentarily   impersonally

REFERENCES

1. Deighton, Lee C. *Vocabulary Development in the Classroom.* New York: Teachers College Press, Columbia University, 1959.
2. DeStefano, Johanna S. *Language, Society, and Education: A Profile of Black English.* Worthington, Ohio: Charles A. Jones Publishing Company, 1973.
3. Durkin, Dolores. "An Attempt to Make Sense Out of a Senseless Basal Reader Lesson." *Illinois Reading Council Journal* 14 (Spring, 1986), 23–31.
4. Durkin, Dolores. "The Decoding Ability of Elementary School Students." Reading Education Report No. 49. Urbana: University of Illinois, Center for the Study of Reading, 1984.
5. Durkin, Dolores. *Strategies for Identifying Words.* 2nd ed. Boston: Allyn and Bacon, 1981.
6. Morgan, Argiro L. "A New Orleans Oral Language Study." *Elementary English* 51 (February, 1974), 222–229.
7. White, Thomas G.; Power, Michael A.; and White, Sheida. "Morphological Analysis: Implications for Teaching and Understanding Vocabulary Growth." *Reading Research Quarterly* 24 (1989, No. 3), 283–304.
8. White, Thomas G.; Sowell, Joanne; and Yanagihara, Alice. "Teaching Elementary Students to Use Word-Part Clues." *Reading Teacher* 42 (January, 1989), 302–308.

PART IV

The fact that *reading* and *comprehending* are synonymous was underscored in Chapter 1. That everything done in the name of "reading instruction" should contribute to comprehension abilities permeated all the chapters that followed. The thrust behind the persistent criticism of round robin reading, for instance, is its penchant for making reading an exercise in expression, not a meaning-making process. How it turns attention away from connected text to naming individual words is another reason the use of round robin reading has been questioned.

Later in the book, when Chapters 4 and 5 concentrated on the beginnings of literacy, comprehension was not forgotten. The recommendation to start with connected text, not with letters and sounds, reflected concern about making certain that young children realize immediately that reading has something to do with meaning. That

the meaning constructed must make sense was the theme when spoken contexts were discussed as a way to initiate attention to contextual cues.

The four previous chapters that have just delved into the cueing system of written English took it for granted that recognizing individual words is necessary because not to know too many words leads to breakdowns in comprehension. Even the emphasis on dealing with unfamiliar words quickly reflected the continuing concern for comprehension. So, too, did the intermittent reminders about the importance of providing for word practice to ensure that students' sight vocabularies serve them well whenever they need or choose to read.

All this is to say that the decision to call Part IV "Developing Comprehension Abilities" was not motivated by the belief that comprehension has been slighted. Rather, this title reflects the fact

Developing Comprehension Abilities

that the purpose of Part IV is to return to comprehension with two chapters that, like the first one, focus on comprehending directly.

Chapter 11 focuses on comprehending individual words. This is not done to suggest that understanding connected text requires readers to understand every word of which it is composed. In fact, as Chapter 8 explained earlier with the help of *brown, beige, and black,* purposes established for reading may make the meanings of certain words unimportant or at least unnecessary to know. On the other hand, it is equally correct to say that, most of the time, the failure to know the meaning of a relatively large number of words in a piece of connected text makes it unlikely that its comprehension is possible.

Connected text is the focus of Chapter 12. Because some people wonder why comprehension instruction is necessary—given the fact that readers comprehend spoken language—this chapter starts by attending to differences between comprehending spoken language and comprehending written discourse. The differences discussed demonstrate that the ability to decode individual written words is insufficient to guarantee the comprehension of connected text.

Because comprehension instruction needs to be rooted in a correct understanding of comprehension, the latter is defined as the fulfillment of whatever purpose(s) were established for the reading. This explains why purposes for reading receive such generous coverage in Chapter 12.

Topics that provide subject matter for comprehension instruction are identified in this chapter. To ensure that sufficiently specific meaning is given to comprehension instruction, a number of lessons are included in the discussions.

Comprehension: Words

PREVIEW

Just as interest in the comprehension process has been widespread and apparent during the past two decades, so has interest in vocabulary acquisition. This is natural when it is kept in mind that over even more decades, researchers have consistently reported high correlations between knowledge of word meanings and ability to comprehend connected text.

To the extent that is possible, the treatment of vocabulary knowledge in Chapter 11 takes into account the research that has been reported. That is why this chapter assigns importance to the reading that students do on their own, as researchers generally agree that this is a rich source for vocabulary acquisition. You might want to take another look, therefore, at ways in which teachers foster reading, which are described in Chapter 6.

Even though it is heartening to know that what is enjoyable is also productive, one fact needs to be kept in mind: Students who do most of the independent reading are the better readers. (Or, as has been said, "The rich get richer while the poor get poorer.") This point is made because it reinforces the great need to provide all students with the best possible instructional programs year after year.

Now that you know from previous chapters the many specific ways in which comprehension is dependent on oral vocabularies, you should be ready to learn what teachers at all grade levels can do to add to those vocabularies. To get an overview of Chapter 11, examine the graphic display in Figure 11.7 before starting the chapter. It is in the Summary section. Even though not all parts of Figure 11.7 may be meaningful now, the display does show at a glance how the chapter covers Vocabulary Knowledge. The same display also practices what Chapter 11 preaches: Helping students *see* how one word or idea relates to other words and ideas promotes both understanding and retention.

Like other chapters, this one includes a few snapshots of what teachers have done—in this case, to enlarge oral vocabularies. These accounts of classrooms help specify the nature of instruction for word meanings; they also show that doing productive, interesting things with words is not beyond the reach of any motivated teacher.

Teachers who are motivated keep in mind that oral vocabularies are as much caught as they are taught. "Does my own use of language provide a desirable model?" is a question such teachers ask of themselves with some regularity.

ANYONE READING THIS CHAPTER KNOWS from personal experience that the inability to understand the meanings of words causes problems for comprehension. Some may even recall a particular time—for instance, while taking a test—when just one unfamiliar word kept them from understanding what needed to be understood.

To make the greatest contribution to comprehension, the meaning of a word as it is used by an author must be known by a reader at the level of automaticity. Isabel Beck and her colleagues at the University of Pittsburgh refer to this as having an "established" meaning (1). To understand better what is meant by their description, the three levels of word knowledge to which they refer are defined below.

Established: Meaning is quickly, even automatically, accessed.
Acquainted: Meaning is known and can be accessed but "only after deliberate attention has been focused on it" (p. 12).
Unknown: Meaning "has not been established in semantic memory" (p. 12).

Why established meanings are significant for reading comprehension is the same reason that automatic word identification and quick decoding are important: Whenever readers have to attend consciously to individual words, attention is taken away from the meaning of the whole of the text.

As explained in Chapter 3, silent reading that is not hesitant is now referred to as *fluent,* a term once reserved to describe "smooth" oral reading. The importance of fluency for comprehension has implications for instruction with word meanings: Established meanings are rarely achieved with as few as one or two contacts with a word. This is especially true when the learner needs to acquire a new label (new name) for a new concept (new referent). Knowing neither the label (e.g., "plateau," "dam," "harbor," "desert") nor what it refers to is one major reason large numbers of students cannot comprehend content area textbooks.

Being aware of what is not known (label? referent? both?) is important for teachers; consequently, levels of instructional needs are discussed next.

LEVELS OF INSTRUCTIONAL NEEDS

Levels of instructional needs refers to the different tasks that teachers face when they want to expand oral vocabularies. Differences in tasks account, in turn, for differences in difficulty. To illustrate, instructional objectives are easier to achieve when a child knows a referent (a particular flower) but not its label ("daffodil") than when neither the referent nor the label is familiar. Viewing tasks in relation to labels and referents results in five possible kinds of responsibilities for teachers. The five are listed below, after which each is discussed.

Tasks for Expanding Vocabulary Knowledge
1. Teach a label for a familiar referent.
2. Expand the meaning of a familiar referent.
3. Teach an additional label for a familiar referent.
4. Expand the referents for a familiar label.
5. Teach a new label for an unfamiliar referent.

Name for Familiar Referent

Teaching a label for a familiar referent is the easiest of the five tasks just identified. It is something that parents and teachers of young children do routinely. As referred to earlier, teaching the names of colors falls into this category, as does teaching words like *dog, circle,* and *chair.* Later, a child may learn that the name for the very tall buildings he sees whenever somebody takes him downtown is *skyscraper.*

Expanded Meaning for Familiar Referent

Another instructional need, expanding the meaning of a familiar referent, goes on during one's entire life. After all, who really understands the meaning of *death* until a loved one dies? And who truly understands *friendship* until a crisis occurs and it is experienced or sadly missed? Implicit in all this is, first, that the meanings of many words change and grow as people change and grow and, second, that children have not lived long enough to have a full understanding of many words, including some fairly common ones.

However, let's take a common word such as *pillow* to trace how its meaning expands. At first, a child may know a pillow only as something soft that supports his head and makes him generally more comfortable in bed. He may eventually learn that when more than one pillow elevates his head in bed, it reduces the amount of coughing he does. He may also learn that having pillow fights with a sibling is fun but forbidden.

Later, this same individual comes to know that some pillows, such as the ones carefully placed on chairs in the living room, serve a decorative function and are not to be touched by head or hand. Still later, when his mother is caring for an ill and elderly grandparent, the child learns that pillows are used to ensure that someone lies in a variety of positions, thus preventing bedsores.

Expanding the meaning of familiar referents should also result from teachers' efforts. How a kindergarten teacher in a rural community went about expanding the meaning of *brush* is described in Figure 11.1. Her efforts show that nothing needs to be purchased to help with oral vocabularies. This was reillustrated during a classroom observation. With the help of close-at-hand materials, the observed teacher expanded the meaning of *bag* with grocery, sandwich, book, and garment bags. She also used her own purse and was sufficiently humble to close the discussion with a reference to the bags under her eyes.

Additional Name for Familiar Referent

In the examples just described, the names *pillow, brush,* and *bag* remain unchanged even while their meanings are expanding. A different instructional task is teaching additional names—that is, synonyms—for the same referent. Teachers who use manuscript writing, for instance, may be using a new label for the familiar behavior known to children (and parents) as *printing.* Similarly, the furniture salesperson who talks about sofas may not know he is using a new label for what the child accompanying his parents refers to as *couch.* Visits to unfamiliar geographical areas are also common times for acquiring new labels for familiar referents. Even though at home one might carry soft drinks in a bag, elsewhere pop is carried in sacks. All

For Sharing Time this week, I asked each child to bring in a brush. (A note had been sent home earlier that explained the reason for the request.) Recalling our discussion in class about the value of common objects for vocabulary development, I decided to use brushes this week. My hope was that enough different kinds of brushes would be brought that any child who had but one notion of *brush* would have many by the time we finished.

Luckily, a variety of brushes *was* brought to school this morning. Because I have a fairly small class, allowing each child to say something about his or her brush was no problem. Following the comments, we talked about how the brushes were alike and how they were different. (Earlier, one of the children had seen a janitor sweeping the halls, which led to the need to discuss whether a broom is a brush.) From time to time, I posed questions to bring out the various functions that the brushes served. In the end, the brushes available were divided into three groups based on use. One group was for cleaning houses, the second was for animals, and the third group was for what I ended up calling "personal use." (The word *personal* took some explaining on my part. Fortunately, one child helped by saying it sounded like *person,* so "Those brushes must be for persons.")

Once the brushes were grouped and counted, we recorded the results in the form of a simple bar graph. Before I printed *Brushes* at the top, we reviewed what a title is and the fact that the first letter in a title is printed in its capital form.

I always feel special satisfaction when what I plan allows not only for realizing the preestablished objective but also for using what we have been learning.

FIGURE 11.1 Expanding the Meaning of a Word

this suggests that even though the classroom is the setting for the treatment of vocabulary knowledge in this chapter, the productivity of nonschool sources of influence should not be underestimated.

Additional Referents for Familiar Name

Adding to the meanings that a word already has for students was discussed in Chapter 6, when homonyms were placed in the category "text-dependent words." At the time, the discussion was about whole word methodology; the specific point made was that if a word in text about to be read is not in the students' reading vocabulary and it is a homonym, the word should be introduced in the company of other words. This allows for attention to the meaning that matches how it is used in the selection that will soon be read. (You may remember that nine contexts illustrated nine meanings for the word *hand*.)

The important point now is that many words *are* polysemous ("many meanings"). One task for a teacher, therefore, is to make certain that students understand the meaning that needs to be assigned to a word in whatever they will be reading. A linguist who studied basal reader glossaries, William Nagy, reached a conclusion that is both surprising and pertinent here. He found that glossary definitions did not always match how the listed words are used in the basal selections (7).

An assignment seen on a chalkboard in a fifth grade did not acknowledge the existence of homonyms, either. The assignment is probably one that you did some time or even many times in elementary school.

1. Write each word three times.
2. Look up the meaning of each word in the dictionary.
3. Write that meaning after each word.
4. Write a sentence using each word.

This dictionary assignment not only fails to accommodate homonyms but also shows disregard for the most important feature of using dictionaries: *selecting* the meaning that fits a given context. One has to wonder whether assignments like that referred to above led the linguist George Miller to conclude that "most healthy, right-minded children have a strong aversion to dictionaries" (6, p. 97).

Name for Unfamiliar Referent

The influence on oral vocabularies of all that happens in nonschool settings is particularly noticeable when it comes to the fifth and most difficult task teachers face in expanding vocabulary knowledge: teaching a new label for a new referent. It is now that the value of out-of-school experiences for vocabulary development is so apparent. For example, even while one student is giving a glowing, detailed account of the mountains he and his family saw on their vacation, other members of the same class may have experienced nothing taller than the pile of dirt hauled to a city park to allow for sledding in the winter.

The difficulty of teaching names for unfamiliar referents was effectively depicted by Edward Dolch as long ago as 1951:

The average adult tries again and again to tell children with words what things are.... The child asks, "What is a snake?" The adult says, "An animal that crawls along the ground." The child imagines such an animal and asks, "But his legs will be in the way." The adult says, "Oh, he hasn't any legs." So the child takes off the legs and sees a legless body lying there. "But how does he crawl around without legs?" "He wiggles," says the adult. The child tries to make the legless body wiggle. "How does that get him to go forward?" The adult loses his temper. The peculiar way in which part of the snake pushes the other part cannot be described. It has to be seen. Let us go to the zoo. (2, p. 309)

The essence of Dolch's observations can be summed up as follows:

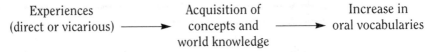

The connections portrayed above are especially relevant for middle- and upper-grade teachers. As mentioned earlier, this is the case because many important words in the textbooks they ask students to read are in the category "unknown name and unknown referent." That one third-grade teacher appreciated the value of experiences for teaching words for which both the name and the referent were unfamiliar is illustrated in the account of classroom activities in Figure 11.2. It was written by an observer.

Admittedly, time does not allow for attending to the meanings of all the words that need to be understood in the ways described in Figure 11.2. On the other hand, anyone familiar with dictionaries should know that a direction like "Look it up in the dictionary" does not usually provide a solution when both the name of the word in question and its referent are unknown. Again, the research done by Nagy is relevant; another of his findings shows that explanations in dictionaries and glossaries may be more difficult to understand than is the word presumably being clarified (7). Nagy specifies his criticisms with precise figures. In one basal reader glossary, for instance, a word listed is *image,* which is defined as "a likeness." Nagy notes that

> "likeness" is a relatively rare word; it occurs less than twice in a million words of text. "Image," the word it is supposed to be explaining, is far more frequent, occurring 23 times per million words of text. (p. 10)

Later in this chapter, better ways to teach word meanings are described.

Now, having read the section "Levels of Instructional Needs," you might be wondering, How can I ever remember all this? Actually, all that has to be remembered is, first, that meanings of words are unknown in different ways and, second, that the differences ought to affect what is done with, and how much time is spent on, any given word. Whether words are important enough that their meanings should be *established* is a third consideration.

TIMES FOR ATTENDING TO WORD MEANINGS

In order to simplify discussions when previous chapters in the book dealt with contextual, graphophonic, and structural cues, an important assumption was made: the meanings of words that figured in the discussions and that served as illustrations

Although I did not find a reading lesson per se when I arrived, I saw a good example of expanding the world knowledge and oral vocabularies of third graders. The teacher was showing a movie in which Marcel Marceau was demonstrating pantomime. Afterward, the teacher discussed the word *pantomime* and how it is done.

One preplanned activity to give the children a chance to pantomime was called "mirroring." The teacher asked a child to help her demonstrate the activity. Facing the teacher, the student became a mirror. Her job was to copy the slow, steady movements that the teacher made as if she really were a mirror. As the two demonstrated pantomiming, the teacher emphasized that it required concentration. She stressed with the onlookers that they should watch their partner's eyes at all times and that they would be able to see side movements that a partner made because of their peripheral vision. She then explained peripheral vision and gave examples of times when it is used without our even knowing it.

The students then paired up. Everyone seemed to be concentrating as they followed the directions of the teacher. The teacher walked around the room, complimenting certain pairs of students who were working especially well. Eventually, the partners switched roles so that everyone had a turn to be a mirror. At the end, the teacher called the children together to discuss what it was like participating in the act of pantomiming.

Because of all the wonderful things this teacher did, the fact that she never wrote either *pantomime* or *peripheral vision* was unexpected. Writing *mirror* might have added one more word to the children's reading vocabularies. Showing *mirroring* directly under *mirror* would specify their relationship. The experience of observing in this room reinforced the fact that even superior teachers need to ask, "*Why* am I doing what I'm doing?" In other words, a little reflection never hurts anyone.

FIGURE 11.2 Experiencing the Meaning of New Words

were known. Now it is time to be more realistic and to acknowledge that life for conscientious teachers is never that simple. In fact, as grade level increases and texts become more difficult, attending to word meanings can be an encompassing responsibility. It is also the case that more and more words are in the category "unknown name, unknown referent."

One time when meanings ought to receive attention is during the prereading preparations made for assigned reading—this includes reading done with content area textbooks. Other times for helping with meanings become apparent whenever classrooms at any grade level are observed. Inevitably in the course of a day, something happens or is said that identifies one or more words whose meanings need to be taught or clarified.

In the section that follows, the focus is prereading preparations. Later, the need to respond to, and take advantage of, teachable moments is the concern.

WORD MEANINGS AND PREREADING PREPARATIONS

The fact that instruction for word meanings may enter into prereading preparations is referred to explicitly in the previous chapter when factors that ought to affect decisions about new words are listed:

Factors Affecting Decisions about a New Word
1. Words in students' oral vocabularies.
2. Context in which the new word appears.
3. Spelling and pronunciation of the new word.
4. Students' ability to use contextual, graphophonic, and structural cues.
5. Words in students' reading vocabularies.

The primary importance of word meanings is acknowledged by the fact that the list urges teachers to consider, first, whether words that are new in their visual form have meanings that are known. For instance, if *icon* is unfamiliar visually and thus shows up on a "new word" list, the first question requiring attention is whether students know the meaning of *icon*. If it happens that the meanings of an excessive number of words are not likely to be known, teachers have to choose for prereading attention the words that (a) must be understood if the assigned material is to be comprehended adequately well and (b) are not explained in the selection. (Ways in which contexts offer help with meanings are discussed later in the chapter.) How this two-pronged guideline functions is illustrated below with the help of three words:

Swan
> For a selection whose purpose is to explain how *swan song* came to mean "a last effort" or "a final piece of work," students should have some idea of what a swan is. However, because two illustrations in the selection show swans, it is only necessary to provide the correct pronunciation for *swan*, because it is irregularly spelled. (*Cygnet* is listed as another new word but is not of major importance. In addition, the selection identifies the referent. Because *cygnet* is regularly spelled, students should be able to reach a correct conclusion about the pronunciation.)

Probe

This regularly spelled word is important to understand in a story about an adolescent who gets into trouble when he tries to keep his best friend out of trouble. In this case, redundancy in the text permits students to infer the meaning, which can be discussed after the selection is read. Whether students reach a correct conclusion about the meaning can also be determined by posing a question about the story that can be answered only if *probe* is understood.

Apprentice

The main character in a story is an apprentice serving under an experienced silversmith. Although *silversmith* is explained in the text, *apprentice* is not. This is a word, therefore, meriting prereading attention.

The first guideline can now be summed up as follows. Words that are not in students' oral vocabularies and are not explained in the text for which preparations are being made are candidates for instruction. Because extensive prereading preparations may have a negative consequence on students' interest in doing the reading, such candidates sometimes have to be reduced in number. Whenever this is the case, words should be selected for instruction not on the basis of their difficulty but in relation to their importance for understanding the text about to be read (14).

The second guideline stems from the fact that superficial understandings do not contribute to comprehension. The second suggestion, therefore, is to make sure that students end up with an in-depth knowledge of the selected words. In some instances, in-depth knowledge has already been acquired, as when the instructional task is to teach a name for a familiar concept. (For example, children have seen objects that are either square or rectangular in shape. The task for the teacher, therefore, is to help them learn that one shape is called *rectangle*, the other *square*.) In-depth knowledge also exists when the need for students is to learn that another name for *scold*—something they have experienced on a number of occasions—is *reprimand*.

A different task faces teachers when the need is to help students understand the meaning of *smoke* used in an expository selection that tells of various ways in which food is preserved. The same comment applies to *cure*, also in the selection.

A more difficult task is helping students achieve an understanding of such words as *disenchantment, awe,* and *wistful*. Unlike other words in which both the referent and the label are also unfamiliar (e.g., *crescent, winch, dam, barge, dwarf, meadow*), these kinds of words cannot usually be explained with pictures. As a result, the tendency is to try to explain a word such as *awe* with other words, which may be as unfamiliar as *awe*. Some time ago, Albert Harris (4) effectively described the hazards of this all-too-common practice:

> One difficulty with this procedure is the danger of relying on superficial verbalizations. Words that are clear to the teacher may be quite hazy to the child. Many of the classical boners are due to a superficial and inadequate grasp of word meanings. It is not sufficient to tell a child that *frantic* means *wild,* or that *athletic* means *strong;* he may try to pick *frantic flowers* or pour *athletic vinegar* into a salad dressing. (p. 409)

The second guideline for the attention given to word meanings during prereading preparations can now be stated as follows. The goal is in-depth, not superficial, understanding. The time required to realize this objective depends not only on the ability of the students but also on the exact nature of the instructional task. Teachers can define the task for each selected word by considering what it is that is unknown—the label, the referent, or both.

The third guideline is to check up on students' retention of meanings once the reading is done. This is the time, too, to learn how the students did on their own with words that the author explained directly or indirectly. Whether words used figuratively in the selection were understood is another question that might require postreading attention. One more possible topic pertains to the need for students to know when words do not have to be understood with exactness. As mentioned earlier, to be aware that *beige* is a color is sufficient under certain circumstances. At another time, inferring that *dulcimers* are musical instruments (*They were familiar with fiddles, dulcimers, and banjos.*) may be all that is needed for adequate comprehension. Students need to be aware of this.

CHARACTERISTICS OF EFFECTIVE INSTRUCTION

As noted, instruction that stands a chance of succeeding takes into account what it is about a word that is unfamiliar. Three other features of instruction that give it the potential to achieve its goal merit attention, too. They are listed below.

Effective Instruction with Word Meanings
1. Relates what students know to the word receiving attention.
2. Shows the relationship of the word targeted for instruction to other words.
3. Provides opportunities for students to use the word they are learning in thoughtful ways.

Each feature is now discussed.

Uses What Students Know

Because learning can be viewed as moving from what is known to what is new but related, attempts to instruct about words with unfamiliar meanings are improved by encouraging students to talk about what they know that is related. With that in mind, a teacher might initiate prereading preparations for a selection about *smoking* and *curing* as preservative processes with a comment like, "I don't know why, but twice this week I've had to return milk to the store because it was sour. Has that ever happened in your family?" Guided by the teacher, the student discussion identifies the fact that very cold temperatures help keep certain foods fresh, including dairy products. It is only natural for the teacher to ask next, "Do you know of other ways to keep something like meat and fish from spoiling?" Responses let a teacher know what does or does not need to be done with the words *smoke* and *cure*. In one case, she might end up writing on the board students' existing knowledge about smoking and curing. Now, one purpose for the reading to be done is to see whether the students learn something new—or contradictory—about the two processes. To help students keep this purpose in mind, it should be written in some form. Questions such as the following achieve that end:

What did you learn about smoking and curing that you already knew?
What new information did you get?
Did your reading suggest you had any incorrect information?

If an instructional group appears to know nothing about smoking and curing as preservative processes, prereading preparations proceed differently. In this case, the teacher might ask the students for the more common meanings of *smoke* and *cure* (which are printed on the board), after which she tells them that both words have different meanings in the selection they will soon read. Because refrigeration has already been discussed as one way to keep foods fresh, the teacher explains that *smoke* and *cure* also have something to do with food preservation. Because both processes are clearly explained in the text, nothing else is done with the two words now. How the meanings of *smoke* and *cure* are extended as a result of the selection is discussed after the reading is done.

Shows Relationships among Words

One suggestion in the previous chapter pertained to new words in assigned reading that are derived or inflected. The specific recommendation is to introduce students to such words—assuming they are unable to deal with them themselves—in their simplest form and to build from there to the new word:

> perfect
> perfectly
> imperfectly

The use of word families, then, is one way to work with words not as isolated bits and pieces but as something with family ties.

Earlier, in Chapter 6, you were reminded that when words are not yet in students' reading vocabularies, it is helpful to present together any words that have related meanings. This illustrated what is now commonly referred to as *semantic webs, semantic maps,* and *conceptual sets.* Another semantic map was the basis for the first Review question in Chapter 6. Even though references were made in these earlier chapters to meaning-based groups of words, a few additional examples are offered here because making connections not only helps clarify meanings but also fosters retention.

Let me continue the discussion of related words with a reference to two uses of semantic webs in classrooms, one seen by an observer and the other reported by the teacher herself. The observer's report of a first-grade teacher is in Figure 11.3. The description shows how a semantic web provides for word practice, thus contributing to sight vocabularies, at the same time that it attends to oral vocabularies.

A third-grade teacher's account of a use of a web shows it to be a means for reviewing in order to prepare for a test. Even though it is generally agreed that discussions by students in conjunction with the development of a web or map is the most important part of their use (12), the account (see Figure 11.4) does not refer to any discussion. Some might say it merely portrays memorization and mindless copying. Even so, the described use of a web is a start. What teachers eventually accomplish with something new is more significant than how it was used the first time.

It was time for art. The teacher began by distributing real leaves to the children. The group then talked about how the leaves looked and felt. As these first graders named descriptive words, the teacher began making a web on the board around the word *leaf.* This was the end result:

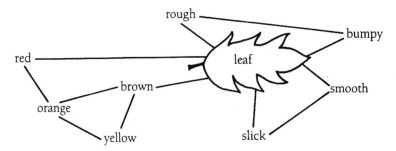

Although the web seemed complex for these young children, they were excited about the way it took shape. They told the teacher where to put words and what words to connect to others. (It was clear that the children had done webbing previously.)

When the web was done, the teacher asked what the word in the center said. The students answered correctly. The teacher then erased the outline of the leaf and reprinted the word, again asking all what it said. They responded correctly once more—even though not all looked at *leaf.* (I kept wondering whether the teacher thought the shape was an irrelevant cue, thus wanted to get rid of it.)

The teacher next asked the class if they remembered the word *rub* from a story she had read to them recently. They said they did. She picked up a red crayon and asked for a volunteer to point to the word on the board that named this color. The teacher then rubbed the red crayon on a sheet of paper that had a large sycamore leaf beneath it. She asked the students what they saw. All called out, "A leaf!" The teacher continued, "Tell me the color of the leaf that you see." They did. She then printed *a red leaf* on the board and asked everyone to read what she wrote, first silently and then aloud. They did.

All this provided a suitable and productive introduction to leaf rubbings, which were labeled by the children when they did their own at their desks.

At the end, before any of the words on the board were erased, all were read aloud several times by everyone as the teacher pointed to the words in a random order.

FIGURE 11.3   Use of a Semantic Web in First Grade

We have just finished a unit on teeth. To review what has been covered in preparation for a test, I made a web to organize some of the content.

In the center of a transparency that I planned to show on an overhead projector, I printed *Teeth.* Subtopics were written on what I referred to as "legs" that extended out from the word *Teeth.* The subtopics I chose and printed were *care, sets, parts,* and *kinds.* Close to each subtopic I drew lines to allow the students to supply related information.

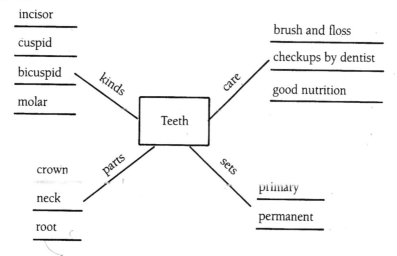

We have used semantic webs before for stories; this was the first time I attempted one for expository material.

After the group supplied information for subtopics, each student received a copy of the same web but on which the information just referred to was omitted. I asked them to fill in the lines on their copy, explaining that copying the information would help them remember the important details better than just reading it from the transparency. As they copied, I circulated among them making sure that no words were misspelled. I did not want anyone studying misspelled words tonight in preparation for the test. Although the test covers more than these particular points, I believe this was a good way to review some of the things we've been discussing.

FIGURE 11.4 Review Information about Teeth

One teacher I'm acquainted with, who recognizes the value of relating one word to others, frequently posts charts showing semantically related words such as the following:

Movement		
walk	dash	scamper
run	stroll	
skip	strut	

As the chart shows, places have been left for *stalk* and *swagger,* two words in selections not yet assigned.

Should *gaunt* be a new and important word in a story and the gaunt person is not pictured, its meaning can be clarified with the help of what is called *scaling.* (Use of scaling is appropriate when word meanings differ from each other by degree.) In this instance, students know *thin, skinny,* and *bony,* which makes the following continuum meaningful:

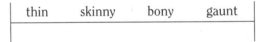

thin   skinny   bony   gaunt

If the same students have been taught the prefix *mal-,* the word *malnourished* might be added to the board and discussed in relation to *gaunt.* The fact that words with similar meanings convey different messages might also be considered. Now, words like *skinny, thin, slim,* and *slender* are appropriate. The question, "How would you prefer to be described, and why?" can be the start of attention to connotative and denotative meanings and to the fact that words sometimes mean more than they appear to say.

As is seen in these illustrations, discussing words in relation to other words does more than just prepare students to comprehend a particular selection. It also allows for contacts with words that are frequent enough to put their meanings into the category referred to by Beck et al. as "established" (1).

Uses Newly Acquired Vocabulary

Once students seem to understand the meanings of words selected for instruction, they should have the opportunity to use them in thoughtful ways. Not to be overlooked is that the most meaningful use is provided by reading the selection in which the words appear one or more times. Before or after the selection is read, other contacts should be provided that encourage further thinking about meanings. A few ways in which students can be encouraged to use, rather than just state, meanings are illustrated below.

Questions:
What does it mean when someone says, "The countryside is so gaunt in winter?"

Multiple-choice items:

A hungry squirrel is likely to   stroll

strut   when he sees a nut.

scamper

True-false statements:

He is an ambidextrous talker. _____

Definitions:

Define *stock:*

a. as a chef might explain it.

b. as a farmer might explain it.

c. as a merchant might explain it.

Completing sentences:

There was a paucity of rain. Therefore,

Analogies:

A _____ is to a cygnet what a horse is to a foal.

Word categories:

Underline all the words below that make you think of your ears rather than your eyes.

bleating   retorted   glared   coastline   stethoscope

Ideally, whenever students are asked to respond to requests like those suggested above, the chance to explain responses should be available. I'm reminded of this need because of what occurred in a first grade in which a group was just completing a page in a workbook. The task was to read the three words listed in each of nine boxes and to cross out the word that did not belong with the other two. One box listed *dog, bird,* and *car.* When a girl was asked why she crossed out *bird*—the Answer Key said the correct answer was *car*—she explained, "You need a license for a dog and a car but not for a bird."

RESPONDING TO NEEDS AND OPPORTUNITIES FOR INSTRUCTION

Thus far, attending to word meanings when preparations are made for assigned reading has been the focus. Another time to be concerned about oral vocabularies was identified earlier in the chapter. At the time it was said that observers of classrooms almost inevitably hear comments, questions, and answers from students that show a need to teach or clarify meanings. The following sections discuss those needs.

Confusion about Meanings

Even though confusion about meanings often adds to the enjoyment of visiting classrooms, teachers do need to respond in ways that result in clarification. Four examples of observed confusion follow.

- In one fourth grade, a group of ten students was beginning a unit of stories entitled "South of the Border." Asking, "What does 'border' mean?" the teacher quickly heard, "It means somebody who lives with you, but he's not in your family." "No," continued the teacher, "it means something else." "I know," volunteered another child. "It means when you feel bored, like you're bored playing the same game."
- Elsewhere, the meaning of "bold" (applied to whoever had burglarized a student's home) was getting attention. One child explained its meaning by saying, "It's like when you go bowling." Disagreeing, another proposed, "It's like when a man doesn't have any hair on the top of his head."
- In a third grade, the teacher inquired about the meaning of "idle" found in the sentence *The children were idle.* Almost before the question was completed, one child said, "It means a statue." "No," said the teacher, "That's a different word. Who can tell us the meaning of *this* word?"
- In another instance, a class had been studying reptiles in science. To supplement the text, the teacher was showing a film called "Reptiles." Because the narrator used the word "viper" several times, the teacher asked one child in the postviewing discussion, "What *is* a viper?" Without hesitation, the boy answered, "It's what's on a car window to keep it clear when it rains."

These four examples were selected from a large number that could have been chosen because they have three things in common. First, the confused words have either the same pronunciation (border, boarder) or similar pronunciations (viper, wiper). This common characteristic makes the second shared feature unexpected: In none of the cases did the teacher show the words. Applied to the examples of confusion cited, "showing" means printing the following on the board as the first step in clarifying meanings.

border	bold	idle	viper
boarder	bowled	idol	wiper,
bored	bald		

The third common feature is that all the misdefined words were part of a context that, seemingly, was ignored by the students. Specifically, the word *border* entered into the theme of stories about to be read, "South of the Border." In the case of *bold,* the context was the behavior of a person who had burglarized the home of a classmate. *The children were idle* was the context for *idle,* and a narrated film provided the context for *viper.*

One further example of confusion about meaning is described for the purpose of emphasizing the following.

Students need:

- To realize that words commonly have multiple meanings.
- To consider the context in which a word is embedded before reaching a conclusion about its meaning.
- To know that "context" may be as brief as a couple of words or as long as an expository article or a story.

The additional example of confusion is described below.

> During a discussion of a character in a story, the teacher commented, "She certainly was a patient person, wasn't she?" Everyone agreed. The teacher then asked, "What does 'patient' mean?" Immediately one child explained, "It means when you're sick and you go to the doctor and he tells you that you have to go to the hospital."

Using this example as an illustration, three guidelines for dealing with confusion about meanings are now listed.

1. To begin, show students the words.
2. Use the words in the context in which they occurred so the dependence of meaning on context can be underscored (e.g., "But the story wasn't about anyone who was sick. Remember, I used 'patient' to describe the kind of person that Melissa was. I said she was patient. What does that say about her? Think about the kind of person Melissa was in the story.").
3. In order to encourage thoughtful responses, do not call on anyone immediately. As another writer has observed, "Students often perceive a discussion as a contest to see who can answer the teacher's question first" (3, p. 145).

With all the attention that goes to reading-writing connections, it is appropriate to end this discussion of confused meanings with a reference to a prewriting discussion in one observed classroom. Again, the incident showed the need for chalkboard teachers—for teachers who follow the advice, "Don't just talk about it—show it!" In this case, the writing was to be about an ancestor. Nothing was on the board when I arrived, nor was anything written by the time the discussion ended and the writing began. Given the unused chalkboard, the title used by one girl for her composition was particularly interesting: "My Auntsister."

Unexpected Happenings

In Chapter 2 when different kinds of instruction were discussed, it was said that some of the most effective teaching seen is in the category "unplanned but intentional." Such instruction has to do with what are commonly referred to as "teachable moments." How some observed teachers have taken advantage of the unexpected to advance students' vocabulary knowledge is described next.

Unfortunately, the unexpected opportunity in one case was the result of a badly damaged school building that had been vandalized the previous night. Even though some teachers might have been mentally paralyzed by the mess left in the classroom, the observed teacher used the occasion to discuss with her first graders the meanings of *vandal, vandalism,* and *vandalized.* (At first, one child thought Mr. Vandal had done the damage.) Because acoustical tiles had been torn from the ceiling, the meaning of *acoustics* and *acoustical* was not overlooked, nor was the need to write the words for all to see, say, and discuss, even though the teacher had a difficult time getting to the chalkboard because of the disarray.

In another classroom, the Monday following a three-day weekend revealed a half-empty fish tank. "Did the fish drink all the water?" wondered one child. In response, the teacher filled two plates with water; by Wednesday, she was able to use them to explain *evaporate* and *evaporation* in a way that reinforced the fact that vocabulary development has to do with learning concepts, not just words.

Teachers who appreciate the need to narrow the gap between school and life outside its doors have also been seen doing productive things with vocabulary. At the time of a serious gasoline shortage, one teacher helped students understand *ration, depleted,* and *emergency,* using contexts taken from newspapers. Another teacher used heavy rains and nearby rivers to teach *flood, crest,* and *tributary.* A teacher of younger children recognized the forthcoming spring vacation as an opportunity to contrast *solid* and *hollow* as these concepts are realized in chocolate bunnies. Finally, another teacher used an attractive bulletin-board display of Hallowe'en masks made by students to extend the meaning of *mask* with discussions of its use in skiing, scuba diving, surgery, and keeping warm. (The students added robbing to the times when masks are useful.)

INDEPENDENT READING AND VOCABULARY GROWTH

Because of research findings (5, 8, 14), a chapter devoted to ways to extend oral vocabularies cannot omit attention to what some authors have called "incidental learning from reading" (5, p. 785). Or, as Nagy, Herman, and Anderson put it so well, "our results strongly suggest that the most effective way to produce large-scale vocabulary growth is through an activity that is all too often interrupted in the process of reading instruction: reading" (9, p. 252).

Why regular, extensive reading produces increases in vocabulary reflects the characteristics of effective instruction that are discussed earlier. More specifically, extensive reading allows for using what is known to acquire new learnings. Second, reading connected text presents many opportunities to experience the relationships among words. Third, a meaningful use of words learned earlier is occurring all the time. And, finally, by supplying repeated contacts with words, reading changes a partial knowledge of meanings into in-depth knowledge.

Reflecting all these incidental opportunities to learn and practice words, recommendations for teachers are to:

1. Provide as much direct vocabulary instruction of the type described as time permits.
2. Encourage, and allow time for, students to read.
3. Do whatever is possible to increase students' ability to learn the meanings of words on their own when they do read.

As the previous chapter demonstrates, instruction for affixes is one means for increasing students' ability to reach conclusions about the meaning of derived and inflected words on their own. How contexts provide other help is the topic dealt with next.

CONTEXTUAL HELP WITH MEANINGS

Agreement exists about the contribution that contexts make in helping students recognize words that are familiar orally but not in their written form. It is assumed in Chapter 7, for example, that anyone familiar with the term *touch football* is likely to recognize *touch* if they see it in the sentence *The boys are playing touch football* and all the words but *touch* are in their reading vocabulary. Agreement also exists about the influence of contexts on the meaning to assign to homonyms. The influence they have on determining the pronunciation, thus the meaning, of homographs is equally important. All of this explains not only the attention that contexts have received in this book thus far, but also the encouragement to teachers to allot instructional time to contexts.

In contrast, whether contexts reveal word meanings often enough to warrant instructional time for this topic receives mixed responses (7, 8, 10). Even so, on at least two points, agreement does exist. The first point is that the contrived text in sources like workbooks, which provides practice in using contexts for help with meanings, is just that—contrived. It bears little relationship to naturally occurring prose. The second point of agreement—one important for teachers—is that contexts may appear to be more helpful than they actually are. Consider the following context as an example.

Jason and Andrew are brothers. They are siblings.

For students already familiar with the meaning of *siblings,* the context seems to be helpful. For readers who have no idea what *siblings* means, however, the context merely indicates that *siblings* is a noun or an adjective that pertains to both Jason and Andrew. Therefore, it could have something to do with their minds (scholars?), with their motor skills (athletes?), with their behavior (delinquents?), or with their occupation (security guards?).

At this point, you may sense a contradiction between the questions being raised about the value of contexts for word meanings and the earlier contention that regular, extensive reading is a rich source of vocabulary knowledge. With that possibility in mind, let me point out that extensive reading allows individuals to encounter words over a long period of time and in a wide variety of contexts. Understanding, therefore, may accumulate slowly but steadily. To be remembered, too, is that extensive reading provides contexts that far exceed a sentence or paragraph. Sometimes, in fact, it may be a whole story or article that gives precise meaning to such words as *dependent, superstitious, loathe,* and *ambition.*

The question now is, What is the significance of all this for teachers? It suggests, first, that students should know that, *at times,* the words they can read help them with the meaning of unfamiliar words. Within this realistic framework, students can be taught that the assistance may come gradually or, on the other hand, immediately and directly. Students should also be helped to know that when an author explains a word that appears to be important, they should take the time to make sure they understand the meaning, because the word is likely to recur. They should also know that when an author uses a word that seems important, but it is not explained either directly or by other known words, it is time to seek help in the best dictionary available. Well-taught students are aware that a meaning that fits a certain context needs to be selected from the dictionary.

For teachers and prospective teachers who want to know how contexts may provide help with meanings, the following categories are offered. Examples of each category show in italic print the word whose meaning is not known to the reader.

The most helpful classroom work with contexts makes use of examples taken from materials students have read or are about to read. It is taken for granted that collections of these examples may result in classifications different from the eight that are listed and illustrated below.

1. **Definition.** The most obvious source of help is the context that acts like a dictionary and defines a word. The following example is used to show that sometimes a definition helps only if other key words are understood:

> The *nucleus* is the center of the atom.

The next context is less like a dictionary than the previous one but is more helpful:

> After they crossed the mountains, they flew over the *desert*. It was very dry because a desert doesn't get much rain. There were no rivers or even creeks, and the soil looked like dry dust and sand.

2. **Synonym.** Providing synonyms is another way contexts help with meanings. The example below reveals the significance of the word *too* for reaching a conclusion about the meaning of *surrendered.*

> When the major *surrendered,* the others gave up too.

3. **Summary.** Sometimes a troublesome word is one an author uses to summarize what preceded it. What comes first, therefore, may help with its meaning:

> When John heard the noise, his knees began to shake. His hands were wet and cold. He felt as if he couldn't move. He was *terrified.*

4. **Simile.** A simile is a figure of speech that compares unlike things. Now, the relevant point is that comparisons may clarify a word's meaning. The following contexts illustrate this:

> The cat's eyes *glowed* in the dark as if they were little lights.
> The sports car *lurched* forward like a dog starting out to chase a cat.
> The speaker's voice *droned* on like the humming of a bee.

At times, neither *as* nor *like* is in a context; however, the comparison is implied with a metaphor:

> He took the money with the *deftness* of a pickpocket.

The illustration just cited reinforces the importance of experiences and world knowledge. Specifically, if a reader knows nothing about the characteristics of successful pickpockets, the context just referred to reveals nothing about *deftness.* In contrast, even a little knowledge of horses makes the following context helpful:

> Barry's horse trotted along the path *jouncing* him from side to side.

5. ***Example.*** More prosaic than the simile or metaphor but more explicitly helpful are examples:

> Joan is a very *selfish* child. For instance, she never lets any of the other children play with her toys or look at her books.

6. ***Appositive.*** Enclosed with commas, an appositive is another direct source of help:

> The *minutes,* a written record of the meeting, were kept by the secretary.

> *Etymology,* a branch of language study dealing with word origins, ought to be viewed as one way to help students expand their vocabularies.

7. ***Antonym.*** As the term "antonym" suggests, this contextual help comes through contrasts, which are communicated in a variety of ways:

> There is a great difference between the *tumult* on the outside and the peace inside.

> She always is so disorganized and disorderly. She never does anything in a *methodical* way.

> I wonder whether the money will be a blessing or a *bane.*

8. ***Groupings.*** As suggested before, the appearance of a word in a series often assigns it a general classification, which may be sufficient for a reader's purpose:

> I had to shop for dinner and bought bread, meat, tomatoes, and *yams.*

> The wallpaper was so colorful that I can only remember seeing yellow, *aqua,* and black.

INSTRUCTIONAL MATERIALS

As would be expected, numerous references have already been made in this book to instructional materials, and more are in later chapters. As the many examples already described suggest, *instructional materials* are defined here as anything that displays text. (As was the case with brushes in the kindergarten—see Figure 11.1—common materials with no text can make their own contribution to vocabulary knowledge.) Types of texts that are especially fruitful for expanding oral vocabularies are considered next.

Environmental Text

The value of environmental text for various aspects of literacy development has been demonstrated. The contribution it can make to extending oral vocabularies is illustrated in Figure 11.5, which displays newspaper headlines. Its potential for that purpose is also shown in Figure 11.6, where other kinds of environmental text are cited along with descriptions of their instructional value.

Our chefs have a beef

Records will leave
taxpayers in spin

Humidity puts damper on forest fires

Cases will
house local
memorabilia

Weather service sends
false tornado warning

Fire sparks
questions

Overcoming insomnia: Tips from A to Zzzzzz

Crafters, florists bloom in spring shows

Stifling voice
of the people

Resource Center
searching for persons in
non-traditional careers

Push on
for arms
accord

Foreign films theater's new fare

Age no barrier to beauty

Builders think small
as land prices zoom

Midwest excursions
crowd the calendar

Misplaced loyalty

Door repair can unhinge you

FIGURE 11.5 Newspaper Headlines for Developing Oral Vocabularies

Text	Source	Instructional Value
Don't gamble on quality. See us first.	Advertisement for a new furniture store	Difference in meanings of *quality* and *quantity*. Different uses of *gamble*. (*Don't gamble on quality* versus *Don't gamble on horses.*)
Don't bank it in your sock. Sock it in the bank.	Advertisement for a bank	Multiple meanings of *bank* and *sock*.
Let your fingers do the walking.	Advertisement for Yellow Pages in telephone directory	Figurative use of language.
I'm so poor I can't even pay attention.	Sign in college dormitory	Multiple meanings of *pay*.
Prices do not exceed maximum allowable price.	Sign at gasoline pumps	Meanings of *exceed, maximum,* and *allow*. Effect of suffix *-able* on meaning of root.
No commuter parking.	Sign in lot near train station	Meaning of *commute*. Effect of suffix *-er* on meaning of root.
Completely immersible.	Label on electric skillet	Meaning of *immerse*. Effect of suffixes *-ly* and *-ible* on meaning of root.
Bad news is a depressant.	*Peanuts* cartoon	Meanings of *depress* and *depressant*.
A unique blend of citrus fruits.	Label on bottle of juice	Meanings of *unique, blend,* and *citrus*.

FIGURE 11.6 Environmental Text: Help for Oral Vocabularies

Environmental text can also contribute to students' understanding the value of *nonverbal* contexts for assigning appropriate meanings to words. Examples of environmental text that have this potential, plus descriptions of where each was found (situational context), are listed below.

1. We refuse no refuse.   Garbage truck
2. I hope we don't meet by accident!   Bumper sticker on car
3. Body by Effort   T-shirt on board in gym

4. So glad you could   Hallowe'en poster welcoming
   bewitch us.   guests
5. Give us a break.   Sign for glass company
6. Slow down.   Highway sign near
   Give us a brake.   construction

Mythology and Etymology

Anyone acquainted with mythology is aware of its presence in our language. A reason for a teacher to start reading myths to students might originate in other environmental text—in product names like Atlas tires, Venus pencils, and Hercules fencing.

Signs in the environment such as "Pedestrian Crossing" provide a starting point for dealing with etymology, another valuable source for learning about the origins and meanings of words. Take *pedestrian* as an example. Its origin is the Latin word *pedalis,* meaning "pertaining to the foot." That origin is reflected in a number of English words:

Word	Meaning
pedestrian	One traveling on foot
peddler	One walking about attempting to sell something
pedal	Part of a bicycle or tricycle where the foot is placed
pedicure	Professional care given the feet
pedestal	Stand on which the feet of a statue are placed
centipede	A hundred-footed insect
biped	A two-footed animal

The content of Table 11.1 explains the origins of other words.

Because the likelihood of attention to origins as a way of expanding vocabularies depends on a teacher's knowledge of etymology, references are listed below.

Mathews, C. M. *Words, Words, Words.* New York: Charles Scribner's Sons, 1980. Starting out by noting "Human beings are talkative creatures," Mathews goes on to tell in seven chapters how words become available for humans to use. In the telling, the author relates some history of the English language as well as interesting accounts of how certain words made their way into English.

Miller, Casey, and Swift, Kate. *Words and Women.* New York: Anchor Press, 1979. Linguistic sexism is the underlying theme of this book. That it has existed in English for centuries is documented with interesting examples.

McCormack, Jo Ann. *The Story of Our Language.* Columbus, Ohio: Charles E. Merrill Books, 1957. Written for intermediate-grade students, this paperback traces the development of American English. A section in the back lists references that will be useful to anyone who wants to supplement this brief history.

Root	Meaning	Example	Prefix	Meaning	Example
audire	to hear	audience	auto	self	autograph
calor	heat	calorie	bi	two	biped
folium	leaf, sheet	folio foliage	bio	life	biography
dicere	to speak, tell	predict	geo	earth	geology
gram	letter	monogram	heter(o)	different, other	heterogeneous
graph	writing	autograph	homo	man	homicide
logos	speech reason study of	monologue logic geology	homos	same, equal	homogeneous
manualis	of the hand	manual	hydro	water	hydroelectric
mare	sea	marine	inter	between, among	international
meter	measure	thermometer	mal	bad, badly	maladjusted
mimeo	imitate	mimic	micro	small	microfilm
mittere	to send	transmit	mini-mus	little, small	miniskirt
mobilis	movable	mobile	mono	one, alone	monogram
pedis	foot	pedestrian	omni	all, everywhere	omnipresent
phobia	fear or hatred of	phobia	photo	light	photograph
phonos	sound	phonics	poly	many	polysyllable
portare	to carry doorway	portable portal	post	after	postscript
scribere	to write	postscript	sub	under, further division	submarine subcommittee
sonus	sound	sonorous	super	above, beyond	supersonic
spectare	to see, look at	spectacles	tele	distant	television
tenere	to hold, have	tenacious	therm	heat	thermometer
visio	sight	television	trans	across	transmit

*Suffixes are not included because so many indicate part of speech rather than meaning. Some that do suggest meaning are presented in Table 10.1.

TABLE 11.1   Latin and Greek Roots and Prefixes: Common Meanings

Nelson, Francis W. *The History of English*. New York: W. W. Norton Co., 1963. This is a forty-one page account of our language by a professor of linguistics. Its straightforward style makes it easy to read.

Kaye, Cathryn B. *Word Works: Why the Alphabet Is a Kid's Best Friend*. Boston: Little, Brown and Company, 1985. As the author explains in the introduction, this is a book about words—why we have them, why we need them, and how we use them.

Funk, Charles E. *Thereby Hangs a Tale*. New York: Harper and Brothers, 1950. This book focuses on words that "acquired their meanings in an unusual manner."

Lambert, Eloise. *Our Language*. New York: Lothrop, Lee and Shepard, 1955. Like so many of the other books that deal with the history of English, this one can be read by middle- and upper-grade students, yet adults will enjoy the interesting content.

Laird, Helene, and Laird, Charlton. *The Tree of Language*. New York: World Publishing Company, 1957. This is written for children with middle- and upper-grade reading abilities. Some of its most interesting pages tell how individual words came to mean what they do now. Prior to these accounts, other chapters recall some of the early history of English.

Epstein, Sam, and Epstein, Beryl. *The First Book of Words*. New York: Franklin Watts, 1954. The simplicity of this book is disarming, for it offers accurate and interesting information about many aspects of words: prefixes, suffixes, compound words ("stuck-together words"), and brand names. Not many adults will read it without learning more about etymology; yet its simple style, combined with illustrations, makes it suitable for middle- and upper-grade students.

Quinn, Jim. *American Tongue and Cheek*. New York: Random House, 1980. A current look at English by a less serious author, this book defends the use of a number of words and phrases that scholars have been "trying to stamp out." In the process, it provides much information about English and its history.

Sperling, Susan K. *Tenderfeet and Ladyfingers*. New York: Viking Press, 1981. This account of the sources of selected words and expressions divides the content on the basis of body parts. Under "finger," for instance, the following expressions are covered: *thumbs down, rule of thumb, keep one's fingers crossed, knuckle down,* and *all thumbs*.

McCrum, Robert. *The Story of English*. New York: Viking Press, 1986. How English became a language that is now spoken by approximately one-tenth of the world's population is the theme of this book.

Clairborne, Robert. *Word Mysteries and Histories*. Boston: Houghton Mifflin Company, 1986. Words appear in alphabetical order. Middle- and upper-grade students can read about their histories and mysteries.

How etymology gets students interested in language, underscores relationships between words, and helps with meanings can be demonstrated by an account of one fifth grade. On the day I was observing, trials in Washington, D.C., were everyone's concern. As a result, the students were discussing *indict*. Questioned about its meaning, they offered wordy definitions, all vague. The teacher, therefore, told of the many languages from which English words have come and explained that *indict* is from the Latin word *dicere*, meaning "to speak," and from the Latin prefix *in*, whose multiple meanings include "against." She then concluded, "The word *indict* means "to speak against someone." The discussion next moved to the connection between that meaning and events in Washington, D.C.

Subsequently, the teacher redirected the students' attention to *indict* (which she had printed on the board), reminded them it had to do with speaking or speech, and asked whether they could think of other words that contained *d, i, c, t*. One child immediately proposed *dictionary*, eventually defined as a book containing words people use when they speak. Another student, whose mother was a secretary, added to the examples by offering *dictate, dictation,* and *dictaphone,* all of whose meanings were clarified. Writing *dictator,* the teacher asked why it was correct to call someone who ruled without asking for advice a "dictator." One student promptly explained, "What he says goes." "Yes," the teacher added, "his word is law."

To show how attention to etymology is possible even at a first-grade level, let me describe what was seen when a small group was being instructed in the use of a type-writer. As the teacher typed, the children watched what appeared on the paper. "What's that?" one child inquired as soon as he saw an asterisk. In response, the teacher typed *asterisk*, pronounced it, and explained that it meant "little star." Directly under *asterisk* she typed *aster*, read that, and explained it was the name of a flower that evidently had reminded someone of a star because that was what *aster* meant. After promising to bring in pictures of asters, the teacher continued with the typing; the children, with their looking.

SUMMARY

One summary of Chapter 11 is in Figure 11.7, which provides a map of the content. A second summary, which follows, refers to the map intermittently.

Because Chapter 11 treated vocabulary instruction as a means for improving reading comprehension, the need for *established* meanings was emphasized. This is a description that refers to words whose meanings are known so well that they can be accessed automatically. The point was made that this level of understanding requires much more than one or two contacts with a word. It also calls for something far superior to a definitional approach for advancing oral vocabularies. This raises questions, therefore, about traditional practices like relying on glossaries and dictionaries to teach meanings.

Because of the connection between vocabulary knowledge and reading comprehension, the amount of research concerned with vocabulary acquisition has increased. Based on data from research, two sources for increasing vocabulary were identified: direct instruction and the reading that students do on their own. Features of instruction that make it effective were discussed and are shown in Figure 11.7. Because what needs to be done with any given word is affected by the kind of new

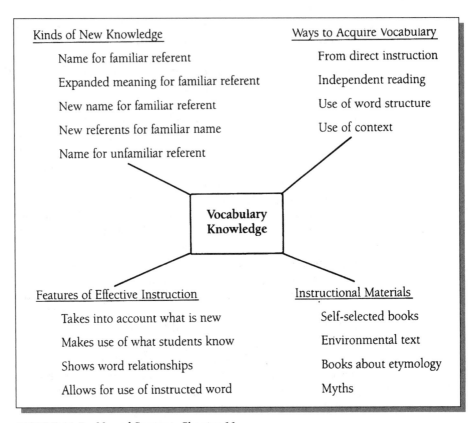

FIGURE 11.7   Map of Content: Chapter 11

knowledge that must be imparted, different types of required learnings were discussed. Again, they appear in Figure 11.7 under the heading "Kinds of New Knowledge."

To maximize the growth in oral vocabularies that results from students' own reading, giving attention to word structure and contexts was recommended. The previous chapter dealt with structure; the present one with contexts. The present chapter also showed with a number of examples how students often explain the meaning of a word without giving any thought to the context in which it occurs. What teachers can do to remedy this omission was illustrated.

Because the importance of motivation for learning should never be minimized, Chapter 11 gave considerable attention to environmental text, as it evokes more interest than do textbooks. Using examples from a variety of sources, the chapter pointed out some of the potential of such text for enlarging oral vocabularies. Keeping student interest in mind, Chapter 11 also urged teachers to get students involved with mythology and etymology. To help teachers who would like to follow the recommendation but feel unready to do so, books were recommended that are both interesting and informative about our language in general and about certain words and expressions in particular.

REVIEW

1. Explain why the two following statements about words are both correct.

   Pronunciations without meaning are useless for reading.
   Meaning without pronunciation is useful for reading.

   What is the implication for instructional programs of the correctness of both statements?

2. Having read Chapter 11, you should know why the dictionary assignment on a chalkboard in a fifth grade that was referred to in the chapter is of questionable value.
   a. For what reasons does the assignment need to be questioned?
   b. Describe how the assignment could be improved.

3. Because the topic of Chapter 11 is word meanings, it is appropriate to request definitions and examples for each term below.

antonym	homonym	synonym
homograph	homophone	polysemous word

4. Chapter 11 distinguishes among five instructional tasks, all of whose goals are to enlarge oral vocabularies.
   a. Using examples for each, describe the five tasks.
   b. It is said in the chapter that the difficulty of the five tasks varies. What does this mean? Again, use examples in your explanation.

5. Prereading preparations for assigned reading often include attention to the meanings of words as they are used in the selection. Summarize the guidelines that Chapter 11 provides both for that part of prereading preparations and for postreading obligations.

6. Chapter 11 acknowledges that much can be learned about the meanings of words when students read books and articles on their own. Specify exactly how this reading contributes to vocabulary knowledge.

7. Students' interest in environmental text explains the generous attention it received in Chapter 11. Six pieces of environmental text were used, for example, to explain nonverbal contexts.
   a. What *is* a nonverbal context?
   b. For what instructional objective could each of the six examples be used?

8. Four examples of students' confusion about words are listed in the chapter, starting with some about *border*. Describe how each of the four teachers who witnessed the confusion should have responded to it.

9. Describe the times in your own reading when problems with word meanings are most common. How do you remedy the problems? Do you make use of a dictionary? Why (not)? Can you recall from your days in elementary school any interesting uses of dictionaries?

REFERENCES

1. Beck, Isabel L.; McCaslin, Ellen S.; and McKeown, Margaret G. *The Rationale and Design of a Program to Teach Vocabulary to Fourth-Grade Students*. Pittsburgh: University of Pittsburgh, Learning Research and Development Center, 1980.

2. Dolch, Edward W. *Psychology and Teaching of Reading*. Champaign, Ill.: Garrard Press, 1951.

3. Gambrell, Linda B. "Think-Time: Implications for Reading Instruction." *Reading Teacher* 34 (November, 1980), 143–146.

4. Harris, Albert J. *How to Increase Reading Ability*. New York: Longmans, Green and Co., 1961.

5. Jenkins, Joseph R.; Stein, Marcy L.; and Wysocki, Katherine. "Learning Vocabulary through Reading." *American Educational Research* 21 (Winter, 1984), 767–787.

6. Miller, George A., and Gildea, Patricia M. "How Children Learn Words." *Scientific American* 257 (September, 1987), 94–99.

7. Nagy, William E. *Teaching Vocabulary to Improve Reading Comprehension*. Urbana, Ill.: National Council of Teachers of English, 1988.

8. Nagy, William E., and Anderson, Richard C. "How Many Words Are There in Printed School English?" *Reading Research Quarterly* 19 (Spring, 1984), 304–330.

9. Nagy, William E.; Herman, Patricia A.; and Anderson, Richard C. "Learning Words from Context." *Reading Research Quarterly* 20 (Winter, 1985), 233–253.

10. Schatz, Elinore K., and Baldwin, R. Scott. "Context Clues Are Unreliable Predictors of Word Meanings." *Reading Research Quarterly* 21 (Fall, 1986), 439–453.

11. Scott, Judith A., and Nagy, William E. "Understanding Definitions." Technical Report No. 528. Urbana: University of Illinois, Center for the Study of Reading, 1991.

12. Stahl, Steven A., and Vancil, Sandra J. "Discussion Is What Makes Semantic Maps Work in Vocabulary Instruction." *Reading Teacher* 40 (October, 1985), 62–67.

13. Stanovich, Keith E. "Mathew Effects in Reading: Some Consequences of Individual Differences in the Acquisition of Literacy." *Reading Research Quarterly* 21 (Fall, 1986), 360–406.

14. Wixson, Karen K. "Vocabulary Instruction and Children's Comprehension of Basal Stories." *Reading Research Quarterly* 21 (Summer, 1986), 317–329.

Comprehension: Connected Text

••••••
PREVIEW

Chapter 6 states that the reading done in classrooms in which round robin reading is omitted commonly divides among (a) *shared reading,* in which students and teacher read together for enjoyment or to acquire information; (b) *independent reading* by students, often of self-selected material; and (c) *guided reading,* for which teachers make preparations that enable students to do the reading. Chapter 12 directs your attention to the last type of situation while considering comprehension instruction. This is not done to suggest that such instruction is confined to guided reading. After all, a shared poem may provide a perfect opportunity to impart information about metaphors or, for instance, to pinpoint the ways in which poets use words to provide mental imagery. All that *is* being said is that the comprehension instruction discussed in Chapter 12 revolves around guided reading.

Because the reason to teach comprehension is to maximize the successful comprehension that students experience, the forthcoming chapter allots a generous amount of space to purposes for reading. This is required by the fact that successful comprehension is the fulfillment of whatever purpose motivated the reading. The connection between purpose and comprehension monitoring and between purpose and comprehension assessment is discussed, too.

Because research shows that confusion between teaching comprehension and assessing it is common (9, 23), the remaining parts of Chapter 12 concentrate on illuminating the nature of comprehension instruction. Among the points made is that different kinds of text require different subject matter for instruction. That some topics are relevant for any type of text is explained, too. All the while, a number of topics that can figure in efforts to teach comprehension are identified. To make the discussions meaningful, examples of comprehension instruction are provided intermittently.

Reading the Summary section is recommended before the chapter is begun.

••••••

FROM READING **C**HAPTER **7** you know that the use of contextual cues can begin before children are able to read. The same is true of comprehension. Teachers can provide help with listening comprehension before the focus shifts to processing written text. That is why a few comments about listening comprehension get the chapter started.

LISTENING COMPREHENSION

The purpose of the present discussion is to show with examples that listening activities can be carried out in ways that are likely to contribute to children's later ability to comprehend text. The suggestions made, however, are not based on the assumption that comprehending spoken language and comprehending written text are identical. In fact, one major similarity and several important differences between listening and reading are considered next.

Major Similarity between Listening and Reading

The major similarity is hardly subtle: The listener and reader attend to language for the purpose of getting or constructing a message. Both are thus engaged in language-processing behavior. Because the basic similarity is obvious, an *erroneous* conclusion is commonly drawn:

listening comprehension ability + decoding ability = reading comprehension ability

Why the equation is an oversimplification is clarified in the following section, which identifies differences between spoken and written language that are relevant for comprehending.

Differences between Spoken and Written Language

Unlike written text, spoken language is fleeting. It is not retrievable unless it is recorded. In contrast, written language makes words a possible subject for study and even permits behaviors like backward checking and forward scanning. For reasons such as these, the reader is more in charge than is the listener.

Listeners, however, are not totally at the mercy of speakers. Failing to understand, they can express puzzlement with a facial expression or direct question. Because speakers routinely monitor the success of their efforts to communicate, these responses typically lead to such adjustments as more careful enunciation, a slower rate of speaking, some repetition, more elaboration, and/or additional illustrations.

The nature of spoken language offers further assistance to the listener. Features like intonation and stress are helpful—much more helpful than are their substitutions in print: underlining, italics, boldface type, question marks, and exclamation marks. Equally significant for communication is the way speakers segment sentences with pauses into meaningful units like phrases and clauses. Evidently, the commas, semicolons, and periods in print are not of equal help because research has shown that instead of processing print into conceptual units, poor comprehenders often read as if a page of text were lines of unrelated words (17, 21).

Even though spoken language does have built-in features that foster communication, it commonly lacks the elegance of carefully constructed prose. Just how *inel-egant* spoken language can be is apparent whenever a conversation or even an interview is recorded and then played back. Too obvious to miss are the hesitations, repetitions, corrections, and abandoned or poorly constructed sentences.

Differences in the kinds of sentences that characterize speech and written text have an important implication for teachers who spend time on listening comprehension as a means for preparing for reading comprehension. The implication is suggested in Figure 12.1. Because written text is not—as is sometimes claimed—"talk written down," the material most suitable for listening comprehension is not everyday conversation but what Figure 12.1 refers to as "written text presented orally." This suggests that reading to students is a relevant topic for illustrating how listening activities may contribute to reading comprehension abilities.

Sample Listening Activities

Reading to children in school customarily starts with stories. Consequently, how to use stories in ways that might contribute to reading ability later is described in Figure 12.2.

Hopefully, a sufficient number of listening activities are in Figure 12.2 to make the point that attention to comprehension need not be delayed until children have acquired reading vocabularies. It should also be kept in mind that the suggestions for listening comprehension can be adapted later to help with comprehending text.

FACILITATING THE COMPREHENSION OF WRITTEN TEXT

Because the underlying concern of the whole of this book is for reading comprehension, much that has been written not only in Chapter 1 but also in all subsequent chapters has something to do with promoting comprehension abilities. Several times, for example, the suggestion is made to replace round robin reading with something that *will* advance comprehension: well-prepared, uninterrupted silent reading of appropriately difficult material. You can recall that from a teacher's perspective, prereading preparations divide among (a) new vocabulary, (b) activating, or adding to, relevant world knowledge, and (c) establishing purpose(s) for the reading.

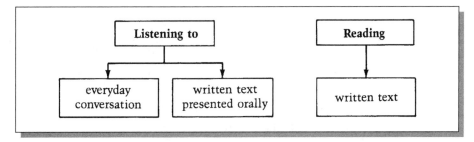

FIGURE 12.1 Processing Spoken and Written Language

Comprehension Requirements	Possible Procedures
Constructing mental images revealed through text	Omit showing illustrations. After the story is read, encourage the children to tell what they think the main character looks like (and *why*). Compare their versions with the author's by showing the illustrations. For another story, the children can draw their own versions.
Following a sequence of events	Stop before the story ends. Ask the children what they think will happen next (and *why*). Afterward, compare their predictions with what did come next. After discussing the order in which events of a story occurred, show children a scroll-like paper with a division for each important event. Help the children decide the kind of picture that can go in each division so that as the paper is unrolled, the plot is revealed. For another story, use similar procedures, this time pulling the paper through a television screen (box with opening on side). As the pictures are displayed, the children retell the story. (The ability to retell what was heard—or read—is reliable evidence of successful comprehension, especially when children do the retelling in their own language. The translation demonstrates that the listener [or reader] has successfully reconstructed the author's message into a form that is personally meaningful.)
Distinguishing between fact and fancy	After reading a fictional account of an animal, read an encyclopedia article about the same animal to allow for a comparison of the two versions. What is factual and what is make-believe in the story should be emphasized through discussion. If the make-believe account deals with an animal that is familiar to the children, draw on their experiences for the comparison.
Evaluating authenticity	Whenever appropriate, encourage children to think critically about characterizations in stories. Pose questions like, "Is that the way children *really* act? If your little sister took something of yours, would *you* smile?" A story about a rabbit might make it natural to inquire, "Would a real rabbit feel sorry for a gardener and not eat his plants?"

FIGURE 12.2   Reading to Children to Help with Comprehension

As Figure 12.3 shows, the preparations can be combined under the heading "Facilitating Comprehension."

The primary focus of the present chapter is comprehension instruction, whose goal is to help students learn how to construct the meaning of connected text. This goal requires attending now to the part of prereading preparations that has to do with establishing one or more purposes for assigned reading. The need for this can be explained as follows:

1. Successful comprehension is the realization of the purpose(s) established for reading.
2. Therefore, students have to be helped to understand the connection between why they are reading and how they should do the reading.

The early attention to purposes and comprehension should make clear why the purposes established for students' reading must be better than, "Read this by tomorrow. Be ready to discuss it."

COMPREHENDING: A PURPOSEFUL PURSUIT

As early as the Introduction to *Teaching Them to Read,* the point is made that little comprehension is likely to result if an individual wanders aimlessly through a piece of text. Instead, adequate comprehension is the product of a journey guided by a prespecified destination.

Like travelers, successful readers sometimes slow down or even stop, perhaps to think about something of interest. Like travelers, too, they may encounter problems that need to be remedied before their reading proceeds. Throughout all this, the destination—that is, the purpose of the reading—is not forgotten. That is why reading was defined earlier as *intentional thinking.* The reference to travelers explains why it was also said that successful reading is *not* one unchanging kind of behavior.

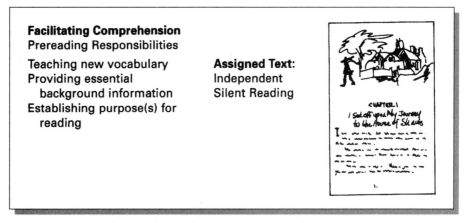

FIGURE 12.3 Facilitating Comprehension with Prereading Preparations

When discussing the need to have a purpose, the Preview for Chapter 1 lists three questions and suggests you keep them in mind as a way of minimizing the possibility of your reading the chapter without a purpose. Posing prereading questions is something classroom teachers can also do to facilitate comprehension. Regardless of how purposes *are* established, they should have an effect on the kind and the rate of reading that ensues. The reading done to find a certain date, for instance, ought to be very different from the reading whose aim is to distinguish between facts about a topic and an author's opinions about it.

Because prereading questions are used so frequently in classrooms to establish purposes for assigned reading and, second, because purpose should affect the kind of reading done, a sequence like the one portrayed in Figure 12.4 merits periodic use in order to clarify for children that reading encompasses a wide range of behaviors.

From time to time, postreading discussions that center on students' responses to prereading questions should deal explicitly with the fact that answers to questions have three origins: (a) the text itself, (b) inferences derived from the text, and (c) inferences stemming from the reader's relevant knowledge. Instruction designed to teach students about the three origins can have them draw pictures based on the content of sentences in much the same way that you did in the course of reading Chapter 1. The fact that some questions call for opinions should be clarified, too.

Depending on the students, other procedures dealing with questions may be required. Slower children, for example, often need help with what it means to answer a question. To achieve that objective, one third-grade teacher who works with poor readers sometimes lists prereading questions in the order in which a selection answers them. Taking one question at a time, she asks the children to stop

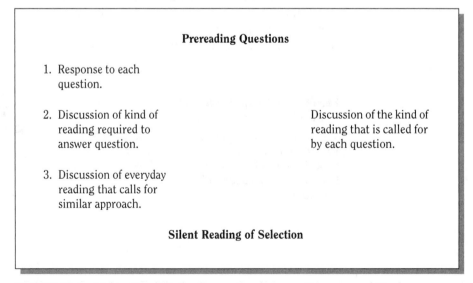

Prereading Questions

1. Response to each
   question.

2. Discussion of kind of   Discussion of the kind of
   reading required to   reading that is called for
   answer question.   by each question.

3. Discussion of everyday
   reading that calls for
   similar approach.

Silent Reading of Selection

FIGURE 12.4   Making Explicit the Connection between Purposes and Kinds of Reading Required

their silent reading when they think they have the answer. After a child proposes one, other probes from the teacher follow: "What made you think you found the answer? Did you think you found it earlier, then decided you hadn't? Can the answer be shortened and still be correct?" Finally the teacher states, "Before you start reading to find the answer to the next question, I'll read this first question again. Then someone can tell us the answer."

Another possibility available to teachers is to model how to go about answering questions. In this case, a teacher again starts with questions that the text answers directly. After posing the question answered first, the teacher reads the material aloud while the children follow it silently. When she reaches the answer, the teacher stops, repeats the question, then rereads the response in the text. A teacher may also choose to provide a think aloud for a time when she believes she has an answer but learns when she rereads the question that she is mistaken.

In order to discourage anyone from concluding that posing prereading questions is the only way to establish purposes, procedures that a second-grade teacher used are described in Figure 12.5. Figure 12.6 describes the thoughts of someone else during her first year of teaching. She has a third-grade class and is making plans for reading a narrative account of a mother who is deaf.

PURPOSE AND COMPREHENSION MONITORING

As the Introduction to *Teaching Them to Read* explains and as the name itself suggests, *comprehension monitoring* is the process of checking up on, or supervising, one's own comprehension. It is an example, therefore, of *metacognition,* which means "thinking about one's own thinking."

Peter Johnston effectively portrays the connection between purposes for reading and comprehension monitoring when he states that monitoring requires readers to decide "on the basis of their purpose for reading when to remove their processing from 'automatic pilot', take conscious control, and instigate the appropriate alternative strategies" (12, p. 27). "Alternative strategies" are the fix-up strategies mentioned earlier. As the name suggests, a fix-up strategy is a plan for fixing or remedying a breakdown in comprehension that is thwarting the accomplishment of goals set for the reading. Depending on both the breakdowns and the goals, remedies include rereading, reading ahead to see whether subsequent text provides a remedy, looking up the meaning of a word in a dictionary, and examining graphics (e.g., a pie graph) more carefully. If the problem is a loss of concentration, the remedy is obvious.

Researchers who have studied comprehension monitoring divide it into two parts (2). One part is *evaluation,* which is the reader's recognition that a problem exists. The second part is *regulation.* This refers to how the reader resolves the problem.

To make the explanation of comprehension monitoring more specific, Figure 12.7 lists three examples of evaluation; underneath, a fix-up strategy for each problem is described.

After our discussion in class about using common objects to enlarge oral vocabularies, I decided to approach the next story for the best readers in a different way. The basal story is called *Magic Mirror,* so I asked whether anyone in the group had a mirror here at school. I myself had brought four. The first had a handle, the second was in my compact, the third stood up and had a magnifying mirror on the back of a regular mirror, and the fourth was in a book that belongs to my son. (It is called *Mirror, Mirror* because each two-page spread has a large hole in the middle that allows a reader to see herself or himself in a mirror. Since each page has a picture of an animal, readers see themselves as a different animal every time they move to the next page.)

As it turned out, one girl in the group had a mirror in a case; another said she had one in her school bag. When she took it out, she produced a spoon!

We then discussed the characteristics of mirrors while each kind was examined. I listed on the board how they were alike or different. In the end, the students decided that the spoon *could* be considered a mirror because it reflects an image. The group concluded that mirrors are made of different materials but that most "real" mirrors are glass with something painted on the back.

To conclude, I asked the group to reread the title of my son's book, as *mirror* is not a word they seemed to have in their reading vocabulary. As soon as it was read, a few children spontaneously added, "on the wall." When I asked why, they recalled *Snow White,* which has a magic mirror in it. I asked why the mirror in that story was magic; the children recalled that it talked to the queen. Then I asked if the mirror in my son's book was magic. The group decided it was not, because the reader didn't turn into animals. This brought us back to the basal story, *Magic Mirror.* We talked about what might happen in a story with that title. Some thought it would be about a magic mirror; others disagreed. This is when I distributed an assignment sheet that had two columns. One started with *The mirror is magic because;* the other, with *The mirror is not magic because.* I told the group that as they read the story, they should look for reasons that show the mirror *is* magic and write them in the first column. Reasons why they think the mirror is *not* magic were to be written in the second column. After one child repeated what was to be done, the children returned to their desks to begin reading.

FIGURE 12.5   Establishing Purposes for Reading a Story

The basal selection that one group will read tomorrow tells of a mother who is deaf. She and her husband have two children. This is an interesting account of the adaptations she makes to compensate for the disability. What does a person do who cannot hear the telephone and doorbell? Is this person able to drive a car? Many interesting questions and answers are in the selection. I think the group will find it interesting even though I don't believe any of them have a deaf person in their immediate family. But, I could be wrong.

I plan to introduce the new words in the framework of being deaf. That will allow me to raise questions like: Do you know anyone who is deaf? What are some of the problems a deaf person might have that we don't have? How do you suppose they solve the problems?

All this will provide a good lead into the account. I plan to prepare a sheet that will divide into (a) problems described, and (b) how the deaf woman solved them. I'll ask the children either to read the account once, and then reread it so that they can complete the sheet; or, if they prefer, they can fill out the sheet while they read. I'm going to encourage use of the first option because, if they're like me, they will find this to be interesting reading. It deals with a number of things that I had not thought about before.

Next year when we get to this selection, I'm going to have other books available that deal with deafness and deaf people. For this year, I plan to get to school a little early tomorrow to see what's available in the library. If nothing else, I may find something I can read to the whole class. I vaguely recall an account called something like *Through Grandpa's Eyes* in which a boy tried to "see" the world in a way that matched how his blind grandfather "saw" it.

FIGURE 12.6   Preparations for a Selection about Deafness

Identifying Breakdowns in Comprehending

1. *Failure to understand the meaning of a word*

    Student encounters the sentence *The Ogden Valley is a large oasis* and realizes he doesn't understand it because he doesn't know what *oasis* means.

2. *Failure to make sense*

    While reading *Fran got a sliver in her finger when she was sweeping,* an individual reads *sliver* as "silver." Reaching the end of the sentence, the person realizes it doesn't make sense.

3. *Failure to realize preestablished purpose*

    A student is reading an assigned biography, is enjoying it, and suddenly realizes he has forgotten the assigned reason for the reading: to find those parts of the text that provide evidence that the biography is, at times, fiction rather than fact.

Fix-Up Strategies for Breakdowns

1. *Failure to understand the meaning of a word*

    Not knowing the meaning of *oasis,* the reader continues on the assumption that subsequent text may clarify the meaning. In this instance, the sentence following the one causing problems helps sufficiently by stating, *Unlike the desert that surrounds it, the Valley has many farms with good green pastures for animals.* (If the later text had not suggested a meaning clear enough to allow the reader to proceed and *oasis* is a word that seems important, appropriate remediation is to seek assistance in a dictionary.)

2. *Failure to make sense*

    Realizing that *Fran got a sliver in her finger when she was sweeping* does not make sense, this individual rereads the sentence. The mistake is corrected, and the reader proceeds.

3. *Failure to realize preestablished purpose*

    Because enjoyment replaced looking for evidence that a biography combines fact and fiction, the reader decides to go back to the beginning in order to start again. Fairly quickly, one type of evidence is found, namely, Harriet converses with her brother even though the author could never know exactly what she said. Having noted that piece of evidence, the reader continues with the hope of finding additional kinds of evidence. (Given the importance of fostering interest in reading, the preestablished purpose was unsuitable for the initial reading of the biography. The evidence sought might have been dealt with during a postreading discussion or could have provided the purpose for a second reading. This is not to suggest the purpose was unimportant but, rather, to question the timing.)

FIGURE 12.7   Comprehension Monitoring: Evaluation and Regulation Components

One fix-up strategy not used in the examples in Figure 12.7 is adjusting the rate of reading. This remedial procedure is important and, apparently, uncommon. Its *in*frequent use is attested to by research data showing that individuals tend to read at a constant rate regardless of what they are reading or why they are reading it (6). With that fact in mind, this is an appropriate time to reexamine Figure 12.4. Note there the suggestion to teachers to use postreading time to make comparisons between the reading just done and everyday reading that calls for a similar approach. One example of a comparison is (a) reading a story for the purpose of identifying traits that describe the main character, and (b) reading descriptions of the three nominees for president of the Student Council in order to decide for whom to vote. In both instances, the purpose means that parts of the text can be skipped or scanned quickly, whereas other parts need to be read carefully.

Making comparisons like the one just described between in-school and out-of-school reading is necessary for transfer. That is, if teachers want to enable students to transfer to their own reading what they are learning in school about the relationship between purpose and type of reading called for, time must be taken intermittently to do what Figure 12.4 depicts. Teachers also need to keep in mind that establishing purposes for the reading done in school should, at times, be the responsibility of students themselves.

None of this suggests that anyone expects—or wants—people to say to themselves each time they pick up something to read, "Now let me see. What is my purpose?" On the other hand, what *is* wanted are students and adults who read newspapers, recipes, novels, and information about a recently banned insecticide to carry out those behaviors in different ways, each determined by the reason that motivates the reading.

PURPOSE AND COMPREHENSION ASSESSMENT

Thus far in the chapter the direct connection that exists between purposes for reading and comprehension assessment has been implied. It was said, for example, that "Successful comprehension is the realization of the purpose(s) established for reading." The significance of this for teachers is that efforts to determine whether comprehension of assigned reading has been achieved must reflect purposes:

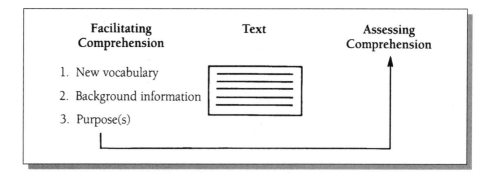

The display on p. 301 is not meant to suggest that postreading time is confined to learning whether purposes established for reading were realized. It does indicate, however, that students should not be asked to read for one kind of purpose and then be evaluated in unrelated ways.

PURPOSE AND TYPE OF TEXT

As has been emphasized, teachers interested in improving students' comprehension abilities help them understand—with instruction and practice—that reading is a purposeful pursuit and, further, that preestablished purposes permit them to monitor their own comprehension. They also help students understand the effect of purpose on the kind of reading that ought to be done. That purpose and type of text are also closely connected is the concern now. That the two *are* directly connected is demonstrated routinely in our everyday lives where the following sequence is so common as to be taken for granted:

Need to read ⟶ Material selected that ⟶ Material read in a way
arises   can fulfill the need   that satisfies the need

Examples of purposes (needs) determining suitable material are listed below.

Purpose	Suitable Material
To learn a person's phone number	Telephone directory
To learn how to dye a white blouse	Directions on box of dye
To relax before going to bed	Light fiction
To learn the stand a newspaper has taken on a city crisis	Editorial in the newspaper
To learn how the fourth-grade manual in a newly adopted basal series provides comprehension instruction	Fourth-grade manual
To write a paper on the topic "An Uncommon Fruit"	Article in *National Geographic* about kiwis

The important point these examples make is that purpose comes into existence first; it then creates the need to find and read certain kinds of materials. The result is "authentic" reading, something associated with the whole language movement (1, 22) that anyone *should* want. Two examples of authentic reading follow.

A teacher reads *Stone Soup* to the class. Afterward, one girl immediately says her mother read *Stone Soup,* and it was different. The teacher explains that many stories from the past end up being told in different ways. She says that with the librarian's help, she'll see how many versions of *Stone Soup* are available. Volunteers can then read the books, tell the class about the version they read, and the class can consider which they like best, and why.

During a discussion of how the sun is setting earlier as winter approaches, one student claims there are times in Sweden when there is nothing but daylight and other times when it is always dark. Not everyone agrees. Because none of the students knows anybody who lived in Sweden, a decision is made to collect articles and books from the library in order to uncover the facts. Depending on what is found, the materials will either be read to the class or summarized so that correct conclusions can be drawn.

One major impediment to having more authentic reading in school than is usually found is the requirement to use certain materials—basal readers and content area textbooks, for example. The expectation that such texts *will* be read results in a contrived sequence that is contrasted below with the one that characterizes out-of-school reading:

Everyday reading: purpose   ⟶   selection of material
                                                                            to be read

School reading: required   ⟶   purpose for reading it
                                        text

The contrived sequence of "school reading" leads to a problem that is common *but not inevitable:* Everything read is read the same way—carefully. To promote "careful" reading, many questions are posed. Overanalyzed material, regardless of its nature and value, is one consequence. Because it seems safe to assume that required textbooks are not going to vanish from classrooms soon, a question to be addressed is what can be done to improve how required material is used.

One remedy is for teachers to differentiate among required materials in order to ensure that both they and their students adopt an appropriate stance toward whatever it is they are about to read (18, 24). To add specificity to the recommendation, the next sections look at the macrostructure of stories and expository text, two common kinds of required materials. Implications of each kind of overall structure for what is done with stories and informational text are considered.

NARRATIVE TEXT: STORIES

Not all narrative texts are stories. Like sentences, narration that does tell a story has a certain structure. (*Story structure* is sometimes referred to as *story grammar.*) The parts or components of the most simple story are named below.

Elements of a Story

			Attempt to	
	Main Character		*Resolve*	*Resolution of*
Setting	(Protagonist)	*Problem*	*Problem*	*Problem*

With the help of a story in a basal reader, which is summarized below, the elements are illustrated. The story also shows why it was said that the elements named above describe the most simple of stories.

Peter, the youngest in his pioneer family, wants more than anything else to be as big as his siblings. Recalling that someone once said that dipping a hand in a certain pool made wishes come true, Peter seeks out the pool, states his wish to grow, dips his hand into the water, and inadvertently falls into it. Lying on the nearby grass to allow his clothes to dry, Peter falls asleep. When he awakes, his clothes, having shrunk considerably from the heat of the sun, make him think his wish came true. Although he is elated at first, the walk home allows for unhappy thoughts about the possibility of being too big—too big to get into his own house, for instance. Once Peter arrives home, he is relieved to find he has not grown. Now he is content just to be able still to curl up in his mother's lap.

As you no doubt noticed, the story about Peter requires expanding the story elements named earlier:

Setting and Protagonist	Problem	Attempt to Resolve Problem	Resolution of Problem	New Problem	Resolution of Problem
Peter, a pioneer boy, lives in a small town.	Wants to be big.	Dips hand in magic pool.	Shrunken clothes suggest growth.	Worry about excessive growth.	Awareness that clothes have shrunk and he has not grown.

When adequate comprehension of a story is the concern, purposes established for reading it should deal with the elements. This is the case because they define "adequate" comprehension. Indirectly, therefore, they identify *un*important details. One teacher who understood this composed four questions for the story about Peter to replace the 26 questions that the basal reader manual suggested. The four questions are in Figure 12.8. They show how the teacher avoided revealing too much about the story, something the neophyte is prone to do.

The teacher's decision to cover "setting" with a brief, prereading discussion of when and where the story takes place is also indicated in Figure 12.8. *When* the

Structure	Possible Questions
Setting	(Cover when background information is provided.)
Problem	1. *Question:* What wish did Peter make?
Attempt to resolve problem	2. *Question:* What did Peter do to get his wish?
Resolution of problem	(Discuss in postreading discussion, because too-small clothing is clearly portrayed in two illustrations.)
New problem	3. *Question:* Was Peter glad that he got his wish? Why (not)?
Resolution of problem	4. Q*uestion:* How does the story end?

FIGURE 12.8   Story Structure and Prereading Questions

story occurred is important because it explains Peter's wearing buckskin clothes and the fact that the sun shrank them when they were wet. (Students brought up in a polyester era might know little about fabric shrinkage from heat.) Because two illustrations in the basal reader show Peter wearing clothes that are obviously too small, the same teacher scheduled a consideration of why Peter thought he had grown for the postreading discussion.

The four questions listed in Figure 12.8 are distributed to members of the instructional group before they start the story. In time, students should understand that they are expected to keep such questions in mind as they read and, further, that if they are unable to answer any, rereading—at least certain parts of the story—is required. This is important, as it moves students toward monitoring their own comprehension.

Because of the current interest in graphic displays of related parts, *story maps* show up frequently—sometimes too frequently—in such sources as manuals. Instead of using the story about Peter to illustrate a map, let me use a fable. The map for the fable is in Figure 12.9. The fable itself faces Figure 12.9.

In addition to providing a visual representation of the major events in a story, a map can serve other purposes. At first, it can be a tool for helping students summarize or retell a story. (Sometimes, free recall without a prompt is better, as it allows for learning what students think is important.) Eventually, constructing a map can be a prereading assignment. In this case, the need to construct the map establishes a purpose for reading, helps students learn what to attend to as they read, and makes their efforts more fruitful (5, 19).

From a teacher's perspective, maps constructed by students allow for assessing comprehension; they also permit attending to connections among story elements. Where a story takes place, for instance, may have major effects on both its characters and the plot. Some teachers also use maps to help students write their own stories (15, 20).

Even while the benefits of students' knowing about story maps are being heralded, the fact that they are sometimes misused cannot be denied. The most blatant misuse known to me occurred in a second grade. At the time, the whole class had been asked to prepare a story map to summarize whatever library book they were currently reading. The tears of one girl caught my attention. Asked why she was crying, she managed to explain that the cows in her story didn't have a problem. As it turned out, the "story" she was reading was an expository selection about a dairy farm where, apparently, life for cows was tranquil.

The moral of this is clear: If story structure and story maps do receive attention, teachers must make certain that they are used with stories. Not to be forgotten either is that nothing is so good that it should be done all the time. Said differently, means should not be allowed to become ends in themselves.

STORIES: APPROPRIATE TOPICS FOR INSTRUCTION

As suggested, story structure is a suitable topic for comprehension instruction if it is not abused through misuse or overuse. Two more suitable topics are discussed

THE COCONUT GAME

One day Elephant fell into a pit. "Help!" cried Elephant. The animals ran and looked into the pit. "We can't help you, Elephant," they said. "You are too big. And the pit is too deep." The animals could not help Elephant. One by one they went away.

"Elephant!" called Monkey from the top of the pit. "I'll get you out."

"But how?" asked Elephant. "You are so little."

"Not too little," said Monkey. And away she ran.

Soon Monkey came back. She had a ladder with her. Elephant tried to climb up the ladder. But when he got on it, the ladder broke.

"It's no use," said Elephant. "How will I get out of this pit?"

"You will see," said Monkey. And away she ran.

Soon Monkey came back. She had a rope with her. Elephant took hold of the rope. Then Monkey pulled on it. But Monkey could not pull Elephant out of the pit.

"It's no use," said Elephant. "How will I get out of this pit?"

"You will see," said Monkey. And away she ran.

Soon Monkey came back. Many, many monkeys were with her. Each monkey had a coconut. "Let's play the Coconut Game," said Monkey. Monkey began to roll a coconut into the pit. All the other monkeys began to roll coconuts into the pit.

"Why are you rolling coconuts into this pit?" cried Elephant.

Elephant was very angry. He stomped on the coconuts. He jumped up and down on the coconuts. Elephant grew more and more upset. But still the monkeys rolled coconuts into the pit.

All at once Elephant found himself close to the top of the pit. He walked right out of it! All the monkeys laughed and jumped.

"Didn't you know that someone small can help someone big?" asked Monkey.

"No," said Elephant. "But now I do!"

Source: From *Inside and Out of Pathfinder*—Allyn and Bacon Reading Program by Robert B. Ruddell and others, © Copyright, 1978, by Silver, Burdett & Ginn Inc. Used with permission.

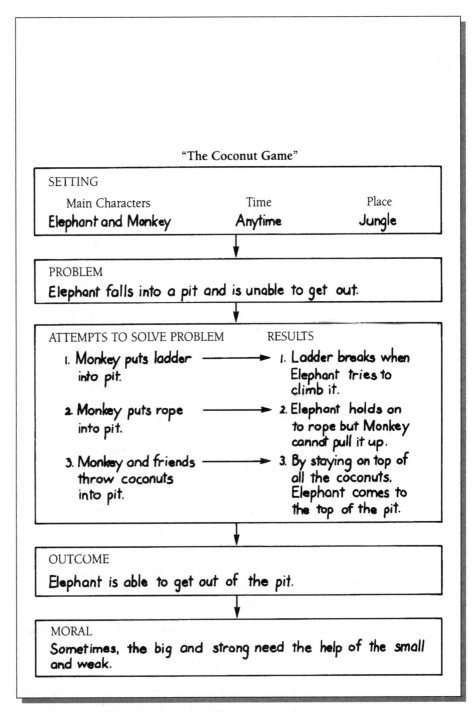

"The Coconut Game"

SETTING

| Main Characters | Time | Place |
| Elephant and Monkey | Anytime | Jungle |

PROBLEM

Elephant falls into a pit and is unable to get out.

ATTEMPTS TO SOLVE PROBLEM   **RESULTS**

1. Monkey puts ladder into pit. — 1. Ladder breaks when Elephant tries to climb it.

2. Monkey puts rope into pit. — 2. Elephant holds on to rope but Monkey cannot pull it up.

3. Monkey and friends throw coconuts into pit. — 3. By staying on top of all the coconuts, Elephant comes to the top of the pit.

OUTCOME

Elephant is able to get out of the pit.

MORAL

Sometimes, the big and strong need the help of the small and weak.

FIGURE 12.9 A Story Map

next: flashback and perspective. Like story elements, they are concerned with the whole of a story—that is, with its macrostructure.

Flashback

Anyone who reads novels knows that authors do not always relate events in chronological order. Often, in fact, they use flashbacks. A *flashback* is an interruption in the narration with a reference to the past. Commonly, the earlier event took place before the story begins. Although authors sometimes use flashbacks to add variety and interest to their tales, a reference to the past may also explain an event in the present.

For some students, explicit instruction about flashbacks is unnecessary. Even their initial experience with stories that have flashbacks is successful. In such cases, the stories allow for a discussion of flashbacks and for introducing the term *flashback*. With other students, explicit instruction is essential in order to eliminate or at least to minimize problems in following plots. A sample lesson, which is provided before the instructional group has its initial experience with stories that have flashbacks, follows. The teacher uses for the instruction a story the group read recently, which was told in chronological order.

Teacher: We've read quite a few stories this year. In all the stories we've read together, the author tells various things that happen in the order in which they happen. For instance, in the story we just finished, the author writes about two girls who live in a tall apartment building. The interesting part occurs when the girls are in the elevator and can't get to the apartment of one because neither is tall enough to reach the button that has *18* printed on it. How they go about solving that problem is quite clever; but the point I want to make now is that the author of the story tells us what happened in the order in which it happened. She starts at the beginning when one of the girls finally gets permission from her mother to go to a friend's apartment without having her older sister take her. The writer next describes how the girls go into the elevator only to find they are unable to reach the right button. The rest of the story tells about the interesting way in which they reach it and finally arrive at their destination.

Displaying a chart, the teacher shows the events she just reviewed, each numbered. This allows her to point out how the events are arranged in chronological order. She continues:

Teacher: Let's pretend that *we* are the authors of this story and want to tell the same story a little differently. To do that, I'll start the story, then you keep it going. In the new version, the beginning tells about the girls sitting in the apartment on the eighteenth floor, resting up a bit from the troubles in the elevator. The older sister of the girl who lives on the eighteenth floor comes in and says, "You look as if you've been into mischief. What did you do now?" That's the beginning of the story. Who wants to tell us what happens next?

Unexpectedly, the group decides unanimously and with persistence that the best thing is to say nothing in order to avoid being punished. Believing that the group is unable to understand the request, the teacher decides to tell the new version of the same story herself.

Teacher: I know why you think silence might be the best thing; however, if the girls say nothing, there is no story. I'm going to suggest something else. I'm going to suggest that the two girls do tell what happened. Afterwards, the bigger sister is so impressed that the two little girls feel more convinced than ever that they really are growing up. I know my story isn't very interesting, but I told it the way I did in order to explain that some authors tell a story by going back and forth between the present and the past. This is what I did in my version of the story. On this other chart—please look here—I've shown the new version. See how I went back and forth from the present to the past and then back to the present again.

The chart being examined displays the following:

Beginning			Return to Past	Back to Present
Girls are in eighteenth floor apartment.	Sister of one girl arrives.	Sister wants to know what girls have been up to.	Girls tell how they were able to reach the button.	Sister is impressed with how they solved the problem.

After discussing the chart, in particular the flashback, the teacher continues:

Teacher: I promise you that the next story in your reader is more interesting than mine. But the two are alike because, in each case, the story starts in the present, after which the characters tell something that happened in the past. In the story I want you to read now, the main character is a boy named Andy. He is lying in a hospital bed so covered with bandages that his own family might not recognize him. As he lies there, Andy thinks of the past, in particular of what caused him to be taken to the hospital in an ambulance. I want you to read only the first two pages. Stop reading when you get to the bottom of page 118. Don't turn the page. Just wait until everyone has finished reading the first two pages.

Once all the students have done this, the teacher comments:

Teacher: Before Andy starts thinking about the past—which he does on the next page—let's see what *you* think happened earlier to put Andy into the hospital. Who has an idea?

Carolyn: I think he was swimming, and he went out too far and almost drowned. If it wasn't for the man near him, he'd probably be dead.

Teacher: Carolyn, when a person almost drowns, he might have to go to the hospital, but would he end up being bandaged from head to toe? What did the two pages you just read tell you about how Andy looks?

After it is established that bandages covering one's body are not usually required when a person comes close to drowning, other more plausible notions of earlier events are offered. When the descriptions move to violence, the teacher ends the discussion:

Teacher: You certainly thought of a lot of things that might have injured Andy, but now let's see what in fact did happen.

The teacher distributes copies of an assignment sheet (see Figure 12.10). A volunteer reads the three assignments aloud. Because everyone appears to understand the responsibilities, the teacher suggests that the students return to their places to finish the story.

Why this teacher did what she did is explained next.

1. Because the quality of the story about Andy is mediocre at best, the teacher used it primarily as a vehicle for introducing flashbacks as well as for adding to the students' reading vocabularies.

Assignments

1. When you finish reading, you should be able to answer the question, <u>Why is Andy in the hospital?</u>
2. When you know the answer to this question, <u>do page 43 in your workbook</u>. If necessary, you can look at the story about Andy. Be sure to read the directions at the top of the workbook page before starting.
3. The next job is to answer another question. This one was asked of a girl named Nell. <u>Read what follows. Then write how Nell answers</u>. When we meet again, you can read to the others the words you put in Nell's mouth. <u>Write what she said below</u>.

Nell felt tired and grouchy. Seeing how tired she looked, Fran inquired, "How come you're so tired, and it's only 11 o'clock in the morning?"
Nell explained, "

FIGURE 12.10   An Assignment Sheet

2. Having students think of possible reasons for Andy's trip to the hospital creates interest in finding out what did occur. It thus provides a reason for continuing beyond the first two pages of the story.

3. A basal workbook page was assigned because it has the students arrange eight sentences describing events in the story about Andy in the order in which they actually occurred. The students then check any statement that tells about an event told with a flashback. Directions for both tasks are clearly stated at the top of the workbook page.

4. The assignment to put words into Nell's mouth was given for several reasons. First, checking it later will allow for further attention to flashbacks. (This is when the teacher plans to introduce the term *flashback*.) Second, because the group learned about figurative expressions earlier, "putting words into Nell's mouth" permits a review of literal versus figurative uses of language. Third, earlier attention also went to authors' uses of synonyms for words like *said* and *asked* in conversations (e.g., *stated, uttered, inquired, wondered*). This topic will also be reviewed.

5. All the assignments were stated in writing to ensure that none is forgotten. Using an assignment sheet also demonstrates one reason for learning to read: to be able to follow written directions in procedural text.

Perspective

All of us have heard, said, and experienced, "Every story has at least two sides." As with life, so it is with the stories we read: How they unfold depends at least in part on who is doing the telling. Perspective (and its effect on stories) is another suitable topic, therefore, for instruction designed to help students understand stories. The subsequent discussion of perspective starts with easy text, then moves to consider more difficult stories.

Easy Text. How perspective may make life difficult for readers of supposedly easy stories can be illustrated with as few as two sentences:

1. "June," said Patty, "get the dime in my jacket."
2. June said, "Patty, get the dime in my jacket."

As can be seen, reading the first sentence must be done from Patty's perspective. That is, Patty is doing the talking, is making the request, and is the girl with a jacket. In contrast, comprehending the second sentence requires understanding that June is central, because she directs Patty to get the dime.*

One more example of dialogue, which seems simple on the surface, suggests other problems related to perspective:

"Don't tease my dog," Al said. "If you don't stop, I'll tell your dad when he gets home tonight."

---

*You may recall the recommendation in Chapter 3 to have dialogues like these read aloud in order to clarify any misunderstanding they may generate.

In this instance, the reader must view life from the perspective of someone named Al. It is unclear whether Al is talking to one or more persons; more clear is that the other person is neither his sibling nor an adult. To comprehend this supposedly simple text, the reader must further conclude that *my* refers to Al, and that *you* and *your* refer to the person(s) to whom Al is giving a direction and then a warning. Also necessary is the understanding that *tonight* refers to a time period in Al's life, not the reader's.

If nothing else, all this should clarify for teachers of beginners that dialogues in stories often provide subject matter for instruction. This point is made to dispel the myth that comprehension instruction can be delayed until about third or fourth grade.

More Difficult Stories. Commonly, stories are told from a third-person perspective. When they are, the teller of the tale is able not only to look down at the characters to describe their activities and relationships to others but also to get inside their heads so that thoughts and feelings can be described.

Eventually, students need to deal with a mix of third-person and first-person narration. Their initial contact with first-person narration can be an appropriate time (a) to compare first-person stories with the third-person perspective, and (b) to discuss words that signal a first-person perspective—*I, my, we,* and so forth. Later, reading another first-person narrative allows for the opportunity to pinpoint possible effects on a story when it is told from one person's point of view.

Initially, to get a discussion of such effects underway, students can be asked to read narration like the following:

How I Got a Ticket

I was driving on the highway. I made sure I didn't go faster than 65 miles an hour, because that is the limit. Even so, I was soon stopped by a police officer in an unmarked car. He said his radar showed I was going 72 miles an hour. I explained I was on my way to see my mother, who is ill, but was careful not to speed. I still got a ticket.

Once members of the instructional group read the paragraph, a line of questioning might go as follows, given the fact that the teacher's intention is to deal with possible effects on content when it is written from one person's perspective.

1. To what kind of a ticket does the title refer?
2. Who is telling about the driver who got the ticket?
3. How do you *know* that the person who got the ticket is the one who is telling how he or she got it?
4. Why do you think the driver mentioned to the police officer that he or she was driving to see a sick person?
5. Why do you suppose the driver mentions that the police officer was in an unmarked car?... By the way, what *is* an unmarked car?... I'll repeat the question I

asked earlier. Why do you think the driver referred to the fact that the police car was unmarked?

At the end, the teacher asks, "Do you think this incident about getting a ticket would be described the same way if the police officer were telling what happened?" Immediately, the group responds, "No!" This is a perfect time, therefore, to distribute the assignment sheet shown in Figure 12.11.

The assignment to tell how the officer explains why he gave a speeding ticket is part of the preparations being made for a story whose plot is summarized in Figure 12.12. When the instructional group meets the next day, some of the time with the teacher will be spent on having volunteers read their accounts of how the officer did the telling. The point the teacher plans to emphasize is the significance of who does the telling on content. This provides an introduction to the story summarized in Figure 12.12. (A suitable postreading assignment is to have the students retell the same story, this time from the perspective of Bonnie's brother.)

Assignment

Now that you have read the driver's explanation of how he or she got a ticket, pretend you are the officer who gave the ticket. Use the space below to tell <u>his</u> side of the story. To get you started, what he says at first is typed below. The title is there, too.

Why My Job Is Tough

I'm a police officer. This morning

FIGURE 12.11 Perspective: An Assignment

Nobody Likes Me
A Summary

Bonnie, the narrator, is unhappy because she feels nobody pays any attention to her. Recalling that her mother once commented that people who are different get attention, Bonnie puts together The Different Plan. She borrows her mother's fanciest hat, wears it to school, but attracts only the attention of the teacher, who directs Bonnie to take off the hat and put it away.

Bonnie's next plan, The Mysterious Plan, leads her to smile without any apparent cause and then to loud laughter in the presence of her brother. Bonnie asks, "Don't you want to know why I'm laughing?" "No," her brother responds, and leaves the room.

The indifference of her brother leads Bonnie to make one final plan called The Lively Plan. It is prompted by her cousin's observation that lively people get attention. Later, while visiting at the home of her aunt and uncle, Bonnie unexpectedly tap dances, sings, and finally does a cartwheel. By the time she is done, she is alone in the room. Bonnie then resigns herself to the fact that nobody will ever care enough to pay attention to her.

At school the next day, Bonnie's ever-growing curiosity about why a classmate, Jack, always has a pickle in his lunch box prompts her to inquire. Jack, surprised that someone noticed and was interested enough to ask, is proud to explain that his dad makes pickles. He then asks Bonnie why she wore such a funny hat to school the previous week. Soon the two children are enjoying each other's company, telling one another about all the things they like to do.

FIGURE 12.12   First-Person Narration

EXPOSITORY TEXT: APPROPRIATE TOPICS FOR INSTRUCTION

Because textbooks are supposed to provide information, they also provide one example of expository text. That is why, many pages back, the Introduction reviewed strategies for acquiring information from this book. Now, only brief pieces of expository material are looked at because learning how to learn from textbooks is the subject of Chapter 15.

Macrostructure

Expository text in sources like magazines, encyclopedias, trade books,* and basal readers have a macrostructure composed of one or more central ideas. Often, the central (or main) ideas are revealed with headings scattered throughout the text. In the case of a magazine article, the title commonly announces the topic (e.g., "The

---

*A *trade book* is written for the library and bookstore market rather than for schools.

Exquisite Beauty of Australian Rainforests"); headings then point out the main ideas about the topic that the article covers.

Knowing that the body of text about to be read *is* expository in nature is important, as this establishes an appropriate mental set for reading it (18). Aware, for instance, that what is about to be read is a factual description of bluebonnets in Texas, a proficient reader adopts a stance that is different from the one appropriate for reading an Indian legend that explains why bluebonnets are so plentiful in Texas.

For teachers, all this suggests that providing background information, which is part of "facilitating comprehension," includes attending to the nature of the text for which preparations are being made. It also means that if the text is exposition, preparing students to read it includes examining headings and, perhaps, making predictions about the kinds of information that each section provides. Now, comparing predictions with the information that the author actually gives provides a reason for the reading.

All this is to say that one kind of comprehension instruction has to do with the macrostructure of expository text and, further, that the preparations and the purposes for reading expository text are not identical to those suitable for stories.

Microstructure

A second kind of comprehension instruction linked to expository discourse focuses on its microstructure—that is, on the parts that make up the whole. In brief pieces of text, such as magazine articles, paragraphs fall under the heading "microstructure." Often, but not inevitably, paragraphs in expository material communicate main ideas that are embellished with related details. Even though it is traditional for basal reader manuals to assume that a paragraph has not only a main idea but also a main idea that is told with a topic sentence, that is not the case (7). Examining authentic text—as opposed to the contrived text in workbooks—shows something else. Specifically, some paragraphs *are* made up of a main idea and related details; however, when this occurs, variation such as the following is characteristic:

- The main idea is stated directly with a sentence, which occurs at the beginning, or the end, or in the middle of the paragraph.
- The main idea is implied rather than stated.

Not to be overlooked are other kinds of paragraphs—some, for example, that consist of a continuation of details that the previous paragraph introduced.

Dorothy Hennings makes other points worth noting:

> Unfortunately,...the attention given [in school] to reading for main ideas occurs primarily in relation to discrete paragraphs in workbooks. Students analyze individual paragraphs that are not part of a continuous text and that have been written for the express purpose of helping them glean main ideas. Such clearcut paragraphs are not typical of authentic texts, and the points being expressed are relatively bland and insignificant. (11, p. 347)

Teachers who correctly attend to main ideas only in the framework of expository text should not overlook the need to demonstrate to students that getting or constructing main ideas is helpful because it (a) identifies important content,

(b) helps to organize it, (c) allows for summarizing the content, and (d) aids in remembering it (4). All this should remind you of advice offered in previous chapters: Help students to see the value for their reading of what they are asked to learn or do.

ESTABLISHING PURPOSES FOR READING EXPOSITORY TEXT

Inherent in expository text is the reason to read it: to acquire information. To specify the acquisition, teachers can do a variety of things as part of prereading preparations in order to maximize the likelihood that comprehension is achieved. Three possibilities are discussed.

Outlines

Let's assume that a selection in a basal reader is informational text dealing with minerals. Let's further assume that it tells about their characteristics, how minerals differ from plants and animals, where they are found, and their uses. Before the reading gets started, the teacher distributes the following outline with directions to fill in the missing information either in the course of reading the article or afterward.

    I. Characteristics of Minerals
       A. _____
       B. _____
       C. _____
       D. _____
    II. Differences between Minerals and Plants
       A. _____
       B. _____
   III. Differences between Minerals and Animals
       A. _____
       B. _____
       C. _____
    IV. Where Minerals are Found
       A. _____
       B. _____
    V. How Minerals Are Used
       A. _____
       B. _____
       C. _____

Obviously, the use of an unfinished outline to encourage students to attend to important content is possible only when previous instruction helped them understand the connection between outlines and the composition of informational material.

K-W-L

Another strategy for specifying purposes for reading expository material and that also promotes comprehension is referred to as K-W-L (14). This plan starts with brainstorming as a means for activating existing knowledge about a topic. It also encourages students to express what else they'd like to learn. Finally, the plan allows for comparing what students had hoped to learn from the reading with what in fact the author told them.

To keep all this in mind, the following should help.

K: What I <u>k</u>now.
W: What I <u>w</u>ant to learn.
L: What I have <u>l</u>earned.

When the V-W-L strategy is used, an assignment sheet is as simple as a three-column page:

What I Know	What I Want to Find Out	What I Learned

If an article happens to be about harmonicas, students might already know that a harmonica is a musical instrument; that it is small and rectangular in shape; that it has holes on one side; and that blowing through the holes produces sounds. All this is recorded in the first column prior to the start of the reading, as is the additional information that students want to acquire. What they want to find out establishes a purpose for the reading, which is to compare what they wanted to find out with what they actually learn. What *is* learned can be recorded in the third column by individuals or, perhaps, by pairs of children. The postreading discussion centers on the comparison.

True-False Statements

Another way to provide a specific purpose for reading informational material involves the use of true-false statements both before the reading is done and afterward. Statements are based on the information provided. If an article deals with air, for instance, statements like those listed in Figure 12.13 are possibilities.

Once the article is completed, each student rereads the ten statements and decides on the basis of the article whether a statement is true or false. The postreading discussion centers on comparisons between pre- and postreading judgments.

COMPREHENSION INSTRUCTION: ADDITIONAL SUBJECT MATTER

To help clarify "comprehension instruction," the following sections name additional topics that are not confined to one type of text. The topics listed—although hardly exhaustive—should help teachers when they examine text that students will read in order to identify the kind of comprehension instruction that is relevant and that

---

Air

Mark with a T any sentence below that you think makes a correct statement. Mark with an F any sentence that you believe is not correct. Do this now. Write the letters in the column that says "Before" to show that this is what you think about air before you read the article that tells about air.

Before	After	
_____	_____	1. Air is all around us.
_____	_____	2. Air is also in lakes and oceans.
_____	_____	3. Air cannot be seen.
_____	_____	4. Air has no smell.
_____	_____	5. Air has weight.
_____	_____	6. In a room of average size, the air weighs about 75 pounds.
_____	_____	7. Cold air is lighter than warm air.
_____	_____	8. Airplanes fly in the air.
_____	_____	9. Space ships do not fly in the air.
_____	_____	10. People need air in order to live.

FIGURE 12.13   An Assignment to Establish a Purpose for Reading about Air

might be needed. The additional topics are identified in the framework of what writers do and use in order to communicate.

Typographic Signals

Typographic signals are first discussed in Chapter 3, where the need to have certain kinds of text read aloud is of concern. Authors' constant reliance on the typographic features of text means that readers need to interpret these signals in appropriate ways. Over a period of time, therefore, students should be taught the following guidelines:

Period:
   signals the end of a thought.
   indicates an abbreviation.

Comma:
   keeps units of meaning together.
   sets off an appositive.
   indicates the person being addressed.

Question Mark:
   signals a question.

Exclamation Mark:
  indicates emotions.
  suggests emphasis (as do italics and underlining).

Capitalization:
  indicates a title, the start of a sentence, or a proper name.

Semicolon:
  suggests that what follows is related to what preceded.

Colon:
  signals that a series of related items follows.

Paragraph Indentation:
  suggests a possible shift in focus.

Descriptions

Describe is something else authors do routinely. For this reason, students need to be helped to understand the variety of ways in which writers do describe. Examples are listed below.

Adjectives:
  The cool weather is <u>refreshing</u>.

Adverbs:
  <u>Eventually</u>, the work was done.

Phrases:
  The baby walked <u>with hesitation</u>.

Clauses:
  Our house, <u>which is on a hill</u>, stayed dry.

Appositives:
  Angela, <u>the oldest in the family</u>, has her first job.

Authors may use language in figurative ways to describe. Figures of speech that merit instructional time include:

Idiom:
  Inferences require reading between the lines.

Hyperbole:
  The tall trees reached to the sky.

Simile:
  He's as thin as a twig.

Metaphor:
  Raising taxes is a minefield for politicians.

Personification:
  As the wind blew, the chimes on the porch sang.

A writer's descriptions may deal with sequence, simultaneously occurring events, or, perhaps, causes and effects. When they do, readers profit from knowing that certain words provide help in clarifying the descriptions:

Signal words for sequence:
    first, next, before, later, afterward, earlier, eventually, finally, at the end

Signal words for simultaneous events:
    while, meanwhile, at the same time, simultaneously

Signal words for cause-effect relationships:
    because, hence, therefore, as a result, for that reason, that is why

Pronoun and Adverb Referents

Writers' frequent use of referent words makes them a suitable topic for comprehension instruction. Even when writers are careful and editors are diligent, research indicates that ambiguous referents—and even some that are not—are major sources of problems for readers (3, 16). The two pieces of text below are offered to illustrate both pronoun and adverb referents.

> The day was wet and cold. <u>It</u> was windy, too. Still,
> <u>that</u> did not keep <u>him</u> from being outdoors.
> Play in the backyard. If <u>you</u> stay <u>there</u>, <u>you'll</u>
> be safe.

Cohesive Ties

When Chapter 1 defines connected text, cohesive ties figure in the discussion. That is natural because it is words that serve this function that allow for connected text. Like referent words—which may also be cohesive ties—this feature of text is a common cause of comprehension problems.

Pronoun and adverb referents functioning as cohesive ties are illustrated first:

> We have reading chairs in the study. <u>They</u> are really
> comfortable.
> Park the car <u>here</u>. The driveway is the only place I've
> had time to shovel.

When Chapter 6 discusses whole word methodology, it points out that certain function words serve as cohesive ties. This is illustrated next:

> I know that vase is expensive. Buy it <u>anyway</u>.
> He has the legs of a wading bird. <u>Nevertheless</u>, he wears
> nothing but shorts in the summer.

To show why dealing with cohesive ties can be difficult for readers, the following illustration is presented in two forms. The first shows how the text appears normally. In the second form, cohesive ties are made explicit.

A higher animal has feelings for other animals of its kind. It forms close attachments. Dogs and chimpanzees do this. Lower animals, like rats, do not. Dolphins also have such feelings.

Why teachers need to view text not from the perspective of an accomplished reader but from the viewpoint of the student who has been asked to read it is demonstrated in the analysis below.

$$\overset{1}{A}\ [\text{higher animal}]\ \text{has}\ \overset{2}{[\text{feelings for other animals of}\ \underline{\text{its}}\ \text{kind}]}.\ \overset{1}{\underline{\text{It}}}$$

$$\overset{3}{[\text{forms close attachments}]}.\ \text{Dogs and chimpanzees}\ \overset{3}{\underline{\text{do}}\ \underline{\text{this}}}.\ \text{Lower}$$

$$\text{animals, like rats,}\ \overset{3}{\underline{\text{do}}\ \underline{\text{not}}}.\ \text{Dolphins also have}\ \overset{2}{\underline{\text{such}}}\ \text{feelings}.$$

Elliptical Sentences

Elliptical refers to sentences in which words omitted by the speaker or writer have to be inferred by the listener or reader. The implied content in elliptical sentences provides more subject matter for comprehension instruction. In the following illustrations, the elliptical sentences are underscored.

"Are you going to the game?" asked Joel. "Yes," answered Beth.
The windows in the garage are dirty. The car is, too.
All the children in the family are sick. So is their mother.
Alan may be late. If so, start the meeting without him.

Inferences

The pervasive need for readers to make inferences is suggested by the fact that many of the illustrative texts used for topics just discussed required inferences. Now, two more pieces of text are used for the following purposes. The first is to emphasize that inferences are required even in simple text. The second purpose is to remind you that inferences are both text-based and knowledge-based, which is something students need to be helped to understand.

The dog is chasing a cat. He is barking his head off.
(The inference that he refers to dog is based on the word barking and on the knowledge that dogs, not cats, bark.)
Jeff is learning to be a flutist. He thinks it is a beautiful instrument.
(The inference that it refers to the unstated word flute is based on the word flutist and on the knowledge that a flutist plays an instrument called a "flute.")

COMPREHENSION INSTRUCTION: ANOTHER EXAMPLE

In order to clarify "comprehension instruction" still further, one more example is described. The lesson that follows is presented in a format that reflects the components of planned, intentional instruction described in Chapter 2. Similes in the selection for which the students are being prepared account for the two objectives of the instruction:

1. To teach the function of similes.
2. To teach that the construction *as…as* may signal a simile.

Instruction

The teacher starts by displaying the following text, which is printed on chart paper.

> as white as snow
> as rosy as blood
> as black as ebony

She explains that the words describe someone in a movie recently shown on television. Because nobody is able to think of the person, the teacher continues, "These words describe 'Snow White.'" Immediately, comments about the movie *Snow White and the Seven Dwarfs* ensue. The teacher then calls the group's attention back to the chart, explaining, "It was said in the film that Snow White's skin is as white as snow. In fact, that's why she's called 'Snow White.' It was also said that her cheeks are as rosy as blood. Of course, we know that her cheeks and blood are different, but comparing the color of her cheeks with the color of blood does help us see what her cheeks are like: very red, indeed. Writers use comparisons like 'as rosy as blood' to help us see in our minds what their words are describing. The author of the story you'll soon be reading uses these kinds of descriptions, too. That's why I wanted to talk to you about them.

"There's one more description of Snow White on the chart that hasn't been read yet. To understand what it tells about Snow White, we need to know what 'ebony' is. Does anyone know?…Nobody?…Ebony is a very hard and very dark wood. In fact, it's deep black in color. That's why the person describing Snow White says that something about her is 'as black as ebony.' Picture Snow White in your mind. What about her is 'as black as ebony'?" Everyone immediately responds, "Her hair!"

The teacher then summarizes: "The person telling us about Snow White describes her by saying that her skin is as white as snow, her cheeks are as rosy as blood, and her hair is as black as ebony. Those words certainly help us see Snow White in our minds. Let's take a look now at descriptions of some other things."

The teacher writes two sentences on the board:

> The boy jumped high.
> The boy jumped very high.

With questions and discussion, the point is made that *very high* indicates a height greater than *high*. Then the following dialogue takes place.

Teacher: I'm going to write some words that mean higher than *very high*. What do you suppose they'll be?

Katrina: Very, very high!

Teacher: No, better than that. [Writes *The boy jumped as high as the sky.*] When I say that the boy jumped as high as the sky, do I mean that he was up in the clouds?

Group: No!

Teacher: No, I'm just trying to impress you with the fact that his jump was *really* high. To do that, I compared it with something that all of us know is about the highest thing around. With the comparison, I hoped you'd get the feeling that this is a person who can *really* jump high. I'll write another sentence that uses a comparison to make a point. This time I want to tell you that somebody came and went very, very quickly. [Writes *They came and went as quick as a wink.*] In this case, why is a wink a good comparison? Chad?

Chad: It's about the fastest thing you do. You do it so fast, you don't even know you do it.

Teacher: Right. I can wink so quickly that it would be hard to know how long it takes. I certainly wouldn't want to have to time it. Here's another good comparison. [Writes *The baby's skin is as soft as silk.*]

After the sentence is read, members of the group get to feel a piece of silk. Then, the teacher summarizes: "Authors use these kinds of comparisons to give you a better feeling for what they're trying to say. They want to make sure you get the point. For the comparisons, they use the word *as* twice—for instance, 'as rosy as blood' or 'as soft as silk.' Now when you see those words, you'll know that the writer is making a comparison. He or she is comparing two very different things, yet the comparison really makes the point. For example, if I wanted to tell you how tough the meat was that we had for dinner last night, I might say something like, 'It was as tough as leather.' When I say that, I don't really mean leather. Meat and leather are different. What I *do* mean is that eating the meat was pretty much like trying to chew leather. In other words, I want to be sure you know just how tough that meat was."

Supervised Practice

Each student receives a paper that lists the following sentences.

> 1. His booming voice is as loud as thunder.
> 2. As quickly as a rocket, she took off in her sports car.
> 3. Today is as windy as a big electric fan.
> 4. Her dress is as colorful as a spring garden.

Guided by the teacher, the students (a) read each sentence silently, (b) identify the simile and explain why the comparison is a good one, (c) underline the simile, and (d) draw a second line under *as*.

Application

Once the students read the assigned story in their basal reader and respond to four questions posed before the reading began, they will be asked to reread the selection in order to find sentences that have similes with the *as...as* construction. The sentences are to be copied and the similes underlined. The page number on which each simile was found is to be noted, too.

Subsequent Instruction

Material containing similes signaled by *like* provides another opportunity to deal with comparisons. Now, examples such as the following are useful.

> The visor on his cap is like an awning.
> My little brother keeps following me. He's like my shadow.
> After a week of rain, the sun is like pure gold.

Once the two kinds of similes are taught, "simile" can be used to refer to both. To be emphasized, however, is that it is much more important for students to recognize and comprehend similes than it is to know the name for the comparisons. This point is made because teaching manuals often show more concern for defining terms (e.g. first-person narration and third-person narration) than for explaining to students the significance for reading of what is being defined (8).

As soon as authors of material that students are expected to read use metaphors, they provide other subject matter for instruction. Because metaphors are implied similes *(Our cat is as stubborn as a mule* vs. *Our cat is a stubborn mule.),* similes and metaphors should be compared at some point. A song known to many children serves well to introduce metaphors:

> Make new friends,
> But keep the old.
> One is silver,
> And the other is gold.

WHEN TO PROVIDE COMPREHENSION INSTRUCTION

A question about when comprehension instruction should be offered needs to be preceded by another: Is such instruction necessary? Because efforts to teach comprehension have had positive results, the general answer is "Yes." However, like any other teaching, it should be offered *only if needed.* Said differently, just as it is indefensible to withhold instruction from students who require it, so is it senseless to "teach" others what they already know or are able to do. A general guideline that wins the support of anyone who has taught elementary school is that no matter what the topic, slower children require more explicit instruction than do others because their ability to self-instruct or discover is less. This does not mean that they should be bombarded with dull instruction dealing with something that will not be useful in the near future. Nor does it mean that poorer readers should be assigned practice that is tedious and, as is sometimes the case, irrelevant for improving reading abilities.

Based on the conviction that all students need some instruction and that certain ones require larger amounts, this book has already demonstrated with numerous examples how instruction can be made useful and that practice need not be drudgery. With this specific help in the background, it is now time to consider when preplanned comprehension instruction should be scheduled. The answer is displayed on p. 325.

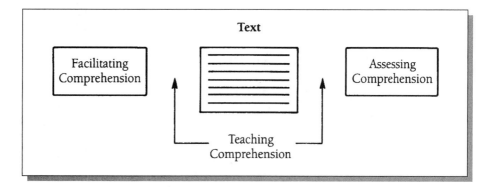

As the display indicates, offering comprehension instruction can be a pre- or postreading activity. Teaching members of an instructional group about similes before they encounter them initially, for instance, makes sense. If it happens that a sizable number of new words in the selection that has similes require a teacher's attention, and, in addition, some background information has to be imparted, such instruction might have to be scheduled for the next day. On this second day of pre-reading preparations, the previous day's work is reviewed, after which the instruction about similes is offered. Assuming purposes for reading have been identified, the group is now ready to begin the selection.

Let's take one more example. In this case, a group is asked to read their first tall tale. The teacher has already called attention to exaggeration but has confined the discussion to sentences and paragraphs. (A newspaper account of interest to the whole class prompted the attention to overstatements.) Because of the earlier discussion, the teacher decides to do nothing with the genre "tall tale" until members of the group have read the one soon to be assigned. Afterward, it can serve as an illustration during the postreading instruction.

If it happens that more than one student has trouble comprehending the tall tale because of the failure to adopt the appropriate mental set for the reading, the teacher may make different decisions the next time one is read for the first time. In other words, experience is the best of teachers for teachers. Coupled with the knowledge of what constitutes "teaching reading," experiences and reflection about them lead to teachers who are capable of making wise decisions about the timing of instruction—in this case, of comprehension instruction.

SUMMARY

Chapter 12 began by stating that comprehension can receive attention before children are able to read. Elaboration of this point took the form of samples of listening activities in which the focus was on comprehension. Attention then shifted to, and stayed with, reading comprehension.

Initially, a number of sections in the chapter dealt with the significance of purposes for reading. This reflects the fact that successful comprehension is the realization of whatever purposes were established for the reading. One implication of the linkage is the need for students to view competent reading as something that encompasses a wide range of behaviors that ought to be determined not only by what they are reading but also by whatever it is they want, or need, to accomplish with the reading.

Purposes continued to be discussed because they permit students to monitor their ongoing comprehension and teachers to assess it afterward. The importance of helping students become not only proficient but also independent readers accounts for the somewhat detailed treatment of comprehension monitoring. Once the two components of this self-checking process were identified—evaluation and regulation—the chapter cited examples of breakdowns in comprehension, which were followed by descriptions of suitable fix-up strategies.

Attention then shifted to teaching students how to go about constructing the meaning of connected text. This discussion of comprehension instruction began by making the point that certain subject matter is suitable for stories whereas other topics are linked to expository text. Still others are more generic. Presumably, finding inferences in this third collection of topics was not a surprise. Deliberately, examples used to illustrate the need for inferences included very easy text in order to re-emphasize that inferential comprehension needs to be a concern of teachers of beginners as well as of those who work with more accomplished readers. Other topics in this more broadly based group included typographic signals, pronoun and adverb referents, cohesive ties, and elliptical sentences.

At various points in Chapter 12, examples of comprehension instruction were inserted. Again, they were included to make discussions specific enough to help both teachers and prospective teachers.

At the end, the question of when to provide comprehension instruction was addressed. That it might be a prereading or a postreading endeavor was the point made. Not overlooked was the following: Only teach what needs to be taught. Or, as Chapter 12 stated, "Just as it is indefensible to withhold instruction from those who need it, so is it senseless to teach others what they already know or are able to do."

REVIEW

1. The title of Chapter 12, "Comprehension: Connected Text," suggests two questions:
   a. What is connected text?
   b. What is comprehension instruction?

2. Purposes for reading received generous attention in Chapter 12. Give four reasons that justify such attention in a chapter generally concerned with comprehension and specifically concerned with teaching comprehension.

3. In a way that makes clear distinctions among the three, explain (a) facilitating comprehension, (b) teaching comprehension, and (c) assessing comprehension.

4. Explain with examples the two statements below, each of which has to do with subject matter for comprehension instruction.
   a. Different kinds of text—for instance, stories and exposition—make some topics suitable for comprehension instruction and other topics unsuitable.
   b. Some topics for comprehension instruction are suitable for just about every piece of connected text—assuming it is a topic for which students need help.

5. One reason for the attention that comprehension monitoring received in Chapter 12 has to do with the importance of independence. What is the meaning of "independence" in this context?

6. Assessing comprehension is often thought of only in the framework of asking questions. In order to correct such a narrow perception, Chapter 12 shows with a number of examples that assessment can be accomplished in a variety of ways. Describe four procedures referred to in the chapter for assessing comprehension that do not center on asking students postreading questions.

7. Chapter 12 states that, much too often, students are expected to read required texts in an identical way: carefully. To counteract this questionable practice, the need for teachers and students to "adopt an appropriate stance" toward whatever is read was emphasized. Exactly what does "appropriate stance" mean applied to both teachers and students?

REFERENCES

1. Altwerger, Bess; Edelsky, Carole; and Flores, Barbara. "Whole Language: What's New?" *Reading Teacher* 41 (November, 1987), 144–154.
2. Baker, Linda, and Brown, Ann L. "Metacognitive Skills and Reading." In P. David Pearson et al. (Eds.), *Handbook of Reading Research.* New York: Longman and Co., 1984, 353–394.
3. Barnitz, John G. "Syntactic Effect on the Reading Comprehension of Pronoun-Referent Structures by Children in Grades Two, Four, and Six." *Reading Research Quarterly* 15 (1980, No. 2), 268–289.
4. Baumann, James (Ed.). *Teaching Main Idea Comprehension.* Newark, Del.: International Reading Association, 1986.
5. Beck, Isabel L., and McKeown, Margaret G. "Developing Questions That Promote Comprehension: The Story Map." *Language Arts* 58 (November/December, 1981), 913–918.
6. Carver, Ronald P. "Is Reading Rate Constant or Flexible?" *Reading Research Quarterly* 18 (Winter, 1983), 190–215.
7. Durkin, Dolores. "Comprehension Instruction in Current Basal Reader Series." Technical Report No. 521. Urbana: University of Illinois, Center for the Study of Reading, 1990.
8. Durkin, Dolores. "Reading Comprehension Instruction in Five Basal Reader Series." *Reading Research Quarterly* 16 (1981, No. 4), 515–544.
9. Durkin, Dolores. "What Classroom Observations Reveal about Reading Comprehension Instruction." *Reading Research Quarterly* 14 (1978–79, No. 4), 481–533.
10. Durkin, Dolores. "What Is the Value of the New Interest in Reading Comprehension?" *Language Arts* 58 (January, 1981), 23–43.
11. Hennings, Dorothy G. "Essential Reading: Targeting, Tracking, and Thinking about Main Ideas." *Journal of Reading* 34 (February, 1991), 346–353.
12. Johnston, Peter. "Implications of Basic Research for the Assessment of Reading Comprehension." Technical Report No. 206. Urbana: University of Illinois, Center for the Study of Reading, 1981.
13. McConaughy, Stephanie H. "Developmental Changes in Story Comprehension and Levels of Questioning." *Language Arts* 59 (September, 1982), 580–589.

14. Ogle, Donna M. "K-W-L: A Teaching Model That Develops Active Reading of Expository Text." *Reading Teacher* 39 (February, 1986), 564–570.

15. Piccolo, Jo Anne. "Writing a No-Fault Narrative: Every Teacher's Dream." *Reading Teacher* 40 (November, 1986), 136–142.

16. Richek, Margaret Ann. "Reading Comprehension of Anaphoric Forms in Varying Linguistic Contexts." *Reading Research Quarterly* 12 (1976–77, No. 2), 145–165.

17. Rode, Sara S. "Development of Phrase and Clause Boundary Reading in Children." *Reading Research Quarterly* 10 (1974–75, No. 1), 124–142.

18. Rosenblatt, Louise M. "Writing and Reading: The Transactional Theory." Technical Report No. 416. Urbana: University of Illinois, Center for the Study of Reading, 1988.

19. Spiegel, Dixie L., and Fitzgerald, Jill. "Improving Reading Comprehension through Instruction about Story Parts." *Reading Teacher* 39 (March, 1986), 676–682.

20. Stark, Constance G. "A Story Writing Map." *Reading Teacher* 40 (May, 1987), 926–927.

21. Steiner, Robert; Wiener, Morton; and Cramer, Ward. "Comprehension Training and Identification for Poor and Good Readers." *Journal of Educational Psychology* 62 (December, 1971), 506–513.

22. Watson, Dorothy J. "Defining and Describing Whole Language." *Elementary School Journal* 90 (November, 1989), 129–141.

23. Wendler, David; Samuels, S. Jay; and Moore, Vienna K. "Comprehension Instruction of Award-Winning Teachers, Teachers with Master's Degrees, and Other Teachers." *Reading Research Quarterly* 24 (Fall, 1989), 382–400.

24. Wittrock, M. C. "Generative Teaching of Comprehension." *Elementary School Journal* 92 (November, 1991), 169–184.

PART V

In a book about reading and reading instruction, it is not accidental that instructional materials entered into discussions as early as the first chapter. You now know that such materials are everywhere. It should be equally clear at this point in *Teaching Them to Read* that any text, be it a bumper sticker or a beautifully illustrated story told with magnificent prose, is good to the extent that it fulfills a purpose that is important or necessary for as few as one student or as many as a whole class. Not to be overlooked is that realized purposes include enjoyment and relaxation, inspiration, an increase in world knowledge, as well as an increase in self-knowledge.

It has already been recognized that certain materials are used in classrooms not because they are the best means for realizing laudable objectives but because they are—or are perceived to be—required. Materials in this category frequently end up merely being "covered." Getting through them, in fact, becomes an end in itself.

Materials commonly required are featured in two chapters that make up Part V. Chapter 13, "Basal Reader Series," deals with collections of materials that a majority of elementary teachers use. More recently, parts of basal programs have also made their way into kindergartens. Because of the widespread influence that basal programs thus enjoy, anyone unacquainted with them was encouraged many pages ago to examine one or more series. Individuals who have not done that should do it before progressing to Chapter 13 because this chapter takes it for granted that part of the background information readers bring to the chapter

Materials

· ·

stems from their familiarity with one or more basal programs. The origin of other related information is your own use of these materials when you attended elementary school.

It seemed appropriate to follow up Chapter 13 with a chapter that deals with nonrequired materials, in this case, trade books. A trade book is one originally written for the library and bookstore market. Even though Chapter 14 is about the use of trade books in classrooms, deciding on its title presented problems. Specifically, calling it "Children's Trade Books" raised the question, "But is the meaning of 'trade book' widely known?" On the other hand, calling the chapter "Children's Literature" prompted the question, "Will this be interpreted to mean that the focus is confined to storybooks and poems?" The second

title was chosen for Chapter 14; but with this decision came the resolution to note in its Preview that the concern was for fiction and nonfiction. Making this point is important because, as stated earlier in the book, the bulk of the literature that students are encouraged to read in school is narrative in nature. In fact, some equate literature with fiction only.

Chapter 15, "Content Area Textbooks," returns to required materials, in this case, for subjects like social studies, science, and health. The objective of the chapter is to illustrate how all these textbooks can serve as a means not only for teaching subject matter but also for teaching students how to acquire information from text on their own.

Basal Reader Series

Those of you who have read this book from the beginning are aware of the many references to basal reader materials. You also know that the frequency does not imply an endorsement but, rather, a recognition of the widespread use of these materials.

The influence enjoyed by basal reader series accounts for a chapter that focuses on them exclusively. Chapter 13 initiates the concentrated attention by dealing with the four major components of every series. The first is the readers. They are the textbooks containing the selections that students read. The second component is the manual. A manual accompanies each reader; all manuals are made up of recommendations to teachers for using the readers. Never missing from any manual are references to workbooks, the third major part of every series. At least one workbook is said by publishers to be necessary for every reader. Other exercises also are available, including blackline masters. The fourth major part of a basal series is its tests. They are of two kinds. End-of-unit tests are supposed to be given after a specified number of selections in a reader are finished. The administration of end-of-level tests is recommended after a reader is completed. Manuals often state which parts of a basal lesson are covered in the tests.

Criticisms of basal series in this book and elsewhere make it appropriate to consider before Chapter 13 is begun whether these materials *ought* to be used. Answers vary. My own opinion is that new teachers need to use them some of the time. That they should use them only as one of several kinds of materials is a point made repeatedly in previous chapters. Equally clear is that the use of basal programs by any teacher, new or experienced, needs to be shaped by teachers themselves. Altered use is required not only by flaws in basal programs but also by the fact that no author of any material knows the particular students for whom each teacher is responsible. This means that every teacher must strive to become a knowledgeable decision maker, whether using basal materials or something else.

• • • • • • •

To start the chapter, the four basic components of basal programs are described. The fact that persistent and very vocal complaints from customers and other individuals and groups have resulted in some improvements starting in the late 1980s is acknowledged (1, 3, 6, 8, 13, 16, 17). Nevertheless, the following descriptions are essentially correct even though they do not reflect publishers' calling their readers "anthologies" and their workbooks "journals."

COMPONENTS OF A BASAL READER SERIES

As the Preview states, the core parts of basal programs are readers, manuals, workbooks, and tests. Each is considered with both descriptions and commentary.

Student Textbooks

The book that contains the selections that students read is referred to as the student textbook or the pupil textbook or simply the reader. Currently, it may even be referred to as an anthology. Publishers spend sizable amounts of time and money on this part of their program because school personnel responsible for selecting—or, as it is usually called, for adopting—a series typically examine readers more carefully than other components (15).

Traditionally, basal readers have been available for grades 1 through 8. The readers targeted for first grade start with three soft-covered, very easy readers that have been called preprimers (rhymes with "swimmers"). Next comes the primer, which is followed by the first reader. The two subsequent textbooks are said to be for second grade; the two following, for third grade. After that, one reader is prepared for each grade.

For a long time, first-grade materials marked the beginning of a basal series. That is not the case now, however. In the 1960s, when interest developed in fostering readiness for reading among kindergartners, publishers responded with one—sometimes two—reading readiness workbooks. Taking advantage of the more recent interest in emergent literacy, all the series available now start with so many materials for kindergarten that it is difficult to keep track of them. In addition to providing big books, little books, and workbooks, one series has 23 kinds of supplementary materials for kindergarten. This should help explain why the description of basal programs is confined to the core parts.

Manuals

However publishers choose to describe them—for instance, as *Teacher's Edition* or *Teacher's Book,* or *Teacher's Guide*—every series has manuals composed of suggestions for teachers when they are using a selection in a reader. Some critics of basal programs portray their manuals as scripts for teaching (8). Because they do suggest what teachers should say, and even how students will respond, the description is not inaccurate.

Anybody who merely skims the manuals in a series soon notices that the format is so similar from one grade to the next that it is possible to identify the name of the publisher by examining a few pages in any one of its manuals. Even though publishers claim that identically labeled segments for each lesson in each manual result in "consistency" and "ease of use," the recurring formats help explain the small amount of change that some students experience during the reading period as they move from one grade to the next.

Because the preparation of basal manuals (and workbooks and tests) is subcontracted to curriculum-development companies, the observations of an employee of one such company are worth repeating. Made in the late 1970s, the comments remain relevant because rigidly formatted manuals continue to be produced. This employee states:

> To my mind, the single gravest problem…, a weakness that leads to most of the other problems, is the matter of format…. Time is money, and formats help publishers make and maintain timetables…. The trouble is, very little learning material logically…divides into rigid, repeatable forms. But the publishers hold firm, so authors are compelled to twist and bend…the material to make it fit the arbitrary, predetermined form. (19, pp. 44–45)

Preestablished formats, with all of their undesirable consequences, warrant advising teachers to conceive of manuals as lists of suggestions that can be used, altered, resequenced, or bypassed. Admittedly, the problem with the advice is that following it is a time-consuming activity because suggestions are so numerous. Publishers, on the other hand, urge teachers to believe that all the "options" are a way of empowering them by not limiting possibilities.

Workbooks

Because it is safe to assume you did not get through elementary school without completing sizable numbers of workbook pages (plus commercially prepared and teacher-made ditto sheets), there may be no need to state that the third component of basal reader programs is the workbook. A minimum of one workbook accompanies each reader; the use of others is referred to and recommended in manuals. In addition to being more numerous than ever, current workbooks are more colorful. Even though workbook pages decorated in color do make them more attractive, the decorations take up space. This means that when a workbook page is worth doing, brevity limits its pedagogical value. The value of workbooks for publishers lies in the fact that, like tests, workbooks are consumable. That is, because students write in them, they are repurchased yearly.

Tests

Just as interest in accountability has remained and even increased, so has the number of basal reader tests. Publishers consider consumable tests to be a very important part of the packages they produce. Visits to schools and conversations with teachers support the conclusion that many administrators take the tests seriously, too.

Schools using a basal series typically administer not only an annual standardized reading achievement test but also the end-of-unit and end-of-level tests that a basal company supplies. End-of-unit tests are given after students finish a group of selections in a reader. Once the whole of the reader is completed, an end-of-level test is supposed to be administered.

Not unexpectedly, workbook exercises and test items are similar. Manuals usually tell teachers which parts of a basal lesson—which words, for example, and which topics—are tested. This is done because both publishers and schools want high scores. After all, who is going to purchase a series whose use yields low scores? In schools in which basal tests *are* taken seriously—sometimes scores are even passed on to parents—teachers have a compelling reason to use basal workbooks.

CHANGES IN BASAL READER SERIES

Like any business, publishers of basal reader programs try hard to please customers. Finding out exactly what the customer wants is revealed indirectly by criticisms of existing materials and directly through sophisticated procedures that the marketing division of each company uses.

When either widespread criticisms or, on the other hand, needs and interests are identified, change results (10). In other words, publishers do not lead the crowd—they follow it. On the assumption that knowing about factors that have accounted for change makes teachers more circumspect consumers, two factors that explain many of the alterations in existing series will be discussed. The first has to do with the concept "readability." The second is related to statewide adoptions of instructional materials, which makes certain states especially important customers for publishers.

READABILITY

One feature of basal programs that has made them attractive to educators over the years is the claim that the readers provide a school with a succession of textbooks that gradually become more difficult. *Readability* is the term customarily used to refer to text difficulty. The readability level of easy text is thus lower than that of more advanced text.

In earlier decades, when reading was still conceived of as an objective translation of an author's words, the interest that developed in measuring readability in a numerical way was natural. So, too, were the readability formulas that began to emerge in the early 1930s (18). This was another consequence of the desire among psychologists and educators in the 1920s to make their work scientific.

To illustrate the general nature of readability formulas, let me use one that George Spache recommended in the 1950s for use with primary-grade materials (20):

> Grade level of text = .141 average sentence length per 100 words + .086 percent of words outside the Dale 769 Easy Word List + .839.

As the formula indicates, a passage of about 100 words is randomly chosen from a longer selection. The average number of words in the sentences that make up the shorter passage is calculated and multiplied by .141. The number that results is added to the number resulting from multiplying .086 by the percentage of words in the selected passage that are not in the list of 769 words compiled by Edgar Dale as being "easy." The result of these calculations is then added to .839. Supposedly, the end product describes the readability of the larger body of text translated into a grade level.

When readability formulas began to be used, questions were soon raised about their accuracy for such reasons as the following. If two or more randomly selected parts of the same text were analyzed with a formula, different conclusions about the readability level were common. Differences also resulted from the use of two different formulas with the same passage. In spite of all this, basal reader publishers flaunted their use of readability formulas in preparing readers because textbook adoption committees considered it to be a positive feature (15). Why all this has changed is explained next.

READABILITY FORMULAS: MAJOR PROBLEMS

As has been emphasized, using "appropriately difficult material" with students is an important responsibility of teachers. Why readability formulas are unable to function as a means for matching student ability and materials has to do with the incorrect understanding of the reading process on which the development of the formulas was based. Another reason formulas are rarely discussed now is rooted in a contradiction between how the formulas were intended to function and how they came to be used by publishers of instructional materials. An elaboration of each of these problems follows.

Misconception of the Reading Process

Starting as early as Chapter 1 in this book, everything said about comprehension suggests a lack of correspondence between the nature of the comprehension process and the factors that readability formulas take into account—average sentence length, for instance. In order to review some factors that contribute to the mismatch, variables missing from formulas are listed below.

Text: Missing Variables in Readability Formulas
1. Knowledge that author assumes reader possesses.
2. Purpose(s) for which text was written.
3. Number and complexity of ideas presented.
4. Rate at which new ideas are introduced.
5. Availability in text of direct and indirect help with word meanings.
6. Number and complexity of required inferences.
7. Overall coherence of text.

When comprehending is viewed as an interactive process between text and reader, variables related to readers count for something, too. Even when they are omitted from consideration, however, the inadequacy of readability formulas remains transparent. Here, let me refer to one study whose findings document flaws in formulas (3). The title of the report of the study pinpoints the concern of the research: "Improving the Comprehensibility of Stories: The Effects of Revisions That Improve

Coherence." *Coherence* refers to the degree to which the events in a story (or the ideas in expository text) are clearly interrelated. For example, in a coherent, well-formed story, pieces fit together in a way that produces a meaningful whole.

To achieve meaningful wholes, the researchers who conducted the study revised two basal stories by clarifying ambiguous referents, rewriting sentences to improve their syntax, replacing implicitly stated relationships with explicit statements, removing excessive irrelevant details, and replacing unclear material with more clearly stated content. While making the revisions, the researchers were careful to avoid altering plots. Even though the revisions were longer than the two original basal stories and had readability levels (according to a readability formula) that exceeded the original selections by two years, subjects in the study were more successful in comprehending the revised versions.

Misuse of the Formulas

In addition to significant omissions in readability formulas, one other factor explains why they are now of greater interest to historians than to publishers and educators. This second problem has to do with misapplication.

From the start, readability formulas were intended to determine the difficulty of existing text. Why basal reader publishers replaced the expected use with another relates to the importance that textbook selection committees assign to selections in readers during their deliberations. Specifically, in order to respond to requests from these groups for good literature, publishers used the variables in readability formulas as a guideline for rewriting and shortening tales such as "The Hare and the Tortoise" and "The Little Red Hen." The result was altered versions that bore little resemblance to the unabridged tale. With their easy words and short, disconnected sentences, the adaptations turned out to be not only less interesting but also less comprehensible (7).

All this led to complaints about "dumbing down" textbooks (5) and ruining good literature. The latter concern, expressed most often by whole language supporters, helps account for the noticeable increase in literary selections in basal series and for the claim by publishers that they now have literature-based programs. Their additional claim that unabridged versions of well-known stories have been kept intact awaits objective verification.

STATEWIDE TEXTBOOK ADOPTIONS

As explained, a second reason for changes in current basal readers has to do with statewide textbook adoptions. This refers to a centralized process that some states use to evaluate and select instructional materials submitted for review. Naturally, the interests expressed by these states is a major consideration whenever a publisher undertakes a new or revised product. Getting on a state's list of approved materials is especially critical when the state has a large population (15).

All this explains one impetus for the extensive changes that occurred in basal programs in the late 1980s. The changes were clearly affected by criteria originating with the California State Department of Education in 1987 (4) prior to its adoption of basal programs in 1989. The summary of California's preferences, which is in Figure 13.1, reflects interest in literature-based series; it also shows the influence of the whole language philosophy with the attention given to making connections not only among the language arts but also across the entire curriculum.

One positive result both of the California initiative and the whole language movement is a much enlarged number of literary selections in basal readers. Other changes, however, are characterized by overkill—that is, by what seems like an excessive eagerness to display in every manual everything recommended. One consequence is excessively large manuals that, in some cases, had to be divided into Part I and Part II. Predictably, complaints about the amount of material means that subsequent revisions will be shorter. Other consequences of the California recommendations, a few of which are noted, are relevant for anyone concerned about instruction.

To begin—this point is made earlier—materials said to be for kindergarten are so plentiful in newer series as to make it necessary to ask how any teacher could ever begin to use what each company offers (11). It should be noted that, just as Mother Goose receives an unusual amount of attention in beginning materials, so does phonics. Like the earlier readiness workbooks, the new materials allot many pages to teaching consonant sounds, which, in a number of programs, are taught in alphabetical order. Regardless of usefulness, each letter-sound correspondence receives identical attention. (This exemplifies a result of the rigid, repetitive formatting referred to in the earlier section about manuals.)

Adhering to California's request, phonics ends at the end of grade two (12). While being taught, decontextualized instruction is not uncommon. In subsequent grades, those responsible for manuals fail to encourage the use of phonics even when new words are regularly spelled. One series, in fact, recommends nothing but direct identifications for new vocabulary at the same time that it is busy teaching phonics from kindergarten through grade two (12).

Expectedly, comprehension instruction appears everywhere in manuals, as does the term *strategy*. (The use of *strategy* illustrates a point made before: What is

1. A literature-based language arts program.
2. Phonics instruction that ends in grade two.
3. Comprehension instruction that makes strategies explicit with the help of modeling.
4. Writing activities that emphasize the process of writing and that vary in their purpose.
5. Suggestions for organizing a class that include cooperative learning groups.
6. Suggestions for relating content subjects to the language arts.

FIGURE 13.1 Requests for a Statewide Adoption of Basal Programs

desirable can be abused through both misuse and overuse.) Topics like story structure and main idea are introduced as early as kindergarten and continue to receive attention throughout the whole of a series (9). This is accomplished through repetition, much of it verbatim repetition. Heavy reliance on computers probably accounts for seeing identical words in descriptions of lessons not only within a manual but across several manuals. At the same time, one manual in a series may promise that something will be taught in a later manual, but the promise is not fulfilled.

More than ten years ago, the lack of coordination both within and among manuals was cited as a major flaw in basal programs (13). Time has not remedied the problem, nor have increasingly large manuals made it easier for publishers to resolve the flaw.

BASAL READER LESSONS

As just suggested, improvements in basal reader selections have not been accompanied by any major improvements in manuals. The same is true of workbooks. Yet, even though workbooks are the most problematic component in basal programs, manual segments with labels like "Reteaching," "Review" and "Providing for Individual Differences" repeatedly aim directly toward suggestions to assign additional exercise sheets.

Because of the widespread interest in writing, references to that appear everywhere in manuals. Unfortunately, the quantity of suggestions for writing greatly exceeds the quality. The decision, for instance, to have at least one writing assignment for every selection in a reader must account for such questionable recommendations as having students write a persuasive letter to parents requesting permission to adopt a camel as a pet. This follows an expository piece about camels who are described in ways that bear no relationship to those seen in places like Saudi Arabia.

All this is to say that teachers who are capable of making informed decisions are as necessary as ever. To help clarify some decisions required of teachers who use basal programs all or part of the time, Figure 13.2 provides an overview of a basal lesson. Please examine the details now, as subsequent sections refer to Figure 13.2.

Overall Composition of Basal Lessons

You are asked to examine Figure 13.2 not because it portrays all lessons in basal manuals but because it provides a model of what basal lessons ought to be. Any characterization of what each lesson ought to be starts with a selection that is worth reading and that is written at a level of difficulty that, with adequate prereading preparations, makes its comprehension possible. Such material is usually said to be at students' *instructional level,* whose meaning is further illuminated with two contrasting descriptions of material: *independent level* and *frustration level.* (Benefits derived from reading independent-level material, not the least of which is meaningful practice, are identified in Chapter 6.)

With a worthwhile selection at the core, an acceptable basal lesson is an accumulation of instruction, practice, application, and reflection over the span of several

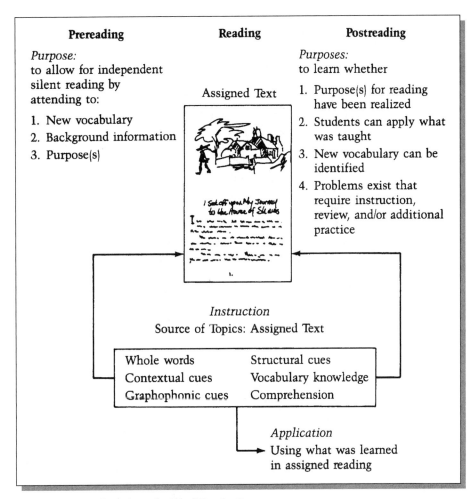

Prereading

Purpose:
to allow for independent silent reading by attending to:

1. New vocabulary
2. Background information
3. Purpose(s)

Reading

Assigned Text

Postreading

Purposes:
to learn whether

1. Purpose(s) for reading have been realized
2. Students can apply what was taught
3. New vocabulary can be identified
4. Problems exist that require instruction, review, and/or additional practice

Instruction
Source of Topics: Assigned Text

Whole words	Structural cues
Contextual cues	Vocabulary knowledge
Graphophonic cues	Comprehension

Application
Using what was learned in assigned reading

FIGURE 13.2 Overview of a Basal Reader Lesson

days that results in a successful, well-integrated experience for students (21). It is taken for granted that coherent lessons show close ties between the text students read and the topics selected for instruction and practice.

Having looked at the whole of a basal lesson with the help of Figure 13.2, let's now consider the parts.

Prereading Preparations

So much has been said about both the components and the importance of what has been called facilitating comprehension that little needs to be added. Because the specific focus now is preparations for basal selections, additional comments are confined to points meriting attention because of the content of basal manuals. To make the discussion specific, recommendations in a third-grade manual for an Indian legend are featured. The discussion shows what a Teacher B would do and, further, how a Teacher A might choose to omit, alter, resequence, or add to manual recommendations.

Background Information.   All the lessons in this particular basal series start with a manual segment for prior knowledge. For the legend, it concentrates on the word *resourcefulness* as a way of getting students to talk about the trait that figures prominently in the forthcoming tale. The recommendation to conclude the discussion with a summary chart is questionable because of the two columns suggested. The first, "Problem and Solution," is for listing examples offered by students of resourceful solutions to problems. Two examples are cited. The second column for the chart, one labeled "Qualities," wanders away from the topic under consideration, for the qualities listed in the manual as examples are "smart," "brave," and "quick thinking." It is likely, then, that a Teacher A will either revise the suggestion by omitting the second column or replace it with something different and better.

New Vocabulary.   The format in this basal series moves from a section for prior knowledge to one for new vocabulary. As explained before, those who prepare manuals either put new words in lists or place all of them in contexts. For the legend, contexts are used. Why this is unnecessary can be explained with the 12 words said to be new:

canoe	fierce	howled	murmured*
dare	flee*	icy	north
determined	freeze	lonely	starve*

The three words marked with asterisks(*) are described as "untested," which presumably is the reason they are excluded from suggestions for prereading preparations. Because these 3 words are as important for understanding the legend as are any of the other 9, a Teacher A assumes 12, not 9, words need to be considered.

In this manual, the nine tested words are placed in sentences, which, as suggested, is not required. All the words receive the same amount of attention even though elsewhere in the manual *freeze, howled, icy, lonely,* and *north* are correctly described as "decodable." You should now know that *dare* and *determined* (as well as the three "untested" words) belong in the same category. That leaves *canoe* and *fierce* as the only words that might require a teacher's attention.

Purpose for Reading.   The sequence for prereading preparations in the manuals for this basal series is: Prior Knowledge, New Vocabulary, and Setting a Purpose. Suggestions for the first two have been reviewed. The recommendation for setting a purpose for reading the legend is to have students recall the earlier discussion of resourcefulness as a way of getting them to make predictions about the "qualities and skills" of the protagonist, a young Indian boy. Judging that such a request is not likely to elicit much of a response, a Teacher A is likely to follow a different course that is influenced by the new words. This is suggested by the fact that, unlike many collections of new vocabulary, the 12 in this legend allow for asking students, "What do you suppose the legend will be about?" Having chosen this way to set a purpose for the reading, Teacher A first has the students name the new words that are decodable. This allows her to know whether what they have been learning is functioning successfully. Next, she herself names *canoe,* whose referent is likely to be familiar. The word *fierce* then receives attention not only to name it for the students but also to discuss its meaning applied to wind. This is important, as a fierce North Wind is the challenge that the protagonist in the legend faces.

Now the students are ready to make predictions about the tale, prompted by the new words. Their predictions can be written and kept to serve as a starting point for the postreading discussion. Or the predictions might be organized around a scheme that starts as follows:

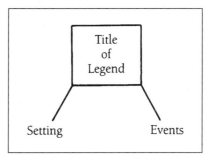

Having made some educated guesses with the help of the new vocabulary about a likely setting for the story and possible events, the students should be able to prepare a fully developed account once the legend is read. To do that, a worksheet like the one in Figure 13.3 can be used. Written assignments are helpful for both specifying and remembering responsibilities. They also provide a possible focus for postreading discussions. In addition, they let a teacher know what is or is not being comprehended.

A Summary. Revised prereading preparations for reading the legend proceed as follows. The teacher first announces that the next selection in the reader is an Indian legend. (This genre is now either reviewed or explained, depending on what is known.) The students then read the decodable words. Following this, the teacher identifies *canoe* and *fierce* using the latter to introduce North Wind, the antagonist in the tale. Finally, students make predictions about the legend with prompts from the new words, which can now be reviewed. Once the legend is read, students retell the legend by completing the worksheet shown in Figure 13.3. Their responses will be part of the postreading discussion.

Instruction

The manual under consideration makes no recommendation for comprehension instruction—or for any other kind of instruction—prior to the reading of the legend. One section does provide information about Indian legends for the teacher, which

Title is _____

Main character is _____

Setting for the story is _____

Season when the story takes place: _____

Problem to solve is: _____

What does the Indian boy do to solve the problem?

    a. _____

    b. _____

    c. _____

    d. _____

Tell how the problem is solved at the end: _____

_____

Now that you have read the tale about the Indian boy, list some words below that tell what kind of person he is.

FIGURE 13.3 An Assignment for a Legend

will be helpful whenever students are unfamiliar with this genre. That students know they will be reading a legend is important, as this allows for adopting an appropriate stance for the reading. Such a stance includes accepting the fact that North Wind, which is referred to as "he" in the text, is treated in a human way. This prompts the question, What about personification? Has it been taught? If not, the legend provides an opportunity to deal with personification with a reference to North Wind. Because essential prereading preparations are not overly time-consuming, attending to personification prior to the reading should not diminish students' interest in the legend.

Reading the Selection

Having been adequately prepared, the students are now ready to engage in what has been referred to so often: uninterrupted, silent reading of appropriately difficult material. As suggested, this promotes comprehension in a way that neither oral reading nor interrupted silent reading succeeds in doing (2).

What about the basal manual? It lists three possibilities for reading the six-page tale—options recommended for every selection in the reader regardless of length or difficulty. The first is uninterrupted silent reading. The second suggestion to the teacher is to stop the children's silent reading at two specified places in the legend in order to encourage them to predict what might happen next. The third suggestion is to divide the legend into three, two-page parts. Questions—a total of 11—are listed for each part.

Postreading Activities

As is indicated in the overall composition of a basal lesson shown earlier in Figure 13.2, one postreading need is to assess comprehension of the legend. A worksheet like the one in Figure 13.3 allows for this. Because of the close link between the new vocabulary and the setting and the events of the story, a next step might be to review the 12 new words. In order to review the prereading attention given to personification, the teacher can have the students move quickly through the legend again, this time to find evidence of the human qualities ascribed to North Wind. Finally, why the tale *is* a legend can be summarized. One highly satisfactory conclusion is to make other Indian legends available. This is not difficult because a large number are on library shelves, some written at fairly low levels of difficulty. They thus allow for independent reading which, in this case, can add to the students' understanding and enjoyment of this genre.

OTHER USES OF BASAL MATERIALS

To provide even more examples of how basal materials can—and have been—used and altered, reports of classrooms are in Figures 13.4, 13.5, and 13.6. Figure 13.4 describes the work of a second-grade teacher that centers on a story with a multiculture theme; it teaches a lesson to which second graders can relate. Figure 13.5 shifts to an observer's account of a third-grade teacher preparing an instructional group for reading a brief biography about Alexander Graham Bell. This account makes correct distinctions between praiseworthy procedures and others that could be improved. The last report, in Figure 13.6, tells how a fourth-grade teacher tried to avoid decontextualized instruction and, in addition, to bring school and out-of-school reading closer together.

The basal selection that one group discussed today is a two-part story about a little Mexican-American girl who feels she doesn't have anything of interest to tell her classmates during sharing time. Over the weekend, however, one of her classmates visits the import store that her parents own. The great interest shown in what is displayed helps this girl realize that what she takes for granted is new and interesting to other people. Although the basal manual suggests reading the story in two parts, I have found that the interest that builds in the first part is lost, unless we continue.

Yesterday, we spent most of the instructional period on new vocabulary. I kept in mind that what is done before reading begins is more important than what occurs afterward. I also distributed written questions—not too many—keeping in mind that reading ought to be purposeful. I did not require written answers. Instead, I asked the children to read the story, keeping the questions in mind. I also said they should make sure they can answer the questions before we discuss the story today. To help them find answers should they be forgotten, one further recommendation was to note the page on which answers are found.

When we did discuss the story this morning, I called on various children to read a question from the list and to respond. As children answered, parts of the story not directly covered by the questions were referred to. This is a big group (N = 12), and I am doing my best to involve as many students as I can whenever we discuss something. The discussion this morning went quite well. I participated, I think, just enough to keep things going but not so much as to dominate the discussion.

Earlier, I had taught about cause-effect events in stories. Today, after the discussion, I reviewed causes and effects as they occurred in the story. The basal manual segment had suggested the review but did not relate it to the story. In fact, the suggestions in the manual did not relate the review to anything in particular except to workbook pages that were recommended for assignments. As you have mentioned in class, there is a real need to show children the connection between what is taught and how to get the most out of their reading.

FIGURE 13.4   Using a Basal Reader Story in Second Grade

The teacher started with several prereading activities, attending first to vocabulary. She used a basal chart, showing ten sentences, each with a new word underlined. To deal with the words, the teacher read a sentence, reread the new word, then asked for an explanation of its meaning. (Sentences showed no connection with the selection for which the group was being prepared.) For the few words that were problems, all derivatives, the teacher effectively related parts to meanings. With *accidentally,* for instance, she first wrote it on the board, after which the suffixes were systematically removed one at a time. After calling attention to the meaning of "accident," the teacher replaced the suffixes. Although she failed to eliminate regularly spelled words and any others that may have occurred in the selection in a helpful context, this teacher did work well with the few words that were troublesome. Having a group reread all the words might have been a helpful addition.

A consideration of biography came next. The teacher explained its meaning but failed to write the word on the board. She then asked whether anyone knew of a biography. Quick-to-come responses referred to George Washington, Abe Lincoln, and Brian Piccolo. This was followed by a brief discussion of Alexander Graham Bell, named as the subject of the biography to be read. Bell's interest in studying sound was especially emphasized. No mention was made of the telephone.

Sounds were then featured in what I think was a teacher-made worksheet that was divided into six boxes with labels that included "School," "City," and "Nature." Students were asked to quickly list in each box any items that made sounds in places identified by the labels. The discussion of responses seemed to spark interest in sounds, thus paving the way to reading the biography.

Purposes for reading it took the form of questions listed on another sheet. Students were asked to read the questions, then the biography. To answer the questions, each member of the group was to meet with a preassigned partner both to discuss the biography and to consider answers. Each set of partners was responsible for one set of written answers. I liked this purpose-setting assignment because it allowed for independent silent reading as well as for the opportunity to discuss the reading soon after it was done. The need to reach agreed-on answers would probably promote a discussion of the biography.

I left this room favorably impressed with the preparations made by the teacher. It seemed she had read the biography carefully and made plans accordingly. Although the basal manual may have affected the plans, it was not consulted—in fact, the manual was not seen during the observation.

FIGURE 13.5　An Observer's Account of Prereading Preparations

The objective of the lesson I'll describe was to help students distinguish between facts and opinions. Our class discussion about the need to match objectives and materials prompted me to write some text myself. This was necessary because the basal program we use deals with facts and opinions out of context. They don't relate them to anything, in fact. The children in this instructional group can easily do the exercises provided, yet when I have them read longer pieces of text—for instance, paragraphs—they respond by calling everything a fact. There seems to be no transfer from the workbook exercises.

The children met at a table near a chalkboard. The words *fact* and *opinion* were already tucked into the pocket chart, so we began by reading both. The meanings were then reviewed. To set the stage for the lesson, I started with what is familiar. Sentence strips were placed in the chart one at a time, and the children responded individually by telling which had to do with facts and which were opinions.

We then discussed clue words such as "I think" and "I believe," and also talked about the fact that opinions do not always go along with key words like these. I also explained that writers sometimes mix facts and opinions. I further explained that facts are sometimes given only when they support the author's opinions and that everything else is left out. When I asked *why* a writer might do this, the students recognized an author's motive to convince the reader to accept her or his opinion.

Then we discussed *when* it is important to distinguish between facts and opinions. I was pleased—"relieved" is a better word—when one child mentioned "reading a newspaper" as an example, because my plans included *Scholastic Newstime.* Our class discussion about showing the relationship between school and real life had reminded me to use *Scholastic Newstime* articles because of their similarity to real newspapers. I've also learned that *Scholastic Newstime* contains subject matter that interests children.

To provide practice in distinguishing between facts and opinions, *Scholastic Newstime* articles ranging over a wide variety of topics had been glued to tagboard and laminated. I distributed them to members of the group. The children were asked to read an article first, then to read it a second time in order to find sentences that seemed to give facts and others that were the opinions of whoever wrote the article. I wrote *Facts* on the board, after which I put the word *blue* in parentheses. I then wrote *Opinions,* after which I put the word *red* in parentheses. I explained that sentences that dealt with facts should be underlined in blue, whereas those that expressed an opinion should be underlined in red. Everything else was to be left alone.

This activity was to be done by the children working independently, after which they were to put their cards in an envelope on which I had written their name. I told the group that the next selection in our basal reader, which was about an exploration at the South Pole, has interesting facts about that very cold and icy place and also some interesting opinions held by the author.

FIGURE 13.6   A Teacher Working to Be Better Than a Basal Manual

SUMMARY

Chapter 13 looked at sets of instructional materials known as basal reader series or basal reader programs. It did this by focusing on their four major parts: readers, manuals, workbooks, and tests. This summary starts by reviewing the major points made about the readers.

At one time, the chapter explained, the collection of readers in each series started with some for first grade and ended with one reader for eighth grade. Because of changed views about the responsibility of pre-first-grade programs for literacy development—this was discussed in earlier chapters—all available series now begin with materials for kindergarten.

In its discussion of readers, Chapter 13 highlighted problems and changes related to the concept "readability." To start, it was said that one feature of basal programs that always appealed to educators was their "carefully graded" readers. Knowing that controlled difficulty was taken into account by groups like textbook selection committees, basal publishers never hid the fact that they used readability formulas to assess text difficulty. However, as soon as new, more complete descriptions of the reading process surfaced, the unrealistic simplicity of readability formulas was questioned. So, too, was their misuse. Questions about misuse were directed to individuals responsible for basal readers who relied on the formulas not only to determine the difficulty of existing text but also to rewrite, and presumably simplify, good literature. The purpose now was to satisfy potential customers who wanted better selections than basal companies were providing. The result was dull, often incomprehensible adaptations.

Chapter 13 continued the discussion of basal readers by pointing out that complaints about dumbing down textbooks and ruining good literature originated in a variety of sources. It then stated that the most noticeable and persistent criticism came from advocates of the whole language philosophy opposed to having students read text viewed merely as a tool for instructing. Some of their concerns were reflected in requests made of basal companies by the California State Department of Education in 1987 (see Figure 13.1). The requests preceded by two years California's plans to judge which basal series were acceptable for use in schools in that state. The fact that basal companies took the requests seriously was not surprising. As Chapter 13 explained, California has not only a large population but also a statewide textbook adoption policy. The results of all this are substantially changed readers portrayed by publishers as "literature-based."

Chapter 13 had much less to say about current manuals, workbooks, and tests, as none of the three is characterized by substantive change. It was pointed out that manuals *are* much more encompassing in what they cover; however, the more important point is that each manual in a series still conforms to one format. Even though an unchanging format expedites the preparation of manuals, Chapter 13 emphasized that it does not encourage adapting recommendations to particular selections in the readers. The chapter acknowledged that the difficulty teachers will experience in matching suggestions to a selection has increased to the same extent that manual pages have increased in number. To demonstrate that changes are still both possible and desirable, Chapter 13 used for illustrative purposes suggestions in a manual for a legend in a third-grade reader. The discussion reinforced the need for a Teacher A at the same time that it showed what a Teacher B might do. In order to specify adaptations made by three teachers, the chapter includes three reports of classrooms.

Like manuals in the newer series, an increase in quantity characterizes workbooks. Because of their continued use of brief, repetitive exercises, it is only natural to wonder why knowledgeable teachers use them. To provide one explanation, Chapter 13 referred to the similarity of workbook exercises and basal test items. This means that when administrators take basal test scores seriously, members of their faculty have a compelling reason to assign workbook pages, like it or not.

REVIEW

1. Presumably, persons unfamiliar with basal reader programs examined one or more series before reading Chapter 13. Now that the chapter has been read, compare its content with what you might write were you the author. Specifically, what would you add, delete, or change in a chapter about basal reader materials.

2. Review Figure 13.2, which depicts a cohesive basal reader lesson. Why is it correct to think of such a lesson as a collection of minilessons, each of which avoids decontextualized instruction?

3. Any Teacher A who uses basal selections some of the time starts by reading the selection that she plans to have students read. Why is knowing the selection the first essential step in making plans for how the selection will be used? Include specific examples in your response.

4. One point made in Chapter 13 is that selections in basal readers have been improved, starting with series that have copyright dates of 1989 or later. The chapter identified factors that account for the change.
   a. How did misuse of readability formulas by basal companies figure in improvements?
   b. How did supporters of the whole language movement contribute to the switch to better selections?

5. Chapter 13 criticized basal manual formats that are the same from one level to the next.
   a. What is meant by "manual format"?
   b. With examples—preferably found in a basal series—explain how an unchanging format contributes to questionable manual recommendations.

6. Chapter 13 discussed statewide textbook adoption policies.
   a. Explain the meaning of these policies.
   b. In your opinion, what are their advantages and disadvantages?

REFERENCES

1. Altwerger, Bess; Edelsky, Carole; and Flores, Barbara. "Whole Language: What's New?" *Reading Teacher* 41 (November, 1987), 144–154.
2. Armbruster, Bonnie B., and Wilkinson, Ian A. G. "Reading to Learn." *Reading Teacher* 45 (October, 1991), 154–155.
3. Beck, Isabel L.; McKeown, Margaret G.; Omanson, Richard G.; and Pople, Martha T. "Improving the Comprehensibility of Stories: The Effects of Revisions that Improve Coherence." *Reading Research Quarterly* 19 (Spring, 1984), 263–277.
4. California English-Language Arts Committee. *English-Language Arts Framework.* Sacramento: California State Department of Education, 1987.
5. Chall, Jeanne S., and Conard, Sue S. *Should Textbooks Challenge Students?* New York: Teachers College Press, 1991.
6. Daines, Delva, and Reutzel, D. Ray. "The Instructional Coherence of Reading Lessons in Seven Basal Reading Series." *Reading Psychology* 8 (1987, No. 1), 33–44.
7. Davison, Alice, and Kantor, Robert N. "On the Failure of Readability Formulas to Define Readable Texts: A Case Study from Adaptations," *Reading Research Quarterly* 17 (1982, No. 2), 187–209.
8. Duffy, Gerald G.; Roehler, Laura R.; and Putnam, Joyce. "Putting the Teacher in Control: Basal Reading Textbooks and Instructional Decision Making." *Elementary School Journal* 87 (January, 1987), 355–366.
9. Durkin, Dolores. "Comprehension Instruction in Current Basal Reader Series." Technical Report No. 521. Urbana: University of Illinois, Center for the Study of Reading, 1990.
10. Durkin, Dolores. "Influences on Basal Reader Programs." *Elementary School Journal* 87 (January, 1987), 331–341.
11. Durkin, Dolores. "New Kindergarten Basal Reader Materials: What's a Teacher Supposed to Do with All This?" Technical Report No. 475. Urbana: University of Illinois, Center for the Study of Reading, 1989.
12. Durkin, Dolores. "Phonics Instruction in New Basal Reader Programs." Technical Report No. 496. Urbana: University of Illinois, Center for the Study of Reading, 1990.
13. Durkin, Dolores. "Reading Comprehension Instruction in Five Basal Reader Series." *Reading Research Quarterly* 16 (1981, No. 4), 515–544.
14. Durkin, Dolores. "What Classroom Observations Reveal about Comprehension Instruction." *Reading Research Quarterly* 14 (1978–79, No. 4), 481–533.
15. Farr, Roger; Tulley, Michael A.; and Powell, Deborah. "The Evaluation and Selection of Basal Readers." *Elementary School Journal* 87 (January, 1987), 267–281.
16. Goodman, Kenneth S. "Basal Readers: A Call for Action." *Language Arts* 63 (April, 1986), 358–363.
17. Goodman, K.; Shannon, P.; Freeman, Y.; and Murphy, S. *Report Card on Basal Readers.* Katonah, N.Y.: Richard C. Owen, 1988.
18. Gray, William S., and Leary, Bernice. *What Makes a Book Readable.* Chicago: The University of Chicago Press, 1935.
19. Pseudonymous, Scriptor. "The Ghost behind the Classroom Door." *Today's Education* 67 (April–May, 1978), 41–45.
20. Spache, George. "A New Readability Formula for Primary-Grade Reading Materials." *Elementary School Journal* 53 (March, 1953), 410–413.
21. Winograd, Peter N.; Wixson, Karen K.; and Lipson, Marjorie Y. (Eds.). *Improving Basal Reading Instruction.* New York: Teachers College Press, 1989.

Children's Literature

Earlier chapters describe the multiple ways in which teachers help their students learn to read. If, while doing that, the chapters fail to demonstrate that the same help can—and should—contribute to students' interest in reading, they have not achieved their purpose. After all, individuals who *can* read but never choose to do so is not an effect that anyone wants. Said differently, aliteracy (can but does not read) is not much better than illiteracy (12).

Unlike the previous chapters, the forthcoming one is primarily concerned with ways to encourage students to want to read. Its secondary goal is to illustrate how trade books function not only in stimulating interest but also in advancing abilities. Trade books, you recall, are written not to serve as textbooks but to provide materials for the library and bookstore market. Thoughtfully selected, trade books allow for the variety recommended in Chapter 1, when it said that students need to read a mixture of narrative, expository, and procedural texts. Prose-poetry, fiction-nonfiction—these are other ways to describe the recommended mix.

One assumption of Chapter 14 is that its two central goals can be attained without the use of long lists of children's books. (Sources where recommended books *are* listed are noted in the chapter.) Titles are named, therefore, only when doing so helps specify certain points or recommendations.

Even though Chapter 14 does deal with children's literature, it makes no pretense about providing a minicourse in this topic. A second of its assumptions, in fact, is that the individuals reading the chapter have taken, or are taking, or will be taking, a course in children's literature. How to help students enjoy that literary treasure even as they improve their ability to read is the focus of the following chapter.

● ● ● ● ● ● ●

As THE PREVIEW STATES, THIS CHAPTER dwells on ways to encourage students to read. The ultimate goal of such efforts is to foster an interest in reading that persists long after students leave school. Actually, this ultimate goal assigns importance to all the chapters in *Teaching Them to Read* that attempt to foster effective instructional practices. This is the case because nobody can expect an individual to like to read if efforts to acquire that ability have been a long series of unsuccessful struggles. Nor can anyone expect much interest if what is done with reading in school compels students to equate it with a daily routine of naming words, answering questions, and completing exercise sheets.

To sum this up, one of the most reliable ways for teachers to promote interest in reading is to offer year after year the best possible literacy programs they can assemble. This recommendation reflects the fact that, like everyone else, students want to do what they do *well*.

READING TO STUDENTS

In addition to making superior instruction available, reading to students is high on any list of ways for making books attractive. This use of a teacher's time was discussed at some length in Chapter 5, when beginning literacy was the concern, and it has been referred to intermittently ever since. Reading to students is sufficiently important, however, as to merit reconsideration now.

As explained, the benefits that students derive from being read to at home or in school are many. At first, the reading can foster positive attitudes toward books as well as an interest in becoming a reader. The same experience brings children into contact with the language of literature and, if stories are read often enough, helps them acquire a tacit understanding of story structure. That some books answer questions viewed to be important is another lesson available to learn; that others raise questions will be discovered, too. Not to be forgotten is that contacts with books help young children achieve an understanding of metalanguage and the conventions of print. And all along the way, both fiction and nonfiction enhance oral vocabularies and increase world knowledge regardless of the reader's age. With such an array of benefits, is it any wonder that teachers and parents alike are constantly urged to read to children every day?

In spite of its obvious value, reading to students has not always been in the schedules of teachers beyond the primary level. It was almost as if it were a "little kid" activity. In recent years, however, many teachers of older students are reading to their class on a regular basis. This can have nothing but positive consequences.

To make certain that the full potential of reading to students has a chance to be realized, let me add guidelines that reflect recommendations for read-alouds that come from such well-known individuals as Jim Trelease, author of the highly regarded paperback *The New Read-Aloud Handbook* (16). He and others support recommendations like the following.

Recommendations for Daily Read-Alouds by Teachers
1. It is generally best to set aside one certain time for the reading. Otherwise, it is all too easy for other pressing needs to crowd the reading out of a day's activities.

2. A certain place should be established in a classroom for read-alouds. With younger children, teachers often sit near a carpeted area on a low chair, as this facilitates showing illustrations. Children sit nearby on the carpet. Older students can gather close to a teacher by quickly rearranging chairs or finding space on the floor. Regardless of age, students always need a few minutes for what Trelease calls "settling-in time."

3. The importance of establishing readiness at a cognitive level should not be overlooked. At times, this can easily be done by naming the book and its author, after which the teacher poses one or more questions: "Does the title remind you of another book I read recently?" or "What do you suppose the story might be about with a title like this?" or "Can anyone remember other books I've read this year that had the same author?" If, on the other hand, one purpose for a read-aloud is to introduce an unfamiliar genre—let's say, tall tales—a teacher may decide to promote cognitive readiness by imparting information about some of its essential features.

4. Teachers, too, need to be ready for the reading. Charlotte Huck, a specialist in children's literature, offers this advice:

> Anyone reading a story…should have read it in preparation for sharing it orally. In this way, the reader can emphasize particularly well-written passages, read dialogue as conversation, anticipate the timing of amusing remarks, and be able to look up from the book…to see children's reactions. (6, p. 716)

Sometimes, well-written passages contain too many descriptive details for the audience a teacher has in mind. In such cases, she should be prepared to summarize the details when the passage is reached; this allows events in the story to unfold without prolonged delays. On the other hand, should the details include one or more figures of speech that older students have been learning, the same passages are useful in demonstrating authors' common use of figurative language. Now, brief comments about similes or whatever might be in order. If mental imagery has been discussed in connection with reading or writing, stopping the reading to suggest to students that they close their eyes in order to "see" what is about to be described illustrates another time when it is appropriate to pause.

5. For whatever reason interruptions in the reading do occur, they should not be so numerous as to impede the flow of the story or, in the case of expository text, to interfere with the communication of interrelated pieces of information. This is not to suggest that read-alouds ought to be teacher-centered with students expected to "sit up straight" and listen. After all, comments and questions from an audience usually promote rather than decrease interest. Nonetheless, teachers need to be on guard to avoid letting comments from themselves or students become so frequent that they reduce both interest and comprehension.

6. Anything worth reading is worth discussing. Postreading discussions that are not quizlike in nature are times for students to have their say. Free-flowing reactions should be encouraged even though some comments may have to be redirected to avoid moving too far away from the text read. Any connection between the text and the audience should be highlighted, for seeing themselves in others is one way students' self-knowledge increases.

7. With older students, read-alouds should include novels. This is especially important for children brought up on basal readers for which selections are kept brief. Short novels with short chapters are a suitable starting point because they permit reading a chapter a day. If a chapter turns out to be too long, stopping at a suspenseful place gives students something to look forward to the next day.

   Unaccustomed to reading novels to a class, some teachers are reluctant to begin. Anyone in this group can find help for getting started in a chapter in the Trelease book referred to earlier (16). Entitled "Treasury of Read-Alouds," this chapter lists a number of short novels. For each title, Trelease includes a summary of the plot along with the range in grade levels for which the book seems appropriate. He does the same for all five categories of books included in the chapter: predictable books, wordless books, illustrated books, short novels, and novels.

8. Other advice for teachers in the process of becoming knowledgeable about children's literature is in an article by Arlene Pillar called "Resources to Identify Children's Books for the Reading Program" (10). One resource sometimes overlooked is described by Pillar this way:

   > Frequently, students are overheard saying, "I just finished reading this great book!" Those are the books teachers probably should read first. We should be taught by our students. (p. 158)

   Lest we forget, students can also be taught by other students. This is effectively demonstrated in the description of a kindergarten reported in Figure 14.1.

CLASSROOM LIBRARIES

It does not make sense to entice students to want to read if they are then left with nothing to quench their thirst. A natural progression, therefore, is to follow a discussion of reading to students with another that looks at classroom libraries.

A good classroom library serves well whatever functions it is meant to serve. On the assumption that one standard purpose is to allow students to engage in self-selected, independent reading, good libraries have collections of books that vary in content, length, and difficulty. It is essential, in fact, that the range in difficulty is wide enough to accommodate both the poorest and the best readers. Because other functions are more varied, further suggestions about desirable content are made when possible functions are considered. Now, let me point out guidelines for assembling libraries regardless of the contributions they are expected to make.

Recommendations for Classroom Libraries

1. Large classes and small classrooms do not allow for the amount of space that libraries merit. The task for a teacher, therefore, is to use as much space as circumstances permit.

2. Where a library is located in a classroom is as important as its size. To start, the selected area should be one to which students can go and return without disturbing others. If one or more of its functions require students to work there,

I observed this kindergarten class of 16 children while they were having a free-time period and saw many fine examples of opportunities for literacy development. A group of five children were performing a play based on the book *Goodnight Moon.* All had assigned parts and had made stick puppets of the characters. Each had memorized a couplet from the book. Another group was busy in the block area building local shops. A parent volunteer was printing signs to identify the buildings. Another group was listening to a tape of songs entitled "Singable Songs for the Very Young" by Raffi; some were acting out parts of the songs spontaneously.

While I was observing, a third-grade boy came in carrying the book *Brown Bear, Brown Bear, What Do You See*? by Bill Martin, Jr. He was greeted with a shout of glee and a hug by a small girl, Sarah. She immediately asked, "What are we going to read today? Can I see it first?"

Brian, the third-grade student, sat with Sarah on a large pillow in a corner near the teacher's desk. (Brian, I learned later, was diagnosed as learning disabled. Why he was reading in this kindergarten was not clarified.) I moved closer so that I could listen to the interaction. Sarah quickly browsed through the book commenting on the pictures. She then handed the book back to Brian who opened it to the title page. He read aloud the title and the names of the author and illustrator.

Brian read the book through; however, by the time he reached the fourth spread, Sarah had figured out the pattern. As Brian turned the page and pointed to the text, Sarah "read" with him, "Green frog, green frog, what do you see? I see a..." (then she flipped ahead to get a clue for the next word) "I see a purple cat looking at me."

Sarah asked if there was time to read the book again. Brian looked at the clock, shrugged his shoulders, and said he would have to go ask his teacher.

Sarah's excitement about reading was so apparent. She had quickly understood the pattern of the book and, in doing so, was constructing meaning. Whether Sarah was attaching a pronunciation to each group of letters was less important than was the fact that she considered herself a reader. The good things that were occurring for Brian cannot be underestimated, either.

FIGURE 14.1   Literacy in a Kindergarten

minimizing distractions by closing off the area with something like portable bulletin boards is helpful. (The same bulletin boards can display materials that contribute to a literate environment—for instance, posters, book jackets, student-designed bookmarks, and samples of their writing.) Where students are to do the work is another point to consider when plans are made for a library.

3. At the start of the year, plans should be fairly specific but sufficiently fluid that students' suggestions can be considered. (The more they have to say about the library, the more will they perceive it to be *theirs*.) Early-in-the-year discussions with students should pose such questions as: When is the library to be used? Is there a limit on the number of students who can be at the library at any one time? How will books be checked in and out? Who is responsible for keeping track of loans and returns and for keeping the library in good order? Can books be taken home?

4. A classroom library should reflect ongoing activities; consequently, as activities and interests change, so should its contents. At any time, nonetheless, students should be fairly well acquainted with what is available. Therefore, additions made for whatever reason need to be announced and then displayed for a while in some special way. New or old, books should be organized so that students wanting a particular book, or a particular kind of book (e.g., riddles, wordless picture book), know where to find it.

5. Because one reason teachers read to students is to encourage them to read themselves, the book read on any given day ought to be placed in the library whenever possible. Multiple copies are even better. Should the book be a new genre (e.g., tall tale) or one with special appeal (e.g., mysteries), more books of the same genre written at various levels of difficulty are other desirable additions. If a story is to be shown on television over the weekend, the most perfect additions on Monday are copies of the book displayed in a way that highlights their presence.

STUDENTS' SELF-SELECTED READING

Although it took place some time ago, I still recall a dialogue between a teacher and an unoccupied student that went something like this:

Teacher: Did you finish all the workbook pages?
Student: Yes.
Teacher: Did you write the spelling words ten times each?
Student: Yes.
Teacher: What about math? Is that done?
Student: Yes.
Teacher: Well, then, go get a library book!

Fortunately, it is unlikely that a similar dialogue would be heard in a classroom now even though it must be recognized that some adults outside school—and they include students' parents—look on reading books as a questionable use of time.

In school, what came to be known in the 1970s as Sustained Silent Reading (9) was an effort to assign to self-selected reading the importance it deserves. Having everyone in a school building—principal, secretary, custodian, teachers, students—stop whatever they were doing at a prearranged time in order to read was even recommended (17). Although some teachers still choose to use special names,* contrived ways of highlighting the reading have been replaced for the most part with less dramatic but more effective, natural practices. The one meriting discussion is as simple as scheduling time daily when students are free to read self-selected material.

Knowing that they lead by example, some teachers read when students read. Others elect to use this time to talk quietly with individuals about their current choice and, possibly, to recommend titles for future selections. Teachers in this second category generally try to meet with every student in the course of a week.

Two questions often asked about self-selected reading pertain to sharing and accountability. Each is addressed separately even though the two overlap.

Sharing

Like adults, most children enjoy sharing with other people what they have been reading. This is why some teachers make every effort to meet with students weekly. Sharing in writing is another possibility. In this case, students might keep *reading-response logs* in which they record reactions to, rather than summaries of, whatever they are reading. In other instances, students turn in weekly *dialogue journals* to which the teacher responds in writing. Whenever either way of sharing is used, students need to know that negative reactions are as welcome as glowing reports.

When more than one student is reading the same book, an opportunity exists for discussions. Depending on the students and their prior experiences, appointing a discussion leader for the group may or may not be necessary. Discussions are also possible when more than one student is reading the same genre (5).

Whenever more than one *is* reading a biography, a myth, or whatever, a mural that combines different but now related content is another way to share. Bulletin boards that display advertisements—reasons a certain book should be a must on everyone's reading list—serve the same purpose.

Something like the display in Figure 14.2 is useful if the content of a book read by more than one student is revealed with flashbacks. In this case, when all students have finished the book, they can meet to decide how to retell the content in chronological order. (The number of events naturally varies from book to book.) A special color can be used to show any sequential events that illustrate a cause-effect relationship.

Students who have read the same book can also convey its content with pictures. In this instance, the group decides who will do which picture. The outcome should be a display of pictures arranged in an order that reflects the book they read.

---

*During recent visits to classrooms, I heard names like the following: STAR (Silent time at reading); DEAR (Drop everything and read); and WEIRD (We enjoy independent reading daily.).

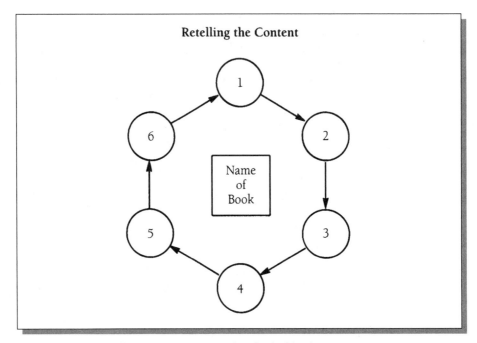

Retelling the Content

FIGURE 14.2   Retelling Content Narrated with Flashbacks

The most important point to make to teachers is this: Avoid any type of sharing that students view more as a chore than as an opportunity to tell others what a book has to say and what they think about what it says. In Figure 14.3, an observer reports how one fourth-grade teacher provided such an opportunity.

Accountability

Keeping track of which books have been read and how many each student has read is not a new practice. In fact, displays of "how many" have been in classrooms for a long time. Most teachers explain the displays in the framework of motivation; nevertheless, whether counting what is read is desirable is debatable. Clearly questionable is a practice like the one described in Figure 14.4.

Teachers' keeping track of who is reading what for such purposes as making recommmendations for the future is another matter. Now, something as simple as providing students with index cards on which they write about a finished book is all that is needed. In one classroom, cards with holes punched in them are hung on hooks placed in a row; each child has a hook. Above the hooks are the words *Hooked on Books*. In another classroom, the same kinds of cards are kept in shoe boxes organized with alphabetically arranged student-name dividers. In both cases, the teachers read the cards regularly to learn what is being read and also to consider the desirability of more variation if only to encourage students to taste something different. Occasionally, vague or overly brief remarks on cards result in quiet talks with students.

This afternoon I saw a fourth-grade teacher introduce a unit on storytelling. She explained that everyone was going to have the opportunity to read a story and retell it in their own words to a first grader. To prepare, the students would take notes on the story they chose and also practice telling it to a classmate.

The teacher began by reviewing different types of stories and describing the characteristics of each one. For example, she first discussed fairy tales and showed the students a copy of *Cinderella*. She quickly reviewed the plot and why it *was* a fairy tale. She wrote *fairy tale* on the board and listed the characteristics—with help from the class—directly below. She continued with fables, folktales, myths, and legends, all the while sharing an example of each type of tale with the students. The teacher listened attentively to their comments and questions throughout.

She then gave the class time to browse through a sizable collection of books. Within a short time, the students had picked their stories. The teacher continued by asking how they were going to remember all of the important content. They replied that they would take notes. The teacher stressed that they were only supposed to write *brief* notes to highlight important events. She also emphasized that they were not to recopy a story. At this point, the fourth-graders began reading.

I enjoyed seeing this involvement with books. My one reservation has to do with the absence of explicit attention to taking notes. Unless the students had done this before, just saying, "*Don't* copy the story!" would be of little help.

FIGURE 14.3 Sharing Literature with Others

Where I am student teaching, encouraging independent reading is viewed as a priority. Each student is required to read a minimum of four books each month chosen from a list that matches his or her ability level. The books are read during free time in school and also at home. For each book, the student takes a computerized test that includes ten multiple-choice questions. With a score of seven or higher, the student passes the test and the book is "counted." Lower scores require students to retake the test until they pass. It is my understanding that the program is a commercial computer package used in a number of schools as a way to increase the number of books students read and to eliminate the responsibility of record keeping from the teacher.

Although the program is successful in achieving the two goals, I question its use. To begin, all items on the reading lists that I have seen are narrative texts. Even though the books are of high quality, the students are not encouraged to read the wide variety of expository materials available in the school's library. Many of the fourth-graders in my class are interested in expository text, but they naturally give a book on their reading list priority attention.

I also wonder about the students' perceptions of why they are reading the books. Is the purpose only to pass a ten-question, multiple-choice test? On one occasion, when students were selecting books, a boy—one of the best readers in the class—asked me to help him. I recommended *Sounder* as a book that I had read and found deeply moving. With that, the boy checked it out.

The next week, the same boy asked me for another recommendation. Pleased, I asked him how he had liked *Sounder*. To my surprise, he said he had never finished it; instead, he watched the movie and passed the test. From his perspective, it seemed, the ability to pass the test was the purpose for reading, and if he could do that without reading, all the better. Are these the attitudes we want to cultivate? I think not.

FIGURE 14.4   Questionable Motivation for Reading Literature

Occasionally, too, accounts that are especially praiseworthy are read aloud to the class. This is done both to encourage improvement by other students and to illustrate the many different ways in which reactions to books can be communicated.

The point to stress about accountability is this: If students hesitate to admit they have read a book because of the consequences, the consequences need to be reconsidered. "You don't want to admit you've read a book with all the things they make you do about it" (13) is not a response that any teacher should be prompting.

LITERATURE AND INSTRUCTION

The idea that students should have time for reading self-selected trade books in the course of a school day rarely meets with much resistance. Those who know that the out-of-school lives of some students come close to making reading impossible can even be counted on to endorse the idea with enthusiasm. Agreement does not exist, however, when the question of using literature for instruction is raised.

One kind of answer is illustrated in a publication entitled "Responses to Literature" (8). The three co-authors claim that accomplished reading "can be best achieved when reading instruction occurs within the context of literature, rather than through the fragmentation and teaching of isolated skills." They go on to urge teachers "to replace mindless worksheets that 'drill and kill' with literature-based instruction" (p. 2). Readers of *Teaching Them to Read* should realize by the time this chapter is reached that something other than the two alternatives referred to by these authors is available. Teachers do not have to choose between the two.

Among the teachers who have chosen to replace basal readers with literature, some seem to believe that instruction is no longer necessary. (This is illustrated in Chapter 2 in Figure 2.5.) Not all meet the criteria, therefore, that I would establish for making such a change. My advice, based on observations in classrooms, is this:

> Those who abandon basal readers in favor of an exclusive use of trade books and environmental text should do so gradually. It is assumed that any teacher who contemplates this change is knowledgeable about reading and reading instruction; is widely read in the field of children's literature; and is industrious and well-organized. In addition, she or he must ask continuously, Is my new literature-based program effective with the poorest readers in the class?

Other teachers using literature have changed materials but not what they do with them. (This is illustrated in Chapter 3 in Figure 3.9.) Some authors characterize the practices of teachers in this group as "the basalization of literature" (13). For instance, Dixie Lee Spiegel (14) wonders what the difference is between using basals and a literature-based program if the latter:

- Uses material that is hardly better than basal selections.
- Treats literary selections with a multitude of questions and worksheets.
- Uses busy-work activities that draw children's attention away from central ideas in order to focus on trivia.

As Bernice Cullinan correctly points out, "There is a fine line between using children's literature to teach reading and destroying the literature we use" (3, p. 7).

In classrooms that I visited recently, practices ranged from highly dependent uses of a basal series to a reliance on one trade book. In the latter case, nothing that resembled instruction was seen even though the book was excessively difficult for some students. This visit reminded me of comments that Ira Aaron (1) made, because they are concerned with balance. He notes:

> The timeworn statement that "children learn to read by reading" would be more ac-curate if it were changed to "children's reading ability is maintained and enhanced by reading." Certainly, just reading without systematic instruction will not accom-plish the task; children must be taught to read. However, in order to maintain profi-ciency in reading, students must use the skills they have learned. Extensive reading leads to increased vocabulary, enlarged knowledge, broadened interests, greater ap-preciation of writing techniques, and improved comprehension. (p. 127)

If you reread Chapter 2 in this textbook, you can find statements that parallel those by Aaron. For instance:

> Practice should be connected with, not detached from, meaningful reading. This calls into question the heavy reliance on workbook exercises still seen in some classrooms.... One of the best ways to provide both practice and application is to allow students time for self-selected, uninterrupted reading.

In the Preview for the chapter that precedes this one, you can find other state-ments such as: "New teachers need to use basal materials some of the time. That they should use them only as one of several kinds of materials is a point made repeatedly in earlier chapters." An addition to this statement might go something like, "The same advice applies to experienced teachers who, over the years, have been a Teacher B."

To move away from dependent reliance on basal materials, the initial step is making knowledgeable choices from manual suggestions and workbook exercises. This is illustrated in the previous chapter with an Indian legend. Supplementing basal selections with other materials is a step that should soon follow; consequently, how basal selections can be combined with literature, both fiction and nonfiction, is the topic considered next.

LITERATURE AND BASAL READERS

Whenever literature is used, whether selected by students or assigned by a teacher in conjunction with basal selections, the difficulty of the text has to be taken into account. Three terms that pertain to difficulty relative to reading ability are used earlier but not directly defined. Definitions follow.

Difficulty in Relation to Reading Ability

Independent level: Student is able to achieve comprehension (relative to pur-pose) without assistance.

Instructional level:	Reader is able to achieve comprehension with assistance generally provided with prereading preparations.
Frustration level:	Student cannot achieve comprehension even with assistance.

Teachers attracted to literature-based programs need to keep in mind that the better the book, the more frustrating it is for a student not to be able to read it.

Using literature in conjunction with a basal series is now considered by looking at some objectives that the trade books can help attain. Selected goals pertain to:

Understanding different genres
Understanding cultural diversity
Promoting appreciation of good literature
Understanding third-person and first-person perspectives
Identifying themes in narrative text
Identifying main ideas in expository text

Understanding Different Genres

One of the more obvious reasons to combine basal selections with trade books is to extend students' understanding of various genres with additional examples. (For anyone unacquainted with narrative genres, they are named and briefly described in Figure 14.5.) The abridged, six-page Indian legend referred to in the chapter on basal readers illustrates an opportunity for reallocating time usually spent on too many exercise sheets to having students read other legends.

Attending to various genres is not done so that students can memorize and recite the characteristics of each. Rather, the central purpose is to allow them to know what to expect in some general way before they read a particular genre. Knowing what to anticipate, students are able to adopt an appropriate mental stance that helps with comprehension.

In order to specify what can be done to establish appropriate mental sets for different kinds of narration, fables are used. They were chosen because they have readily recognizable features: Animals are usually the protagonists, and a lesson or moral lies beneath the surface of the tale.

The best known fables are those supposedly written centuries ago by a man named Aesop. Using Aesop's fables at the start is recommended for several reasons. To begin, they are found in every library. They are also sufficiently popular that different versions of the same tale are available. This allows for attention to differences, in particular to those that *make* a difference—that is, to differences that have to do with important parts of the story's structure. Not to be overlooked, either, is that many Aesop fables are available in easy-to-read text that is often supplemented with excellent illustrations.

Because fables are usually short, some teachers introduce children to this genre by reading fables to them. After a sufficient number have been read, children readily pick out the unique features. In the case of fables by Aesop, students also learn that the three most popular animals in his fables are the fox, the wolf, and the lion, all of whom display predictable traits.

Folklore
Old tales passed on orally from one generation to the next. Folklore includes:
Fable: Animal characters with human traits who solve problems in ways that
teach lessons usually concerned with how human beings ought to behave.
Folktale: Humanlike animals, kings, princesses—these are among the
imaginary characters who act in brave or unusual or even magical ways.
How something came to be what it is might be "explained." A moral may be
emphasized.
Tall tale: Exaggerated events involving people who are bigger than life are
central to this genre.
Myth: Supernatural beings performing superhuman acts eventually explain
either an event that took place at the beginning of time or how a reality
came to be.
Legend: Main character is usually portrayed in a mysterious or heroic way.
May be a tale that was originally true but, in retellings, has changed
substantially. Often "explains" something.
Fantasy
Characters, setting, and plot are imaginary. Characters commonly have
special powers.
Realistic fiction
A story that could happen in real life.
Science fiction
Mixes realism with the impossible as the author uses features of reality as the
basis for imaginary events.
Historical fiction
Setting, time, characters, and events are based on historical facts, which are
altered to various degrees and in various ways.
Mystery
A story that centers on something—often a crime—with an unknown
perpetrator. Key elements are a detective, suspects, clues, suspense, and a
solution.
Autobiography
An account of the author's own life.
Biography
An account of a person's life told by someone else.
Play
A script written to be performed for an audience. May include not only
dialogue but also references to scenes, acts, and stage directions.
Poetry
Form of writing that usually has one subject or theme revealed with lines of
text often characterized by rhythm and/or rhyme. Uses words that allow for
imagery.
Epic
A long narrative poem that tells about a legendary or historical figure.

FIGURE 14.5 Narrative Genres

Preparing children for fables by reading some helps when this genre appears in a basal textbook. I was recently reminded of the help during a classroom observation. In this case, the teacher was preparing an instructional group not for a fable but for a legend. Because it was the students' first encounter with legends, the teacher spent considerable time on certain of their features. As a result, insufficient time went to the many words described as being new—even to words central to the important parts of the legend. The consequences were both clear and predictable: As soon as the students took turns reading the legend aloud, many words could not be identified. The point to be stressed, then, is that the kinds of narratives that are in basal textbooks should, *at times,* affect what teachers elect to read to students.

It should also be noted that whenever purposes for students' own reading are established with questions, teachers who take genre into account are likely to ask more appropriate questions than are teachers who ignore it. When students are reading mysteries, for example, questions like the following match the genre:

1. How does the author create suspense?
2. Does the author try to mislead the reader about the guilty person? If so, how is this done?
3. Is the ending what you expected? Is it realistic or contrived?

Teachers who keep genre in mind also know that experiences with poetry require oral reading; how else can students learn to appreciate the rhythm and rhyme and the careful choice of words unless they hear them? As Louise Rosenblatt reminds us (11), this is *not* the time for teachers to ask, "What facts does this poem teach you?"

Understanding Cultural Diversity

Just as the use of literature can extend students' understanding of the various genres included in basal readers, it also can contribute to their understanding of the cultural and racial diversity that characterize our society.

As most readers of this textbook remember, the "melting pot" metaphor was once routinely used to describe the mix of people called "Americans." In more recent times, the mix has increased in both numbers and origins; more significant, however, is that the many different groups now want to retain their identity and to communicate their own traditions and experiences. The relevant point here is that some communication can be achieved with literature. For example, behind every cultural and racial group is folklore. Growing out of oral tradition, folktales are particularly suitable for read-alouds by teachers. In this case, something like Joanna Cole's collection, *Best-Loved Folktales of the World* (Doubleday, 1982), provides a suitable starting point; the stories are both short and international in scope. These folktales cover such regions as East Europe, the Middle East, Africa, and Central and South America.

Eager as they are to take into account current interests, the people responsible for deciding what will be included in basal readers have not overlooked the theme of diversity. For example, the Indian legend referred to in the previous chapter is just one of many stories selected by all the publishers from this genre. Teachers who want to have students read more Indian legends can find attractive possibilities in books by Paul Goble. One, *The Girl Who Loved Wild Horses* (Bradbury Press, 1978), received the Caldecott Medal in 1979 for the illustrations. Other books by the same author that deal with Native Americans—all with beautiful art—are *Buffalo Woman* (Bradbury Press, 1984), *The Great Race of the Birds and Animals* (Bradbury Press, 1985), and *Iktomi and the Berries* (Orchard Books, 1989).

Chapter 13 also refers to a basal story about a Mexican-American girl who felt that nothing about her was special enough to be of interest to other people (see Figure 13.4). This theme identifies one of the most important reasons for using multiculture literature: to show that all of us share certain feelings and fears. That all of us, for example, must learn to accept ourselves is the theme developed in Laurence Yep's story about Chinese Americans entitled *Sea Glass* (Harper Row, 1979).

That we all have days of special celebration can be communicated with literature, too. For this goal, one starting point can be the many books available that tell about the Chinese New Year. Well-known for his stories about Mexican Americans in California, Leo Politi has also written about the Chinese New Year in a book called *Moy Moy* (Scribners, 1960). The photo essay *Chinese New Year* by Tricia Brown (Holt, 1987) provides a factual account of the same celebration.

Teachers interested in communicating about diversity should not overlook an observation made by Rudine Sims Bishop in an article entitled "Extending Multicultural Understanding through Children's Books" (2). She notes, "A logical place to begin.... is with nonfiction" (p. 61). It is true that some selections in basal readers do attempt to provide information about different cultures and races; however, the text is so brief that not much is offered. An 11-page version of a biography of Harriet Tubman, for instance, can hardly make a significant contribution; nor will a 15-page excerpt of *Dragonwings* by Laurence Yep, when the original version about Chinese people living in San Francisco is four times longer (Harper & Row, 1975). Considerably more informative are the historical accounts by Milton Meltzer that deal with African Americans, Chinese Americans, Hispanic Americans, and Jewish Americans. More recommendations for nonfiction are found in *Multicultural Children's and Young Adult Literature* (7). Other categories in this reference book include "Seasons and Celebrations," "Issues in Today's World," and "Poetry."

Promoting Appreciation of Good Literature

Good literature in its original form is now said by publishers of basal series to characterize selections in the readers. Is this correct?

It *is* true that original versions are more common; however, alterations of various kinds are still easy to find. In one series, for example, a third-grade manual states that seven words in a seven-page story are new. Reading it prompts the conclusion that the new words appear so often that the story must be an abbreviated adaptation. Curious, I found a copy of the original story, *The Horse Who Lived Upstairs* by Phyllis McGinley (Lippincott, 1944). Unexpectedly, it turned out to be a 48-page picture book. Unexpectedly, too, the text had not been changed; however, spread out over this number of pages with many illustrations to enjoy, the words said to be new in the basal manual no longer seemed to occur with a contrived frequency.

Typically, the alterations made in basal readers have to do with reducing the text. To illustrate, the well-known folktale *Stone Soup* appears in one basal series in the format of a 6-page play with seven characters. In this version, one hungry person arrives in the town that is the setting for *Stone Soup*.* An unabridged version of the same tale by Marcia Brown (Scribner's, 1947) features three hungry soldiers and uses 48 pages plus many illustrations to tell how they tricked some townspeople into making soup. Obviously, differences in the two versions are not difficult for children to discern.

Sometimes, unstructured discussions are the most effective way to have students contrast two (or more) versions. If the text is a story, a written assignment like the one in Figure 14.6 might also be used, to be followed later by a discussion. In this case, the completed assignment provides a starting point for the discussion, after which other, perhaps more important, differences are highlighted. The differences might pertain to illustrations, interest appeal, development of characters, and choice of words used for descriptions.

For teachers, the important point to keep in mind is that the reason for the recommended comparisons is not to criticize basal readers but to help students acquire from their reading experiences an appreciation of text that is *worth* their time and effort.

Story Elements	Basal Adaptation	Original Version
Setting		
Characters		
Problem		
Events		
Ending		

FIGURE 14.6 Assignment for Making Comparisons

---

*The manual suggests using the topic "Community helpers" to promote a prereading discussion. This was not expected given the fact that the theme in *Stone Soup* is trickery. Teacher A, it seems, is as necessary as ever.

How one second-grade teacher used television to make comparisons is described by an observer in the report in Figure 14.7.

Understanding Third-Person and First-Person Perspectives

When Chapter 12 discusses suitable topics for comprehension instruction, perspective is named as one possibility. A basal story entitled "Nobody Cares about Me" illustrates a first-person perspective. The map in Figure 14.8 reviews the story.

Sometimes postreading assignments are useful in clarifying for students how who tells a story makes a difference. To illustrate, if a basal story is written from a character's point of view, as is the story just referred to, a teacher can have members of the instructional group read easy, familiar tales—something like "Little Red Riding Hood," for instance—all of which are told with a third-person perspective. (Using easy text allows everyone to do the assignment independently.) Afterward, the job for the students is to rewrite the story they read from the point of view of a character. Told by the wolf, for example, "Little Red Riding Hood" might go something like this:

Little Red Riding Hood
by
The Wolf

Life is hard for a wolf like myself. I get into trouble because I have a very big appetite. I'm always hungry.

Last week I met a cute little girl in the woods. She was taking some food to her grandmother, which smelled very good. Do you think she'd give me some? Not on your life. Some kids are really selfish. I ran off to the grandmother's house. I thought <u>she</u> might share some food with me, once her granddaughter went back home. I made the mistake, though, of peeking in her window. As soon as the grandmother saw me, she hid in a closet.

By then I was ready for a little fun. I found some clothes in another closet and dressed up to look like a grandmother. I was sure I could fool the little girl into giving <u>me</u> the food. But, again, I had problems. She screamed as loud as she could the minute she saw me. Soon, a nasty looking man holding an axe appeared. That was enough for me. I yanked off the clothes and ran for my life.

Now I'm <u>really</u> hungry. In fact, I'm thinking right now of how to get some food. Maybe I can find a few tasty pigs somewhere.

With a variety of reading experiences, students should be able to conclude that with first-person perspectives, identified with revealing words like *I* and *me* and *we* and *us,* narrators are part of the story and tell it in ways that are affected by their own opinions and feelings. An author's use of a third-person perspective, on the other hand, makes the narrator omniscient. Now, how characters feel and even what

When I walked into the classroom, I was surprised to see the teacher setting up a television set in the middle of the room. I had expected to find groups reading. The teacher explained that they were going to watch "Reading Rainbow," after which she established with the children a purpose for watching the program. She held up a copy of *Rumplestiltskin* and asked if anyone remembered who had written this version of the folktale. (The teacher had read it to the class the day before.) A few students raised their hands; one answered. The teacher wrote the author's name on the board and then referred to the previous day's discussion of how folktales are retold by different authors and illustrated by different artists. She explained that *Rumplestiltskin* was the featured book on today's "Reading Rainbow" tape and suggested to the children that they look for two things: differences in authors and differences in content.

When the program concluded, the teacher asked who remembered the author's name of the version on the tape. Most raised their hands; many, in fact, had taken the time to write it down. After hearing the name, the teacher wrote it on the board next to the other author. She then asked if anyone had read still other versions of *Rumplestiltskin*. Unexpectedly—at least to me—two students took paperback versions out of their desks, each written by different authors. Again, the names were added to the board.

After this, the class discussed similarities and differences in the two versions all had heard thus far. Differences mentioned dealt with particular words, dialogues, and illustrations. Finally, the teacher asked the children to tell her in writing which version they preferred, and why. They seemed more than willing to do this.

I liked what I saw. It was interesting for the students and added to their knowledge of folktales. It was obvious that the teacher had planned ahead, set objectives, and proceeded to attain them. However, one thing was missing: If she expected the students to write about their preference and to explain why they liked the version they chose, the expectations should have been written somewhere to serve as a reminder. This would also give the children practice in following written directions.

FIGURE 14.7   Comparing Different Versions of *Rumplestiltskin*

"Nobody Cares about Me"

SETTING

Main Character	Time	Place
Bonnie	Anytime	Anyplace

PROBLEM
Bonnie feels neglected and wants attention

UNSUCCESSFUL EFFORTS TO SOLVE THE PROBLEM

1. Bonnie wears her mother's fanciest hat to school.
2. Bonnie smiles and even laughs aloud for no apparent reason.
3. Bonnie dances, sings, and even turns a cartwheel during a visit to the home of an aunt and uncle.

SUCCESSFUL EFFORT TO SOLVE THE PROBLEM
Bonnie gives her attention to a classmate, Paul.

OUTCOME
Bonnie receives attention from Paul.

MORAL
Do unto others as you would have them do unto you.

FIGURE 14.8   Story Map: First-Person Perspective

they are thinking can be told. Students need to keep in mind, however, that authors are still in charge and write a story as they wish to tell it.

Identifying Themes in Narrative Text

When story structure is discussed in Chapter 12, a selection in a basal reader about a pioneer boy named Peter illustrates story elements. The map in Figure 14.9 reviews the plot and the fact that the underlying theme of the story goes something like this: Be satisfied with who you are.

Themes often convey important messages that can be reinforced by reading more than one story. In conjunction with "Peter, the Pioneer Boy," for instance, two other stories might be read. One, written at an easy level, is entitled *I Want to Be a*

"Peter, the Pioneer Boy"

SETTING

Main Character	Time	Place
Peter	Pioneer days	Rural area

PROBLEM
Peter wants to be bigger than he is.

ACTION TO SOLVE PROBLEM
Peter dips hand into magic pond and wishes to be bigger.

SOLUTION OF PROBLEM
Shrunken clothes suggest to Peter that his wish came true.

NEW PROBLEM
Peter believes himself to be so big he won't be able to get into his own house.

SOLUTION OF PROBLEM
The ability to walk through the doorway of his home and fit on his mother's lap shows Peter he is the same size.

ENDING
Peter is satisfied with his size.

FIGURE 14.9   Map for "Peter, the Pioneer Boy"

Bird by Joanne Kaiser (Houghton Mifflin Company, 1964). This is about a baby hippopotamus who, as the title of the book indicates, wants very much to be a bird. When Herbie the hippo becomes a bird in a dream, he learns the hard way that it really is better to be what he is, a hippopotamus. The other story, slightly more difficult, is *Dandelion* by Don Freeman (Viking Press, 1964). Again, an animal is the protagonist. After receiving an invitation to a party, the lion decides to make himself more handsome by getting a new hairdo. It alters his appearance so much, however, that on the night of the party the hostess refuses to admit him because she does not recognize Dandelion. A rainstorm solves the problem by ruining what, at first, this lion thought was an elegant hairstyle.

Once the stories about Peter, Herbie, and Dandelion are read, discussed, and understood, a subsequent step is to help students recognize that tales that are different on the surface may teach the same lesson. Initially, direct comparisons like the one in Figure 14.10 help clarify what is meant by "same message" or "same theme."

Because it is themes that often last after a story is read, they should receive regular, intermittent attention. Students can identify many with themes, such as the importance of friendship and the consequences of guilt feelings. This identification leads to thoughtful discussions in which increased self-knowledge and renewed appreciation of what is taken for granted may be some of the valuable products.

Identifying Main Ideas in Expository Text

Like themes in narrative text, main ideas should be retained when expository material has been read. At one time, expository selections in basal series occurred relatively infrequently, but that is not the case now. The current problem is the use by basal authors of both expository and narrative selections when "main idea" receives attention (4). The result of this indiscriminant mix of texts is confused and confusing recommendations for instruction. Any Teacher A who is using a basal series knows enough to confine main idea instruction to expository selections.

Like trade books, basal selections that provide information commonly have excellent photographs. More often than not, they also deal with topics of interest to

Somebody	Wanted	So	But	At the end
Peter	to be big.	he dipped a hand in the pool.	he thought he was too big.	he was glad to be the same size.
Herbie	to be a bird.	he dreamt he was a bird.	being a bird caused problems.	he was glad to be himself.
Dandelion	to be handsome.	he got a new hairdo.	he was kept out of a party.	he was glad to be recognized by the hostess.

FIGURE 14.10   Comparing Three Stories to Highlight a Common Theme

children. This combination serves well in permitting students to see that reading-to-learn need not be the dull task it often turns out to be when content area textbooks are used.

To supplement expository selections in basal readers with trade books that provide information, a variety of procedures can be used. For instance, once the main ideas in the basal selection are reviewed, trade books that focus on the same topic can be read. Now, comparing main ideas from the different sources is one possibility. Details that relate to the main points might be compared, too. If the topic is of sufficient interest, writing a synthesis of the main ideas from the different sources is another possibility. Now, the fact that not every detail needs to be included should be emphasized, especially with students who have been in other classrooms in which distinctions were not made between content worth remembering and unimportant details.

Other ways to supplement expository basal selections are possible, too. If the selection explains something like why camels survive so well in a desert, trade books that tell about other desert animals or about vegetation that grows there are appropriate choices. A book like Barbara Bash's *Desert Giant* (Little, Brown, 1989) covers both topics; it provides information with text and photographs about the saguaro cactus. That the branches of this plant reach 50 feet into the air and that it provides a home for a number of small animals are among the book's interesting facts. As students read the book, the referents they have for *tree* are also being expanded.

Sometimes, narrative text in a basal reader may provide a reason to have students read expository text in trade books. To illustrate, one fable in a basal series centers on two chipmunks and develops a theme about the importance of friendship. In this instance, having one or more students read informational material about chipmunks can suggest that they are not the most appropriate animal for such a tale because, compared to other animals, chipmunks are loners. Assessing authenticity with the help of information in trade books can also focus on something like the setting in a basal story.

Expository trade books should not be forgotten when it is time for teachers to read to a class. Young children who have a gerbil or two in their classroom will enjoy having *Gerbils* by Kate Petty (Gloucester Press, 1989) read to them. Should the consequences of an oil spill on animals in the ocean be featured in current newspapers or on television, older students will be interested in having someone read aloud *Sea Otters* by Ruth Ashby (Macmillan, 1990). As is typical of trade books that offer information, these two are colorfully illustrated with superb photographs. (Trade books with expository text are discussed further in Chapter 15.)

Teachers who bear in mind both the significance of world knowledge for comprehension and the interest of students in informational material also make certain that magazines are available. A reference at the end of the chapter (15) offers an annotated list of suitable magazines along with the address of each publisher.

Comments by a fifth-grade teacher, which are in Figure 14.11, provide a suitable conclusion for this discussion of expository material. She wrote them at the time of the Persian Gulf War.

One way I try to increase students' familiarity with materials other than textbooks is by bringing to school articles that relate to topics we have discussed. Currently, the students are especially interested in the crisis in the Middle East and our troops in Saudi Arabia. They have had two opportunities to write to a service person, and the topic has been discussed frequently.

Today I brought the current issue of *Newsweek,* whose subject is "Letters in the Sand." This issue deals extensively with the service people in the Persian Gulf, and, in particular, with communication between them and their families and friends in the United States. I selected portions of articles that I thought would be interesting and read those aloud to the class. One article was written by a serviceman to a fifth-grade class in response to their letters to him. Because my class had also written letters, they were particularly interested in this man's response.

Having given them a preview of the magazine's content, I let the students know that it would be available to read if they were interested. Throughout the day, I saw at least five students reading articles.

The experience was significant, for it reminded me of the importance of making available a wide variety of materials. It also helped me see that it is not necessary to rely on artificial incentives to encourage independent reading. There are enough things that genuinely interest my students to provide the motivation. I am further reminded of the value of reading aloud to the class and of the desirability of choosing more than just stories.

FIGURE 14.11   Magazines in a Fifth-Grade Classroom

SUMMARY

The fact that teachers who had read to the class daily may be a person's fondest memory of earlier years spent in school helps explain why Chapter 14 started with teachers' daily read-alouds. Because one main benefit of this use of a teacher's time is encouragement to students to read on their own, the next two topics covered in the chapter were trade books for classroom libraries and schedules that include time for self-selected, uninterrupted reading.

Whether trade books should provide subject matter for reading instruction is another matter—one that always generates controversy. Less controversial is the contention that teachers who use basal readers should take for granted the need to supplement them with other materials. The remaining parts of Chapter 14 illustrated how the accomplishment of worthwhile goals can be advanced with the additions.

Using trade books to promote a better understanding of the various genres was discussed initially. The most important point made in this section is that knowing the characteristics of each type of text is not what is important. What *is* important is a reader's use of that knowledge to adopt an appropriate stance. More specifically, how one ought to go about reading historical fiction differs substantially from the mental set that should be adopted for acquiring information from text presenting well-documented facts about stars.

Extending students' contacts with people of different cultures and races through books was the next topic considered. The diversity of our population makes this goal mandatory.

The continued inclusion of adapted literature in basal programs accounts for the next section in the chapter, "Promoting Appreciation of Good Literature." The fact that illustrations as well as text can differ in basal versions of literary selections was demonstrated. One main point in this segment is that the recommended comparisons serve the purpose of helping students acquire an appreciation of books worth reading.

The next two sections dealt with topics that Chapter 12 referred to when comprehension instruction was the subject. The first, "Understanding Third-Person and First-Person Perspectives," showed how the combined use of basal selections and trade books can illuminate the effects of first-person and of third-person perspectives on the content of a story. The second section, "Identifying Themes in Narrative Text," offered help with how to show students that texts that are different on the surface may have the same underlying theme. Because themes may be the most important—and long-lasting—outcome of reading narrative text, teachers were urged in this section to plan activities for highlighting themes on a regular basis.

Just as narrative text may communicate a theme, so may expository text convey main ideas. This fact accounts for the focus of the final section, "Identifying Main Ideas in Expository Text." One fact emphasized is basal authors' misguided use of both narrative and expository selections for main idea instruction. This practice makes it essential for teachers to do better; otherwise, confusing instruction is the inevitable consequence.

Because reading done by adults is often confined to newspapers and magazines, the section on expository text included a reminder to make magazines available in classrooms. How one teacher fostered interest in reading a magazine was described. Like the other accounts of classrooms that appeared intermittently in Chapter 14, the purpose of this description was to specify the meaning of recommendations.

REVIEW

1. Explain the following statements.
   a. Chapter 14 has more to do with aliteracy than with illiteracy.
   b. Providing effective instructional programs is the best means for producing adults who read.

2. The many benefits that accrue from being read to ought to make reading to a class a mandatory procedure for teachers. Specify the benefits, starting with those for the youngest students.

3. Were you the teacher, what advice would you give to a newly employed aide, one of whose responsibilities is to read to the class?

4. What does Ira Aaron say about the frequently heard observation, "Children learn to read by reading"?

5. Chapter 14 reminds teachers to *avoid* asking students to share what they are reading in ways they view to be chores.
   a. Exactly what does this mean?
   b. What is an example of sharing likely to be thought of as a chore?

6. What do you think about the practice described in Figure 14.4?

7. Teachers who want to encourage students to read trade books need to keep in mind the three terms referred to in Chapter 14 that describe difficulty of text in relation to a student's reading ability: independent level, instructional level, and frustration level.
   a. Define each term.
   b. Explain why teachers interested in getting students to read literature need to keep these terms in mind.

8. The importance of a Teacher A who routinely asks, "*Why* am I doing what I'm doing?" was reinforced in Chapter 14. Review why such a question is important by completing each of the following statements.
   a. Comparing adaptations of literature found in basal readers with the original text is not done to foster negative attitudes toward these textbooks. Instead, the purpose is…
   b. Teaching students about the characteristics of such genres as fable and autobiography is not done to have the characteristics memorized. Instead, the purpose is…

c. The reason to have students read expository text is not to have them attend to, and remember, everything an author says about a topic. Instead, the purpose is...

9. Whenever a teacher elects to use trade books to advance students' reading ability by attending to topics like flashbacks or, for instance, figurative uses of language, the books should be read as a whole before anything is done with its parts. Why is this the case?

REFERENCES

1. Aaron, Ira E. "Enriching the Basal Reading Program with Literature." In B. Cullinan (Ed.), *Children's Literature in the Reading Program.* Newark, Del.: International Reading Association, 1987.

2. Bishop, Rudine Sims. "Extending Multicultural Understanding through Children's Books." In B. Cullinan (Ed.), *Children's Literature in the Reading Program.* Newark, Del.: International Reading Association, 1987.

3. Cullinan, Bernice E. "Inviting Readers to Literature." In B. Cullinan (Ed.), *Children's Literature in the Reading Program.* Newark, Del.: International Reading Association, 1987.

4. Durkin, Dolores. "Comprehension Instruction in Current Basal Reader Series." Technical Report No. 521. Urbana: University of Illinois, Center for the Study of Reading, 1990.

5. Heine, Patricia. "The Power of Related Books." *Reading Teacher* 45 (September, 1991), 75–77.

6. Huck, Charlotte. *Children's Literature in the Elementary School,* 4th ed. New York: Holt, Rinehart and Winston, 1987.

7. Kruse, Ginny M., and Horning, Kathleen. *Multicultural Children's and Young Adult Literature.* Madison: University of Wisconsin, 1989.

8. Macon, James M.; Bewell, Diane; and Vogt, Mary Ellen. *Responses to Literature.* Newark, Del.: International Reading Association, 1991.

9. McCracken, Robert A., and McCracken, Marlene J. "Modeling Is the Key to Sustained Silent Reading." *Reading Teacher* 31 (January, 1978), 406–408.

10. Pillar, Arlene M. "Resources to Identify Children's Books for the Reading Program." In B. Cullinan (Ed.), *Children's Literature in the Reading Program.* Newark, Del.: International Reading Association, 1987.

11. Rosenblatt, Louise M. "What Facts Does This Poem Teach You." *Language Arts* 57 (April, 1980), 386–394.

12. Sanacore, Joseph. "Encouraging the Lifetime Reading Habit." *Journal of Reading* 35 (March, 1992), 474–477.

13. Silvey, Anita. "The Basalization of Trade Books." *The Horn Book Magazine* 65 (September/October, 1989), 549–550.

14. Spiegel, Dixie Lee. "Literature Resource Materials Revisited." *Reading Teacher* 44 (December, 1990), 336–340.

15. Stoll, Donald R. *Magazines for Children.* Newark, Del.: International Reading Association, 1990.

16. Trelease, Jim. *The New Read-Aloud Handbook,* 3rd ed. New York: Penguin Books, 1991.

17. Yatvin, Joanne. "Recreational Reading for the Whole School." *Reading Teacher* 31 (November, 1977), 185–188.

Content Area Textbooks

Two familiar facts affected the content of this chapter. One is that subject area textbooks are not made up of consistently well-written, interesting prose. Some content is so irrelevant for elementary school students as to make it necessary to ask why an author decided to include it. The second fact is that some students who are expected to acquire information from these textbooks do not even come close to having the reading ability or the experiences that the expectation assumes.

These two facts create problems for teachers and students alike. They also cause problems for authors writing about the topic that is the title of Chapter 15. To alleviate some problems for the present author, two decisions were made. One was to use social studies textbooks to exemplify expository text. This decision is justified by the fact that most points made can be applied to a variety of informational texts. The circumscribed focus also keeps Chapter 15 from covering an excessive amount of material.

The second decision was to confine the chapter to recommendations that are reasonable—that is, that can be followed by teachers who, first, do not spend all their waking hours either teaching or preparing to teach and, second, have students who cannot read textbooks without help.

Even if Chapter 15 were addressed to teachers who work only with successful readers, two assumptions would remain the same:

1. It is impossible to find a textbook that deals with nothing but well-written, highly important content that is relevant for elementary school students. In part, this reflects the fact that easy reading is hard writing.
2. At the elementary level, it is more important to teach students how to acquire information from text than it is to cover all the content in a textbook.

These two assumptions are not meant to suggest that teachers should take lightly their responsibility to teach *important* content. After all, its acquisition increases students' knowledge about the world. Rather, the two assumptions stated above are intended to make the points that, first, selections from all the content in a textbook need to be made and, second, that both the selected content and how it is written provide subject matter for instruction.

Chapter 15, then, has two main purposes. First, it is meant to help teachers and prospective teachers instruct about content thought to be important. Second, it is intended to show how the textbooks that convey the content can be a vehicle for helping students learn how to learn from expository discourse.

IN PREVIOUS CHAPTERS, DETAILED ATTENTION went to a substitute for round robin reading: *well-prepared, un*interrupted silent reading of *appropriately difficult* material. This substitute is pertinent now for several reasons. First, content area textbooks may be "appropriately difficult" for very few of the students who are expected to comprehend them. In addition, each chapter often has to be read not as a whole but in sections, because an entire chapter deals too quickly with too much unfamiliar content. "Well-prepared" comes to the foreground because the difficulty of textbooks makes prereading preparations mandatory.

Features of content area textbooks such as those just referred to affected decisions made for the content to include in the present chapter. So, too, did data from observations in middle- and upper-grade classrooms during social studies (1, 8, 15). Findings from this source are summarized next.

CLASSROOM PRACTICES WITH CONTENT AREA TEXTBOOKS

To begin, various numbers of students in all the classrooms were unable to read the assigned textbook. Nonetheless, nothing was seen that could be called comprehension instruction. Instead, the concern was to cover content even when it was dull, unimportant, or out-of-date.

Because covering content *was* the goal, teachers often relied on procedures that "told" the content to the poorest readers. A round robin reading of a chapter or of part of a chapter by the best students was a common means for doing the telling. At such times, the teacher stopped the oral reading intermittently in order to provide an explanation or pose a question.

In other classrooms, everyone was asked to read a specified section of a chapter silently, after which the content was discussed. Only certain students participated, probably because others had not been able to read the text. In a few classrooms, students were expected to respond in writing to questions about a chapter; however, because some could not do the reading, they could not be expected to do the writing.

Elsewhere, teachers had taken the time to rewrite a chapter in a simplified form. In other instances, substantial amounts of material supplemented textbooks. Even in these classrooms, however, the focus was still confined to learning the content.

All these findings make it necessary to highlight the following: Teachers have *two* responsibilities when content area textbooks are the concern. The first is to select and teach important content. The second, equally important responsibility is to teach students how to go about comprehending expository material. Put differently, if elementary teachers (and others at the high school level) continue to give all their attention to content, when will students learn how to learn from text?

CONSEQUENCES OF CLASSROOM PRACTICES

One consequence when students do not learn how to acquire information from expository material is effectively portrayed in tongue-in-cheek comments by Robert

Ireland (12). These remarks underscore the consequences when reading is not *strategic*—that is, it is not purposeful and planful:

> Often, the child who tries the hardest suffers most in reading textbooks. He thinks he must read carefully and remember all the information. He starts a textbook chapter on the Plains Indians. The first paragraph names nine different tribes. He rereads and "studies," trying to memorize all nine. The second paragraph names five rivers and two mountain ranges. Again, "study," memorize. By this time, he's getting pretty well fed up with the book and with reading in general. The next paragraph describes the buffalo. It is high shouldered, shaggy. He thinks it looks like his brother and then goes on. The buffalo has hair like a lion and a hump like a camel. Picture that! By this time, he has been reading for fifteen minutes and has covered three paragraphs. (p. 586)

That the passing of years does not necessarily bring improvement is supported in a portrayal of the reading habits of older students enrolled in a highly regarded university. The conclusions reached by William Perry, a researcher, were quoted as early as the Introduction to this textbook and are worth repeating:

> The typical approach of 90 percent of these students was to start at the beginning of the chapter and read straight ahead. No attempt was made to survey the chapter, note marginal headings, or first read the recapitulation paragraph in which the whole structure and summary of the chapter was given. Thus, none of the clues and signals provided as a basis for raising questions were used to identify specific purposes for reading. (16, p. 196)

COMPREHENSIBILITY OF CONTENT AREA TEXTBOOKS

Implied in the observation just quoted is that textbooks are considerate in the help their authors provide for understanding the content they present. However, the opposite conclusion has been reached when texts are analyzed. In fact, one result of this body of research is the description *inconsiderate text* (3).

Factors that make text "inconsiderate," thus difficult to comprehend and remember, are discussed next. The discussion proceeds not by noting what makes text inconsiderate but, to the contrary, by focusing on factors that facilitate understanding. This perspective is taken because it allows for attention to text features that teachers should encourage students to use to help themselves understand. Attending to the positive can also help teachers choose more wisely if they find themselves on a committee responsible for selecting new textbooks.

Although the following discussion features the positive aspects of helpful text, it shows indirectly that the problems some students have in understanding textbooks are not necessarily the result of deficiencies in reading ability. Instead, they may originate in the composition of the text they are struggling to understand.

Considerate Textbooks

As Chapter 12 points out, how the content of a body of text is put together is called its *macrostructure*. The fact in need of emphasis now is that the macrostructure of considerate expository text makes it possible for readers to understand how the topics covered are interrelated. Or, as Bonnie Armbruster and Thomas Anderson have stated, in coherent text "central ideas across the entire discourse are woven together in such a way as to make relationships among the ideas clear and logical" (3, p. 47). A student's ability to see how the content of a chapter is organized and fits together promotes both understanding and retention.

Authors of considerate text also omit irrelevant content because it takes attention away from central ideas. On the other hand, the same writers include graphic aids such as tables and maps whenever they help explain or, perhaps, summarize. Once the decision is made to use these aids, text that is user-friendly informs readers not only about their function but also about the appropriate time to examine them.

In the most considerate text, readers are further helped by introductory sections that orient them to the whole of the chapter. More assistance is in summaries that underscore the key ideas. Between all this are headings and subheadings that preannounce forthcoming topics, thus establishing expectations.

Looked at in smaller segments (*microstructure*), considerate text contains not only clear, well-constructed sentences but also cohesive ties that make apparent intersentence and interparagraph connections. The content of one sentence or paragraph thus flows smoothly into the content of an adjacent sentence or paragraph. Easy-to-understand definitions of terms that are both important and likely to be unfamiliar are further sources of help in considerate text. Terms that are of special importance commonly appear in italic type.

Interest Value of Textbooks

Not to be overlooked is that the best organization and writing cannot compensate for dull content. I make this point because my own review of social studies textbooks has left the impression that a sizable amount of the material is deficient in comprehensibility not only because of factors like poor organization and excessive detail but also because many topics are uninteresting. Such topics, plus others that are far removed from the lives of students, often keep the best readers in a class from deriving either new knowledge or enjoyment from their textbooks (10).

Enjoyment cannot be expected when the content is not only dull but also difficult and excessive in amount. Researchers who have attempted to make textbooks more comprehensible reach conclusions similar to those stated by Beck et al. (4). She and her colleagues have noted that even methodical efforts to rewrite and improve textbooks are never totally successful because the nature of the information is often inherently difficult for elementary school students.

That authors are prone to tell readers too little about too much is another reason students may not enjoy, or learn from, their textbooks. In this case, blame is usually assigned to the eagerness of publishers to satisfy content requirements issued by groups responsible for purchasing textbooks in the most populous states and cities. For example, Tyson and Woodward (19), who have examined textbooks, drew the following conclusion:

> It is not surprising that American textbooks have become compendiums of topics, none of which are treated in much depth. The aggregate volume of material re-

quired by many states and localities simply cannot be put into a standard-sized text-book unless the material is compressed to the point of incomprehensibility. (p. 15)

These conclusions about the content of something like social studies text-books—dull, unrelated to students' lives and experiences, difficult, superficial—makes it natural to wonder about the persistence of some teachers to give almost all their time to content and practically none to instruction for understanding expository discourse. This is the case even though it is the latter instruction that will allow students to learn from, *and* enjoy, all the interesting expository trade books that sit on the shelves of libraries everywhere. When it is kept in mind that a "major impediment to effective learning is a deficient knowledge base" (5, p. 19), the importance of helping students acquire information on their own cannot be taken lightly.

EXPOSITORY TEXT: BASAL READERS AND TRADE BOOKS

Not too many years ago, expository selections in basal readers were a rarity. This meant that students often went from reading nothing but narration in grades 1 through 3 to having responsibility for learning from textbooks in grade 4. This helped to account for what was sometimes referred to as the "fourth-grade slump"—students who seemed to read adequately well in third grade appeared to have serious limitations in fourth.

Now that all the basal series include more expository text than was once charac-teristic, both basal selections and informational trade books allow for a transition to the much longer content area textbooks. The combination also gives teachers ample opportunities to ensure that students understand not only the significant differ-ences between expository and narrative text but also the implications of the differ-ences for how they should go about reading a story and reading something whose purpose is to inform. To assign importance to the differences, some teachers prepare charts that highlight contrasts (9).

One word of caution for users of basal reader manuals needs to be underscored: Even when excellent suggestions are made for working with a forthcoming exposi-tory selection, it will probably be called "a story" (7). In fact, in manuals at the earli-est levels, it is not uncommon to have text as brief as one sentence referred to as "a story." Again, Teacher A can be counted on to be more careful and correct than are some authors of basal manuals.

Because ways for teachers to deal with expository text like that in basal readers and trade books are discussed in some detail in Chapter 12, they are not repeated here. Instead, you are urged to reread the earlier material before proceeding with the present chapter. The two sections "Expository Text: Appropriate Topics for Instruction" and "Establishing Purposes for Reading Expository Text" are particu-larly relevant. It is also advisable to reread in the same chapter the section called "Comprehension Instruction: Additional Subject Matter" because the topics named are as pertinent for content area textbooks as they are for novels.

USE OF RECIPROCAL TEACHING

One topic not named in Chapter 12 is *reciprocal teaching* (14). The briefer pieces of expository text in basal readers and trade books are especially suitable for this way of helping students learn how to go about extracting information from text. As with any other help, time should be allotted to reciprocal teaching only if certain students are likely to profit from its use.

Reciprocal teaching is a procedure whose purpose is to help students learn how to learn from text. Once each of its components is explained and modeled by the teacher—perhaps more than once—and then practiced by students, all are used together. The six components are:

1. **Predicting**
   To initiate the procedure, a prediction is made about the content likely to be in the passage all students will read silently. The passage may be as limited as one paragraph or could include whatever appears under a subheading or heading. If the focus is the start of the text, predictions can be made with the help of a title. If a previous passage was read and discussed, the prediction is based on its content.

2. **Reading**
   Everyone—teacher and students alike—read a specified piece of text silently.

3. **Questioning**
   Whoever is functioning as teacher (teacher or student) poses one or more questions about the passage just read.

4. **Clarifying**
   If any misunderstandings are apparent, they are clarified.

5. **Summarizing**
   After the question(s) is answered, the one acting as teacher summarizes the passage.

6. **Predicting**
   (See #1 above).

The goal of the components just outlined is to help students take charge of their own learning. With that in mind, teachers eventually withdraw, allowing members of collaborative learning groups to use reciprocal teaching on their own but only if some still need this kind of help.

Comments by Annemarie Palincsar and Ann Brown about the clarification component of reciprocal teaching are worth quoting:

> Clarification is particularly important with students who have a history of comprehension difficulty.... These students very likely believe that the purpose of reading is saying the words correctly; they may not be uncomfortable with the fact that...the passage is not making much sense. When students are asked to clarify, their attention is called to...reasons why text is difficult to understand, e.g., unfamiliar vocabulary, unclear referent words, new and perhaps complicated concepts. They are taught to be alert to the effects of such impediments...and to take the necessary measures to restore meaning, e.g., reread, ask for help. (13, pp. 772–773)

OVERVIEW OF REMAINING PARTS OF THE CHAPTER

Because previewing is one important means for preparing students to read expository text, this is an appropriate time to go over the remaining sections of the present chapter.

The first section deals with a teacher's need to be very familiar with the text that students are expected to read. What the teacher should be looking for when she herself reads the material is identified. The next section describes a teacher's responsibilities for preparing students for a chapter, viewed as facilitating comprehension. Four prereading responsibilities are discussed. Subsequently, how one teacher helped the poorest readers in her class deal with text that they were unable to comprehend independently is described. After that, postreading activities are the focus. At the end, Chapter 15 concentrates on a way to help students know how to go about learning from textbooks on their own. It thus supplements the earlier discussion of reciprocal teaching.

A TEACHER'S PREPARATIONS

The following discussion of teachers' preparations assumes that textbooks are covered one chapter at a time. In no way, however, does this mean that a chapter is always the best unit to use. What *is* best is something each teacher must decide after taking into account students' abilities and interests and the characteristics and content of the text.

A second assumption is that teachers must also decide how much time to spend on a chapter, should that be the unit selected to study. Now, importance of content should be the primary consideration.

The content also accounts for a third assumption, namely, that teaching procedures that are suitable for one chapter may be inappropriate for another. Nobody should conclude, therefore, that the suggestions made here are suitable for every chapter—or for every group of students. Instead, the suggestions serve the more modest function of providing illustrations.

Chapter Preview

It should go without saying that a teacher's responsibilities start with reading whatever it is that students will read. A helpful beginning is to preview the material first to see how it is organized. At this time, topics and subtopics are pertinent, as are features of the text that show the procedures the author selected for communicating information. For instance:

- Is the text composed of main ideas, each amplified with supporting details?
- Did the author select a question/answer format?
- Is the basic organization one of comparisons and contrasts?
- Does the text concentrate on causes and effects?
- Is it necessary to understand content presented first in order to comprehend information covered later?

Meriting attention, too, is evidence of considerate or inconsiderate text, as instances of both should be brought to students' attention. It is helpful for them to know, for example, that key terms are presented initially in italic type and are then defined and often illustrated. Students should also be aware of an author's penchant for using pronouns to refer to large chunks of previous text. Not to be overlooked are examples of out-of-date information, oversimplification, and an author's possible bias. Also important to note are passages that do not make clear distinctions between facts and opinions.

Decisions: Content, Background Information, Vocabulary

Once a teacher has a sense of the whole of a chapter, selecting content that is worth understanding and remembering comes next (17). With social studies, interrelationships between where people live and how they live (occupations, transportation, homes, clothing, recreation) may be important. At other times, both the indirect and immediate causes of certain events merit attention. Sometimes, comparisons and contrasts among different countries need to be the focus. The overall point is that some content is important; other content is not.

After important content and related concepts are determined, a teacher needs to consider the author's assumptions about students' existing knowledge. In turn, this identifies what needs to be activated or taught. The selected content also identifies key vocabulary.

Now that the teacher's own preparations have been outlined, let's shift the focus to look at how students can be prepared for a chapter.

PREREADING PREPARATIONS FOR STUDENTS

Anyone familiar with earlier chapters in this book should feel at home with the preparations for expository text depicted in Figure 15.1. The one addition to the earlier discussions of facilitating students' comprehension is previewing the text.

As is true of the earlier attention to facilitating comprehension, the prereading responsibilities listed in Figure 15.1 are not meant to suggest a sequence for dealing with the four components. Nor does the list mean that each is separate and distinct

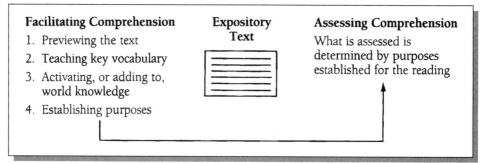

Facilitating Comprehension
1. Previewing the text
2. Teaching key vocabulary
3. Activating, or adding to, world knowledge
4. Establishing purposes

Expository Text

Assessing Comprehension
What is assessed is determined by purposes established for the reading

FIGURE 15.1   Prereading Preparations for Expository Text

from the other three. To illustrate, previewing the text with students may provide highly suitable times for dealing with some key vocabulary. Vocabulary is also likely to overlap with what is done to activate, or add to, essential background information. Now, however, for purposes of discussion, the four kinds of preparations are covered separately in the order in which they are shown in Figure 15.1.

Previewing the Text

Procedures for previewing a chapter—or whatever amount of text is to be read—vary depending on (a) what has already been done with previewing, and (b) the nature of the text. Regardless of what a teacher does decide to do, it is important to keep in mind that teaching students about the structure of a chapter is less helpful than is explaining directly how they should use the structure to help themselves understand (18).

For times when a preview is thought to be necessary, or when the students in question are beginning to learn about previewing, the following summary should be a helpful guide for teachers.

Possible Procedures for Previewing a Chapter

STEP ONE: *Title and Introductory Paragraph*

Direct students to read the title silently. The introductory paragraph might then be read aloud either by you or an able student. Even this brief contact with the chapter might elicit responses, especially if you probe a bit: Does anyone know something about this already? Does it remind you of anything we talked about earlier?

Having students think and talk about a topic, often referred to as *brainstorming,* is important because, first, it activates prior knowledge and, second, it helps students see the connection between what they already know and what they will be learning. The discussion might also reveal misunderstandings.

STEP TWO: *Structure of Chapter*

To help students see how the chapter has been assembled, have them look at headings and subheadings. If either includes words in need of clarification, take the time to discuss them. Should one or more footnotes be used, their purpose ought to be clarified.

STEP THREE: *Graphics*

Students might next be asked to leaf through the chapter to find graphic material. Again, questions should provide a focus so that the students do not view what is being done as aimless browsing. Questions about pictures, for instance, can call attention to details that might be overlooked or, perhaps, assist in estimating the actual size of what is pictured. Queries about other graphics might lead to responses that suggest students need help. For example: How are the lines and arrows to be interpreted in a diagram? If the chapter introduces a new type of graphic aid—let's say a time line—more careful attention is necessary.

STEP FOUR: *Summary*

To wrap up the overview, the summary at the end of the chapter should be read. If questions are included, either at the end or intermittently throughout the chapter, they should be examined, too. If, for the first time, students are using a textbook in which questions are interspersed throughout a chapter, they should be shown how to use the questions.

Afterward, students can be asked if *they* have questions they hope the chapter answers. Their questions can be either incorporated into purposes established for reading the chapter or discussed later during postreading activities.

Attending to Key Vocabulary

Words that figure prominently in the content judged to be important merit prereading attention. Not to be overlooked are familiar words that are used in unfamiliar ways. For instance:

> mouth of the river
> bed of rock
> shrinking world
> school of fish
> farming the seas

Not to be overlooked, either, is the help an author may provide for key terms. Help often comes, for instance, from appositives (*Climate, the weather an area has over a long period of time, varies from one part of the country to another.*). It goes without saying that students' ability to repeat an author's definitions verbatim does not provide reliable evidence of understanding. That this is not always recognized has been verified. To illustrate, the following exchange was heard during an observation in a fourth grade, when social studies was receiving attention (8):

Teacher: Who can tell us what a continent is?
Child 1: A really big place with states and countries and stuff.
Teacher: Can anyone give us another description?
Child 2: It's a large land mass.
Teacher: Fine. Good.

Because vocabulary is often a major problem for students, chapters from two textbooks are used to continue the discussion. Each chapter is concerned with terminology important for geography. Each is also the initial chapter in a textbook that covers the history and geography of the United States.

The first of the two chapters exemplifies considerate text. Covering the bottom portion of two successive pages is a colorful graphic display that clarifies the terms students are expected to learn. Above the display are fairly good definitions. (Figure 15.2 shows the first of the two pages. The bottom of the page is in color, which contributes to the clarification of the terms.)

Further clarification might come from the students themselves with specific examples—Lake Tahoe and the Adirondack Mountains, for instance, when the words *lake* and *mountain* receive attention. Subsequent pages in the same chapter provide more examples, some of which are supplemented with photographs.

Because the vocabulary in the chapter lends itself to topically related sets of words, graphic displays can serve as summaries. *Semantic webs,* sometimes called *concept clusters,* are illustrated in Figure 15.3. They help to develop what researchers refer to as a *schema* (skē-mə). A schema is "an organized network of concepts embodying some aspect of knowledge" (11, p. 266). In the case of the semantic webs in Figure 15.3, the knowledge pertains to water and land.

Words for Land and Water

basin the land drained by a river and the streams that flow into it; land surrounded by higher land

bay part of a larger body of water that extends into land

canyon a narrow valley with high, steep sides

cape a point of land that extends into water

coast land along the ocean

delta land built up by deposits of soil which collect at the mouth of a river

divide the highest ridge of land that separates two regions drained by different river systems

gulf part of a body of water that extends into land, often larger than a bay

harbor an area of deep water that is protected from winds and ocean currents, forming a place of shelter for ships

hill a raised part of Earth's surface, smaller than a mountain

inlet a narrow body of water, smaller than a bay, that extends into land

island a body of land surrounded by water, smaller than a continent

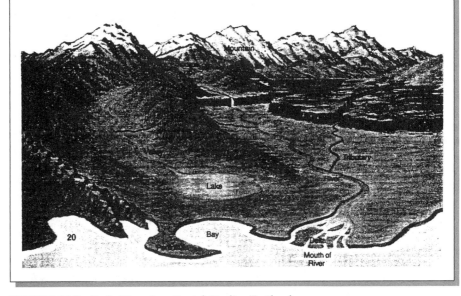

FIGURE 15.2 Definitions in a Social Studies Textbook

Scaling, referred to in Chapter 11, can be used with some of the terms discussed, as their meanings differ from each other by degree. This is illustrated in Figure 15.4.

Having focused on a considerate chapter, let's switch to the second one. This chapter also introduces terms needed for geography. Now, however, students are expected to read the pages that explain the terms at the same time that they are supposed to refer to an assortment of maps on later pages. Used as is, this poorly organized chapter is likely to result in little learning and much frustration.

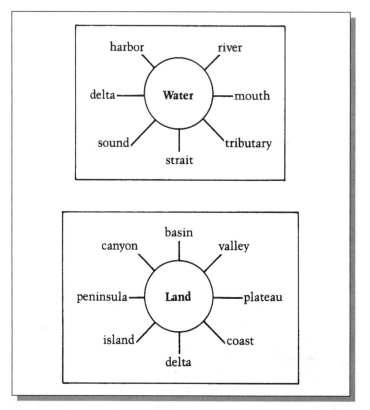

FIGURE 15.3   Semantic Webbing

For teachers, an alternative procedure is to list on the board any key term likely to be familiar so that meanings can be reviewed. How many *are* familiar determines how many new terms to teach. (The words not dealt with can be taught in subsequent chapters as the need for them arises.) Explanations for new terms should be supplemented with maps and photographs scattered throughout the textbook. Again, specific examples from students are helpful. Again, too, graphic displays like those in Figures 15.3 and 15.4 can function in interrelating and summarizing the terms covered.

To conclude this discussion of work with key vocabulary, some points made in earlier chapters are now reviewed.

Guidelines for Teachers: Work with New Words
1. Whenever possible, relate new terms to words already understood. If students know about mountains, discuss the new word *plateau* in relation to mountains.
2. Rapid lexical access (meaning is recalled promptly and effortlessly) is essential for comprehension. For that reason, time spent on vocabulary should concentrate on words connected with important content in order to ensure that they receive ample attention.

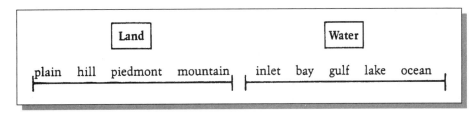

FIGURE 15.4   Scaling to Help Explain Meanings

3. Extra attention is required for unknown words whose referents are also unknown. This means that teaching *harbor* to students who have no idea what a harbor might be is more difficult and time-consuming than is teaching it to other students who are familiar with the referent but do not know the label. Whenever possible, pictures should be used when both the label and the referent are unknown. Fortunately, one prominent part of current content area textbooks is highly effective photographs, most of which are in color.
4. Key terms should be in students' sight vocabularies before a chapter is begun.

Activating or Adding to Relevant Knowledge

Because what is known affects what is comprehensible, making sure that students have the prerequisite knowledge for understanding a chapter is an important responsibility. Usually, at least part of what students know or, as the case may be, misunderstand, surfaces when new vocabulary is discussed. Attending to vocabulary typically allows, too, for activating, or adding to, world knowledge.

All this is illustrated with a chapter about Canada, in which some of the vocabulary expected to get attention is *Parliament, Senate, House of Commons, prime minister, Supreme Court,* and *province.* With students living in the United States, who, if they are using this textbook, have just finished an extensive treatment of their own country, promoting comprehension with analogy can be accomplished by discussing the words just named in relation to other words the students should know: *Congress, Senate, House of Representatives, president, Supreme Court,* and *state.*

Because the same students should also be familiar with the geography of the United States, attending to a large wall map of North America or to the smaller one in the textbook might be the next step in developing background information for the chapter about Canada. The fact that the two countries share more than an extensive border should be emphasized. Specifically, how the two share the Great Lakes, Niagara Falls, the St. Lawrence River, the Rocky and the Appalachian mountains, and the Great Plains can be shown.

The fact that some students have visited Canada or learned about it from books or television provides additional sources of information that should always be used.

Because the first part of the chapter highlights differences as well as similarities between Canada and the United States, activating previously acquired information can be accomplished with questions about the topics covered in the chapter as they pertain to the United States—for instance, "The First Settlers," "The First European Settlers," and "Effects of the American Revolutionary War."

Establishing Purposes for Reading

Because the first major section of the chapter deals with similarities and differences between the United States and Canada, purposes established for that section should have the same two-sided focus. One possible prereading assignment, therefore, might use teacher-made ditto sheets on which the topics covered appear as headings. The first topic is listed at the top of a sheet as shown:

Similarities and Differences
between the United States and Canada

The First Settlers

As the first section of the chapter about Canada is read, students write under each heading how the United States and Canada are alike or different. Enough blank space separates headings to allow for the writing. Responses are discussed during postreading activities.

EXTRA HELP FOR POOR READERS

The second major section of the chapter covers Canadian provinces. As is often the case with textbooks, the attention is needlessly detailed. One defensible decision, therefore, is to deal with the second major section as follows. Only students capable of comprehending the second part without help will be asked to read it. (The whole class heard the names of the provinces earlier when *province* was contrasted with *state.*) Directions to the better students will be to skim two worksheets provided by the publisher before the second section is begun. Completing the exercises requires matching the names of the provinces with described characteristics and with the occupations of the inhabitants. The completed worksheets will figure in postreading activities in order to make one important generalization: Where people live affects how they live.

The decision to assign the second part of the chapter only to students who can read it independently allows the teacher to spend time with the other students on the first part, judged to be more important. Depending on both the ability of the poorer readers and the composition and content of the text, help that enables these students to comprehend the first part, taking one topic at a time, might include (a) a review of one or more terms discussed earlier with the entire class, (b) further attention to a map or graph that helps clarify the content, and (c) instruction that focuses on any part of the text that may be problematic.

Following the extra assistance, the less able students will be asked to read silently about the initial topic covered—in this case, "The First Settlers." A volunteer then reviews the content orally. Anything that impeded comprehension is discussed or explained. Finally, the students write their own responses on the assignment sheet under the appropriate heading. Adhering to this procedure, the teacher has time in between topics to help the better readers with problems or questions that may arise as they work with the second part of the chapter.

RATIONALE FOR PROCEDURES USED

When the fifth-grade teacher read the chapter about Canada, she reached three conclusions. First, certain of her students are unable to comprehend the material without assistance. Second, the initial part of the chapter is useful because it allows for a review of information acquired earlier about the United States and, further, for a comparison of the United States with a close, important neighbor. The third conclusion is one this teacher often reaches about chapters in social studies textbooks: The detailed account of each Canadian province in the second part of the chapter is excessive and likely to be of little interest to fifth graders in the United States. Therefore, in addition to making sure that all the students understand *province* and can pronounce the names of the Canadian provinces, all she wants to stress with the detailed descriptions is the interrelationship between where people live and how they live.

It should go without saying that if the teacher in question had access to large, colorful pictures of various parts of Canada or to a videotape or to trade books that tell about Canada in relevant ways, they would be used to add both information and interest to the textbook's bland content. Current news about Canada that might be of interest would be discussed, too.

POSTREADING ACTIVITIES

As explained earlier, the objectives established for reading a chapter affect the nature of postreading activities. Because prereading objectives should divide between some that pertain to the content of the chapter (e.g., similarities and differences between the United States and Canada) and some that are intended to improve students' abilities to acquire information from text (e.g., understanding that a pronoun can refer to a chunk of text), postreading activities should be planned to cover both kinds of objectives. The reading side of the picture has been dealt with extensively in previous chapters; the focus now, therefore, is objectives having to do with content selected as being sufficiently important to merit serious attention.

Two points need to be made about such objectives. The first is that postreading activities should deal with important content in ways that synthesize any bits and pieces of information that have been acquired. As stressed earlier in the chapter, if all or certain students are asked to read about the characteristics of Canadian provinces, time spent on each province during postreading activities should not obscure the main reason for the reading: to help students understand that the geography of an area has a direct effect on how people live, earn a living, and spend their leisure time. If some able readers were asked to do additional research on the Eskimos living in Canada because the chapter said too little about them, their reports could highlight the same cause-effect relationship. The relationship will assume even greater meaning by having the students discuss how where they themselves live affects their lives.

To cite another illustration, if certain students were asked to prepare picture dictionaries for the geographical terms introduced in a chapter, having the opportunity to examine this material allows for bringing together the individual terms through comparisons and contrasts, plus specific examples supplied by students. At other times—depending on the nature of the chapter, in particular on the nature of the important content—materials like semantic maps, displays of captioned pictures, a filmstrip or videotape, an outline, or a time line may also serve to synthesize what has been learned.

The second major point to be made about postreading activities has to do with assessment. As is true of any assessment worthy of a teacher's time, what is learned during postreading activities should be used to make informed decisions for the next chapter to be studied. What were various students able or unable to do and learn? What do the students seem to enjoy? On the other hand, what is tedious? What could I as a teacher have done to facilitate even more the students' ability to comprehend the important content? These are some of the questions that should have answers once the plans for postreading activities have been executed.

To sum up, then, postreading activities should function in (a) integrating for students the various kinds of information they have acquired, and (b) allowing a teacher to see what might be done to make the study of the next chapter more productive and interesting. It goes without saying that postreading activities should also allow for clarifying any misunderstandings that students may have.

How another fifth-grade teacher chose to deal with postreading activities is described in Figure 15.5.

TEACHING STUDENTS HOW TO STUDY

Procedures teachers can use to help students learn from expository text have been discussed. Of no less importance are other procedures whose purpose is to teach students how to go about learning *on their own*. One possible procedure for realizing this goal is referred to as SQ3R (survey, question, read, recite, review).

Typically, SQ3R is covered in basal reader programs. The problem is that it is introduced in conjunction with one expository selection, is reviewed once or twice, and is never referred to again. An additional deficiency is that the help offered teachers to initiate the procedure is insufficient. The aim of the following sections, therefore, is to provide enough help so that teachers will know exactly how to go about introducing SQ3R. The assumption is that SQ3R will be used and reviewed more than once; otherwise, it does not have a chance to be of lasting help to students (6).

The description that follows should bring to mind two topics discussed in earlier chapters: comprehension monitoring and fix-up strategies.

We have just begun to study the New England colonies. Two chapters of the textbook deal with New England geography, town life, and home life. To help the students see the organization of the information in their textbook, I made a bulletin board. It included a map of the thirteen colonies, with the New England colonies all labeled in the same color. An arrow linked the New England colonies to a concept map showing the text's organization.

While introducing the topic, I used the bulletin board to guide our discussion. Because the students had already studied the Pilgrims in Plymouth, Massachusetts, I asked them to use what they knew about how the Pilgrims lived to make predictions about life in the New England colonies. (Making predictions is not something that students should be asked to do every time they read. In this case, however, I thought the students had enough prior knowledge to make fairly accurate predictions.)

The organization of the text permitted it to be divided into sections and studied separately. I assigned two or three students to study each topic. I told them they were to read their assigned section (approximately one page) and discuss with their partners what they thought the most important information might be. They were to list the central points and then select a way to present this information to the class.

I gave the students about 35 minutes to prepare their section of the material. The students did an excellent job carrying on discussions in their small groups and deciding what information represented the main ideas. The presentations to the whole class were a bit rough but, as it was the first time the students had been asked to do anything like this, I thought they did a fairly good job. I did, however, find it necessary to summarize each group's presentation, highlighting the most important points.

I believe there were several benefits from this type of activity. First, the students started out understanding the text's structure; as a result, they could see the relationship of each section to the whole. Second, the procedure divided a large piece of text into manageable units for study. Third, students were asked to take responsibility for one part of the information and to help their peers learn it. This encouraged involvement from every student as well as growth toward independence in learning from social studies textbooks.

FIGURE 15.5 Procedures Used by Another Teacher

A Strategy for Studying: SQ3R

Even though the outline of studying presented below focuses on a chapter, early use by students of SQ3R under a teacher's guidance ought to deal with something shorter than that—with a magazine article, for example. Participants in the initial uses of SQ3R ought to be as few in number as is possible.

Procedures for Studying Expository Text: SQ3R

Survey: Skim through the chapter to get the general gist of both the organization and the content. Attend only to headings and subheadings, captions, graphics, and summaries.

Question: Return to the start of the chapter. Taking one section at a time, turn the heading or subheading into a question. "How do people use magnets?" is the question to pose if the heading or subheading is "Use of Magnets." To keep the question in mind, write it.

Read: Read the section to answer the question.

Recite: Looking away from the book, recite the answer to yourself. If this is difficult or even impossible, reread the section, keeping the question in mind.

Review: After using the above procedures with each section, review all the questions to see whether they can still be answered. If any cannot, reread the section that is causing problems.

Having looked at the use of SQ3R from a student's perspective, let me conclude with reminders for teachers who may be working for the first time with this systematic way to study.

Reminders for Teachers

Survey: To foster the type of reading that a survey warrants, only a prescribed amount of time should be allowed. Otherwise, students are likely to read too slowly for the stated purpose. (This allows for giving explicit attention to the need for flexible reading that takes into account the relationship between [a] purpose for reading and [b] kind of reading done.)

Question: Typically, students require help when headings are first turned into questions. Provide examples to specify transformations. For instance:

Heading	Question
Provinces	What is a province?
Prairie Provinces	What are prairie provinces?
Problems of Rapid City Growth	What are the problems when a city grows fast?

Recite: When a group is involved, the recitation is done aloud by individuals. When students use SQ3R themselves, it is done silently.

Review: Comments about the recitation part of the pattern apply to the review as well.

Further reminders to teachers pertain equally to SQ3R and to reciprocal teaching. The first reminder is that students who are consistently successful in learning from text on their own have no need to spend time on either procedure. Some students in this group *may* profit from SQ3R by making their studying a little more systematic; others will not.

The second reminder is that less advanced readers cannot benefit from participating in either procedure if the text from which they are supposed to acquire information is routinely at a frustration-level of difficulty. The best procedures cannot achieve the impossible.

SUMMARY

Because of features like colorful, sophisticated formats and excellent photographs, current content area textbooks are much more attractive than their predecessors. Students in large numbers, nevertheless, continue to have trouble comprehending and remembering the information that these books present. Chapter 15 identified a number of reasons for the persistent problems. One is that the content is both inherently difficult and, in many instances, foreign to the lives and experiences of elementary school students. In spite of this, numerous topics are covered quickly, and thus superficially. Commonly, the decision to do this reflects the determination of publishers to include all the topics that are of interest to—or demanded by—potential customers, especially those residing in areas with large school populations.

The problem of difficult content covered quickly cannot be resolved when the text itself is flawed. Chapter 15 referred to less-than-helpful writing as being "inconsiderate." It also suggested some characteristics of such text: connections between related topics are not made clear; important details are mixed with trivial information; graphic aids do not always contribute to the clarification of descriptions and explanations.

Chapter 15 then acknowledged that in spite of the content in subject area textbooks, teachers do not always sort out the parts worth understanding and remembering. Teachers who do should use their own reading of a chapter to accomplish the following:

1. Identify the concepts and vocabulary that students must know if the important content is to be understood and retained.
2. Learn what the author assumed students already know about the selected content.
3. Identify features of the text that might be confusing (e.g., figurative uses of language) or that might be a roadblock to comprehension (e.g., pronouns with ambiguous referents).
4. See whether any graphic aid (e.g., map, diagram, graph) is included that students may not be able to interpret.

When the four objectives stated above are realized, teachers are in a position to establish other objectives—in this case, for the reading that students will soon do.

Because the structure of expository text is less familiar and also more complex than that of narrative discourse, Chapter 15 recommended previewing chapters. The recommendation lies in the fact that a preview gives students a bird's eye view of a body of text that allows them to see not only its parts but also how the parts fit together. How to do the previewing was described in detail. Other recommended pre-reading preparations are not new; they include attending to key vocabulary, providing essential background information, and establishing purposes for the reading. Because the vocabulary often includes semantically related words, how to highlight the relationships was illustrated.

Chapter 15 acknowledged that one major problem that teachers face when working with content area textbooks is the limited reading ability of some of their students. That is why Chapter 15 attended to ways to help poorer readers acquire information from text. The first procedure described was reciprocal teaching. Its use was recommended for shorter expository text, such as that found in basal readers and trade books. The special contribution of reciprocal teaching is the attention it gives to a portrayal of reading that correctly views it as a process of constructing meaning. The second procedure recommended, SQ3R, is for longer pieces of text, such as chapters in content area textbooks. SQ3R can be especially effective in helping students achieve more systematic study skills that can maximize the amount of information they acquire and remember.

REVIEW

1. Early in Chapter 15 you were urged to reread specified sections in Chapter 12 because they discuss topics that pertain to facilitating and teaching comprehension.
   a. Summarize the content in the section "Expository Text: Appropriate Topics for Instruction."
   b. Do the same for the section "Establishing Purposes for Reading Expository Text."
   c. What topics are named in the section "Comprehension Instruction: Additional Subject Matter" that are relevant when teachers want to improve students' ability to understand expository material?

2. Under the heading "facilitating comprehension," earlier chapters in this book discussed how teachers should prepare students for assigned reading. Chapter 15 highlighted preparations that teachers themselves must make before they are ready to work with a chapter in a content area textbook. Reread the section "A Teacher's Preparations" so that you can summarize how teachers can ready themselves.

3. To ready students for a chapter, Chapter 15 recommends previewing. Describe a preview. Explain its central purpose.

4. While discussing oral vocabularies, Chapter 11 stated that the most difficult words to explain are those whose names and referents are both unknown. Chapter 15 stated that such words are common in content area textbooks prepared for elementary school students. Skim through at least one such textbook (social studies, science, health) and list examples of words likely to be in this category. Be prepared to explain how you would go about clarifying the meaning of at least one word selected.

5. A major theme underlying Chapter 15 is that teachers need to help students learn how to acquire information from expository text. Both reciprocal teaching and SQ3R demonstrate to students how to read-to-learn. Describe each procedure.

6. Contrast your own study habits with recommendations that Chapter 15 makes for learning from text.

REFERENCES

1. Alvermann, Donna E. "Creating the Bridge to Content-Area Reading." In P. Winograd, K. Wixson, and M. Lipson (Eds.), *Improving Basal Reading Instruction.* New York, N. Y.: Teachers College Press, Columbia University, 1989.

2. Alvermann, Donna E. "The Discussion Web." *Reading Teacher* 45 (October, 1991), 92–99.

3. Armbruster, Bonnie B., and Anderson, Thomas H. "On Selecting Considerate Content Area Textbooks." *Remedial and Special Education* 9 (January/February, 1988), 47–52.

4. Beck, Isabel L.; McKeown, Margaret G.; Sinatra, Gale M.; and Loxterman, Jane A. "Revising Social Studies Text from a Text-Processing Perspective: Evidence of Improved Comprehensibility." *Reading Research Quarterly* 26 (1991, No. 3), 251–275.

5. Brown, Ann L.; Campione, Joseph C.; and Day, Jeanne. "Learning to Learn: On Training Students to Learn from Texts." *Educational Researcher* 10 (February, 1981), 14–21.

6. Call, Patricia E. "SQ3R + What I Know Sheet = One Strong Strategy." *Journal of Reading* 35 (September, 1991), 50–52.

7. Durkin, Dolores. "Comprehension Instruction in Current Basal Reader Series." Technical Report No. 521. Urbana: University of Illinois, Center for the Study of Reading, 1990.

8. Durkin, Dolores. "What Classroom Observations Reveal about Reading Comprehension Instruction." *Reading Research Quarterly* 14 (1978–79, No. 4), 481–533.

9. Englot-Mash, Christine. "Tying Together Reading Strategies." *Reading Teacher* 35 (October, 1991), 150–151.

10. Guzzetti, Barbara J. "The Reading Process in Content Fields: A Psycholinguistic Investigation." *American Educational Research Journal* 21 (Fall, 1984), 659–668.

11. Herman, Patricia A.; Anderson, Richard C.; Pearson, P. David; and Nagy, William E. "Incidental Acquisition of Word Meaning from Expositions with Varied Text Features." *Reading Research Quarterly* 22 (Summer, 1987), 263–284.

12. Ireland, Robert J. "Let's Throw Out Reading!" *Reading Teacher* 26 (March, 1973), 584–588.

13. Palincsar, Annemarie S., and Brown, Ann L. "Interactive Teaching to Promote Independent Learning from Text." *Reading Teacher* 39 (April, 1986), 771–777.

14. Palincsar, Annemarie S., and Brown, Ann L. "Reciprocal Teaching of Comprehension-Monitoring Activities." Technical Report No. 269. Urbana: University of Illinois, Center for the Study of Reading, 1983.

15. Pearson, P. David, and Gallagher, Margaret C. "The New Instruction of Reading Comprehension." Technical Report No. 297. Urbana: University of Illinois, Center for the Study of Reading, 1983.

16. Perry, William G. "Students' Use and Misuse of Reading Skills: A Report to the Faculty." *Harvard Educational Review* 29 (Summer, 1959), 193–200.

17. Peters, Charles W. "You Can't Have Authentic Assessment without Authentic Content." *Reading Teacher* 44 (April, 1991), 590–591.

18. Pressley, Michael; Goodchild, Fiona; Fleet, Joan; Zajchowski, Richard; and Evans, Ellis D. "The Challenges of Classroom Strategy Instruction." *Elementary School Journal* 89 (January, 1989), 304–342.

19. Tyson, Harriet, and Woodward, Arthur. "Why Students Aren't Learning Very Much from Textbooks." *Educational Leadership* 47 (November, 1989), 14–17.

Like other professional persons, teachers are charged with the responsibility of making knowledgeable decisions. In their case, critical decisions have to do with what to teach, to whom to teach it, how to teach it, and when to teach it. Deciding when instruction is *un*necessary is equally important.

The collection of decisions just referred to explains why many pages ago, the need for teachers to be introspective about their work was emphasized. The same decisions explain why it was said more than once that the most important question teachers can learn to ask of themselves

is, *Why* am I doing what I'm doing?

Because some decisions teachers make have to be dealt with before a school year begins, you may wonder why a concentrated look at decision making was left until now. The delay was deliberate and is based on the fact that all the professional decisions just referred to require the individual making them to be *knowledgeable*. On the assumption that previous chapters have initiated, or added to, your knowledge of literacy and literacy instruction, this is the appropriate time to focus on the decision-making role of teachers.

As acknowledged earlier, some teachers do

Making Professional Decisions

permit commercial materials to make decisions for them. This fact accounts for references in previous chapters to Teacher B. Most teachers, however, want to be professionals and know that, as such, their primary responsibility is to make decisions that result in students' realizing their full potential.

Achieving that goal calls for *diagnostic teaching*. This refers to the mental set of classroom teachers who routinely look for evidence both of what students know and of what they still have to learn. Inevitably—but sometimes as quickly as the first day of school—these teachers conclude that students in the same grade and classroom are not the same in what they know and can do. It is such differences that make teaching difficult and challenging for a Teacher A. At the same time, it is success in dealing with the differences that makes the efforts of a Teacher A so rewarding.

How classroom teachers with a diagnostic outlook go about identifying differences is one of the two major topics covered in the forthcoming chapter. How the same individuals organize their classes to accommodate differences is the second topic addressed.

Assessment and Classroom Organization

●●●●●●●

PREVIEW

In the past decade or so, criticisms directed at how schools foster literacy development have been atypical, not because they are more vocal than usual but because so many critics are themselves educators. One favorite target of this group is externally mandated standardized achievement tests.

From the perspective of *Teaching Them to Read,* the most serious shortcoming of such tests is their failure to provide teachers with data that are useful for making instructional decisions. That is why standardized tests are discussed but dismissed fairly quickly in Chapter 16. The same limitation explains why the subsequent treatment of assessment in the chapter dwells on how teachers *can* acquire information that helps them match instruction with students' needs.

My own observations in classrooms demonstrate repeatedly that special assessment efforts are not required to know that students in the same grade are not the same in their ability to read. Traditional efforts to accommodate differences—interclass organizations and intraclass ability groups—have also been the subject of much criticism. Why this is the case is explained in Chapter 16.

To show why it makes sense to have a combination of whole class and smaller group activities is the overall purpose of the sections in the forthcoming chapter concerned with classroom organization. To prepare for the recommendations made, the meanings of *instructional materials* and *assignments* are reviewed in some detail. This is done on the assumption that restricted definitions are one reason classroom organizations have tended to be rigid.

To learn in a general way how Chapter 16 goes about discussing both assessment and classroom organization, you are encouraged to examine the outline facing this page before you start your reading. As has been said more than once, a bird's eye view of a chapter facilitates both comprehension and retention of its contents. Reading the Summary is recommended, too.

●●●●●●●

IT WOULD BE DIFFICULT TO COUNT the number of times and the number of different ways *Teaching Them to Read* has made the following point: Teachers have the responsibility to do whatever is possible to match the instruction (and practice) they provide with students' needs.

As recently as Chapter 15, for instance, reciprocal teaching and SQ3R were portrayed as possible means for improving students' ability to comprehend expository text. They were recommended, however, only for students who need to improve that ability. Elsewhere the statement was made that it is just as questionable to teach what students already know as it is to withhold instruction from those who need it. Earlier, specifically in Chapter 2, it is said that what is taught should be not only something that students need but also something whose usefulness for reading is apparent.

All this can be summed up by saying that a pervasive goal of *Teaching Them to Read* is to maximize the amount of *individualized instruction* offered in classrooms. Because seeing "individual" in "individualized" may prompt the conclusion that the referent is tutoring, let me state immediately that the description "individualized" has nothing to do with the number of students taught. Whether the number is 1 or 100, individualized instruction is marked by the following characteristics: It

- Deals with what the student or students have not yet learned but are ready to learn.
- Is directed toward an objective that, if attained, advances existing abilities.
- Proceeds at a pace suitable for the individual(s) being instructed.

Obviously, achieving individualized instruction is not an overnight accomplishment. It can be said, in fact, that it is as difficult to achieve as it is important to achieve it. In spite of the difficulty, anything less than individualized instruction leads to boredom for able students even as it puts others at risk of not learning—in particular, students who must rely on the school to learn what they need to know.

What students need to learn and how it might be taught provided subject matter for previous chapters. Now, the focus is ways for teachers to become aware of what members of a class do and do not know so they can plan for whatever help is necessary to keep abilities advancing.

STANDARDIZED READING TESTS

Learning what students do and do not know, or what they can and cannot do, defines the assessment that is the concern of this final chapter. Three of its assumptions, therefore, can be stated as follows:

1. The reason for assessment is to improve instruction.
2. Assessment that does not increase individualized instruction is a waste of time.
3. Assessment is a daily occurrence, not a special event.

Even though the statements just made are difficult to dispute, a routine practice of schools is to administer standardized reading tests in spite of the fact that they do not yield information that is directly relevant for instruction. Because their use seems to be taken for granted, standardized tests cannot be omitted from the discussion. They are treated first to get them out of the way so that your attention can be drawn to assessment that can guide decisions for instruction.

Nature of Standardized Tests

Commonly, standardized reading tests evaluate word recognition (rather than identification), vocabulary knowledge, and comprehension. As the meaning of *standardized* suggests, procedures for their administration are described in detail in test manuals and are assumed to be followed carefully by whoever gives the tests. Usually, this is the classroom teacher. Often, procedures include time restrictions.

Standardized tests are also referred to as being *norm-referenced,* because they allow for comparisons of achieved scores with the distribution of scores attained on the same test by a large sample of students elsewhere. These students are called the *norming population.*

Since scoring is done by computers, that, too, is standardized. Computer scoring is less informative for teachers, however. When they scored the tests themselves, teachers had the opportunity to examine responses that, at times, offered help in identifying accomplishments and deficiencies. With computer scoring, schools can request from a publisher multiple kinds of scores—raw scores, percentile ranks, stanines, and grade equivalents, all of which are defined in manuals. Now, only grade-equivalent scores are discussed.

Grade-equivalent scores merit attention because they are sufficiently misleading that the International Reading Association passed a resolution in 1981 urging publishers to eliminate them (14). The resolution resulted from the widespread misconception that when a raw score is converted to a grade equivalent by using tables provided in test manuals, the converted score describes a student's ability in relation to materials. Stated specifically, the fact that prompted the resolution is that a grade-equivalent score, such as 5.2, does *not* signify that students achieving such a score are necessarily able to read fifth-grade material. To take grade-equivalent scores seriously, therefore, results more often than not in a mismatch between students' abilities and the materials they are expected to read.

Criticisms of Standardized Tests

Grade-equivalent scores are not the only feature of standardized tests that have generated criticism. How the tests evaluate comprehension abilities brought out the critics a long time ago. Before both traditional and more recent concerns are enumerated, let me review briefly how the tests evaluate comprehension.

The typical procedure is to have students read short passages, after which they select answers to questions about their content from a list of possible answers. Multiple-choice formats—something likely to persist because of computer scoring— have always prompted criticism if only because they promote and even reward guessing. Equally important, they make it impossible to know when a correct answer was chosen for the wrong reason or when a wrong answer was selected for a defensible reason.

In addition to concerns about multiple-choice formats, other complaints about the way comprehension is assessed have been common for some time. These criticisms are listed first, after which more recent concerns are identified.

Comprehension: Traditional Concerns

- Test passages are prepared and their difficulty assessed with readability formulas. (Why readability formulas are questionable is discussed in Chapter 13.)
- Some questions can be answered without reading the text.
- The meaning of scores is unclear when a test includes difficult questions for easy passages and easy questions for difficult passages.

Comprehension: More Recent Concerns

- What is important to teach is not tested. Bypassed, for instance, are comprehension-monitoring abilities and the selection of appropriate fix-up strategies.
- The pervasive influence of prior world knowledge on comprehension is not taken into account. (To avoid problems created by differences in world knowledge, authors of tests usually rely on questions that are answered directly in a passage. This confines the evaluation to literal comprehension. Test authors also use brief passages that cover a variety of topics on the erroneous assumption that the variety neutralizes the influence of differences in background information.)
- Comprehension scores reveal nearly nothing about the reasons for poor student performance. (Whether comprehension broke down at the word, sentence, or passage level is unknown. Nor can anything be determined about students' uses of text structure to help themselves understand, as the brevity of the passages precludes their having much of a structure. It should be noted that high scores present the same problem: They do little to explain the success.)

Reasons for the Use of Standardized Tests

With all their flaws, it is natural to wonder why administering standardized tests persists in being a taken-for-granted annual ritual. Habit cannot be ruled out when explanations are sought, nor can the fact that many people who happen to be taxpayers believe that standardized tests give correct information about student achievement. Because the believers commonly include school board members, parents, and highly vocal critics of the schools, the use of standardized tests is likely to continue.

Not to be overlooked is that funding agencies often require the administration of a standardized test for purposes of evaluation when they allot money for a special program. Even though school administrators are likely to defend the use of standardized tests as a means for making comparisons or for tracing growth over time, no one who is knowledgeable about the tests can ever claim that the results assist teachers intent on achieving individualized instruction. Authors of the tests, in fact, might be the first to say this is not their purpose. In fairness to the authors, it must also be stated that they should not be blamed either for the misuse or the overuse of their tests.

ASSESSMENT FOR INSTRUCTION: PROCEDURES RECOMMENDED EARLIER

Four kinds of assessment that *can* have a positive impact on instructional decisions are referred to in previous chapters. Each is now reviewed.

Assessment: One Component of Lessons

When Chapter 2 discusses planned, intentional instruction, it names objective, instruction, practice, and application as the four components of lessons. It says of the fourth component, "In a sense, application is the most important part of a lesson because it allows students to use in their reading what they have been helped to learn." It could also have been said at the time that, from a teacher's perspective, application allows for assessment—that is, for the opportunity to learn whether the objective of the lesson was realized so that it is now affecting how students read. As is true of any useful assessment, knowing that an objective was or was not realized ought to help determine where the instructional program goes next (19).

Assessment: Postreading Responsibilities

More than once, this book recommends a substitute for round robin reading: well-prepared, uninterrupted silent reading of appropriately difficult material. The prereading responsibilities that this kind of reading imposes on teachers are identified with references to new vocabulary, essential background information, and purposes for reading. What this substitute for round robin reading requires for postreading activities is considered, too. As Figure 16.1 shows—this is a less elaborate display than the one shown earlier in Figure 13.2—a teacher's postreading responsibilities are largely concerned with assessment. They, too, have the potential to increase individualized instruction.

Assessment: Monitoring Oral Reading

As early as Chapter 1, the portrayal of the reading process makes it clear that, in and of itself, a sizable sight vocabulary is insufficient to guarantee successful comprehension.

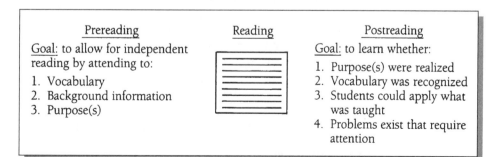

FIGURE 16.1 Postreading Concerns: Assessment Opportunities

Yet, not to know too many words in a piece of connected text puts comprehension out of reach. How students respond to words, therefore, is important for teachers with a diagnostic outlook to know.

Because teachers are not clairvoyant, Chapter 3 proposes oral reading as a means for learning about the strategies that students use with words they cannot identify immediately. Given its goal, another suggestion is to use unfamiliar material. Because using text that has not been seen before is likely to result in less-than-perfect reading, one further recommendation is to conduct the diagnosis as privately as circumstances permit.

To make sure that what is heard when a student reads aloud has significance for instructional decisions, a teacher should look not for mistakes per se but for possible patterns in responses. Stated differently, *how many* misidentifications occur is less important than is the *nature* of the misidentifications.

The significance of type of response has been effectively underscored by John Pikulski (16). Discussing how two children read the sentence *The boy is sitting in a chair waiting for his mother,* he notes:

> In the first [case]…substitutions and insertions did very little to change the meaning of the sentence. He made four scoreable errors. The second child read in a word by-word fashion, needed examiner help with one word and substituted *champ* for *chair* and *water* for *waits.* A very substantial amount of difficulty with word recognition is suggested. Yet, the first child made four scoreable errors and the second made only three. (p. 146)

For teachers interested in monitoring a student's oral reading in order to learn what needs to be fixed with the help of instruction, questions like those in Figure 16.2 are relevant. Which are most relevant depends on where students are in the development of their sight vocabularies and in their efforts to use relevant cues to recognize unfamiliar words.

It would be remiss not to refer in this section to work done by Kenneth Goodman in the early 1960s (10, 11). At the time, Goodman and his colleagues were attempting to learn about the mental processes that take place during reading by analyzing individuals' oral reading of unfamiliar text. For the analyses, each response to a word was catalogued as "expected" (says the word on the page) or "observed" (what the reader said). In turn, observed responses were referred to as *miscues,* which, when analyzed, were said by Goodman to be "windows on the reading process." (The term *error* was avoided, as that has only negative connotations. A *miscue,* on the other hand, may be positive, as when a reader responds to *lad* with "boy," or negative, as when a word like *tried* is called "tired.") Emphasized in Goodman's work is a theme that has been reinforced many times in this book: Reading is not naming words but is, instead, a sense-making process achieved only when readers use both the words on the page and what they know in order to construct something meaningful.

Assessment: Everyday Observations

Goodman's frequent references to teachers as "kid watchers" (12) allow for reviewing the fourth kind of assessment recommended in earlier chapters. This can be

Monitoring Oral Reading to Establish Instructional Needs

Are high-frequency words automatically identified?

Are all available cues being used with unfamiliar words?

Do misidentifications follow any pattern? For instance, are contextual cues overused or, to the contrary, does the use of spelling dominate?

Exactly how are graphophonic cues used? For example, is the sequence of sounds commonly rearranged (*felt* read as "left")? Are sounds added (*pet* read as "pest")? Are sounds commonly omitted (*cart* read as "car")? Is equal attention given to initial, medial, and final sounds?

What is the student's strategy for working out long, seemingly complicated words? Or does a strategy even exist?

What is done with unknown inflected and derived words? Is any attempt made to sort out the root? Do altered spellings of roots cause problems? Are prefixes and suffixes recognized as such?

Are unfamiliar words worked on aggressively and persistently, or is there a tendency either to omit them or to depend on outside help?

FIGURE 16.2 Monitoring Oral Reading

thought of as *naturalistic* assessment because it occurs naturally in the course of everyday classroom events. More recently, it has been referred to by some as *situated* assessment (4) in order to emphasize the importance of carrying out assessment not with externally mandated tests but in the situation in which learning was to have taken place.

Naturalistic assessment is recognized a few pages back in the discussion of diagnostic teaching, said to refer to "the mental set of classroom teachers who routinely look for evidence both of what students know and of what they still need to learn." Naturalistic assessment is also discussed as early as Chapter 2, when "teachable moments" received attention. Subsequently, additional examples of such moments showed up in other chapters. You may recall:

- Kindergartners who responded, "Five" after a teacher pointed to *you* and *me* and asked, How many words did I just write?"
- The student who pronounced *touch* in a way that made it rhyme with "couch."
- Responses like "under" and "uncle" when a teacher was discussing the prefix *un-* and asked for additional examples of words with this prefix.
- The eagerly offered definition, "Somebody who is sick in the hospital" when a teacher asked about the meaning of "patient" in the sentence, *She was a very patient person.*

An example of naturalistic assessment not referred to earlier is described below because it depicts not only assessment of children's responses but also a teacher who engages in *self*-assessment. In this instance, she was introducing an instructional group to a generalization about vowel sounds: When there is one vowel in a word and it is not the last letter, it usually stands for its short sound. Correctly, the teacher used words that the group could read to help explain the new generalization:

> and
> ask
> bad
> can

Later, to summarize the lesson, the teacher inquired, "Can someone tell us what you learned today?" Someone did, observing, "When a word has one vowel, it'll be an *a.*" Recognizing the problem, the teacher started the lesson again, this time using *at, end, big, not, cub,* and *ten* for examples. Now the objective of the instruction was quickly realized.

The lesson about a vowel sound was chosen to conclude the illustrations of naturalistic assessment because it makes an important point: Assessment should serve to improve teaching as well as to evaluate learning.

ASSESSMENT FOR INSTRUCTION: TEACHER-DEVISED TESTS

Two more ways to identify both achievements and problems are described, the first of which is called "teacher-devised tests." This description refers to preplanned efforts to learn about instructional needs. All the examples of this assessment that follow have something to do with a basal reader series; and, as you will see, the illustrations reveal still more about the stance of a Teacher A toward these materials.

Guidelines for Teacher-Devised Tests

Whenever teachers plan assessment, two guidelines need to be kept in mind. The first is to restrict the focus to something specific. This suggests that a suitable focus is the ability to understand similes signaled by the *as...as* construction. It further suggests that the ability to understand figurative language is too broad.

The second guideline also pertains to the focus of the assessment. It is the reminder to evaluate only what can soon be taught or reviewed, should it turn out that the assessment reveals a need for help. Said differently, having diagnostic information about many topics is not the goal of assessment that is relevant for instruction. A little assessment followed by teaching, followed by more assessment followed by teaching—this sequence permits assessment to have a positive impact on instructional programs.

Illustrations of Teacher-Devised Tests

The four descriptions of teacher-devised assessment that follow show the close connection that should exist between the objective of the evaluation and how it is done. The connection thus suggests that "*Why* am I doing what I'm doing?" is as important to ask when assessment is planned as it is when instructional decisions are made. You can see, too, that the teachers' concerns are not only for shortcomings but also for abilities. The two-sided focus is necessary, as information about both is needed for planning individualized instruction. Also underlying these teachers' efforts is an interest in reducing the time spent on basal materials, which, in turn, allows more time for reading trade books.

Ms. White. Over a period of five years, Ms. White taught both third and fourth grades. Even though she believed that the basal materials for these grades give excessive, even tedious, attention to dictionary skills, it was only now that she felt sufficiently confident to omit nonessentials. To pinpoint what was unnecessary, she conducted brief, individual tests close to the start of the year—she was now teaching third grade—in which the objective was to learn who was unable to use a dictionary sufficiently quickly. Five words made up the test. Results indicated that only two children had trouble; consequently, they became a special-needs group, and it was only to them that instruction and assignments with location skills would be given. Meanwhile, everyone worked on using a pronunciation key in dictionaries and on choosing meanings that fit particular contexts. Sentences taken from science and social studies textbooks were used to make explicit the connection between the instruction and assigned reading.

Approximately one month later, another test was given. This time the purposes were, first, to see whether the students could pronounce unfamiliar words with the help of pronunciation keys and, second, to learn whether additional help with selecting appropriate meanings was needed. For this test, words were in sentences. One result of the testing was the establishment of a special-needs group composed of 13 students who will receive further help with choosing relevant definitions. The other 16 will get no further dictionary assignments even though the basal reader workbook continues to offer dictionary exercises for what seems like an endless amount of time.

Ms. Paul. This teacher has 26 bright second graders, all of whom read well. Like other teachers in her building, Ms. Paul is obliged to use basal readers and workbooks written for the grade she teaches. Once children complete the materials, anything else is permissible.

To make the best of what she believes is policy that stands in the way of her able readers' getting still better, Ms. Paul started the year determined to eliminate any manual segment, workbook page, or practice sheet that deals with what her students know or with what is not essential for reading. Falling into the latter category are procedures for contractions, specifically, having children write the words for which contractions substitute and having them note the letters that an apostrophe replaces. Aware that all that is required for reading is the ability to identify contractions and to understand their meanings, Ms. Paul decided to begin by eliminating nonessentials for contractions.

She first listed all the contractions that were reviewed or introduced in the basal series she has to use and then composed sentences that included them all. For the testing, each child read the sentences aloud, which permitted Ms. Paul to learn whether they were pronouncing the contractions correctly. Following that, the children told in their own words what each sentence meant. This procedure was used because the meaning of the sentence depended on knowing the meaning of the contraction. In the end, the test confirmed the earlier conclusion: Time did not have to go to contractions because the children knew them as well as their teacher.

Mr. Oliver.   This teacher has a third-grade class in which 11 students are mature in their behavior and proficient in their reading. These two characteristics encouraged Mr. Oliver to give them numerous written assignments at the start of the year. In fact, their time was consumed by basal selections, workbook pages and worksheets, and written reports. Facing up to the monotony of it all, Mr. Oliver decided in November to collect diagnostic information so that suitable instruction could begin.

He started by meeting individually with students to learn what each one does with unknown words. Because the specific goal was to learn what is done when only spellings are available to help, he compiled a list of 20 words, some likely to cause problems. This was mentioned at the start of each session, as was the reason for having it: to learn whether further help with decoding is necessary.

In the initial conferences, only root words were used; for the second, derived and inflected words were listed. By asking the students to do a think aloud whenever they came to a word they were unable to name immediately, Mr. Oliver concluded with a number of notations that pinpointed problems.

In the end, only one student was so proficient as to require no further help. Mr. Oliver offered her the chance to read self-selected trade books while the other students had advanced decoding instruction; however, she preferred to stay with the group. As it turned out, her observations about difficult words (especially derived and inflected words) made useful contributions to the fast-paced work of these advanced students.

Ms. Antley.   This second-grade teacher is just starting the second month of a new year. Earlier, while listening to certain children read in order to organize instructional groups, she noticed that two boys, both spending a second year in second grade, seemed content to say anything whenever they encountered a word they were unable to identify. It was as if they did not realize that reading is a sense-making process. To learn more, Ms. Antley met with each boy separately to see what he knew about contextual cues. With that objective in mind, she had the boys read aloud ten sentences with deleted words—for instance, "When you come in, _____ the door." Any word was accepted for a blank as long as it made sense.

Results of the brief conferences showed the need for attention to the semantic aspects of reading as well as to the use of contextual cues for help with word recognition. Therefore, Ms. Antley plans to concentrate at first on text that she will read to the boys, much like the kindergarten teachers did who are referred to in Chapter 7. Later, written sentences similar to the ones that figured in the original diagnosis will be used. Still later, Ms. Antley plans to learn how the two boys use contextual cues plus minimal graphophonic cues, because they know most letter-sound relationships. Therefore, in a subsequent diagnostic session, she will use written sentences such as *When you come in, cl_____ the door.*

ASSESSMENT FOR INSTRUCTION: PORTFOLIOS

The last type of assessment considered is called *portfolio* assessment. Although interest in portfolio assessment is relatively new, some teachers—especially at the primary levels—have always kept samples of children's work over the course of a year. Their objective, however, had less to do with assessment than with giving children an opportunity to see evidence of progress.

In recent years, attention has turned to the value of keeping samples of work at all grade levels as a meaningful way to assess progress and identify instructional needs (15, 20, 22). Supporters of portfolio assessment are especially critical of the contrived ways in which commercially produced tests evaluate achievement. At the same time, they are enthusiastic about making assessment more authentic—that is, more directly concerned with what we want students to be able to do. The appeal of portfolios, in fact, lies in the close connection between what teachers are attempting to accomplish and what is assessed.

Taken seriously, portfolio assessment raises many questions for reflective teachers: Exactly what should be put into a portfolio? Should students as well as teachers decide what to keep? Should the contents of a portfolio be seen only by a teacher and the student or, for instance, should they be part of the information shared during parent conferences? What is the connection between the contents of portfolios and the report cards that most teachers are expected to use?

For me, the critical question is the one that has teachers ask, *Why* am I thinking about using portfolios? Jerry Johns's advice reflects the same posture:

> One of the real dangers of using portfolios is that they can become an unfocused collection of many pieces of information. Such an unorganized accumulation of bits and pieces will reduce their usefulness. To promote usefulness, you will need to think carefully about the purposes of the portfolio as they apply to your curricular and instructional priorities. (15, p. 5)

Because the usefulness of students' seeing evidence of their progress is indisputable, teachers who bypass portfolios as instruments for assessment should not overlook the value of keeping samples of work for a period of time that need not be year-long. With young children, for example, the chance to see their writing advance from drawings to drawings with brief captions, and from there to writing done at first with invented spelling and then with a more frequent use of standard spelling is a highly motivating experience. Older students feel the same pride and satisfaction when they have the opportunity to see their responses to literature evolve from brief summary statements of a story to prose that gets at the heart of the tale. The point, then, is that we all benefit from at least an occasional pat on the back.

ACCOMMODATING DIFFERENCES: TRADITIONAL PRACTICES IN CLASSROOM ORGANIZATION

Now that ways to learn about students' abilities have been examined, it is time to acknowledge the major reason individualized instruction is no mean accomplishment: *differences* in abilities among members of a class.

Over the years, two procedures have been used routinely as a way of coping with differences. Each is reviewed; each also is critiqued in order to explain why criticisms of taken-for-granted practices have been mounting.

Ability Groups within a Classroom

Until recently, it was fairly safe to assume that observers in grade 1 through 3 classrooms found teachers using ability-based groups during the time allocated to reading. The fact that some students were reading above grade level, that others read below grade level, and that still others were at grade level is the reason three such groups have been common.

Over time, practices that came to be associated with the use of ability groups have elicited criticism (1, 2, 13, 18). It is important to keep in mind that the complaints, some of which are enumerated below, *are not confined to teachers who use ability groups.*

1. In order to keep some students occupied while the teacher works with others, indefensible kinds and amounts of busy work are assigned. Almost always, the assignments are workbook and workbook-like pages.
2. Although some silent reading is done by high ability groups, round robin reading is used routinely with poorer readers. As a consequence, the latter do much less reading for two reasons. First, the reading is oral. Second, many interruptions occur in order to deal with unfamiliar or forgotten words in text for which ample prereading preparations were not made. Remedies offered by the teacher for problems with words focus on spellings, as the number of troublesome words obscures the help that contextual cues provide. The result of all this is that the lowest achievers fail to develop a concept of reading that equates it with a meaning-making process.
3. Once students are assigned to an ability-based group, they remain there for the rest of the year.
4. Ability groups undermine the self-esteem of members of the lowest group.

Before ways to eliminate the *need* for all these complaints are discussed, an interclass organization is considered briefly.

Ability Groups across Classrooms

Beyond the primary level, schools have often attempted to deal with differences in ability with an interclass organization. Sometimes referred to as *tracking,* this way of proceeding has ability groups that cut across classrooms and, very often, also across grade levels. In some schools, for instance, the best fourth-grade readers go to one teacher, the next best to another, and so forth. Elsewhere, a teacher might find herself responsible for a supposedly homogeneous group composed of fourth, fifth, and sixth graders.

It should be noted that interclass organizations have not been fostered by data that show they are effective in advancing achievement (13). Rather, the main impetus for their use is that as grade level increases, the range in students' abilities also increases. This means that individuals in the same grade may differ substantially in what they can read.

As it happens, some complaints leveled at ability-based groups in self-contained classrooms apply equally to interclass organizations. For example, students assigned to the lowest group stand out even more as they travel from homerooms to their reading teacher. Other complaints are more unique—for instance, the common reliance on whole-class teaching, used on the highly erroneous assumption that the group is now homogeneous. Repeatedly, observers find not only obvious differences in such groups but also restless, inattentive students who are as inundated with exercise sheets as are other students in self-contained classrooms (6, 7, 8).

ONE STEP FORWARD: BETTER ASSIGNMENTS

Although documentation is lacking, it seems correct to conclude that criticism of workbook and workbooklike assignments has been as influential as any other criticism in encouraging educators to rethink how schools should accommodate differences in ability. Where documentation is *not* missing is in the area of teachers' concerns about the inevitability of behavior problems, thus of losing control, unless students *are* occupied with something (5). With this fact in the foreground, it makes sense here to begin thinking about better ways to deal with ability differences by reviewing assignments described in previous chapters. The goal of the present discussion, then, is to bring back into focus a sample of earlier recommendations for assignments on the assumption that teachers who are aware of possibilities other than exercise sheets are freer to expand and vary the procedures they use as they try to match instruction with abilities. Said differently, when students are *profitably* occupied, teachers have an opportunity to spend time with individuals and small groups as a way of maximizing the amount of individualized instruction provided.

Many suggestions made earlier for assignments were linked to procedures to establish purposes for reading. For that reason, the samples of possible assignments start with some connected with purposes.

Stories

- The construction of a time line showing the chronological order in which events unfold is helpful when a plot includes flashbacks.
- First-person narration allows for rewriting a story, now told by a character different from the one that the author chose.
- The components of a story can be made apparent with a story map.

Exposition

- Statements and misstatements about a topic are listed, to which students respond with "true" or "false." Once the selection is read, students reconsider the statements in order to see whether earlier judgments need to be changed.
- What students think they know about a topic and what they want to learn from their reading are listed. Afterward, students write what they actually learned in the selection.
- Students list from a selection samples of text that relate facts and other samples that communicate opinions.

Because differences in students' abilities are noticeable as early as the first week of kindergarten, teachers of young children also need to know how to keep some profitably occupied in order to be free to work with groups or individuals. A few possibilities described in previous chapters are listed next.

Young Literates

- At the time they are learning to print their names, children draw self-portraits and sign their signatures.
- Using letters, children design a cover for a three-page Alphabet Book.
- After working with a graph for fruits, children draw and label a picture of their favorite fruit.
- Activities for a rainy day are suggested by the children and written by the teacher. Each child then illustrates one activity, labeling it with words copied from the board.
- Children reassemble words that tell a rhyme, such as "Jack and Jill."
- Children make a book by illustrating captions taken from a rhyme, such as "One, Two, Buckle My Shoe."

The references to nursery rhymes provide a transition to another sample of helpful assignments, all of which have to do with trade books.

Trade Books

- Older students make preparations to read a story to kindergartners.
- Students illustrate the sequence of events in a story. The pictures are pulled through a shoebox television set while the artists relate the tale to others.
- Students record themselves reading. Later, the recording allows for comparing their reading with that of a professional, or for evaluating their reading with help from a checklist.
- Wordless picture books offer prompts for writing text to accompany the illustrations.
- Students read the histories of words, taking notes on the most interesting ones so they can report their findings to classmates.
- The different versions of fables, folktales, and legends that exist permit written comparisons that cover both illustrations and text.

As early as Chapter 1, reading is equated with comprehending. It is appropriate, therefore, to conclude the reminders about possible assignments with two that Chapter 1 suggests.

Inferential Comprehension

- Using brief pieces of text that evoke mental imagery, students draw pictures whose content can serve to differentiate between literal and inferential comprehension. The same activity is useful in making explicit the sources from which questions are answered (17).
- Students write internal texts for brief samples of external texts in order to show what authors are implying.

ANOTHER STEP FORWARD: VARIETY IN MATERIALS

When teachers enlarge not only their notions of assignment but also their definitions of instructional material, more possibilities for matching instructional programs with students' abilities come into view. A more encompassing conception of materials, it should be noted, does not necessarily eliminate the use of a basal series. However, the new perspective does assign it less importance than has been customary, for now it shares the stage with a large number of other materials.

At the forefront of the additions should be trade books, some of which make up the part of the classroom library that is more or less permanent. As Chapter 14 illustrates, other trade books complement basal reader selections. Still others make their way into a classroom because they are by an author who has become a favorite with students or because they deal with thematic units that function not only in integrating reading and writing but also in providing ongoing activities. This latter contribution is important because, combined with briefer assignments, long-term projects help with classroom management.

What, you might be wondering, are the origins of units? In one room, "Opposites" was suggested by Tana Hoban's *Push, Pull, Empty, Full* (Macmillan, 1972), in which large photographs and brief captions deal effectively with all sorts of opposites. In another case, reading *A House Is a House for Me* by Mary Ann Hoberman (Viking, 1977) surprised both teacher and students when they counted the 25 different animal homes referred to in the book. This turned the theme "Houses" into a highly productive unit. Aesop's Fables, Imagination, Sea Animals, Weather, Histories of Words, and Mythology—these are other themes that worked well elsewhere because the teachers using them had thought through the major concepts and ideas to be developed with the help of the themes. (Again, the significance of *"Why* am I doing what I'm doing?" is reinforced.)

Not to be overlooked here is environmental text like that discussed in Chapter 11. The value of newspaper headlines is emphasized, too. Because the individuals responsible for writing headlines for the sports section of newspapers appear to work hard to avoid the use of *win* and *lose,* students in one observed classroom were able to add many words to their oral vocabularies through interesting discussions and displays of synonyms for *win* and *lose* found in headlines heralding the results of sports events. Synonyms for *win* included *overcome, conquer, wallop,* and *hammer.* Losers were *crushed, paralyzed, overpowered, demolished,* and *battered.*

How one fifth-grade teacher used a newspaper for a different purpose is described in Figure 16.3.

During the Thanksgiving season, students encounter many sources of information about the Pilgrims. Because my class just read a chapter on the Pilgrims of Plymouth in their social studies textbook, I thought it might be interesting to have them compare and contrast information from a different source. To do that, I read a fairly lengthy article in a local newspaper. Afterward, the students were eager to discuss the contents—in particular, the new information provided. One interesting point made was that the Pilgrims did not wear wedding bands because they considered marriage to be a legal commitment, not a religious one. The students were also quick to notice that the newspaper article described the Pilgrims in a less rigid way than the textbook. According to the article, for example, the Pilgrims drank beer and sang and danced. (This allowed me to insert the reminder that newspapers often highlight content like this even when it may not be based on verified facts.)

Everyone seemed interested in the article, for clearly it was much livelier than the textbook. The textbook gave only main ideas and a broad overview, whereas the newspaper included the odd and the humorous details that both children and adults find appealing and memorable.

It was interesting to note that, even though the newspaper article was written in a much less simplistic style than is used in the social studies book, the students appeared to have no trouble comprehending it. The contents may be the reason.

Were I to do this again, would I do it the same way? Probably not even though everything went fairly well. Today, for example, I relied on a whole-class discussion. As so often happens with this group, some students were overshadowed by more vocal classmates. Some, perhaps, needed more time to form their ideas. With those possibilities existing, next time I might again read the article, after which the class could meet in small groups to think about the content as a way of preparing for a discussion. Because the article was in a local paper, it would have been easy to find extra copies. That way, each group could have a copy, should members feel the need to check or reread some part of the material.

Based on past experiences, this effort to do better may *not* turn out to be better. But at least I'll have the satisfaction of knowing I tried.

FIGURE 16.3   A Reflective Fifth-Grade Teacher

STILL ANOTHER STEP FORWARD: VARIETY IN CLASSROOM ORGANIZATION

The idea that teachers must use either ability-based groups *or* whole-class teaching does not reflect the ingredient that facilitates offering individualized instruction in classrooms: *meaningful* variety. Support for variety should come as no surprise to anyone familiar with previous chapters. In almost all, references are made to teachers' working with an entire class, to others who were teaching a group smaller than the class—hereafter referred to as *subgroup*—and to other teachers who were with an individual. Then, as recently as the present chapter, you read about Ms. White, who used both whole-class and special-needs instruction in her efforts to eliminate parts of the basal series she was using. At the same time, you read about Mr. Oliver, whose temporary special-needs group included 11 advanced readers, and also about Ms. Antley's intentions to work with 2 second graders who had not yet grasped the essence of what it means to read.

ORGANIZING CLASSES: VARIABLES TO CONSIDER

How and when whole-class, subgroup, and individual instruction ought to be used is affected by a host of variables, not the least of which is the teacher.

Teachers

If a knowledgeable, caring teacher had no more than about eight students who were similar in their ability to read, providing appropriate and successful instruction would be fairly easy. Differences in interests could also be accommodated without too much trouble. As it is, the larger number of students who make up a class, coupled with what may be great variation in reading ability, make individualized instruction difficult but, as superior teachers demonstrate, not impossible to achieve. It seems appropriate to compare these successful teachers to a symphony orchestra conductor who can synthesize into a meaningful, harmonious whole a large number of different musicians and instruments.

Admittedly, I know little about the intricacies of successful orchestration, but I do understand from experience that organizing students in ways that facilitate offering appropriate instruction to everyone is no small feat. A speaker at a conference once expressed my own feelings when he said, "Effective organization is the end product of trial and error." Inherent in his observation is that getting students, materials, and time organized in ways that result in an effective instructional program is an evolutionary process that gradually progresses as decisions are made and remade throughout the whole of a year.

The decision that has an impact on many others is not always made consciously, which means it often escapes reexamination. I refer to the perceptions that teachers have of their responsibilities. Why this affects other decisions can be explained by contrasting two teachers.

The first teacher views her responsibilities as moving students through a basal reader, the workbook that goes with it, and whatever exercise sheets the representative of the basal publisher succeeded in selling. With such a perception, this teacher uses the time assigned to reading in a way that differs markedly from the second teacher, whose priorities are identified in the following statement:

> The major goal of my instructional program is to develop each child's potential for comprehending print via silent reading. To attain it, instruction and practice must focus on whatever it is that will advance each child's abilities. To keep children involved and trying, every effort must be made to help them see the relevance of reading in their own lives. The importance of motivation for learning also makes it necessary to have materials that match not only their abilities but also their interests. In the end, I evaluate myself not just on the basis of how well the children read but also by the frequency with which they *do* read.

Just as teachers' priorities are undeniably significant for how classrooms are run, so, too, are their personalities. On this point, Carl Wallen offers sound advice to teachers:

> You should be frank about the fact that the best degree of structure is largely how you define it. Some teachers cannot tolerate much movement in the classroom. They feel distinctly uncomfortable when a child moves around the room in an apparent search for adventure. On the other hand, some teachers feel the same degree of discomfort if children are too quiet and too still. They enjoy movement and the ambiguity that characterizes it. Because you must live comfortably in the classroom, you should...allow for as much structure as you and the children find comfortable. (21, p. 475)

The differences in teachers that have been referred to, joined with other differences of equal significance (e.g., knowledge about reading, instruction, and materials), make it impossible to offer recommendations for organizing a class that are acceptable to all teachers. A suggestion that is viewed by some as beyond their reach or even as unrealistic might be scorned by other teachers as being excessively modest or too conservative. In spite of the complexity caused by differences, it is still hoped that the following sections can help some teachers and prospective teachers either immediately or eventually.

Students

Just as variation in teachers affect how instructional programs are organized and executed, so, too, should differences among students have their effects. Ordinarily, differences in reading ability among members of a class require working with less than the whole group. Even if differences were small, the difficulty of getting and keeping the attention of a large number of students cannot be overlooked.

Nonetheless, there *are* times when teachers can spend time with an entire class in ways that are profitable. To support this contention, the first section that follows describes circumstances that make it appropriate to involve everyone in an activity. After that, working with individuals is considered, but only briefly because it is difficult for classroom teachers to find time to spend with one student. The treatment of subgroups, which comes next, is longer. It should also be pointed out that even though working with the whole class, with individuals, and with subgroups is each discussed separately, spending time in all three ways is characteristic of accomplished teachers.

WORKING WITH THE WHOLE CLASS

Given the demonstrable fact that teachers who instruct—or try to instruct—an entire class will almost always end up facing inattentive, restless, and even noisy individuals (3, 9), the recommendation is to confine whole-class activities to those likely to be of interest to all students. The teacher who, in Figure 16.3, describes the use of a newspaper article about the Pilgrims illustrated one such activity—although she was sensitive to the fact that whole-class discussions keep some students from participating. Even so, the growing number of teachers at all levels who are now reading to their classes on a daily basis are being rewarded with attentive audiences and excellent reactions.

Without diminishing the pleasure or the interesting information that a book provided, I have also seen teachers who used their read-alouds afterward to discuss with the whole class some small or, as the case may be, some encompassing feature of the book. Authors gifted in evoking mental imagery, for example, allow for talking about sentences like "The wind raked his hair." At another time, an author's clever, humorous use of hyperbole may merit time and also be interesting to everyone. I have also seen teachers who introduced a class to a new genre with daily read-alouds. In another instance, the thematic unit "Aesop's Fables" was introduced to everyone with a videotape for which the teacher provided helpful pre-viewing preparations.

Whole-class instruction is something I myself used not too long ago. In order to provide one-on-one reading for two groups of kindergartners, arrangements were made with two fifth-grade teachers for each of their students to read to a kindergartner weekly. The original plan was to have the teachers provide instruction (or review) about story grammar as a way of helping the fifth graders, first, to know what is important to discuss with the kindergartners and, second, to choose good stories rather than text that merely covers a series of events. (The school librarian agreed to help with selections and to model how to read to young children.) After learning that neither fifth-grade teacher was familiar with story grammar, I did the teaching myself with the help of "The Coconut Game," a story map (see Figure 12.9), and a chalkboard. From what I could tell, all 39 fifth-graders were attentive and certainly eager to begin reading to the younger children. They may have also learned something about stories that will help with the more advanced text they are expected to read in their own classrooms.

When the text is selected with care, choral reading, which is discussed in Chapter 3, is another activity that succeeds with an entire class. Directed by a teacher at first, choral reading preparations can later be undertaken by small groups who, on their own, take the time to get ready to read to the rest of the class. This kind of grouping allows students with different abilities to work together when teachers make sure that the most advanced and the least advanced readers are not placed in the same group.

WORKING WITH INDIVIDUALS

Working with one student seems so inherently valuable and desirable that neither an explanation nor a defense of this use of a teacher's time seems necessary. What should not escape attention, however, are the reasons that motivate individual assistance. This point needs to be made because classroom observations indicate that some teachers are required to help individuals as a consequence of giving the same assignments to the whole class even when the ability of its members to do them is clearly unequal (8). The moral of the story? Private lessons are desirable when the instruction that a student requires deviates substantially from what other students need. Commonly, the requirement will be easier instruction.

Teachers often identify the need for easier instruction or for additional explanations with individual diagnosis that can be done quickly. This is illustrated earlier in the chapter in the section dealing with teacher-devised tests. Another noteworthy example of individual assessment is described when the use of contextual cues for recognizing words is the focus (see Figure 7.2).

Many teachers also find time to meet with individuals when a program allows for self-selected reading. As Chapter 14 points out, these are opportunities for a student to share what is presently being read and for the teacher to make suggestions for future selections.

WORKING WITH SUBGROUPS

The differences in reading ability that are apparent in every classroom call for the use of subgroups some of the time. This is not to say that organizing members of a class on the basis of ability results in homogeneous groups; students and reading are both too complex to expect such a consequence. Nonetheless, smaller groups do give knowledgeable, conscientious teachers opportunities to provide appropriately differentiated instruction.

Groups based on ability can be categorized as general-achievement subgroups and special-needs subgroups. Each is discussed.

General-Achievement Subgroups

Earlier references to well-prepared, uninterrupted silent reading of appropriately difficult material assumed that a general-achievement subgroup was doing the reading. That is, the students were about the same in their ability to read. One further assumption was the likelihood—not the inevitability—that the appropriately difficult material was in a basal reader not only because basal series are still used with considerable frequency but also because the readers are organized on the basis of general-achievement levels.

When teachers use general-achievement subgroups merely as one component in their organizational scheme and, in addition, consider membership in a group as something that may change, large amounts of time need not be spent at the beginning of the year deciding who goes where. This is not an endorsement of casual decisions; rather, the point is that decisions should not consume so much time that the temptation exists to keep all groups intact until the school year ends. The recommendation, then, is to be thoughtful about decisions but not compulsively so. Teachers, for example, who use information about basal readers already completed in order to form general-achievement groups initially need not feel careless or unprofessional. Instead, the procedure should be viewed as a way to get instruction underway as soon as possible at the beginning of a new year.

Special-Needs Subgroups

Observant teachers learn fairly quickly that members of a general-achievement subgroup are not identical in their ability to read. At times, the extent of the differences warrants shifts to different groups. At other times, differences may suggest the need for *temporary* special-needs subgroups to remedy a problem or, as the case may be, to provide suitable challenge.

At one time, working with general-achievement *and* special-needs subgroups was thought to be impossible by many, if not most, teachers. Why such a conclusion was widespread can be understood only when other of their taken-for-granted beliefs are kept in mind. The notions, for example, that instructional material is confined to basal readers; that assignment is confined to skill sheets; and that conducting a lesson is confined to round robin reading, all combined to make it natural to conclude that working with general-achievement groups was the best that could be done. Because of opinions such as these, *Teaching Them to Read* has developed a different conception of lessons and has expanded with many examples the meaning of both "instructional material" and "assignment."

It has also expanded the meaning of "special needs" with the attention given earlier to naturalistic assessment and to teachable moments; for they, too, reflect the importance of responding to needs not just at some preplanned time but also at the moment a need is identified. All this explains why the Introduction to this final chapter highlights the significance of a diagnostic posture on the part of teachers if a maximum of individualized instruction is to be achieved.

SUMMARY

Chapter 16 opened with a definition and discussion of individualized instruction. This was an appropriate beginning, as the two major topics addressed in the chapter, assessment and classroom organization, are both concerned with the essence of such teaching: matching instruction with needs.

Learning what is needed is the purpose of the assessment central to Chapter 16. At the start, four kinds were reviewed. The first is an integral part of lessons, for it is a teacher's attempt to learn whether students are able to use in their reading what she had hoped to teach. The second falls into the category "postreading responsibilities." In this case, the assessment is a teacher's efforts to see whether purposes established for reading were realized and, further, to find answers to questions like: Did any of the new words cause problems? Did the author's frequent use of figurative expressions cause breakdowns in comprehension? Were the students able to see that the theme of this selection is similar to the one in a recently completed story?

Chapter 16 continued by elaborating on the use of oral reading to learn about students' strategies for dealing with troublesome words. This kind of assessment is important for instructional decisions because it allows teachers to learn exactly how students go about solving—or not solving—problems with words in connected text. Naturalistic assessment, introduced under the heading "Everyday Observations," was dealt with next. Use of this kind of assessment was implied many times in earlier chapters when teachable moments were identified and discussed.

A detailed account of what the chapter called "teacher-devised tests" followed. This refers to assessment conducted with individuals as much to learn what they know as to identify what they do not know or cannot do. Underlying this discussion was encouragement to eliminate all nonessentials from recommendations made in basal reader manuals.

Chapter 16 then discussed portfolio assessment more to stress the importance of providing students with opportunities to see evidence of their progress than to promote relying on this type of assessment for making instructional decisions.

Decisions made on the basis of what students need to learn almost always eliminate whole-class teaching as a means for achieving individualized instruction. This is why attention went to ability-based groups, which were divided into general-achievement subgroups and special-needs subgroups. The latter, whose use is not as common as it ought to be, last only as long as it takes to remedy the problem that accounts for the group.

To show that working with subgroups of students is not as difficult as it may at first appear to be, Chapter 16 reminded its readers of the expanded meanings that *Teaching Them to Read* has assigned to "instructional material," "assignment," and "lesson." This was done on the assumption that, in the past, highly restricted meanings have fostered either whole-class teaching or a rigid use of general-achievement subgroups, neither of which is the best means for promoting either advancement in reading or students' interest in doing some.

REVIEW

1. Teachers' assessment efforts, along with how they organize a class, should contribute to offering individualized instruction. Describe the essential features of such instruction.

2. Individualized instruction is also linked to diagnostic teaching, which was discussed in the Introduction to Part VI. Characterize a teacher who assumes a diagnostic stance in the course of a school day.

3. Chapter 16 reviewed four ways to collect helpful diagnostic information that earlier chapters discussed. Describe the four.

4. Chapter 16 told of two additional ways to collect diagnostic information. Describe both.

5. As Chapter 16 pointed out, the use of nothing but general-achievement subgroups in self-contained classrooms has been the target of mounting criticism.
   a. State the criticisms.
   b. What is a remedy for each? That is, counter each criticism with a recommendation that is an improvement.

6. Decisions about placements in general-achievement subgroups are closely tied to other decisions about the materials to use with each group. Explain the connection.

7. Selecting "appropriately difficult material" is no longer as simple as it was when readability formulas were erroneously thought to provide correct information about text difficulty. Review the section in Chapter 13 called "Readability Formulas: Major Problems." Based on the review, explain why selecting appropriately difficult material for students is often more like a best guess than an objective judgment.

8. Psychological and pedagogical factors both support teachers' dividing their time among the whole class, general-achievement subgroups, special-needs subgroups, and individuals. Tell why a mix *is* best for both psychological and pedagogical reasons.

REFERENCES

1. Allington, Richard L. "If They Don't Read Much, How They Ever Gonna Get Good?" *Journal of Reading* 21 (October, 1977), 57–61.
2. Allington, Richard L. "Poor Readers Don't Get to Read Much in Reading Groups." *Language Arts* 57 (November/December, 1980), 872–876.
3. Bossert, Steven T. *Tasks and Social Relationships in Classrooms.* New York: Cambridge University Press, 1979.
4. Brown, John S.; Collins, Allan; and Duguid, Paul. "Situated Cognition and the Culture of Learning." *Educational Researcher* 18 (January/February, 1989), 32–42.
5. Duffy, Gerald G., and Roehler, Laura R. "The Illusion of Instruction." *Reading Research Quarterly* 17 (1982, No. 3), 438–444.
6. Durkin, Dolores. "Is There a Match between What Elementary Teachers Do and What Basal Reader Manuals Recommend?" *Reading Teacher* 37 (April, 1984), 734–744.
7. Durkin, Dolores. "A Six-Year Study of Children Who Learned to Read in School at the Age of Four." *Reading Research Quarterly* 10 (1974–75, No. 1), 9–61.
8. Durkin, Dolores. "What Classroom Observations Reveal about Comprehension Instruction." *Reading Research Quarterly* 14 (1978–79, No. 4), 481–533.
9. Good, Thomas L., and Brophy, Jere E. *Looking in Classrooms.* New York: Harper and Row, 1984.
10. Goodman, Kenneth S. "Analysis of Oral Reading Miscues: Applied Psycholinguistics." *Reading Research Quarterly* 5 (Fall, 1969), 9–30.
11. Goodman, Kenneth S. (Ed.). *Miscue Analysis: Application to Reading Instruction.* Urbana, Ill.: National Council of Teachers of English, 1973.
12. Goodman, Kenneth S. "Whole-Language Research: Foundations and Development." *Elementary School Journal* 90 (November, 1989), 207–221.

13. Hiebert, Elfrieda H. "An Examination of Ability Grouping for Reading Instruction." *Reading Research Quarterly* 18 (Winter, 1983), 231–255.

14. International Reading Association. "Misuse of Grade Equivalents." *Reading Teacher* 35 (January, 1982), 464.

15. Johns, Jerry L. "Literacy Portfolios: A Primer." *Illinois Reading Council Journal* 19 (Summer, 1991), 4–10.

16. Pikulski, John. "A Critical Review: Informal Reading Inventories." *Reading Teacher* 28 (November, 1974), 141–151.

17. Raphael, Taffy E. "Teaching Question-Answer Relationships, Revisited." *Reading Teacher* 39 (February, 1986), 516–522.

18. Reutzel, D. Ray, and Cooter, Robert B. "Organizing for Effective Instruction." *Reading Teacher* 44 (April, 1991), 548–554.

19. Rhodes, Lynn K., and Nathenson-Mejia, Sally. "Anecdotal Records: A Powerful Tool for Ongoing Literacy Assessment." *Reading Teacher* 45 (March, 1992), 502–509.

20. Valencia, Sheila. "A Portfolio Approach to Classroom Reading Assessment: The Whys, Whats, and Hows." *Reading Teacher* 43 (January, 1990), 338–340.

21. Wallen, Carl J. *Competency in Teaching Reading.* Chicago: Science Research Associates, 1972.

22. Winograd, Peter; Paris, Scott; and Bridge, Connie. "Improving the Assessment of Literacy." *Reading Teacher* 45 (October, 1991), 108–116.

Index